A BIBLE HISTORY OF BAPTISM

LECTOR HOUSE PUBLIC DOMAIN WORKS

HAPPY READING!

A BIBLE HISTORY OF BAPTISM

SAMUEL JOHN BAIRD

ISBN: 978-93-93794-49-9

Published: 1882

LECTOR HOUSE LLP
E-MAIL: lectorpublishing@gmail.com

THE GREAT BAPTIZER.

A BIBLE HISTORY OF BAPTISM

BY

SAMUEL J. BAIRD, D. D.

"He shall baptize you with the Holy Ghost and with fire." — MATT. iii, 17.

"This is that which was spoken by the prophet Joel: And it shall come to pass, in the last days, saith God, I will pour out of my Spirit upon all flesh." — ACTS ii, 16, 17.

1882

PREFACE.

Not only does the ordinance of baptism hold a position of pre-eminent honor, as being the door of entrance to all the privileges of the visible church, but it has been distinguished with a place of paramount importance and conspicuity in the transactions of the two grandest occasions in the history of that church, — in sealing the covenant at Sinai, by which Israel became the church of God, and the grace of Pentecost, by which the doors of that church were thrown open to the world. Proportionally interesting and significant is the ordinance, in itself, as symbolizing the most lofty, attractive and precious conceptions of the gospel, and unfolding a history of the plan of God in proportions of unspeakable interest, grandeur and glory. And yet, heretofore, the discussion of the subject has been little more than a disputation, alike uninteresting, inconclusive and unprofitable, concerning the word *baptizo*.

The present treatise is an attempt to lift the subject out of the low rut in which it has thus traversed, and to render its investigation the means of enlightening the minds and filling the hearts of God's people with those conceptions, at once exalted and profound, and those high hopes and bright anticipations of the future which the ordinance was designed and so happily fitted to induce and stimulate.

Eighteen years ago, — in a catechetical treatise on "The Church of God, its Constitution and Order," from the press of the Presbyterian Board of Publication, — the author enunciated the essential principles which are developed in this volume. In 1870, they were further illustrated in a tract on "The Bible History of Baptism," which was issued by the Presbyterian Committee of Publication, in Richmond, Va. The reception accorded to these treatises has encouraged me to undertake the more elaborate disquisitions of the present work. The questions are sometimes such as require a critical study of the inspired originals of the holy Scriptures; and occasional illustrations are drawn from classic and other kindred sources. It has been my study so to conduct these investigations that while they should not be unworthy the attention of scholars, they may be intelligible to readers who are conversant with no other than our common English tongue, the richest and noblest ever spoken by man.

The circumstances and manner of the introduction of the rite of immersion into the post-apostolic church presented a rich and inviting field of further investigation. But the volume has already exceeded the intended limit; the Biblical question is in itself complete, and its authority is conclusive. To it, therefore, the present inquiry is confined.

The fruit of much and assiduous investigation and thoughtful study is now reverently dedicated to the glory of the baptizing office of the Lord Jesus. May he speedily arise and display it in new and transcendent energy; pouring upon his blood-bought church the Spirit of grace and consecration, of knowledge and aggressive zeal, of unity and power; baptizing the nations with his Spirit, and filling the world with the joy of his salvation and the light of his glory.

Covington, Ky., Feb. 8, 1882.

CONTENTS

PART III.
ADMINISTERED BAPTISMS = SPRINKLINGS.

PART IV.
THE RITUAL SELF-WASHINGS.

PART V.
LATER TRACES OF THE SPRINKLED BAPTISMS.

PART VI.
STATE OF THE OLD TESTAMENT ARGUMENT.

BOOK II.
NEW TESTAMENT HISTORY.

PART VII.
INTRODUCTORY.

PART VIII.
THE PURIFYINGS OF THE JEWS.

PART IX.
JOHN'S BAPTISM.

PART XII.
THE BAPTIST ARGUMENT.

PART XIII.
BAPTISMAL REGENERATION.

PART XIV.
THE NEW TESTAMENT CHURCH.

PART XV.
CHRISTIAN BAPTISM.

PART XVI.

THE FAMILY AND THE CHILDREN.

CONCLUSION.

INTRODUCTION.

The history of the ritual ordinances of God's appointment is full of painful interest. Passing any reference to the times preceding the transactions of Sinai,—the institutions then given to Israel constituted a system of transparent, significance, perfect in the congruous symmetry and simplicity of the parts and comprehensive fullness of the whole, as setting forth the whole doctrine of God concerning man's sin and salvation. Designed not only for the instruction of Israel, but for a light to the darkness of the surrounding Gentile world, its truths were embodied in symbols which spake to every people of every tongue in their own language. Copied in imperfect and perverted forms into the rites of Gentile idolatry,—although distorted, veiled and dislocated from their normal relations, they shed gleams of twilight into the gloom of spiritual darkness, and prepared the world for the dawning of the Sun of Righteousness, when he rose upon the nations. To multitudes of Israel, those ordinances were efficient means of eminent grace. With gladness, they saw therein,—as through a glass, darkly, it may be, but surely,—adumbrations of the salvation, grace and glory of the Messiah's kingdom. And, if the fact be considered that at one of the darkest crises in Israel's history, when the prophet cried,—"I, even I am left alone,"—God could assure him,—"Yet have I left seven thousand,"—we may possibly find occasion to revise our preconceptions concerning the history of the gospel in Israel. Still, undoubtedly there were multitudes in every generation of that people to whom the gospel preached in the ordinances brought no profit, for lack of faith. In their earlier history, indifference and neglect, and in the later, a self-righteous zeal for the mere outward rites and forms, were equally fatal. The splendor of the ritual, and the superfluous variety and frequency of the observances, were a poor substitute for faith toward God, and rectitude of heart and life. The result was that when Christ came, who was the end of all the rites and ordinances of the law, those who were the most strict and zealous in their observance were his betrayers and murderers.

When the Lord Jesus ascended the heavens, assumed the throne, and sent forth the gospel to the Gentiles, it was accompanied by two simple ordinances, which were eliminated out of those of the Levitical ritual, by the omission of the element of sacrifice. In them was symbolized and set forth the whole riches of that salvation which was represented in the more cumbrous forms of the Levitical system. By the supper, was signified the mystery of his atoning sufferings, and of the nourishment of his people by faith therein. By baptism, was shown forth the glory of his exaltation, and the sovereignty and power with which he sheds from his throne the blessings of his grace. But very soon, these ordinances, so beautiful and instructive in their simplicity, were corrupted through the misconceptions and ignorance of the teachers of the church. The Mosaic ritual, instead of being recognized, as Paul describes it, as a pattern or similitude of the things in the heavens, was regarded as a type of the New Testament church and of the ordinances therein administered. This one error became the inevitable cause of corruption and apostasy. Respecting the impending defection, Paul assured the Thessalonians, that the mystery of iniquity was already at work; and forewarned the elders of Ephesus of the coming of grievous wolves to rend the flock, and of apostasies among themselves, through the lust of an unhallowed ambition.

We have not the means, from the scanty and corrupted records which remain, of the age immediately following the apostles, of tracing the process of defection. But when, at length, the church emerges into the light of history, it is found to have realized a fatal transformation. The pastors and elders of the apostolic churches, from being simple preachers of the word, have become priests ministering at the altar, and offering better sacrifices than those made by the Aaronic line. For, while the latter offered mere animals, and the worshippers fed upon mere carnal food, the former, in the sacrament of the supper, the supposed antitype of those offerings, were believed to offer the body and blood of the Lord Jesus, and the people, in those elements, imagined themselves to receive and feed upon that very body and blood. So, too, while the "type baptisms" of the ancient ritual accomplished a mere purifying of the flesh, the baptism of water by the hands of the Christian ministry was regarded as the antitype of these, and considered effectual for accomplishing a spiritual regeneration, a renewing of the heart of the recipient.

The same error which thus corrupted the doctrine of the sacraments, was equally efficient in changing their forms. As they were held to be the antitypes of the Old Testament rites, it was sought to develop in them features to correspond with all the details of those rites, and to give them a dignity, a pomp and ceremonial, proportioned to their relations as fulfilling the things set forth in the splendid ritual of Moses and David. The rite of baptism, particularly, was corrupted by alterations and additions which left scarcely any thing of the primitive institution, save the name. The Levitical purifyings were especially observed in connection with the annual feasts at Jerusalem. In like manner, the administration of baptism was discouraged, except in connection with two of those feasts,—the passover, and the feast of weeks, or of firstfruits,—transferred into the Christian church, under the names of Easter, and Pentecost, or Whitsunday; the latter being named from the white garments in which the newly baptized were robed. The administration was connected with an elaborate system of attendant observances. First, was a course of fastings, genuflections, and prayers, and the imposition of hands upon the candidate. Then, he was divested of all but a single under garment, and facing the west, the realm of darkness, was required, with defiant gesture of the hand, to renounce Satan and all his works. This was followed by an exorcism, the minister breathing upon the candidate, for expelling Satan, and imparting the Holy Spirit; then the making upon him of the sign of the cross; anointing him with oil, once before and once after the baptism; the administration of salt, milk and honey, and three immersions, one at the name of each person of the Trinity. Such was the connection in which baptism by immersion first appears. For its reception, the candidate, of whatever sex, was invariably divested of all clothing, and, after it, was robed in a white garment, emblematic of the spotless purity now attained. The rite of baptism by bare sprinkling, however, still survived. And the question is entitled to a critical attention which it has not yet received, whether, always or generally, the more elaborate rite consisted in a *submersion* of the candidate. Against this supposition, is the practice of the Abyssinian, Greek, Nestorian and other churches of the east. In them, the candidate, in preparation for the rite, is placed, or we may say, immersed, naked, in a font of water, the quantity of which neither suffices, nor is intended, to cover him. The administrator then performs the baptism, while pronouncing the formula, by thrice pouring water on the candidate, once at the mention of each name of the blessed Godhead.[1] To the same effect, is the evidence of numerous remains of Christian art, which have been transmitted to us from the early ages. Among these are several representations of the baptism of the Lord Jesus by John; one, of that of Constantine and his wife, by Eusebius; and others. The baptism of Constantine precisely corresponds with the description above given. The emperor is seated naked in a vessel, which if full would not reach to his waist; and the bishop is in the act of performing the baptism by pouring water upon them. In the representations of the baptism of Jesus, he sometimes appears waist-deep in the Jordan, and sometimes on the land. But in all cases, the rite is performed by the baptist pouring water on his head out of a cup or shell. Such is, in fact, the invariable mode represented in these remains of ancient art.

In this connection the analogy of the forms of religious purifying prevalent throughout the east is worthy of special notice. The Brahmin, before taking his morning's meal, repairs to the Ganges, carrying with him a brazen vessel. By hundreds, or by thousands, they enter the stream, and while some take up the water in their vessels, and pour it over their persons, others plunge beneath the stream, for the purging away of their sins. Then filling the vessels, they repair to the temple, and pour the water upon the idol, or as a libation, before it. The Parsee, worshiper of the sun, goes, in the morning, to river or sea, and entering until the waves are waist high, with his face toward the east, awaits the rising of the sun, when, using his joined hands as a dipper, he dashes water over his person, and makes obeisance to his god. On the other hand, the Mohammedan, deriving his usage from the earlier Pharisaic ritual, repairs to the mosque, and from the tank in front, without entering it, takes up water in his hands with which to bathe face, feet and hands, before presenting his prayers.

By the corruptions in the Christian church, before exemplified, the key of knowledge was taken away from the people. The instructive meaning of the sacraments was obscured and obliterated, by the idea of their intrinsic efficacy for renewing the heart and atoning for and purging sin. The preaching of the word was disparaged and ultimately set aside; the preachers having become propitiating priests, working regeneration by the baptismal rite, and making atonement by the sacrifice of the mass. The corruption and tyranny of the clergy of the middle ages,

[1] My authorities are "A voyage to Abyssinia, and travels in the interior of that country, executed under the orders of the British government, in the years 1809 and 1810, etc., by Henry Salt, Esq., F. R. S., etc., London, 1814;" and the personal testimonies of several of our missionaries to the east, who have related to me what they saw.

and the ignorance, slavery and spiritual darkness which for centuries brooded over the people, were the inevitable results.

The reformation came, through the recovery by Luther of the golden doctrine of justification by faith, which had so long been buried and lost under the accumulated mass of ritualistic error. But even Luther was unable to shake off the fetters of superstition and falsehood in which he had been cradled, and to enjoy the full liberty of the doctrine which he gave to the awakened church. In the dogma of consubstantiation, he transmitted to his followers the very error which had corrupted the church for more than a thousand years. And the result in the churches of his confession has added another to the already abundant evidence of the ever active and irreconcilable antagonism which exists between the theory of sacramental grace, and the doctrine, —criterion of a standing or falling church, —of justification by free grace through faith.

Our space does not admit of a critical tracing of the history of the sacramental question in the churches of the reformation. On the one hand, ritualists of every grade, misled by the erring primitive church, and attributing to the sacraments a saving virtue intrinsic in them, render indeed high but mistaken honor to the sacred rites; but fail to enjoy them in their true intent and office, or to view and honor them in their proper character. On the other hand, our immersionist brethren, misguided respecting the form of baptism, by the same erring example, and thus lost to the true and comprehensive meaning of the ordinance, have failed to apprehend the instruction which it was designed to impart, and to enjoy the abundant edifying which it was adapted to minister; and, instead, have found it a potent agent of separation, and an efficient temptation to the indulgence of a disproportionate zeal on behalf of mere outward rites and forms.

Nor do those who have escaped these errors always seem to appreciate the sacraments, in their true design and character, as ever active and efficient witnesses, testifying to the gospel, through symbols as intelligible and impressive as the most eloquent speech. The beauty and rich significance of the supper have, indeed, been in a measure apprehended, and made available in some just proportion, to the instruction and edifying of God's people. But baptism has not held the place, in the ministrations of the sanctuary and the mind of the church, which is due to its office and design, to the richness of meaning of its forms, and to the sublime conceptions and the lofty aspirations and hopes which it is so wonderfully adapted to create and cherish. One efficient cause of this, undoubtedly, is, the reaction induced by the aggressive zeal of immersionists, and the exercise of a false charity toward their erroneous sentiments; as though the charity of the gospel, as toward our brethren, consisted in an acceptance of their errors as equivalents to the truths of God. While they have justly and irrefragably maintained that nothing can be Christian baptism which has not at once the form and the meaning ordained by Christ, we have been weakly disposed to imagine ourselves patterns of charity, in admitting the validity of immersion, while denying it to be the form or to have the meaning which Christ ordained. As if such an ordinance, from the great Head of the Church, could have in it any thing indifferent, or subject to our discretion, whether in doctrine or mode! The immediate and inevitable result is, a low estimate of the ordinance itself; indifference alike to its form and meaning, and to the place it was designed to fill, and the offices which it was to perform, in the economy of grace. As a mere door of entrance into the fold of the church, it is administered and received; with too little regard to its beautiful and comprehensive symbolism; and, once performed, it is almost lost sight of in the instructions of the pulpit, and meditations of the people. Should this representation suggest a doubt, let the reader reflect how often, in the ordinary ministrations of the sanctuary, he has heard the significance of baptism dwelt upon, or even alluded to, for illustrating the great truths of the gospel, on any occasion except that of the administration of the rite; and how seldom, even then, the richness of its symbolic import is unfolded, — its relations to Christ's exaltation and throne, and to all the functions of his scepter; the meaning of the element of water, and of the mode of sprinkling; and the office of the ordinance, as a symbol of the Spirit's renewing grace, and a prophecy and seal to the doctrine of the resurrection. As the initial seal of the covenant, it is discussed and insisted upon. But of these, its intrinsic and most interesting characteristics, but little is heard. No wonder, therefore, that the privilege of its reception is so little appreciated, and its appropriation by parents on behalf of their children, so often neglected.

The recent researches of Drs. Conant and Dale have exhausted the philological argument as concerning *baptizo*. The former, representing the American (Baptist) Bible Union, and the latter, from the opposite standpoint, have come to conclusions which, to all the practical purposes of the discussion, are identical and final. Essentially, they agree (1) that *baptizo* never means, to dip, that is, to put into the water and take out again; but, primarily, to put into or under the water, — to bring into a state of mersion, or intusposition; (2) that it also means to bring into a new state or condition, by the exercise of a pervasive control; as one who is intoxicated is said to be baptized with wine. The former of these meanings is all that remains to the Baptist argument from the word. The latter is all that is desired by those who repudiate immersion. The philological discussion being thus brought to a practical termination, the occasion seems opportune for inviting attention to the real issues involved in the question respecting the form of the ordinance; and to the various and abundant testimonies of the Scriptures, as to its origin and office, its mode and meaning, its history and associations.

In the same line of investigation, it is the expectation of the writer, should time and opportunity concur, to offer to the Christian public, at some future day, a treatise, similar in plan to that now presented, on the ordinances and church of God, historically traced from the apostasy, and the renewal of the covenant in Eden, to the close of the sacred volume.

BOOK I.
OLD TESTAMENT HISTORY.

PART I.

BAPTISM AT SINAI.

Section I.—*Baptism Originated in the Old Testament.*—It was familiar
to the Jews when Christ came. There were "divers baptisms" imposed at Sinai

At the time of Christ's coming, baptism was a rite already familiar to the Jews.
The evangelists testify of them that, "when they come from the market, *except they
baptize (ean mē baptisōntai) they eat not. And many other things there be which they
have received to hold, as the *baptisms (baptismous)* of cups and pots and brazen
vessels and tables."—Mark vii, 3, 4. On account of this rule of tradition, a Pharisee
at whose table Jesus was a guest "marveled that he had not first *baptized (ebaptisthē)* before dinner."—Luke xi, 38. Hence, when John came, a priest, baptizing,
there was no question raised as to the origin, nature, form, or divine authority of
the ordinance which he administered. The Pharisees, in their challenge of him,
confine themselves to the single demand, by what authority he ventured to require Israel to come to his baptism, since he confessed that he was neither Christ
nor Elias nor that prophet. (John i, 25.) Their familiarity with the rite forbade any
question concerning it. Had we no further light on the subject, we might suppose
that this ordinance had no better source than the unauthorized inventions of Jewish tradition. But the Apostle Paul,[2] an Hebrew of the Hebrews, taught at the feet
of Gamaliel, and versed in all questions of the law, excludes such an idea. He declares that in the first tabernacle "were offered both gifts and sacrifices that could
not make him that did the service perfect as pertaining to the conscience; which
stood only in meats and drinks and *(diaphorois baptismois) divers baptisms*—carnal
ordinances imposed on them until the time of reformation."—Heb. ix, 9, 10. The
conjunction "and" ("divers baptisms *and* carnal ordinances") is wanting in the best
Greek manuscripts; is rejected by the critical editors, and is undoubtedly spurious.
The phrase "carnal ordinances" is not an additional item in the enumeration, but
a comprehensive description of "the meats and drinks and divers baptisms" of the
law. Paul thus speaks of them by way of contrast with the spiritual grace and righteousness of the Lord Jesus. A critical examination of this passage will be made
hereafter. For the present, we note two points as attested by the apostle:

1. Among the Levitical ordinances there were not *one* but divers baptisms.

2. These were not merely allowable rites, but were "imposed" on Israel as part

---

[2] I assume what I believe to be demonstrable, that Paul was the author of the Epistle
to the Hebrews.

of the institutions ordained of God at Sinai.

It may be proper to add that they were baptisms of persons, and not of things. They were rites which were designed to purify the flesh of the worshiper. (vs. 9, 13, 14.)

These baptisms were, therefore, well known to Israel, from the days of Moses. This explains the fact that, in the New Testament, we find no instruction as to the form of the ordinance. It was an ancient rite, described in the books of Moses and familiar to the Jews when Christ came. No description, therefore, was requisite. We are then to look to the Old Testament to ascertain the form and manner of baptism.

Section II.—*No Immersions in the Old Testament.*—None in the ritual.
None in the figurative language

Says Dr. Carson: "We deny that the phrase 'divers baptisms' includes the *sprinklings*. The phrase alludes to the *immersion* of the different things that by the law were to be *immersed*."[3] Had this learned writer pointed out the things that were to be immersed, and the places in the law where this was required, it would have saved us some trouble. In default of such information, our first inquiry in turning to the Old Testament will be for that form of observance. We take up the books of Moses, and examine his instructions as to all the prominent institutions of divine service. But among these we find no immersion of the person. We enter into minuter detail, and study every rule and prescription of the entire system as enjoined on priests, Levites, and people, respectively. But still there is no trace of an ordinance for the immersion of the person or any part of it. We extend our field of inquiry, and search the entire volume of the Old Testament. But the result remains the same. From the first chapter of Genesis to the last of Malachi, there is not to be found a record nor an intimation of such an ordinance imposed on Israel or observed by them at any time. Not only is this true as to baptismal immersion performed by an official administrator upon a recipient subject. It is equally true as to any conceivable form or mode of immersion, self-performed or administered. There is no trace of it. But here is Paul's testimony that there were "divers baptisms imposed." By *baptisms*, then, Paul certainly did not mean immersions.

The impregnable position thus reached is further fortified by the fact that, in all the variety and exuberance of figurative language used in the Bible to illustrate the method of God's grace, no recourse is ever had to the figure of immersion. All agree that the sacraments are significant ordinances. If, then, the significance of baptism at all depends on the immersion of the person in water, we would justly expect to find frequent use of the figure of immersion, as representing the spiritual realities of which baptism is the symbol. But we search the Scriptures in vain for that figure so employed. It never once occurs.

Section III.—*The Old Testament Sacraments.*—1. Sacrifice. 2. Circumcision. 3. The Passover. 4. Baptism

As there are no immersions in the Old Testament, we must look for the divers

[3] "Carson on Baptism" (published by C. C. P. Crosby: New York, 1832), p. 117.

baptisms under some other form. Assuming that in this rite there must be a sacramental use of water, we will first examine the ancient sacraments. On a careful analysis of the ordinances comprehended in the Levitical system, we find among them four which strictly conform to the definition of a sacrament, and which are the only sacraments described or referred to in the Old Testament.

1. *Sacrifice.*—The first of these in origin and prominence was sacrifice. Originating in Eden, and incorporated in the Levitical system, it had all the characteristics of a sacrament. In it the life blood of clean animals was shed and sprinkled, and their bodies burned upon the altar. Thus were represented the shedding of Christ's blood, and his offering of atonement to the justice of God. But here is no water. It is not the baptism for which we seek.

2. *Circumcision.*—The second of the Old Testament sacraments was circumcision, whereby God sealed to Abraham and his seed the covenant of blessings to them and all nations through the blood of the promised Seed. Here, again, no one will pretend to identify the ordinance with the baptisms of Paul.

3. *The Passover.*—The third of the Old Testament sacraments, the first of the Levitical dispensation, was the feast of the passover. In it, the paschal lamb was slain, its blood sprinkled on the lintels and door posts of the houses, and the flesh roasted and eaten with unleavened bread and bitter herbs. At Sinai, this ordinance was modified by requiring the feast to be observed at the sanctuary, the blood being sprinkled on the altar, and the fat burned thereon. And, to the other elements appointed in Egypt, the general provisions of the Mosaic law added wine. All peace offerings, free will offerings, and offerings at the solemn feasts, of which the passover was one, were to be accompanied with wine, and were eaten by the offerers, except certain parts, that were burned on the altar. (See Num. xv, 5, 7, 10; xxviii, 7, 14.) This ordinance, eliminated of its sacrificial elements, is perpetuated in the Lord's supper. In it was no water. It was not the rite for which we seek.

4. *Baptism.*—There remains but one more of the Mosaic sacraments. It was instituted at Sinai. In it, water was essential, and by it was symbolized the renewing agency of the Holy Spirit. It was "a purification for sin," an initiatory ordinance, by which remission of sins and admission to the benefits of the covenant were signified and sealed to the faith of the recipients. It occupied, under the Old Testament economy, the very position, and had the significance, which belong to Christian baptism under the New. Moreover, it appears under several modifications, and is thus conformed to Paul's designation of *"divers* baptisms," whilst these, in their circumstantial variations, were essentially one and the same ordinance.

Section IV.—*The Baptism of Israel at Sinai.*—Scene at the mount. The covenant proposed and accepted. A great revival. Baptism of the converts. The feast of the covenant

The occasion of the first recorded administration of this rite was the reception of Israel into covenant with God at Sinai. For more than two hundred years they had dwelt in Egypt, and for a large part of the time had been bondmen there. The history of their sojourn in the wilderness shows that not only was their manhood debased by the bondage, but their souls had been corrupted by the idolatries of the Egyptians (Josh. xxiv, 14; Ezek. xx, 7), and they had forgotten the covenant and forsaken the God of their fathers. They were apostate, and, in Scriptural language, unclean.

But now the fullness of time had come, when the promises made to the fathers must be fulfilled. Leaving the nations to walk after their own ways, God was about to erect to himself a visible throne and kingdom among men, to be a witness for him against the apostasy of the race. He was about to arouse Israel from her debasement and slavery, to establish with her his covenant, and to organize and ordain her his peculiar people—his Church.

Proportioned to the importance of such an occasion was the grandeur of the scene and the gravity of the transactions. Of them we have two accounts, one from the pen of Moses (Ex. xx-xxiv), and the other from the Apostle Paul, in exposition of his statement as to the divers baptisms. (Heb. ix, 18-20.) As to these accounts, two or three points of explanation are necessary. (1) The two words, "covenant" and "testament," represent but one in the originals in these places, of which "covenant" is the literal meaning. (2) Paul mentions *water* (Heb. ix, 19), of which Moses does not speak. The fact is significant, as the apostle is in the act of illustrating the "divers baptisms," of which he had just before spoken. (3) The word "oxen," in our translation (Ex. xxiv, 5), should be "bulls." Oxen were not lawful for sacrifice. Yearling animals seem to have been preferred. Says Micah, "Shall I come before the Lord with burnt-offerings, with calves of a year old?"—Micah vi, 6. Hence Paul indifferently calls them bulls and calves. The goats of which he speaks were no doubt among the burnt-offerings of Moses's narrative. Both "small and great cattle" seem to have been offered on all great national solemnities.

The redeemed tribes came to Sinai in the third month after the exodus. Moses was called up into the mount and commanded to propose to them the covenant of God. It was in these terms: "If ye will obey my voice indeed, and keep my covenant, then ye shall be a peculiar treasure unto me above all people, for all the earth is mine, and ye shall be unto me a kingdom of priests and a holy nation."—Ex. xix, 3-6. This proposal the people, with one voice, accepted. God then commanded Moses: "Sanctify the people to-day and to-morrow, and let them wash their clothes and be ready against the third day; for the third day the Lord will come down in the sight of all the people upon Mount Sinai."—Vs. 10, 11. On the third day, in the morning, there were thunders and lightnings, and a thick cloud upon the mount, and the voice of the trumpet exceeding loud, so that all the people trembled. And Mount Sinai was altogether on a smoke, because the Lord descended upon it in fire, and the smoke thereof ascended as the smoke of a furnace, and the whole mount quaked greatly. And when the voice of the trumpet sounded long, and waxed louder and louder, Moses spake, and God answered him by a voice. And the Lord came down upon the top of the mount; and the Lord called Moses up to the top of the mount, and Moses went up.

In the midst of this tremendous scene, so well calculated to fill the people with awe, and to deter them from the thought of a profane approach, Moses was nevertheless charged to go down and warn the people, and set bounds around the mountain, lest they should break through unto the Lord to gaze, and many of them perish. After such means, used to impress Israel with a profound sense of God's majesty and their infinite estrangement from him, his voice was heard, uttering in their ears the Ten Commandments, prefaced with the announcement of himself as their God and Redeemer. (Compare Deut. iv, 7-13.) At the entreaty of the people, the terribleness of God's audible voice was withdrawn, and Moses was sent to tell them the words of the Lord and his judgments. The people again unanimously declared, "All the words which the Lord hath said, will we do."—Ex. xxiv, 3.

In this sublime transaction we have all the scenes and circumstances of a mighty revival of true religion. It is a vast camp-meeting, in which God himself is the preacher, speaking in men's ears with an audible voice from the top of Sinai, and alternately proclaiming the law of righteousness and the gospel of grace, calling Israel from their idolatries and sins to return unto him, and offering himself as not only the God of their fathers, but their own Deliverer already from the Egyptian bondage, and ready to be their God and portion—to give them at once the earthly Canaan, and to make it a pledge of their ultimate endowment with the heavenly. The people had professed with one accord to turn to God, and pledged themselves, emphatically and repeatedly, to take him as their God, to walk in his statutes and do his will, to be his people.

It is true that, to many, the gospel then preached was of no profit, for lack of faith; whose carcasses therefore fell in the wilderness. (Heb. iii, 17-19; iv, 2.) But it is equally true that the vast majority of the assembly at Sinai were children and generous youth, who had not yet been besotted by the Egyptian bondage. To them that day, which was known in their after history as "the day of the assembly" (Deut. x, 4; xviii, 16), was the beginning of days. Its sublime scenes became in them the spring of a living faith. With honest hearts they laid hold of the covenant, and took the God of the patriarchs for their God. Soon after, the promise of Canaan, forfeited by their rebellious fathers, was transferred to them. (Num. xiv, 28-34.) Trained and disciplined by the forty years' wandering, it was they who became, through faith, the irresistible host of God, the heroic conquerors and possessors of the land of promise. Centuries afterward, God testified of them that they pleased him: "I remember thee, the kindness of thy youth, the love of thine espousals, when thou wentest after me in the wilderness, in a land that was not sown. Israel was holiness to the Lord, and the firstfruits of his increase."—Jer. ii, 2, 3. Until the day of Pentecost, no day so memorable, no work of grace so mighty, is recorded in the history of God's dealings with men as that of the assembly at Sinai.

And as on the day of Pentecost the converts were baptized upon their profession of faith, so was it now. Moses appointed the next day for a solemn ratifying of the transaction. He wrote in a book the words of the Lord's covenant, the Ten Commandments; and in the morning, at the foot of the mount, built an altar of twelve stones, according to the twelve tribes. On it young men designated by him offered burnt-offerings and sacrificed peace-offerings of young bulls. Moses took half the blood and sprinkled it on the altar. Half of it he kept in basins. He then read the covenant from the book, in the audience of all the people, who again accepted it, saying, "All that the Lord hath said will we do, and be obedient." Moses thereupon took the blood that was in the basins, with water and scarlet wool and hyssop, and sprinkled both the book and all the people, saying, "Behold the blood of the covenant which the Lord hath made with you concerning all these words." — Ex. xxiv, 8, compared with Heb. ix, 19, 20.

In the morning Moses had already, by divine command, assembled Aaron, Nadab and Abihu, and seventy of the elders of Israel. And no sooner was the covenant finally accepted and sealed with the baptismal rite, than these all went up into the mount, and there celebrated the feast of the covenant. "They saw the God of Israel; and there was under his feet, as it were, a paved work of a sapphire stone, and as it were the body of heaven in his clearness. And upon the nobles of Israel, he laid not his hand. Also, they saw the God of Israel, and did eat and drink." — Ex. xxiv, 1, 9-11. So intimate, privileged, and spiritual was the relation which the covenant established between Israel and God.

Thus was closed this sublime transaction, ever memorable in the history of man and of the church of Christ, in which the invisible God condescended to clothe himself in the majesty of visible glory, to hold audible converse with men, to enter into the bonds of a public and perpetual covenant with them, and to erect them into a kingdom, on the throne of which his presence was revealed in the Shechinah of glory.

Such were the occasion and manner of the first institution and observance of the sacrament of baptism. In its attendant scenes and circumstances, the most august of all God's displays of his majesty and grace to man; and in its occasion and nature, paramount in importance, and lying at the foundation of the entire administration of grace through Christ. It was the establishing of the visible church.

Section V. — *The Blood of Sprinkling.* — It was a type of Christ's atonement

In all the Sinai transactions, Moses stood as the pre-eminent type of the Lord Jesus Christ; and the rites administered by him were figures of the heavenly realities of Christ's sacrifice and salvation. This is fully certified by Paul, throughout the epistle to the Hebrews, and especially in the illustration which he gives of his assertion concerning the divers baptisms imposed on Israel. See Heb. ix, 9-14, 19-28. In these places, it distinctly appears that the blood of the Sinai baptism was typical of the atonement of Christ. Not only in this, but in all the Levitical baptisms, as will hereafter appear, blood was necessary to the rite. In fact, it was an essential element in each of the Old Testament sacraments. The one idea of sacrifice was the blood of atonement. The same idea appeared in circumcision, revealing atonement by the blood of the seed of Abraham. In the passover the blood of sprinkling was the most conspicuous feature; and in the Sinai baptism blood and water were the essential elements.

Peter states the Old Testament prophets to have "inquired and searched diligently, searching what, or what manner of time the Spirit of Christ which was in them did signify, when it testified beforehand the sufferings of Christ and the glory that should follow."—1 Pet. i, 10, 11. Of the time and manner they were left in ignorance. But the blood, in all their sacraments, was a lucid symbol, pointing them forward to the sufferings of Christ as the essential and alone argument of the favor and grace of God. In it, and in the rites associated with it, they saw, dimly it may be, but surely, the blessed pledge that in the fullness of time "the Messenger of the covenant" would appear (Mal. iii, 2), magnify the law and make it honorable (Isa. xlii, 21), by his knowledge, justify many, bearing their iniquities (Isa. liii, 11), and sprinkle the mercy-seat in heaven, once for all, with his own precious and effectual blood—the blood of the everlasting covenant. (Heb. ix, 24-26; xiii, 20; 1 Pet. i, 11.)

> Section VI.—*The Living Water.*—A type of the Spirit. Living and salt water. The river of Eden. That of the Revelation and of the prophets. The Dead Sea. Rain and fountains. Their symbolic functions

In the Sinai baptism, as at first administered to all Israel, and in all its subsequent forms, living or running water was an essential element. This everywhere, in the Scriptures of the Old Testament and of the New, is the symbol of the Holy Spirit, in his office as the agent by whom the virtue of Christ's blood is conveyed to men, and spiritual life bestowed. In the figurative language of the Scriptures, the sea, or great body of salt or dead water, represents the dead mass of fallen and depraved humanity. (Dan. vii, 2, 3; Isa. lvii, 20; Rev. xiii, 1; xvii, 15.) Hence, of the new heavens and new earth which are revealed as the inheritance of God's people, it is said, "And there shall be no more sea."—Rev. xxi, 1.

The particular source of this figure seems to have been that accursed sea of Sodom, which was more impressively familiar to Israel than any other body of salt water, and which has acquired in modern times the appropriate name of the Dead Sea—a name expressive of the fact that its waters destroy alike vegetation on its banks and animal life in its bosom. Its peculiar and instructive position in the figurative system of the Scriptures appears in the prophecy of Ezekiel (xlvii, 8, 9-11), where the river of living water from the temple is described as flowing eastward to the sea; and being brought forth into the sea, the salt waters are healed, so that "there shall be abundance of fish."

Contrasted with this figure of sea water is that of living water, that is, the fresh water of rain and of fountains and streams. It is the ordinary symbol of the Holy Spirit. (John vii, 37-39.) The reason is, that, as this water is the cause of life and growth to the creation, animal and vegetable, so, the Spirit is the alone source of spiritual life and growth. The primeval type of that blessed Agent was the river that watered the Garden of Eden, and thence flowing, was parted into four streams to water the earth. This river was a fitting symbol of the Holy Spirit, "which proceedeth from the Father," the "pure river of water of life clear as crystal, proceeding out of the throne of God and of the Lamb" (John xv, 26; Rev. xxii, 1), not only in its life-giving virtue, but in its abundance and diffusion. But the fall cut man off from its abundant and perennial stream, and thenceforth the figure, as traceable through the Scriptures, ever looks forward to that promised time when the ruin of the fall will be repaired, and the gates of Paradise thrown open again. In the last chapters of the Revelation, that day is revealed in a vision of glory. There is no more sea; but the river of life pours its exhaustless crystal waters through the restored Eden of God. But the garden is no longer the retired home of one human pair, but is built up, a great city, with walls of gems and streets of gold and gates of pearl and the light of the glory of God. And the nations of them that are saved do walk in the light of it. But still it is identified as the same of old, by the flowing river and the tree of life in the midst on its banks. (Rev. ii, 7; xxii, 1, 2; and compare Psalms xlvi, 4; xxiii, 2; John iv, 10, 14; vii, 38, 39; Zech. xiv. 8.) In Ezekiel (xlvii, 1-12) there appears a vision of this river as a prophecy of God's grace in store for the last times for Israel and the world. In it, the attention of the prophet and of the reader is called distinctly to several points, all of which bear directly on our present inquiry:

1. The source of the waters. In the Revelation, it is described as proceeding out of the throne of God and the Lamb. In Ezekiel the same idea is presented under the figure of the temple, God's dwelling-place. The waters issue out from under the threshold of the house "at the south side of the altar" — the altar where the sprinkled blood and burning sacrifices testified to the Person by whom, and the price at which, the Spirit is sent. (Compare John vii, 39; xvi, 7; Acts ii, 33.)

2. The exhaustless and increasing flow of the waters is shown to the prophet, who, at a thousand cubits from their source, is led through them, — a stream ankle deep. A thousand cubits farther, he passed through, and they had risen to his knees. Again, a thousand cubits, and the waters were to his loins; and at a thousand cubits more it was a river that he could not pass over. "And he said unto me, Son of man, hast thou seen this?"

3. The river was a fountain of life. On its banks were "very many trees," "all trees for meat," with fadeless leaf and exhaustless fruit, "the fruit thereof for meat, and the leaf thereof for medicine." "And there shall be a very great multitude of fish" in the Dead Sea, "because these waters shall come thither." For "it shall come to pass that every thing that liveth which moveth, whithersoever the river shall come shall live. Every thing shall live, whither the river cometh."

4. By these living waters, the Dead Sea of depraved humanity shall be healed. "Now this sea of Sodom," says Thompson, "is so intolerably bitter, that, although the Jordan, the Arnon, and many other streams have been pouring into it their vast contributions of sweet water for thousands of years, it continues as nauseous and deadly as ever. Nothing lives in it; neither fish nor reptiles nor even animalculæ can abide its desperate malignity. But these waters from the sanctuary heal it. The whole world affords no other type of human apostasy so appropriate, so significant. Think of it! There it lies in its sulphurous sepulcher, thirteen hundred feet below the ocean, steaming up like a huge caldron of smouldering bitumen and brimstone! Neither rain from heaven nor mountain torrents nor Jordan's flood, nor all combined can change its character of utter death. Fit symbol of that great dead sea of depravity and corruption which nothing human can heal!"[4] But the pure waters of the river of life will yet pour into this sea of death a tide of grace by which "the waters shall be healed." — Ezek. xxvii, 8.

---

[4] "The Land and the Book." Vol. II, pp. 531, 534.

In the prophecy of Joel (iii, 18,) there is another allusion to these waters. Again, in Zechariah a modified form of the same vision appears. "It shall be in that day that living waters shall go out from Jerusalem; half of them toward the former" (the Eastern or Dead) "sea, and half of them toward the hinder sea" (the Mediterranean). "In summer and winter shall it be;" not a mere winter torrent, as are most of the streams of Palestine, but an unfailing river. (Zech. xiv, 8.)

Such is the type of the Spirit, as his graces flowed in Eden, and shall be given to the world, in the times of restitution. But, for the present times, the symbols of rain and fountains of springing water are used in the Scriptures as the appropriate types of the now limited and unequal measure and distribution of the Spirit. The manner and effects of his agency are set forth under three forms, each having its own significance:

1. Inasmuch as the rains of heaven are the great source of life and refreshment to the earth and vegetation, the coming of the Spirit and his efficiency as a life-giving and sanctifying power sent down from heaven are expressed by water, shed down, poured, or sprinkled, as the rain descends. Says God to Israel: "I will pour water upon him that is thirsty, and floods upon the dry ground; I will pour my Spirit upon thy seed and my blessing upon thine offspring."—Isa. xliv, 3. The Psalmist says of the graces of the Spirit to be bestowed by Messiah, "He shall come down like rain upon the mown grass" (the stubble, after mowing) "as showers that water the earth."—Psalm lxxii, 6. Of this we shall see more hereafter.

2. The act of faith by which the believer seeks and receives more and more of the indwelling Spirit is symbolized by thirsting and drinking of living water. "Ho, every one that thirsteth, come ye to the waters."—Isa. lv, 1. "If any man thirst, let him come unto me and drink.... This he spake of the Spirit which they that believe on him should receive."—John vii, 37-39. "Let him that is athirst come. And whosoever will, let him take the water of life freely."—Rev. xxii, 17. The intimate relation which this figure sustains, responsive to the one preceding, is illustrated by the expression wherein God describes the land of promise: "A land of hills and valleys, and *drinketh* water of the rain of heaven. A land which the Lord thy God careth for."—Deut. xi, 11, 12. With this, compare the language of Paul: "The earth which *drinketh* in the rain that cometh oft upon it, and bringeth forth herbs meet for them by whom it is dressed, receiveth blessing of God; but that which beareth thorns and briars is rejected and is nigh unto cursing; whose end is to be burned. But, beloved, we are persuaded better things of you."—Heb. vi, 7-9. The figure is further illustrated in the sublime description given by Ezekiel of the destruction of Assyria, in which he speaks of "the trees of Eden, the choice and best of Lebanon, all that *drink water*," and so grow and flourish. (Ezek. xxxi, 16.)

3. The duty of the penitent to yield himself with diligent obedience to the sanctifying power and grace of the Holy Spirit, to put away sin and follow after holiness, is enjoined under the figure of washing himself with water. "Wash ye; make you clean; put away the evil of your doings from before mine eyes; cease to do evil; learn to to well."—Isa. i, 16, 17. "O Jerusalem, wash thine heart from wickedness, that thou mayest be saved."—Jer. iv, 14. So, James cries, "Cleanse your hands, ye sinners; and purify your hearts, ye double-minded."—Jas. iv, 8. In the rite of

self-washing, to which these last passages refer, the pure water still symbolized the Holy Spirit given by Jesus Christ; whilst the washing expressed the privilege and duty of God's people conforming their lives to the law of holiness, and exercising the graces which the Spirit gives.

PART II.

THE VISIBLE CHURCH.

Section VII.—*The Abrahamic Covenant.*—It was the betrothal,—not the marriage. Its terms spiritual, everlasting, exclusive. The Seed Christ. It adumbrated the covenant of grace. No salvation but on its terms

The interest attaching to the Sinai baptism is greatly enhanced by its immediate and intimate relation to us. The covenant then sealed is the fundamental and perpetual charter of the visible church. The transaction by which it was established was the inauguration of that church. It was the espousal of the bride of Christ, whose betrothal took place in the covenant with Abraham. So it is expressly and repeatedly stated by the Spirit of God in the prophets. (See Jer. ii, 1, 2; Ezek. xvi, 3-14; xxiii; Hos. ii, 2, 15, 16.) It is true that this is controverted. It is asserted that the relations established by the covenants between God and Israel were secular and political, not spiritual; that the blessings therein secured were temporal; that they conveyed nothing but a guarantee that Israel should become a numerous and powerful nation, that God would be their political king, the Head of their commonwealth, and that the land of Palestine should be their possession and home. How utterly at variance with the teachings of God's Word are these assertions a brief analysis of the record will prove.

The covenant of Sinai was the culmination of a series of transactions which began with the calling of Abram from Ur of the Chaldees. "The Lord had said unto Abram, Get thee out of thy country, and from thy kindred and from thy father's house, unto a land that I will show thee; and I will make of thee a great nation, and I will bless thee and make thy name great; and thou shalt be a blessing; and I will bless them that bless thee, and curse him that curseth thee; and in thee shall all families of the earth be blessed."—Gen. xii, 1-3. Respecting this record, the following points are made clear in the New Testament: (1) That under the type of Canaan, "the land that I will show thee," heaven was the ultimate inheritance offered to Abram; and that it was so understood by him and the patriarchs. (Gal. iv, 26; Heb. xi, 10, 14-16.) (2) That the blessings promised through him to all the families of the earth were the atonement and salvation of Jesus Christ; and that this also was so understood by Abram. (Gen. xvii, 7; Gal. iii, 16, John viii, 56.) Thus, in his call from Chaldea, and the promises annexed to it, God "preached before the gospel unto Abraham."—Gal. iii, 8. So far, certainly, the transaction is eminently spiritual.

About ten years after the coming of Abram into the land of Canaan, the promises were confirmed to him by being incorporated into covenant form, and ratified by a seal. Respecting this first covenant, the record of which is contained in the fifteenth chapter of Genesis, the following are the essential points:

1. The interview was opened by the Lord with an assurance so spiritual and large as to be exhaustive of every thing that heaven can bestow. "The Lord came unto Abram in a vision, saying, Fear not, Abram; I am thy shield, and thy exceeding great reward." Whatever else was promised or given, after an assurance thus rich and comprehensive of time and eternity, must evidently be interpreted in a sense subordinate to it. No minor particulars can ever exhaust or limit the treasury thus opened. Henceforth God himself belongs to the patriarch.

2. An innumerable seed was assured to him, as heirs with him of the promises; and he is told that not to him but to his seed should the earthly Canaan be given. (Vs. 5, 18; and compare xvii, 7, 8.)

3. Abram's faith was the condition of the covenant. "He believed in the Lord, and he counted it to him for righteousness." — Vs. 6.

4. The promises thus made and accepted were confirmed by a sacrifice appointed of God, and his acceptance of it was manifested by the sign of a smoking furnace and a burning lamp, passing between the pieces. (Vs. 8, 9, 17, 18.)

5. It was an express provision of the covenant thus ratified that, so far as it concerned the seed of Abram, its realization was to be held in abeyance four hundred years. (Vs. 13-16.) It was the betrothal, of which the marriage consummation could only take place when the long-suffering of God toward the nations was exhausted and the iniquity of the Amorites was full.

About fifteen years afterward God was pleased to appear again to the patriarch, to renew the covenant, and to confirm it with a new seal. (Gen. xvii, 1-21.) Of this edition of the covenant the principal provisions were: (1) That he should be a father of many nations. (2) That Canaan should be, to him and his seed, an everlasting possession. (3) That God would be a God to him and to his seed after him. By the first of these promises, as Paul assures us, Abraham was made the heir of the world, and the father of all believers; of the gospel day, as well as before it; of the Gentile nations, as well as of Israel. (Rom. iv, 11-18; Gal. iii, 7-9, 14.) Hence the name given him of God, in confirmation of this promise (Gen. xvii, 5), ABRAHAM, "Father of a multitude," Father of the church of Christ. But the central fact of this transaction remains. The covenant was epitomized in one brief word: "I will establish my covenant between me and thee and thy seed after thee, in their generations, for an everlasting covenant, *to be a God unto thee and to thy seed after thee.*" — v. 7.

1. The covenant thus set forth is "an everlasting covenant;" no lapse of time can alter or abrogate its terms.

2. By it the Godhead assumed toward Abraham and his seed relations peculiar, exclusive, and of boundless grace. God, even the infinite and almighty God, can do no more than to give himself. Christian can conceive no more, and the most

blessed of all heaven's ransomed host will know and enjoy no more than this, which was first assured to Abram, in those words, "Fear not; I am thy shield, and thy exceeding great reward;" and is now concentrated into that one word, *"Thy God."* What can there be, not spiritual, in a covenant thus summed? And what spiritual gift or blessing is not comprehended in it? But this is not all. Whilst Paul testifies that all who believe are the seed of Abraham, and heirs with him of the promises, he also declares that Christ was the seed to whom distinctively and on behalf of his people they were addressed: "To Abraham and his seed were the promises made. He saith not, And to seeds as of many, but as of one: And to thy seed, which is Christ."—Gal. iii, 16. It thus appears that the promises in question were addressed immediately to the Lord Jesus, and they indicate all the intimacy and grace of his relation to the Father,—the relation which he claimed, when, from the cross, he appealed to the Father by that title: *"My God! my God!* why hast thou forsaken me?" It follows, that the title of others to this promise is mediate only: "As many of you as have been baptized into Christ have put on Christ.... And if ye be Christ's, then are ye Abraham's seed, and heirs according to the promise."—Ib. 27-29.

It was with a view to this relation of the covenant to the Lord Jesus, that circumcision was appointed as a seal of it. In that rite was signified satisfaction to justice through the blood of the promised Seed, and the crucifying of our old man with him, to the putting off and destroying of the body of the flesh. (Deut. x, 16; Jer. iv, 4; Rom. vi, 6; Col. ii, 11, 12.)

Upon occasion of the offering of Isaac, the covenant was again confirmed to Abraham in promises which do not mention Canaan, but are summed in the intensive assurances: "In blessing I will bless thee, and in multiplying I will multiply thy seed as the stars of heaven, and as the sand which is upon the sea-shore, and thy seed shall possess the gate of his enemies, and in thy seed shall all the nations of the earth be blessed."—Gen. xxii, 16-18. What seed it was to whom these promises were made, we have seen before. The assurance to him of triumph over his enemies renews the pledge made to Eve, through the curse upon the serpent, "Her seed shall bruise thy head."—Gen. iii, 15. Of the same thing, the Spirit in Isaiah says: "Therefore will I divide him a portion with the great, and he shall divide the spoil with the strong; because he hath poured out his soul unto death, and he was numbered with the transgressors; and he bare the sin of many and made intercession for the transgressors."—Isa. liii, 12. Of it, Paul says: "He must reign, till he hath put all enemies under his feet."—1 Cor. xv, 25.

The covenant thus interpreted, was confirmed to Abraham with an oath (v. 16), of which Paul says: "Wherein God, willing more abundantly to show unto the heirs of promise the immutability of his counsel, confirmed it by an oath; that, by two immutable things, in which it was impossible for God to lie, we might have a strong consolation who have fled for refuge to lay hold upon the hope set before us. Which hope we have as an anchor of the soul both sure and steadfast, and which entereth into that within the veil, whither the forerunner is for us entered, even Jesus."—Heb. vi, 17-20. Here, again, it appears that the covenant with Abraham comprehended in its terms the very highest hopes which Christ's blood has purchased,—which he, in heaven, as his people's forerunner, now possesses, and which with him they shall finally share; and that the oath by which it was confirmed contemplated these very things, and was designed to perfect the faith and confidence of his people, in the gospel day, as well as of the patriarchs and saints of old.

It is thus manifest that while the Abrahamic covenant did undoubtedly convey to Abraham and his seed after the flesh many and precious temporal blessings, it was at the same time an embodiment of the very terms of the covenant between God and his Christ; that its provisions of grace to man are bestowed wholly in Christ; and that it is, therefore, exclusive and everlasting. There can be no reconciliation between God and man, but upon the terms of this covenant. There can, therefore, be no people of God, no true church of Christ, but of those who accept and are embraced in, and built upon, that alone foundation, "the everlasting covenant" made with Abraham.

> Section VIII.—*The Conditions of the Sinai Covenant.*—Moses' commission. 1. "If ye will obey." 2. "And keep my covenant."

At length, the four hundred years were past. The probation of the apostate nations was finished. The iniquity of the Amorites was full. God remembered his covenant with Abraham, and sent Moses into Egypt, saying to him: "I am Jehovah. And I appeared unto Abraham, unto Isaac, and unto Jacob, by the name of God Almighty; but by my name, Jehovah, was I not known to them. And I have also established my covenant with them, to give them the land of Canaan, the land of their pilgrimage, wherein they were strangers. And I have also heard the groaning of the children of Israel, whom the Egyptians keep in bondage, and I have remembered my covenant. Wherefore, say unto the children of Israel, I am the Lord, and I will bring you out from under the burdens of the Egyptians, and I will rid you out of their bondage, and I will redeem you with a stretched out arm and with great judgments; and I will take you to me for a people, and I will be to you a God; and ye shall know that I am the Lord your God, which bringeth you out from under the burdens of the Egyptians. And I will bring you in unto the land, concerning which I did swear to give it to Abraham, to Isaac, and to Jacob."—Ex. vi, 2-8. In this initial communication we have the key to the Sinai covenant, and to all God's subsequent dealings with Israel. In it three things are specially observable. (1.) The Abrahamic covenant is designated, "my covenant," in accordance with what we have already seen as to the nature of that covenant, as exclusive and everlasting. (2.) Its scope is stated in those all-embracing terms, "I will take you to me for a people, and I will be to you a God." (3.) The possession of the earthly Canaan is specified as a minor particular, under this comprehensive pledge.

With all this the Sinai covenant was in accord. Its conditional terms we have seen, as propounded through Moses. "Thus shalt thou say to the house of Jacob, and tell the children of Israel: Ye have seen what I did to the Egyptians, and how I bare you on eagles' wings, and brought you unto myself. Now, therefore, *if ye will obey my voice indeed, and keep my covenant.*"—Ex. xix, 3-5. The "voice" which they were to obey they heard on the next day, when God spake to them the words of the law, from the midst of the smoke and flame. Of it Moses afterward reminded the people: "Ye came near and stood under the mountain; and the mountain burned with fire unto the midst of heaven, with darkness, clouds, and thick darkness. And the Lord spake unto you out of the midst of the fire: ye heard the voice of the words, but saw no similitude, only a voice. And he declared unto you his covenant which he commanded you to perform, even ten commandments; and he wrote them upon two tables of stone."—Deut. iv, 11-13. Very great emphasis attaches to the Ten Commandments, in their relation as thus the fundamental law of the covenant. The first overture having been addressed to Israel, in the terms, "If ye will obey my voice," and by them accepted, the next day that voice was heard uttering those commandments. Again the people are called upon, and again respond in pledge of obedience. Moses then wrote in "the book of the covenant" all these words of the Lord, and read them in the audience of the people. And it was not till again they promised obedience to the terms thus set before them that the covenant was ratified, as we have seen. The Ten Commandments were then, by the finger of God, engraved on the two tables of stone, which were thence known as "the tables of the covenant." These were placed in "the ark of the covenant," which was in the holy of holies, in "the tabernacle of the covenant." Both of these derived their names and significance from these tables, which were the very center of the whole system of religion and worship connected with the tabernacle. The lid of the ark which covered these tables was the golden mercy-seat, with its cherubim of gold, between which stood the pillar of glory, the Shechinah, overshadowing the mercy-seat. It thus typified God's throne of grace immovably based upon the firm foundation of his eternal law—mercy to man only possible on condition of satisfaction to that law. Therefore, when remembrance of sins was made every year (Heb. x, 3), it was by the sprinkling of blood upon the mercy-seat and the ark of the covenant. (Ib. ix, 7.) A proper regard to the fact that the moral law was thus the fundamental condition of the covenant, while the ritual law was no part of it, but a later system of testimony, would have prevented much perplexing and erroneous speculation on the subject.

But the covenant had a second condition, "If ye will *keep my covenant.*" This second clause is implied in the first. But it is none the less important and significant, as being a categorical statement of the nature of the obedience required. We have already pointed out the fact that by *"my covenant"* was meant the covenant with Abraham, so interpreted by God himself in his first communication to Israel in Egypt. The covenant thus defined had but one condition and two promises. The promises were, to bring them out of the bondage of Egypt and give them the land of Canaan, and to be to them a God. The condition was, that Israel, in turn, would surrender themselves to be for a people to God. (Ex. vi, 7.) This condition is the only thing that can be meant by the phrase, "If ye will *keep* my covenant." It was the only duty laid upon them by that covenant. We thus find the two fundamental conditions of the Sinai covenant to have been in the terms, "If ye will obey my voice indeed"—the voice that spake in the Ten Commandments—and, "If ye will keep my covenant," to be a willing people unto me, and cleave to me as your God. Such was the foundation-stone on which the church was built.

Section IX.—*The Promises of the Sinai Covenant.* —1. A peculiar treasure. 2. "All the earth is mine." 3. A priest kingdom. 4. A holy nation. 5. Palestine

As were the conditions of the covenant, so were its promises altogether and eminently spiritual.

1. "Ye shall be unto me a peculiar treasure above all people; for all the earth is mine." A treasure is a property, valuable, highly prized, and cherished. It is riches to the owner; his enjoyments largely depend thereon; and over it he therefore exercises a watchful guardianship. Such was the relation which, by the covenant, God conferred on Israel. The expression is strengthened by the qualifying adjective, "peculiar," which means, special and exclusive. "My own special treasure." What was thus implied may be gathered from a single Scripture. Says the Lord, by Malachi: "Then they that feared the Lord spake often one to another, and the Lord hearkened and heard it, and a book of remembrance was written before him for them that feared the Lord, and that thought upon his name. And they shall be mine, saith the Lord of hosts, in that day when I make up my jewels" ("my peculiar treasures." The word in the original is the same), "and I will spare them, as a man spareth his own son that serveth him. Then shall ye return and discern between the righteous and the wicked; between him that serveth God, and him that serveth him not."—Mal. iii. 16-18. By this clause, Israel became the object of God's assiduous watchfulness and constant care as his own peculiar treasure of price.

2. The parenthetic clause, "For all the earth is mine," is of singular interest. The covenant with Abraham conveyed the assurance that in him should "all the families of the earth be blessed." The clause inserted in the Sinai overture was a reminder to Israel of that fact, to certify them and the world that the purpose concerning the latter was unchanged, that the peculiar relation now assumed toward Israel was not incongruous to it; that, on the contrary, whilst Israel was first, it was not alone in the obligations and promises of the covenant. "All the earth is mine;" and the claim which, in such a transaction, God thus makes he will surely vindicate, in his own good time, by taking his own to himself, bringing them, also, within the pale of his covenant, and gathering from them a revenue of praise and glory.

3. "A kingdom of priests." Israel's acceptance of the first condition of the covenant, "If ye will obey my voice," erected them into a kingdom, of which God was the alone sovereign,—the kingdom of God. This promise defines the character and function of that kingdom,—"a kingdom of priests;" or, rather, "a priest-kingdom." Israel was thus ordained to the exalted office of intercessory mediation for the world, and of testimony to it on God's behalf. Had ten righteous men been found in the cities of the plain, they would have been spared, for the sake of those ten. (Gen. xviii, 32.) The angels of destruction could do nothing to Sodom until Lot departed out of it. (Ib. xix, 22.) Had one righteous man been found in Jerusalem in the days of Jeremiah, the city would have been spared for the sake of that one. (Jer. v, 1.) Aaron the priest, with his golden censer—a type of the prayers of the saints (Rev. v, 8; viii, 3)—standing between the living and the dead, stayed the plague in the camp of Israel. (Num. xvi, 46-48.) So, Israel itself was now ordained a mediating priest, to stand for the time then present, between the living and the dead of

the nations, in the ordinances at the sanctuary, uplifting a censer of intercession which stayed the sword of justice that was ready to destroy them; and appointed to become at length the agent of the world's salvation, through atonement made by one of their nation, and the gospel sent forth from Jerusalem to all the world, by the preaching of Israel's sons. Thus was it a priest-kingdom, set apart and sanctified of God, to be for salvation to all the ends of the earth.

This priestly consecration of Israel, moreover, constituted her a witness on behalf of God among the nations. It was the lighting of a lamp to shine amid the darkness of the world. The office to which she was thus ordained was not yet aggressive; for the times of the Gentiles were not come. Yet was hers none the less a public and active testimony, which, if they would, the Gentiles could hear, a gospel light which did, in fact, penetrate far into the darkness, and prepared the nations for the coming of Christ and the gospel day. For the time being, it was the office of Israel to cherish the light, by keeping the oracles and maintaining the ordinances of God's worship, and transmitting them to their children, until the fullness of time.

4. "A holy nation." The word "holy" primarily designates the completeness and symmetry of the moral perfections of God. From hence, it is transferred to those attributes in the intelligent creatures which are in the likeness of God's holiness. And, as the distinguishing characteristic of holiness in a creature is surrender and consecration to God, the word is used to designate all such things as are his by peculiar dedication to his service. Thus, the altar, the tabernacle, and all the vessels and things pertaining thereto, were holy. So the tithe of the land, of the flocks, and of the herds, was holy; and the firstborn of men and of beasts. (Lev. xxvii, 30, 32; Luke ii, 23.) In this sense of accepted consecration, and of appropriation to himself, God here puts upon Israel the designation of "a holy nation." Henceforth, they were so named, and the obligation implied therein constantly insisted upon, as demanding from them real separation to God, and holiness of heart and life. Says the Lord: "Ye shall be holy men unto me, neither shall ye eat any flesh that is torn of beasts in the field." — Ex. xxii, 31. Moses exhorts them to abhor and destroy the idols of the land, "For thou art a holy people unto the Lord thy God; the Lord thy God hath chosen thee to be a special people unto himself, above all people that are upon the face of the earth.... Thou shalt, therefore, keep the commandments and the statutes and the judgments which I command thee this day to do them." — Deut. vii, 6-11. From this article of the covenant, the New Testament designation of the members of the visible church is derived. Says Peter, "Ye are a chosen generation, a royal priesthood, a *holy nation*, a peculiar people." — 1 Peter, ii, 9. Hence, the name of "saints," or, "holy ones," which, familiar in the Psalms, is constantly used in the epistles, as the distinctive title of the members of the New Testament Church.

Thus it appears that in all the provisions of the covenant earthly and temporal blessings are not once alluded to. That clause of the Abrahamic covenant which concerned the possession of Canaan was, indeed, referred to at Sinai, and Israel was assured of its fulfillment. (Ex. xxiii, 23.) But it was then, and ever after, spoken of and treated as already and finally settled by the promise made to Abraham. (Ex.

vi, 3-8; Deut. vii, 7-9; ix, 5, 6; Psalm cv, 8-11.) Moreover, the bestowal of Canaan was in no sense a secular transaction. Not only as a type of the better country was it designed and calculated to awaken and stimulate heavenly aspirations. (Heb. xi, 8-16.) But, like the fastnesses of the Alps, for centuries the retreat and home of the gospel among the martyr Waldenses, Canaan, planted in the very center of the old world-empires, and upon the mid line of march of the world's great history, was chosen and prepared of God as a fortress of security entrenched for Israel's protection, in the midst of the apostate and hostile nations, while tending and nourishing the beacon fire of gospel light which glowed on Mount Zion, and shed its beams afar into the gloom of thick darkness which enshrouded the world. As such, it was assured to Abraham's seed by the covenant with him and the seal set in their flesh.

> Section X.—*The Visible Church was thus established.*—The Church defined. Its name. Its fundamental law. Membership. Family and eldership. Ordinances of testimony. The relation of the ritual law

The Sinai covenant gave origin to the visible church of God. By the visible church, I mean that society among men which God has called and taken into covenant and communion with himself, and ordained to be his witness to the world. Two points are essentially involved in the definition. The first is the relation to God established by the terms—"I will take you to me for a people; and I will be to you a God." The second is the office to which the church is thus called and ordained, to be God's witness, testifying on his behalf against the world's apostasy. Such is Peter's declaration, quoting the terms of the Sinai covenant, and applying them to the New Testament church: "Ye are a chosen generation, a royal priesthood, a holy nation, a peculiar people; *that ye should show forth the praises* of him who hath called you out of darkness into his marvelous light; which in time past were not a people, but *are now the people of God.*"—1 Peter ii, 9, 10. This privilege of communion, and this office of testimony were implied and involved in the whole covenant, and all its terms; but especially indicated by that expression, "Ye shall be *unto me a kingdom of priests, and a holy nation.*" It is the privilege of priests to draw nigh to God, and their office to testify on God's behalf to men.

The manner and meaning of the designation by which, throughout the Greek Scriptures of the Old Testament and of the New, the body thus constituted is known as the *ekklēsia*, the church, is worthy of special notice in this connection. The fact of God having met with Israel at Sinai, and communed with them in an audible voice, is referred to by Moses and emphasized as being a signal demonstration of relations established of extraordinary intimacy. "What nation is there so great, which hath God so nigh unto them as the Lord our God in all things that we call upon him for?... Take heed to thyself, and keep thy soul diligently, lest thou forget the things which thine eyes have seen, and lest they depart from thy heart, all the days of thy life; but teach them thy sons and thy sons' sons, specially the day that thou stoodest before the Lord thy God in Horeb, when the Lord said unto me, Gather me the people together, and I will make them hear my words, that they may learn to fear me all the days that they shall live upon the earth, and that they may teach their children.... And the Lord spake unto you out of the midst of the fire; ye heard the voice of the words, but saw no similitude; only ye heard a voice."—Deut. iv, 7-13. Again, he says: "Ask now of the days that are past, which were before thee, since the day that God created man upon the earth, and ask from one side of heaven unto the other, whether there hath been any such a thing as this great thing is, or hath been heard like it. Did ever people hear the voice of God speaking out of the midst of fire, as thou, hast heard, and live? Or hath God assayed to go and take him a nation from the midst of another nation, by temptations, by signs, and by wonders, and by war, and by a mighty hand, and by a stretched out arm, and by great terrors, according to all that the Lord thy God did for you in Egypt before your eyes? Unto thee it was showed, that thou mightest know that the Lord he is God; there is none else beside him."—Ib. iv, 32-35.

The presence of God with Israel, thus impressively manifested, was not casual or transient. The fires and the terrors of Sinai were indeed withdrawn. But the tabernacle of testimony was erected, and the shechinah there revealed for the express purpose of being a testimony to Israel that God was with them dwelling in their midst. Of the services to be there established, he directed Moses that there should be "a continual burnt-offering throughout your generations, at the door of the tabernacle of the congregation before the Lord, where I will meet you to speak there unto thee. And there will I meet with the children of Israel, and the tabernacle" (or rather, as the margin, "Israel") "shall be sanctified by my glory. And I will dwell among the children of Israel, and will be their God."—Ex. xxix, 42-46.

Thus the gathering of Israel at Sinai was not a mere congregation or assembling of the people to each other, but a meeting with God; and this fact is very remarkably indicated in the Septuagint Greek. In the description of the Sinai scene, given in Deut. iv, in that version, the tenth verse stands thus: "The day that thou stoodest before the Lord thy God in Horeb (*tē hēmera tēs ekklēsias*), *in the day of the assembly,* when the Lord said to me (*Ekklēsiason pros me*), *Assemble to me* the people." Previous to that occasion the word *ekklēsia* is not found in the Greek Scriptures. That day was, by Moses, habitually designated "the day of the *ekklēsia*—the assembly" (Deut. ix, 10; x, 4; xviii, 16), and the reason of the designation is thus, by the Greek translators, stamped upon the face of that version. It was so called because the people on that day met with God, in compliance with the command (*Ekklēsiason*), "*Assemble to me* the people." In accordance with the special meaning to which the word was thus appropriated it is used throughout the Scriptures. In the Old Testament and Apocrypha it occurs nearly one hundred times, and a careful examination fails to discover an instance in which it is used otherwise than to designate Israel in their sacred character as the covenant people of God. In that sense it passed into the New Testament. In one place it is exceptionally used by the town clerk of the Greek city of Ephesus, and by Luke, after him, in its classic meaning, to designate an assembly of the freemen of the city. (Acts xix, 39, 41.) But everywhere else it is employed in the same sense as in the Septuagint. It is thus applied (1) to Israel in the wilderness (Acts vii, 38), and at the temple (Heb. ii, 12); (2) to the religious assemblies of the Jews during the time of Christ's ministry (Matt. xviii, 17), and ever afterwards, in the Acts, Epistles, and Revelation, to the New Testament Church. According, therefore, to the uniform usage of the Scriptures, the word is appropriated to designate an assembly with God, and, in a secondary sense, the people as related to such an assembly. Such is the designation given to Israel as the people of God by covenant and fellowship, among whom he held the communion of mutual converse, he with them in the words of his testimony and the communications of his grace, and they with him in all things in which they called upon him. (Deut. iv, 7. Compare Matt. xviii, 20; Acts x, 33.) In the assembly of Israel, the church of the apostles finds an origin in no wise unworthy her own lofty character and office. Happy she when with conscious experience she can take to herself the glad words of Israel's song, "There is a river, the streams whereof shall make glad the city of God, the holy place of the tabernacles of the Most High. God is in the midst of her, she shall not be moved; God shall help her, and that right early.... The Lord of hosts is with us, the God of Jacob is our refuge."—Psalm xlvi, 4-7.

The following were the essential features of the constitution of the church thus erected:

1. Its fundamental charter was the covenant, embracing the ten commandments, in the reciprocal terms which have been considered in the preceding chapter.

2. The persons with whom these terms were made, and who were comprehended in the society thereupon erected, were all those, whether of Israel or the Gentiles, together with their households, who made credible profession of accepting the covenant, and were thereupon sealed with its baptismal seal. To this point we shall presently return.

3. The radical principle of organization was that of parental headship and family unity. The family is the divine original of all human society, as the parental office is of all human authority. Upon this basis was founded the Abrahamic covenant, and upon it was erected the system of government for Israel. It was administered by the fathers of families, of houses, and of tribes; the first-born son succeeding to his father as head of his house, under the designation of elder. This system was recognized in the first commission of Moses from God, and the elders, or heads of houses, were united with him in his mission to Pharaoh. (Ex. iii, 16, 18; iv, 29.) To them was committed the ordering of the passover on the night of the exodus. (Ib. xii, 21.) At Sinai, before the giving of the covenant, the system was perfected in its details, at the suggestion of Jethro, with the sanction of God. (Ex. xviii, 12-24.) Immediately upon the sealing of the covenant seventy of the elders, who had been previously assembled by the command of God, went up, as already stated, with Moses and Aaron, Nadab and Abihu, into the mount, and there celebrated on Israel's behalf the feast of the covenant. "They saw the God of Israel, and did eat and drink."—Ex. xxiv, 1, 9-11. Afterward, when the covenant was renewed in the plains of Moab, the relation of the elders thereto, in their official capacity, was expressly stated. "Ye stand this day, all of you, before the Lord your God, your captains of your tribes, your elders and your officers, with all the men of Israel, your little ones, your wives."—Deut. xxix, 10.

Such were the essential features of the constitution of the church, as ordained at Sinai. To her, thus organized, were given ordinances of testimony, concerning which a few points only are here necessary. Since she was appointed simply to maintain, in her position in the midst of the nations, the lamp of gospel truth ever shining, until the set time should come for sending it forth through the world, the ordinances of testimony which were intrusted to her were adapted expressly to this office. They were: (1.) The oracles of God, his written word, from time to time imparted through Moses and other holy men, who spake as they were moved of the Holy Ghost. (Rom. iii, 2; 2 Pet. i, 21.) (2.) The holy convocations of the Sabbath days. (Lev. xxiii, 3; 1 Kings iv, 23; Acts xv, 21.) (3.) The priesthood and ritual service. (4.) The sanctuary worship and festivals. (5.) Public professions of faith, occasional and stated. (Deut. xxvi.) (6.) Poetic recitations and psalmody. (Ex. xv, 1-21; Deut. xxxi, xxxii; the book of Psalms.)

It was with a special view to the witnessing office of the church of Israel that the ritual system was constructed. The covenant and the ritual were testimonies to the better covenant and the heavenly realities which belong to it. It is with this view that the word "testimony" is so much used in designating them. Thus the Ten Commandments, the fundamental law of the covenant, were frequently designated "the testimony." (Ex. xxv, 21.) The tables on which they were written were, in like manner, "the tables of the testimony." They were kept in "the ark of the testimony," which was in "the tabernacle of the testimony." In the same way the whole system of ordinances and laws given to Israel is designated "the testimonies of God." Of them, and the office of the church concerning them, the Psalmist says: "He established a testimony in Jacob, and appointed a law in Israel, which he commanded our fathers, that they should make them known to their children, that the generation to come might know them: even the children which should be born; who should arise and declare them to their children; that they might set their hope in God, and not forget his works, but keep his commandments."—Psalm lxxviii, 5-7.

Respecting the ritual system, there are two propositions which are believed to be demonstrable, but are here presented without argument. The *first* is, that these rites were not dark forms, veiling rather than disclosing a new revelation; but were inscriptions in luminous characters, setting forth the doctrines of a faith well understood by the patriarchs and fathers from the beginning, and from them transmitted and known to Israel. *Second.* The ritual forms in which the gospel was clothed in the Levitical system were far more suitable for the purposes of popular instruction and world-wide dissemination than would have been any conceivable exposition of it in writing. The art of writing was in its infancy. A written gospel would have been, even to Israel, a sealed book; how much more to all other people! The history and laws were put in writing and kept at the sanctuary for the direction of the priests and magistrates in the performance of their duties, the administration of justice, and the instruction of Israel. But the gospel, for the people, was clothed in forms which required no interpreter, which meant the same in every language under heaven, and which were calculated, by their appeals to the imagination through the eye and the senses, to stamp themselves indelibly upon the memory and the affections. Thus were they eminently adapted to arrest the attention and impress the minds of strangers, and of the young, for whom especially they were designed. (Ex. xii, 26; xiii, 14; Deut. vi, 20; Josh. iv, 6, 21; 1 Kings viii, 41, 42.)

The fact is of an importance which entitles it to distinct and emphatic mention, that the Aaronic priesthood and the ritual law were no part of the constitution of the church, as it was established by the covenant. They were not in existence when the covenant was made, but were ordinances afterward given to the church, as already existent and organized. They were bestowed as means of fulfilling her witnessing office, means adapted to the times and circumstances of Israel, but subject to be modified, as they were in the temple system, or to be wholly suspended or set aside, without impairing the constitution of the church or the completeness and efficiency of its organization. Not only thus did the covenant precede the ritual law and the priesthood, but when, forty years afterward, the covenant was renewed, and the parties to it were enumerated in detail, the priests were altogether ignored. (Deut. xxix, 10-12.) They were in no wise essential to it.

Section XI. — *The Terms of Membership in the Church of Israel.* — Professed
faith and obedience. The same to Israel and Gentiles. Separating
the unworthy

With some slight circumstantial differences, having reference to the difference in the office of the church under the two dispensations, the conditions of membership were essentially the same as propounded at Sinai and as prescribed under the gospel. While the spiritual blessings of the covenant were from the beginning conditioned upon true faith and loving obedience, the privilege of membership in the visible church was at Sinai bestowed upon those, with their households, who made credible profession of these graces, and upon them only. On "the day of the assembly," all the people professed to take God for their God, and to devote themselves to him as his believing and obedient people. And as on the days of Pentecost, so on this occasion, the profession was accepted, and their admission was sealed with baptism; although doubtless, in both cases, there were false professors included with the true. With certain exceptions, ordained for special reasons (Deut. xxiii, 1-8), the conditions of membership were the same for the Gentile world as for Israel. The law was explicit and most emphatic on this point. "One ordinance shall be both for you of the congregation and also for the stranger that sojourneth with you, an ordinance forever in your generations: as ye are, so shall the stranger be before the Lord. One law and one manner shall be for you and for the stranger that sojourneth with you." — Num. xv, 14-16, and 29; and see ix, 14; xix, 10; Ex. xii, 43-49; Deut. xxxi, 12; Josh. viii, 33, etc.

For eliminating unworthy members, the means provided in the Sinai ordinances were as abundant as those now enjoyed by the church, and would seem to have been as well adapted to the effectual securing of the end proposed. They come under three heads. (1.) Certain offenses were visited with the penalty of death or of utter separation from the communion of Israel. (Ex. xxxi, 14; Num. ix, 13, etc.) (2.) The expenses incident to a faithful performance of the duties required of members of the church of Israel were large and continual. Firstfruits, firstlings, and tithes, trespass offerings, sin offerings, freewill offerings, and other oblations, made up an aggregate which can not have fallen short of one-fifth of all the income of Israel, and probably went far beyond that amount. The law provided none but moral means for enforcing these requirements; and numerous facts in the history of Israel show that by many they were entirely neglected. (Neh. xiii, 10-13; Mal. iii, 8-10.) Those who thus withheld what belonged to the Lord were self-excluded from the fellowship of the covenant society, and were "cut off from the congregation (*ekklēsia* from *the church*) of the Lord." (3.) The irksome and humiliating nature of the regulations concerning uncleanness and purifying were very efficient means of separating between the believing and the profane. As we shall presently see, occasions of uncleanness were of almost daily occurrence, in every house. These required a conscientious watchfulness and assiduity, in guarding against defilement, and in using the appointed rites of purifying, which often involved the interruption and expense of journeys to the sanctuary and offerings there.

The communion of the church of Israel thus consisted of those only, with their families, who added to the obligations of a public profession of faith, a fidelity to all the requirements of the law, its moral precepts, its ritual observances, its tithes and offerings, its rites of purifying and its annual feasts. In a word, the account given of Zacharias and Elizabeth describes the character required, in order to fellowship in the church of Israel: "Righteous before God, walking in all the commandments and ordinances of the Lord blameless."—Luke i, 6. Such, and such only, were the *clean*, to whom the privileges of Israel's communion belonged. To them they were certified by the seal of baptism.

Section XII.—*Circumcision and Baptism.*—The former sealed the Abrahamic covenant. The latter alone sealed the ecclesiastical covenant of Sinai

It is commonly assumed that baptism has come into the place and office of circumcision. This I conceive to be a mistaken view, which involves the whole subject in confusion. Circumcision is the distinctive and peculiar seal of the Abrahamic covenant. While it is true, that in that covenant, as relating to the terms of salvation, all believers were accounted as seed of Abraham, and heirs of the promises, it is equally true that, by its terms, peculiar blessings unspeakably great were assured to the seed of the patriarch after the flesh. Not only was Christ to come of his flesh; not only was the church to be for fifteen centuries constituted of his offspring, but Paul moreover testifies, that richer blessings than they have ever yet enjoyed are to be bestowed on Israel and on the Gentiles through Israel, in the coming future: "If the fall of them be the riches of the world, and the diminishing of them the riches of the Gentiles, how much more their fullness?... For if the casting away of them be the reconciling of the world, what shall the receiving of them be but life from the dead?"—Rom. xi, 12, 15. This the apostle, futhermore, puts upon the ground that "the gifts and calling of God are without repentance."—Ib. 29. It was with a view to this relation of the covenant to Abraham's natural seed, that circumcision was appointed as its seal. Said God: "I will establish my covenant between me and thee and thy seed after thee, *in their generations*, for an everlasting covenant, to be a God unto thee and to thy seed after thee."—Gen. xvii, 7. Hence, by circumcision, the token of the covenant was set in the flesh of the males, through whom the descent is counted. So long, therefore, as the church was, for the divine purposes, restricted to the family of Israel, the rite of circumcision was necessary as a prerequisite condition of admission to its privileges, because it was the seal of incorporation by birth or adoption into that family. But this did not constitute admission into the church. The Sinai covenant had its own baptismal seal. The church consisted, not of Israel, the circumcised; but only of the *clean* of Israel. Of this, baptism was the token and seal. It hence resulted that when the restriction was removed, and the gospel was given to the Gentiles, emancipated from the yoke of circumcision, baptism remained unchanged in place or office, the original and only seal of actual admission to the fellowship and privileges of the church of God. Of all this we shall see more hereafter.

PART III.

ADMINISTERED BAPTISMS = SPRINKLINGS.

Section XIII.—*Unclean Seven Days.*—The meaning. Childbirth. Issues. Contact with the dead. Leprosy. Characterized by (1) inward corruption; (2) seven days continuance; (3) contagiousness; (4) requiring sacrifice and sprinkling

In the laws of Moses there were two grades of uncleanness defined—uncleanness of seven days, and uncleanness till the even. The former was a symbol of that essential corruption which is in us by nature, to which are essential the redeeming blood of Christ and the renewing of the Holy Spirit, without which no man can see God in peace. Uncleanness till the even symbolized those casual defilements to which God's renewed people are liable by contact with the evil of the world. The ritual, concerning the uncleanness of seven days, was designed to signalize the light in which man's apostate nature, and the depravity and sin thence resulting, appear in the sight of a God of ineffable holiness. To this conception the word *unclean* was designed to give expression, the intense meaning of which is liable to escape the casual reader of the Scriptures. It signified, not the mere external soiling of the living person, but death, corruption, and rottenness within the heart, the fermenting source of pollution poured forth in the outward life. To impress us with a just sense of the exceeding evil of this thing the Spirit employs every variety of figure expressive of deformity and loathsomeness. In the primitive faith, of which the book of Job is a record, it is characterized in language which is a key-note to all the Scriptures on the subject. "Behold he putteth no trust in his saints" (his holy angels); "yea, the heavens are not pure in his sight. How much more abominable and filthy is man, which drinketh iniquity like water."—Job xv, 15, 16. Says the Psalmist, "The Lord looked down from heaven upon the children of men, to see if there were any that did understand and seek God. They are all gone aside; they are all together become filthy."—Psa. xiv, 3. Here the word "filthy" is in the margin rendered "stinking." It is the same in the original as in the above place in Job, and means the offensiveness of putrefaction. David, in his penitential Psalm, indicates his sense of this radical evil of his nature. "Wash me thoroughly from mine iniquity and *cleanse* me from my sin.... Behold I was shapen in iniquity, and in sin did my mother conceive me. Behold thou desirest truth in the *inward parts*: and in the *hidden part* thou shalt make me to know wisdom. Purge me with hyssop, and I shall be *clean*; wash me and I shall be whiter than snow.... Create in me a *clean heart*, O God; and renew a right spirit within me."—Psa. li, 2-10. Isaiah and other sacred writers represent the same evil by the figures of the vomit and filthiness of a drunken debauch, and by every kind of abominable and loathsome thing. (Isa. xxviii, 8; Prov. xxx, 12.) By the designation, unclean, the moral deformity and offensiveness of Satan and the "unclean spirits," his angels, are described. And in the accounts of the riches of grace and glory in store for the church, the crowning feature is the exclusion of the unclean. "A highway shall be there, and a way; and it shall be called, The way of holiness; the unclean shall not pass over it." — Isa. xxxv, 8. The church is called upon for this cause to exult: "Awake, awake, put on thy strength, O Zion; put on thy beautiful garments, O Jerusalem, the holy city; for henceforth there shall no more come into thee the uncircumcised and the unclean." — Ib. lii, 1. And again, John, in the vision of the glory of the new Jerusalem, which crowns and closes his revelation, says of her: "And there shall in no wise enter into it any thing that defileth" (literally, "any thing unclean"), "neither whatsoever worketh abomination, or maketh a lie; but they which are written in the Lamb's book of life." — Rev. xxi, 27.

For the purpose of inducing a profound sense of this evil and loathsomeness of sin, as working in the heart, the ordinances respecting the uncleanness of seven days were appointed, each having its own lesson.

1. The birth of a child was the actual propagation, from the parents, of part in the uncleanness of the apostate nature. It was, therefore, attended with natural phenomena, and marked by ritual ordinances which characterized it, and every function connected with it, as unclean and defiling. Emphasis was thus given to the challenge, "Who can bring a clean thing out of an unclean? Not one." — Job xiv, 4.

2. Running issues of all kinds were appropriated as symbols of the corruption of man's nature, festering within, and breaking forth in putrescent streams of depravity and sin in the active life. (Ezek. xvi, 6, 9.)

3. Death is "the wages of sin" (Rom. vi, 23), and physical death is a terrible emblem of its loathsome and accursed nature. And as sin and the curse are diffused to Adam's seed by the very contagion of nature, this, their symbol, was ritually endowed with the same contagious character. He that touched the dead was reckoned no longer among the living but the dead. He was, therefore, cast out from the camp, from his family, the sanctuary, and the privileges of the covenant. To them all he was dead. He was unclean.

Thus, as the loving and bereaved stood by the couch of death, gazed upon the face and form once blooming in health and beauty, and beheld the sightless and sunken eyes, the ghastly features and cadaverous hue — pledges of corruption begun — while the very air of the chamber seemed to breathe the cry, "Unclean!" as they realized the instinctive recoil which love itself must feel from the very touch of the departed, and felt as Abraham, concerning the beloved Sarah, the constraint to "bury his dead out of his sight," — as, in all this, they knew that these last offices even must be fulfilled at the expense of defilement and exclusion from the privileges of God's earthly courts and the society of his people, for seven days, they and all Israel received a lesson of divine instruction as to the exceeding sinfulness of sin, the wages of which is death, its loathsomeness in God's sight, its contagious diffusion and power, and its curse, to which human speech or angel eloquence could have added nothing.

4. No less impressive were the ordinances concerning leprosy. The name designated a class of diseases, some of which would appear to have been altogether miraculous in their origin, and peculiar in their symptoms, while others were attributable to natural causes. The disease was peculiar for the shocking and loathsome appearance of its victim, its poisoning the blood and pervading the whole body, and its incurable and inevitably deadly nature. It was, therefore, employed by God as, at once, an extraordinary punishment of sin, and a most fitting symbol of it, as seated in the heart and nature of man, and pervading and corrupting his whole being. (Num. xii, 10; 2 Kings v, 27; 2 Chr. xxvi, 20.) The leper was accounted as one dead (Num. xii, 12), and, therefore, excluded from his family, from the congregation and ordinances at the sanctuary, and from the very camp of Israel, where the living God walked. (Num. v, 2; xii, 14.) Thus, outcast from the abodes of men and the house of God, "the leper in whom the plague is, his clothes shall be rent, and his head bare, and he shall put a covering upon his upper lip, and shall cry, Unclean! Unclean! All the days wherein the plague shall be in him, he shall be defiled; he is unclean; he shall dwell alone; without the camp shall be his habitation."—Lev. xiii, 45, 46. How dreadful the figure thus presented to the senses of Israel, of the loathsomeness of sin in God's sight, and of its ruinous effects upon the sinner! The person offensive with scabs and sores, the rent garments, the uncovered head, the wailing cry, "Unclean! Unclean!" while the exclusion from the house of God, and from the abodes of men, and the covered lip, proclaimed to Israel that the spiritual leper, yet in his sins, brings danger to his fellow-men with his very presence, and is an offense and loathing to God, before the eyes of whose purity he may not venture to come, save through the cleansing blood and Spirit of Christ. Hence, the cry of Isaiah, when he beheld the glory of the Lord: "Woe is me! for I am undone, because I am a man of unclean lips, and I dwell in the midst of a people of unclean lips; for mine eyes have seen the King, the Lord of hosts." And hence, the coal of fire from off the altar of atonement, and the seraph's assurance, "Lo, this hath touched thy lips; and thine iniquity is taken away, and thy sin purged."—Isa. vi, 5-7.

Thus, every way, under the idea of indwelling defilement, was sin and its source in man's corrupted nature held up to Israel as loathsome in itself, propagated to the race and infecting all, defiling in its contact, deadly in its indwelling power, and abhorrent to the eyes of God.

Four circumstances in the ritual on these defilements are peculiar and characteristic:

1. The first of these exhibits a broad and fundamental contrast between these defilements and those which continued only till the even. The latter, as already intimated, presented the conception of an outward soiling of the living person. But the uncleanness of seven days exhibited the idea, not of surface defilement of the living, but of the loathsomeness and pollution of the dead and decaying carcass, pouring out its own corruption, and infecting all around with its unclean

and abhorrent presence,—a pollution which no extrinsic or surface washing can ever cleanse.

2. The defilement was for seven days. God's work of creation ended in the rest of the seventh day. That day was hence appropriated as a type of the final rest of Christ and his people upon the completed work of redemption. Hence, the argument of Paul: "For he spake of the seventh day on this wise, And God did rest the seventh day from all his works. And in this place again, If they shall enter into my rest. There remaineth therefore a rest for the people of God."—Heb. iv, 4-9. "A rest:" literally, as in the margin, "a keeping of a Sabbath," or, "a Sabbatism." But the Sabbath thus reserved for God's people, coincides with "the day of judgment and perdition of ungodly men." Hence, a seven days' uncleanness was typical of such a corruption of nature as is essential and, therefore, persistent to the end; and the exclusion of the defiled from the camp and the sanctuary signified the sentence of the judgment of the last day, when those whose natures are unrenewed, and whose sins are unpurged will be excluded from the Sabbath of redemption and from the new Jerusalem, and remain finally under the woe of the second death: "He that is filthy, let him be filthy still.... For without are dogs and sorcerers, and whoremongers, and murderers, and idolaters, and whosoever loveth and maketh a lie."—Rev. xxii, 11, 15.

3. The defilement was contagious. If the unclean for seven days touched a clean person, the latter was thereby defiled until the even. For, such is the inveteracy of this native corruption of the race that God's people are liable to defilement from every intercourse and contact with the world,—a defilement, however, which they will leave behind them when the day of earthly life is ended. Therefore, "Come out from among them, and be ye separate, saith the Lord, and touch not the unclean thing, and I will receive you."—2 Cor. vi, 17.

4. This seven days' uncleanness could not be purified without sacrificial rites, and water sprinkled by the hand of one that was clean. For nothing but the atoning merits of Christ's one offering, and the Spirit of life which he sheds down upon his people, can enter and cleanse our defiled nature, and fit us for admission to the presence of God, or for part in the New Jerusalem. All this will more fully appear as we proceed to notice the rites of purifying appointed for the several kinds of this uncleanness, respectively.

Section XIV.—*The Baptism of a healed Leper.*—Seven sprinklings. The self-washings. Meaning of the rites

The rites appointed for the purifying of a healed leper come under two heads,—those administered by the priest, and those performed by the person himself. When a leper was healed, he was first inspected by the priest, who went forth to him to ascertain that the healing was real, and the disease eradicated. This being ascertained, the priest took two clean birds, and had one of them killed and its blood caught in an earthen vessel, with running water. He then took the remaining bird, alive, with cedar wood, scarlet, and hyssop, and dipped all together in the blood and water; "and he shall sprinkle upon him that is to be cleansed from the leprosy seven times, and shall pronounce him clean, and shall let the living bird loose into the open field." — Lev. xiv, 7.

The rite which thus ended by the official decree of the priest, "*He is clean*," completed the purification, properly so called. The man is now clean. The remaining ordinances were expressive of duties and privileges proper to one who is cleansed and restored to the commonwealth of Israel, and the communion of God's house. First of these he was required to "wash his clothes, and shave off all his hair, and wash himself in water, that he may be clean." — Ib., vs. 8. He was now admitted to the camp, but must not yet enter his own tent, nor come to the tabernacle for seven days. On the seventh day he was again required to shave off all his hair, wash his clothes, and bathe his flesh; and "he shall be clean." — Vs. 9.

Now, on the eighth day, he came to the sanctuary, bringing a sacrifice of a trespass offering, a sin offering, and a burnt offering. The rites attendant upon these offerings completed the ceremonial. Thenceforth, the leper resumed all the privileges of a son of Israel, in his family, in the the congregation, and at the sanctuary.

The general signification of these ordinances is evident. The priest, by whom alone the cleansing rites could be administered, was the official representative of our great high-priest, Christ Jesus. The two birds were with the priest a complex type of him who offered himself without spot to God, who was dead and is alive for evermore, and by the merits of whose blood and the power of whose Spirit remission of sins and the new life of holiness are given to men. The first self-washing symbolized the duty of the redeemed to turn from their old ways and walk in holiness. The continued exclusion, for seven days, from his house and the sanctuary was a testimony that for the present we are pilgrims and strangers, and that only at the end of earth's trials and purgations can we enter our "house which is from heaven." The seventh day's washing indicated the final putting off of all evil in the resurrection; and the offerings of the eighth represented the way whereby, in the regeneration, God's redeemed people shall have access to his presence and communion with him, through the blood of Jesus.

We are now able to understand why the cleansing of the healed leper was thus separately ordered, and not included in the provision which we shall presently see was made, in common, for all other cases of seven days' uncleanness. The extraordinary and frequently supernatural character of both the disorder and its cure rendered it proper and necessary to take it out of the category of ordinary uncleannesses, and place it under the immediate jurisdiction of the priests. This was necessary, alike, in order to a judicial determination at first as to the existence of the leprosy, and afterward as to the cure. And the priestly administration of the rites of cleansing was equally important, as constituting an official and authoritative proclamation of the healing and restoration of the leper.

Section XV. — *Baptism of those defiled by the Dead.* — The ordinary seal of
    the covenant. The ashes. Manner of the baptism

The purification of the leper must have been of rare occurrence. All the facts and indications of the Scriptures tend to the conclusion that, except by miraculous agency, the disease was incurable. The baptism of Israel at Sinai was extraordinary in its nature and circumstances, and could not have been repeated except in circumstances equally remarkable, such as that when, in the plains of Moab, the covenant was renewed with the new generation, which had risen up to take the place of those who perished in the wilderness. (Deut. xxix, 1.) But of that transaction the particulars are not recorded. In the water of separation, provision was made for an ordinary rite, essentially the same, in its nature, mode, and meaning, as the Sinai baptism; and so ordered as to serve as a continual memorial and repetition of it, and reiteration of the promises and instructions therein embodied. This rite was appointed for the cleansing of defilements of daily occurrence, and was maintained through all the after history of Israel, until the time of Christ, and the destruction of Jerusalem. It was known to the Jews by the name of *baptism*.

In preparation for this rite, a red heifer without blemish was chosen by the priest, and slain without the camp, whence the priest sprinkled the blood toward the door of the tabernacle of the congregation seven times. The entire heifer was then burned, while the priest cast cedar wood, hyssop, and scarlet into the burning. The ashes were gathered and laid up in a clean place, without the camp. (Num. xix, 2-10.) They were to be "kept for the congregation of the children of Israel for a water of separation."—Ib. 9. By the phrase, "water of separation," is not meant a water to cause separation, but a remedy for it. They were, as Zechariah expresses it, "*for* sin and *for* uncleanness."—Zech. xiii, 1.

The primary case for which they were provided was that of defilement by the dead. (Num. xix, 17, 18.) Whoever touched a dead body or bone of a man, or a grave, was defiled thereby, as was the tent or house where the body lay, and the furniture and utensils that were in it. For the purifying of these, some of the ashes of the heifer were mingled, in an earthen vessel, with running water. A clean person then took a bush of hyssop, and, dipping it into the water, sprinkled it on the persons or things to be cleansed. This was done on the third day, and repeated on the seventh. "And on the seventh day he shall purify himself, and wash his clothes, and bathe himself in water, and shall be clean at even."—Num. xix, 2-19. Thus, as in the case of the leper, the rites for defilement by the dead were divided into two categories,—those administered by the priest or a clean person acting officially, and those performed by the subject himself. The importance of the distinction thus made between rites administered and those self-performed is worthy of repeated and emphatic notice. The former symbolized Christ's and the Spirit's agency; the latter, the active personal obedience and holiness of the believer's life.

It appears from the rabbins that, at least during the later period of Jewish history, the purifying of persons was, whenever practicable, performed at Jerusalem, by the hand of a priest, and with water drawn from the pool of Siloam, which flowed from the foot of the temple mount. For the purifying of houses and other things, the ashes were sent throughout the land, and the rites performed where the uncleanness was contracted.

Section XVI.—*Purifying from Issues.*—The law seemingly incongruous.
      The water of nidda

The remaining forms of major uncleanness are those of childbirth, and of issues. (Lev. xii, 2; xv, 13, 19, 20, 25.) The places here referred to in the book of Leviticus contain the only directions as to purifying which specify these cases. Were our attention confined to those chapters, we might imagine that for these defilements there were no purifyings required, except in one single case, a self-washing for men healed of issues. But there are several things which suggest the propriety of looking farther before accepting that conclusion.

1. The instructions given in these places, if taken by themselves are incongruous. Thus, a man cured of an issue was directed to "number to himself seven days for his cleansing, and wash his clothes, and bathe his flesh in running water, and he shall be clean." But of a woman it is said: "She shall number to herself seven days, and after that she shall be clean."—Lev. xv, 13, 28. In neither of the cases of female defilement is there mention made of any purifying rites whatever, although the seven days of purifying are specified in each of them. And yet if any one had but touched the bed, or the seat of a woman so defiled, he must "wash his clothes, and bathe his flesh, and be unclean until the even."—Vs. 19-23. I do not here account as rites of purifying the offerings which in each case the parties, after being cleansed, were required to make at the sanctuary. In those offerings they claimed and exercised the privilege of communion at his table with the God of Israel—the highest privilege of the clean. Admission to it was, therefore, a formal and conclusive attestation to them as already clean.

2. The manifest analogy between these defilements, and those arising from leprosy and contact with the dead, indicates the necessity of analogous rites of purifying for them all. The intimacy of relation between their several meanings we have seen. It is attested by the whole tenor of Scripture. The same period of seven days marked them all—a period emphasized, even where the uncleanness was prolonged to thirty-three and sixty-six days. (Lev. xii, 2, 4, 5.) They all were included in one decree of exclusion from the camp, except for manifest reasons—women in childbed. (Num. v, 2.) At the end of the seven days of purifying, when they were clean, offerings were to be made at the sanctuary by the leper, the Nazarite defiled by the dead, and all the others, except those purged from the ordinary defilement by the dead. And the offerings were in each case essentially the same. The leper, if able, brought three lambs, one for a trespass-offering, the second for a sin-offering, and the third for a burnt-offering. If he was poor, he brought one lamb for a trespass-offering, and two young turtles or pigeons, one for a sin-offering, and the other for a burnt-offering. This offering of a lamb and two turtles was the same that was required of a Nazarite, defiled by the dead, after his cleansing. (Num. vi, 10, 12.) The two turtles, or pigeons, were alone required of those defiled by childbirth, or by issues, one for a sin-offering, and the other for a burnt-offering. Thus, the only difference in these observances was the trespass-offering which was, for evident reasons, required of the Nazarite and the leper, and of them only. The Nazarite, although by an involuntary act, had trespassed in profaning the head of his consecration. (Num. vi, 9.) As to the leper, his disease seems usually, if not always, to have been a special divine retribution for some specific and aggravated offense, for which, therefore, upon his cleansing, a trespass-offering was required. (Num. xii, 10; 2 Kings v, 27; 2 Chron. xxvi, 19.)

3. The supposition that these defilements all did not call for rites of purifying essentially the same in each case, would involve incongruity and contradiction in the testimonies uttered by them severally. That they all were typical of human depravity in its different aspects can not be questioned by any one who will candidly study the Scriptures, and especially the Levitical and prophetic books on the subject. But, upon the supposition in question, their several representations as to the remedy are irreconcilable. For leprosy, and those defiled with the dead, the rites of purifying declare that there is cleansing for man's moral defilement nowhere but in the blood and Spirit of Christ. But the rites for cleansing a man defiled with an issue would proclaim our own works and righteousness all-sufficient; whilst the silence of the law as to any rites whatever for women, in any form of issue, would declare no cleansing necessary, but that time and death would purify all. Thus, three several testimonies, each contradictory to the others, are incorporated in the ordinances, if complete in those chapters.

The key to these difficulties is found in the general character and intent of the law concerning the water of separation. That law was the latest that was given on the subject of purifyings, and is, therefore, not expressly referred to in the earlier regulations which have been under examination, although the divine Lawgiver intended the later statute to fill up and supplement those which had gone before. Of this there is a very plain indication in the ordinances respecting the Nazarite. "If any man die suddenly by him, and he hath defiled the head of his consecration, then he shall shave his head in the day of his cleansing; on the seventh day shall he shave it." — Num. vi, 9. Here the defiling effect of contact with the dead is not declared, but assumed; although the law to that purpose was not yet given. It is left to the subsequent ordinance (Num. xix) to prescribe the rites of cleansing, which are here, as in the rules concerning issued, alluded to, but not stated.

Those rites might seem to relate only to the case of defilement by the dead. But among the directions as to them, there is one which is unequivocal and comprehensive. "The man that shall be unclean and shall not purify himself, that soul shall be cut off from among the congregation, because he hath defiled the sanctuary of the Lord; the water of separation hath not been sprinkled on him. He is unclean." — Num. xix, 20. Here is no limitation nor exception of any kind. "The man that is unclean;" unclean, from whatever cause. Of all such, we are here certified that no lapse of time will bring cleansing. He must be purified before he can be clean. Till that is accomplished, his presence is a profanation of the sanctuary. It is, moreover, here declared that the one only mode of cleansing for all such was the water of separation, sprinkled according to the law. That this is a true interpretation, is confirmed by the testimony of Philo, of Alexandria, a Jewish writer of the highest reputation, contemporary with the apostles. Giving an account of the Levitical law, he distinguishes between defilements of the soul and of the body; by the latter meaning, ritual defilements. Of them, he says, in unrestricted terms, that the water of separation was appointed for purifying from those things by which a body is ritually defiled.[5]

We shall presently see one notable example of this comprehensive interpre-

___

[5] Below p. 91.

tation of the law, in the case of the daughters of Midian. Their need of the rites of purifying did not arise out of any of the categories specified in the laws which we have examined. They were unclean, because they were idolatrous Gentiles (Compare Acts xv, 9); and were purified with the water of separation, because that was the general provision made for the unclean. This is further illustrated in the fact that all the spoil taken at the same time was also purified with this same water of separation. (Num. xxxi, 19-24.)

A fact remains, which is conclusive of the present point. It is the remarkable name by which the purifying elements are designated. "It shall be kept for the congregation of the children of Israel for a water of (*nidda*) *separation*." This word, *nidda*, occurs in the Old Testament twenty-three times. Its radical idea is exclusion, banishment. Hence, the name of the land to which Cain was driven. "Cain went out from the presence of the Lord, and dwelt in the land of Nod," that is, "the land of banishment." — Gen. iv, 16. Under this general idea of exclusion, the particular form, *nidda*, is appropriated to the separating or putting away of a wife from her husband, and to the uncleannesses which gave occasion to such separation. And inasmuch as God is the husband of his church, the same word is used to designate those apostasies and sins which separate her from his favor and communion. (Lam. i, 17; Ezek. xxxvi, 17, etc.) In the two chapters in Leviticus, which present the law respecting defilement by childbirth and by issues (Lev. xii and xv), the word occurs no less than eleven times. Those who were thus defiled were, *nidda*, "put apart," "separated." Six times, in the directions as to the ashes of the red heifer, the water is called "a water of *nidda*." — Num. xix, 9, 13, 20, 21, 21; xxxi, 23. Once, again, the word is used in the same way by the prophet Zechariah. (Zech. xiii, 1.) "A fountain for sin and for *nidda*." Elsewhere it always has distinct reference, literal or figurative, to the causes of separation here indicated; whilst it is worthy of special mention, that it never designates defilement by the dead.

The conclusion implied in these facts becomes a demonstration when we observe that in the figurative language of the prophets, the defilement of *nidda* is expressly referred to as requiring the sprinkled water of purifying. In Ezekiel (xvi, 1-14) God's gracious dealings with Israel at the beginning are described under the figure of the marriage tie. "I sware unto thee, and entered into a covenant with thee, and thou becamest mine. Then washed I thee with water; yea, I thoroughly washed away thy blood from thee, and I anointed thee with oil." — vs. 8, 9. "I thoroughly washed away." The verb in the original is *shātaph*, which will be critically examined in another place. It signifies such action as of a dashing rain. In another place (Ezek. xxxvi, 17-26), the Lord, under the same figure, describes the subsequent transgressions of Israel: "Their way was before me as *nidda*." — v. 17. Because of this, God declares that he scattered them among the nations. But, says the Lord, "I will take you from among the heathen and gather you out of all countries, and will bring you into your own land. Then will I sprinkle clean water upon you, and ye shall be clean; from all your filthiness and from all your idols will I cleanse you. A new heart also will I give you, and a new spirit will I put within you." — vs. 24-26.

So, says the Spirit by Zechariah: "In that day there shall be a fountain (a flowing spring) opened to the house of David and to the inhabitants of Jerusalem, for sin and for *nidda*."—Zech. xiii, 1. *Nidda*, then, signified a defilement for which that fountain was necessary; and to imagine the ritual uncleanness of *nidda* to have been healed without ritual water of purifying, would be to suppose the ordinance to contradict the doctrine of the prophets.

From these passages it appears: (1.) That the defilement of *nidda* was a figure representing the sins and apostasies of Israel, viewed as God's covenant people, his married wife. (2.) That the sprinkling of water is the ordinance divinely chosen to represent the mode of the Spirit's agency in cleansing from these offenses. (3.) That this defilement and the water of *nidda* were so intimately associated with each other in the usage of Israel as to serve the prophets for a familiar illustration of the gracious purposes of God, indicated in the texts. If the figure of speech used by the prophet is the proper one for illustrating his doctrine in words, the water of *nidda* sprinkled on the unclean was the appropriate form by which to express it in ritual action. When, therefore, in the light of these facts, we read the law that the ashes of the heifer "shall be kept for the congregation of the children of Israel for a water of *nidda*," the conclusion is irresistible, that those defiled with *nidda* were to be purified with that water. And when to this we add the further declaration concerning "the man that is unclean," and is not sprinkled with it, and see it illustrated by the case of the Midianite children, the further conclusion is equally evident that, except the peculiar case of the leper, the water of separation was designed for all classes of seven days' defilement. To all others who were in a state of ritual separation from the communion of Israel, it was essential in order to being restored.

Section XVII.—*The Baptism of Proselytes.*—Talmudic traditions. Question between the Schools of Shammai and Hillel. The Levitical mode exemplified in the daughters of Midian

Maimonides was a learned Spanish Jew of the twelfth century. He wrote large commentaries upon the institutions and laws of Israel. Concerning the reception of proselytes, he is quoted as saying: "Circumcision, baptism, and a free-will offering, were required of any Gentile who desired to enter into the covenant, to take refuge under the wings of the divine majesty, and assume the yoke of the law; but if it was a woman, baptism and an offering were required, as we read, 'One law and one manner shall be for you and for the stranger that sojourneth with you.'—Num. xv, 16. But what was the law 'for you'? The covenant was confirmed by circumcision and baptism and free-will offerings. So was it confirmed with the stranger, with these three. But now, that no oblations are made [the temple being destroyed], circumcision and baptism are required. But after the temple shall have been restored, then also it will be necessary that an offering be made. A stranger who is circumcised and not baptized, or baptized and not circumcised, is not called a proselyte till both are performed."[6] Various similar statements are frequently quoted from the same writer, and from the Talmud. Respecting them the following points are to be noticed:

1. The Hebrew word which is used by Maimonides and the Talmudic writers,

---

[6] Maimonides, Issure Biah, Perek 13, in Lightfoot, Harmonia Evang. in Joan i, 25.

and is here translated, to baptize, is *tābal*, a word which in the books of Moses is never used to designate rites of purifying of any kind.

2. The *tābalings*, or Talmudic baptisms, were self-performed, and not the act of an official administrator. The reception of the person must be sanctioned by the consistory or eldership of a synagogue, and attested by the presence of three witnesses. But it was performed by the person's own act. Being disrobed, and standing in the water, he was instructed by a scribe in certain precepts of the law. Having heard these, he plunged himself under the water; and as he came up again, "Behold he is an Israelite in all things." If it was a woman, she was attended by women, while the scribes stood apart and read the precepts: "And as she plungeth herself, they turn away their faces, and go out, when she comes out of the water."[7] It is perfectly evident that the rite thus described is wholly foreign to any thing to be found in the Mosaic law, and that it belonged to the category of self-washings, and not to that of the sacrament, in which an official administrator was essential to the validity of the rite.

3. This baptism is an invention of the scribes, of post Biblical origin. Our sources of information are (1) the Scriptures and Apocrypha; (2) the writings of Philo and Josephus, authors, the former of whom was contemporary with Christ, and the latter with the destruction of Jerusalem, both of whom wrote largely of the institutions and history of the Jews; (3) the Targums of Onkelos and of Jonathan; (4) the Mishna; (5) the Gemaras.

The Targums are Aramaic versions of the Old Testament. The Jews, at the return from the Babylonish captivity, had lost the knowledge of the Hebrew language. It was, therefore, necessary that the public reading of the Scriptures should be accompanied with a translation into the Aramaic dialect, which they now used. (Neh. viii, 2-8.) The translations thus given were, no doubt, at first extemporaneous and somewhat variable. But they gradually assumed fixed forms, more or less accurate, as they received the impress of different schools of interpreters. At first transmitted orally, they were at length committed to writing, the Targum of Onkelos soon after the end of the second century, and that of Jonathan a century later. The former, as a rule, keeps closely to the text. The Targum of Jonathan indulges more in paraphrase. The Mishna is the text of the Oral law, the traditions of the scribes. It was reduced to writing by Rabbi Judah Hakkadosh, about the end of the first century, and is believed to be a faithful exhibit of the traditions of the Jews, as they stood at that time. The two Gemaras, with the Mishna, constitute the Talmud. They are collections of interpretations and commentaries on the Mishna, or oral law, by the most eminent scribes. The Jerusalem or Palestinian Gemara was compiled in the third and fourth centuries, and that of Babylonia one or two centuries later. The former represents the great rabbinic seminary at Tiberias, in Galilee; the latter that of Sora, on the Euphrates.[8]

From these sources of information, the indications are conclusive that Talmu-

---

[7] Maimonides, as above, in Lightfoot, on John iii, 23.

[8] According to Etheridge, the final revision of the Babylonian Gemara was completed by Rabbi Jose, president of the rabbinic seminary at Pumbaditha, on the Euphrates, in the year 499 or 500. —*Jerusalem* and *Tiberias*, pp. 174-176.

dic baptism came into use after the destruction of Jerusalem. We have seen already part of the evidence, which will be more fully developed in the following pages, that no such rite was ordained in the law, observed by Israel, or recognized in the Scriptures. The Apocrypha are equally silent on the subject. The writings of Philo and Josephus ignore such a rite; as do the Targums and Mishna. In the latter, the word, *tābal*, which is commonly translated, to dip, is used constantly to designate the self-washings of the law, which, as will presently appear, can not have been immersions. In fact, there is sufficient evidence that this word, in addition to its modal sense, was also used to express a washing or cleansing, irrespective of the manner. That it was so employed to describe the cleansing of Naaman, will here-after appear. It is not until we come to the Gemara of Babylonia, dating at the close of the fifth century, long after the destruction of Jerusalem and cessation of the temple service, that we meet with any distinct account of proselyte immersion. After that it is found everywhere.

4. Whilst it is thus evident that the baptisms of the Talmud are wholly without divine warrant, they are nevertheless valuable as constituting an authentic rabbinic tradition that a purifying with water was requisite in the reception of proselytes. A key to the truth on this subject presents itself in a statement found in the Mishna. "As to a proselyte who becomes a proselyte on the eve of the passover" (that is the evening before the day of the passover), "the school of Shammai say, Let him receive the ritual bath" (*tābal*), "and let him eat the passover in the evening; but the disciples of Hillel say, He that separates himself from his uncircumcision is like one who separates himself from a sepulcher."[9] It thus appears that between the two schools of Jewish scribes there was a division on this subject. The one party taught that the uncleanness of the Gentiles was of such a nature as to require seven days of purifying with the water of *nidda*, according to the law for one defiled by the dead. The others held them subject to that minor uncleanness which ceased with the close of the day, upon the performance of the prescribed self-washing. We shall presently see that the former were correct, according to the explicit testimony of the Scriptures. But here we have a clue to the later history of Jewish practice on the subject. Upon the destruction of Jerusalem and the termination of the sacrificial services there, the rites for purifying with the water of *nidda* were of necessity pretermitted, as the ashes of the heifer were no longer obtainable. The rabbins were, therefore, induced to substitute the self-washing which the looser school of scribes had already espoused. At what precise time the self-washings of the law became the self-immersions of the Gemaras does not appear. But at the beginning of the Christian era, causes had been already for centuries at work which were abundantly sufficient to account for the change. From the times of the captivities, the vast multitude of Hebrews who never returned, dwelling in Babylonia and the farther east, had been exposed to the influences arising from the religions of the lands of their dispersion, as embodied in the Zend Avesta and the Shasters, the teachings of Zoroaster and of the Brahmins, and from the related manners and customs and religious rites which have their native seats upon the banks of the Indus and the Ganges. The profoundness of the operation of these influences is seen in the pantheism of the Kabala, traceable as it is to the kindred doctrines of

[9] Tract Pesachim, cap. viii, § 8.

the Zend Avesta and the Vedas.[10] How conspicuous the place held by self-immersion in the religious customs of the people of the East, from the earliest ages, every one knows. The Hebrews dwelling among them were not restricted by the law to any defined mode of self-washing in fulfilling its requirements. It was, therefore, natural and inevitable for them to adopt the mode which was daily practiced before their eyes. The relations between the Jews of "the Dispersion," and those of Palestine, were of the most intimate kind, sustained through attendance upon the annual feasts at Jerusalem (Acts ii, 9), and afterwards by continual correspondence and travel, and by the intercourse of the school at Tiberias with those of Sora and Pumbaditha. If to these facts be added the tendency by which the rabbins would seek to compensate for the absence of the water of *nidda*, by expanding and magnifying the self-washings which were still practicable, there remains no ground of surprise or perplexity in finding self-immersion installed among the imperative observances set forth in the Gemaras. Of the disposition to supply the place of the now impracticable rites by the enlargement of others, the Talmud affords more than one example.

I have said that the Scriptural mode of purifying for proselytes was by sprinkling with the water of *nidda*. Of its use there is a conspicuous example. On account of their licentious wiles against Israel, Midian was doomed to destruction. In the campaign which followed, none were spared, except the female children. These were reserved for bond servants. (Num. xxxi, 18; and compare Lev. xxv, 44-46; and Deut. xxi, 10-14.) But, from the days of Abraham, all bond servants had been by divine authority and command endowed with an equal right and share with their masters in God's favor and covenant. And as Israel itself had been purified from the defilements and idolatries of Egypt, and ordained as the peculiar people of God by the baptism of blood and water at Sinai, so these children of licentious Midian, spared from the destruction incurred by their parents, and about to be joined with Israel as God's people, must be cleansed and admitted in the same manner.

During the expedition, many of the army had become defiled by contact with the slain, and were therefore to be cleansed with the water of separation, according to the law. Moses, therefore, issued orders to the men of the army: "Do ye abide without the camp seven days; whosoever hath killed any person, and whosoever hath touched any slain, *purify* both yourselves and your *captives* on the third day, and on the seventh day." In these directions as to the third and seventh days, we recognize the exact requirements of the law, with respect to the water of separation for the purification of sin. But the narrative is still more specific. "Eleazer the priest said unto the men of war which went to the battle, This is the ordinance of the law which the Lord commanded Moses. Only the gold and the silver, the brass, the iron, the tin, and the lead, every thing that may abide the fire, ye shall make it go through the fire, and it shall be clean. Nevertheless, it shall be purified with *the water of separation*, and all that abideth not the fire ye shall make go through the water. And ye shall wash your clothes on the seventh day, and ye shall be clean, and afterward ye shall come into the camp." — Num. xxxi, 19-24. "The water of sep-

[10] This is clearly shown by Etheridge, in "Jerusalem and Tiberias." Pp. 339 et seq. The same thing is largely illustrated in Blavatsky's "Isis Revealed."

aration," here, is, in the original, "the water of *nidda*,"—the water, that is, in which were mingled the ashes of the red heifer. With this, therefore, it was that these daughters of Midian were baptized and cleansed. There were thirty-two thousand of these captives, thus rescued from the destruction incurred by the licentiousness and crimes of their own people, purged from their uncleanness, engrafted into the family of Abraham, and endowed with the blessings of the covenant. All were "women children" (Num. xxxi, 18); and, undoubtedly, many were mere babes; the first recorded example of distinctive infant baptism.

> Section XVIII.—*The Baptism of Infants.*—The principle of infant membership recognized. Evidence of the baptism of Hebrew children. Example of the infant Jesus

We have seen that in the Abrahamic covenant,—the betrothal of the church,—the infant sons were expressly included on equal terms with their fathers; and that in the Sinai espousal the infants of both sexes were joined with their parents in the bonds of the covenant, and in the reception of its baptismal seal. We have seen the young daughters of Midian purified and admitted to the covenant and church of Israel by the same sacrament. By these unquestionable facts, the principle of infant membership in the church, and the mode of its certification by baptism, are both alike clearly established. The Scriptures contain conclusive evidence that the children of after generations of Israel were received to the covenant and the church in like manner, by baptism with the water of separation.

1. The law of God was explicit that "one ordinance shall be both for you of the congregation and also for the stranger that sojourneth with you, an ordinance forever in your generations; as ye are so shall the stranger be before the Lord. One law and one manner shall be for you and for the stranger that sojourneth with you."—Num. xv, 14-16. From this law, it results as a necessary conclusion, that inasmuch as the Midianite children were baptized, the same must have been the rule for the infants of Israel.

2. Circumcision was the seal of the Abrahamic covenant, but not of that of Sinai. So long as the church was confined to the family of Israel after the flesh, this rite, as being the proof and seal of membership in that family was essential as a condition precedent to the enjoyment of the privileges of the church; but did not, of itself, seal or convey a right to them. Otherwise, every circumcised person would have been entitled to those privileges; whereas they were reserved exclusively for the clean.

3. While such was the case, it was a fundamental article of the faith from the beginning, that men are all natively unclean. Job, Eliphaz, and Bildad, each severally states it as an unquestionable proposition that man born of woman must be so. (Job xiv, 4; xv, 14; xxv, 4.) David cries: "Behold I was shapen in iniquity and in sin did my mother conceive me.... Purge me with hyssop and I shall be clean; wash me and I shall be whiter than snow."—Psalm li, 5-7. He not only recognizes the radical nature of his moral corruption as born in him, but indicates the remedy under the very figure of sprinkling with the water of *nidda,* to which the hyssop refers. The Lord Jesus, speaking at a time when the Old Testament ordinances and

system were still in full force, testifies, "That which is born of the flesh is flesh, and that which is born of the Spirit is spirit. Marvel not that I said unto thee, Ye must be born again."—John iii, 6, 7.

4. To signalize this native corruption of man and the remedy, the ordinances concerning the defilement of *nidda* and its cleansing were appointed. In them the new born infant was regarded as the product of overflowing corruption, and as a fountain of defilement to the mother, who thus became unclean, until purified with the water of separation.

5. The child was identified with the mother in this uncleanness (1) as being its cause in her; (2) as being subject to her touch, which was defiling to the clean; and (3) as being bone of her bone and flesh of her flesh, born of her body.

6. In accordance with the doctrine of man's native defilement, above illustrated, it was characteristic of the law that it recognized none as clean, unless purged by water of sprinkling. The infants at Sinai were so purified and admitted to the covenant, as well as their parents. So it was with the daughters of Midian; and no other principle was known to the law,—no other practice tolerated by it. "The man" (the person) "that shall be unclean, and shall not purify himself, that soul shall be cut off from among the congregation, because he hath defiled the sanctuary of the Lord: the water of separation hath not been sprinkled upon him; he is unclean."—Num. xix, 20.

7. It is a very remarkable fact, that while we have in the Scriptures but one single example specifically mentioned of the purifying of an infant from this ritual defilement of birth, that example occurs in the person of Him respecting whom the angel said to Mary, "That holy thing which shall be born of thee shall be called the Son of God."—Luke i, 35. In the same gospel in which is this record, we read, respecting Mary, in the common version, that "when the days of *her* purification, according to the law of Moses, were accomplished, they brought Jesus to Jerusalem to present him to the Lord."—Ib. ii, 22. But it is agreed by critical editors that this is a corrupted reading, which is wholly without authority from any respectable manuscript. Instead of "the days (*autēs*) *of her* purification," it should read (*autōn*), "the days *of their* purification;" that is, of both mother and child. Beside all the other authorities, the three oldest manuscripts, Sinaiticus, Vaticanus, and Alexandrinus, unite in this reading. How the mothers were purified, we have seen; and, from these facts, we know the children to have shared with them in the baptism.

Section XIX.—*The Baptism of the Levites.*—Sprinkled with "water of purifying."

The case of the Levites, in their cleansing and consecration, was peculiar. They had already enjoyed with the rest of the congregation the purifying rites and sprinkled seal of the Sinai covenant; and were thus, in the ordinary sense of the Mosaic ritual, clean, and competent to the enjoyment of the ordinances and privileges of Israel. But when they were set apart to a special nearness to God, in the service of the sanctuary, they were required to undergo additional ceremonies of purifying. Moses was instructed to "take the Levites from among the children of Israel and cleanse them. And thus shalt thou do unto them to cleanse them. Sprinkle water of purifying upon them; and let them shave all their flesh, and let them wash their clothes, and so make themselves clean." They were then to bring two bullocks; "and the Levites shall lay their hands upon the heads of the bullocks, and thou shalt offer the one for a sin-offering, and the other for a burnt-offering, unto the Lord, to make an atonement for the Levites. And thou shalt set the Levites before Aaron and before his sons, and offer them for an offering unto the Lord. Thus shalt thou separate the Levites from among the children of Israel; and the Levites shall be mine."—Num. viii, 6-14.

Section XX.—*These all were one Baptism.*—The rites were essentially the same. Slight differences explained

The baptism of the Levites was official and peculiar. Its analogies to the other examples will readily occur to the reader, as we proceed. As to them, there is a common identity in all essential points, in form, meaning, and office. The design of the first administration at Sinai, and of all the attendant circumstances, was to impress Israel with a profound and abiding sense of the evil of sin, and of their own utter vileness and ruin as sinners in the presence of a God of infinite power, majesty, and holiness; and to illustrate to them the manner in which grace and salvation are given. In accepting that baptism, Israel professed to submit themselves to his sovereignty and accept him in the offices of his grace, as symbolized in the baptismal rites. On God's behalf, the transaction was an acceptance and acknowledgment of them as his covenant people. The laws of defilement and the rites of purifying were continual reminders and re-enactings of the Sinai transaction, and for the same essential purpose,—the restoring to the fellowship of the covenant of those who came under its forfeiture. In each several case, sacrificial elements—blood or ashes—were applied by sprinkling. In each, those elements were mingled with running water, and the instrument for sprinkling was a bush of hyssop, and in each, scarlet and cedar were used.

The meaning of the scarlet, cedar, and hyssop is unexplained in the Scriptures. Expositors have wandered in conjectures, leading to no satisfactory conclusions. One result of their use is manifest. To us, devoid of meaning, they more distinctly mark the essential identity of the rites, in which they occupy the same place, and perform the same office. This may have been one design of their use.

The essential identity of these rites is altogether consistent with the minute variations in their forms. These had respect to the diversity of circumstances under which they were administered. The inferior dignity of a single person, a leper, as compared with the whole people, explains the acceptance of lambs or birds for his offerings, while bulls and goats were sacrificed for the nation. In the case of ordinary uncleannesses, the circumstances rendered special provision necessary. Sacrifice was lawful only at the sanctuary, which was the figure of the one holy place and altar where Christ ministers in heaven. But death and other causes of uncleanness were occurring everywhere. The ashes of the red heifer were, therefore, provided. They presented sacrificial elements in a form incorruptible and convenient for transportation. They were a most fitting representation of the "incorruptible blood of Christ." And, as the proper place of the priests was at the sanctuary, and their presence could not be expected on every occasion of uncleanness elsewhere, it was appointed that any clean person might perform the sprinkling. This was, in fact, a mere ministerial sequel to the sacrificial rites, performed by the priest, at the burning of the red heifer. The probability of the circumstances, and intimations from the rabbins, lead to the conclusion that, as the priests multiplied and were released from the necessity of constant attendance at the sanctuary, they were commonly called to sprinkle the water of purifying. In fact, the Talmud indicates that in the later times the administration, when practicable, took place at Jerusalem, by the hands of the priests, with water from the pool of Siloam, which, flowing from beneath the temple, was recognized as a type of the Holy Spirit.[11]

The minute variations traceable in these rites only make it the more clear that essentially, in form, meaning, and office, they were one baptism.

Section XXI.—*This Symbol was derived from the Rain.*—Descent from heaven. Life and fruitfulness imparted. Testimonies of the prophets. Carson's doctrine

We have seen, in the prophecy of Isaiah, the source whence the figure of sprinkling or pouring is derived. "I will pour water upon him that is thirsty, and floods upon the dry ground; I will pour my Spirit upon thy seed, and my blessing upon thine offspring; and they shall spring up as among the grass, as willows by the water courses."—Isa. xliv, 3, 4. It is the descent of the rain from heaven, penetrating the earth, and converting its deadness into life, abundance, and beauty.

Herein the rites in question stand in beautiful contrast with the self-washings of the law. The latter accomplished a surface cleansing, by a process which neither could, nor was designed to penetrate the substance, or to affect its essential state or nature. They indicated to God's people the duty of conforming the external life to the grace wrought in the heart by the Holy Spirit. But the rite of sprinkling represented the rain of God, sent down from heaven, penetrating the soil, pervading and saturating it, converting its hard, dead, and sterile clods into softness, life, and fertility, and causing the plants and fruits of the earth to spring forth, saturated with the same moisture, and thus possessed and pervaded with the same spirit of life. Thus was typified the work of the Spirit, entering, pervading, and softening the stony heart, converting all its powers and faculties as instruments of holiness to God, and causing the plants of righteousness to spring up and grow in the life and conduct.

The two words, *sprinkle*, and *pour*, are used throughout the Scriptures with reference to the same figure of rain, the only apparent difference being that the word, pour, expresses the idea of abundance. No phenomenon of nature is of greater manifest importance, or more pervasive and vital in its influences than the rain of heaven, and none more suitable to illustrate the method of grace. The land from which the rains are withheld is without fruit, or beauty, or attraction. It is given over to barrenness, death, and cursing; and, in the language of the Scriptures, is

---

[11] Compare Ezek. xlvii, 2; John ix, 7. "Go wash in the pool of Siloam, which is by interpretation, Sent."

accounted unclean, as being shut out from the favor of God, whose favor is life. Hence, the word of God, to the prophet, concerning Israel: "Son of man, say unto her, Thou art the land that is not *cleansed*, nor *rained upon*, in the day of indignation."—Ezek. xxii, 24. Similar is the significance of our Savior's words: "When the unclean spirit is gone out of a man, he walketh through dry places" (*anhudrōn topōn*, "waterless places"), places congenial to him because unblessed with the Spirit's presence. (Matt. xii, 43; Luke xi, 24.)

Illustrations from the Scriptures might be multiplied, showing this origin of the form of baptism. Isaiah says of the blessings to be bestowed on Israel in the latter days, that the times of desolation shall continue "until the Spirit be poured upon us from on high, and the wilderness be a fruitful field, and the fruitful field be counted for a forest."—Isa. xxxii, 15. In another place he cries, "Drop down, ye heavens from above, and let the skies pour down righteousness; let the earth open, and let them bring forth salvation, and let righteousness spring up together; I the Lord have created it."—Isa. xlv, 8. Hosea says of him: "His going forth is prepared as the morning; and he shall come unto us as the rain, as the latter and former rain unto the earth."—Hosea vi, 3. And again, "Sow to yourselves in righteousness, reap in mercy; break up your fallow ground; for it is time to seek the Lord, till he come and rain righteousness upon you."—Ib. x, 12.

The whole conception thus unfolded is assailed and repudiated by writers who assume that physical phenomena can not be used to set forth spiritual realities. Dr. Carson insists that "Baptism can not be either pouring or dipping, for the sake of representing the manner of the conveyance of the Holy Spirit, for there is no such likeness. Pouring of the Spirit is a phrase which is itself a figure, and not a reality to be represented by a figure."[12] The learned doctor has confounded himself with his own subtlety. On the day of Pentecost, there was a blessed "reality" of some kind experienced by the apostles and converts. There is no absurdity, such as he imagines, in the supposition that the pouring or sprinkling of water may be an appropriate physical representation and symbol of that spiritual reality, and that words descriptive of that symbol may be appropriate for the verbal designation of the thing signified. If the assertion of Dr. Carson is to be accepted, it is fatal not to baptism only but to the other sacrament also. "Except ye eat the flesh of the Son of man and drink his blood, ye have no life in you."—John vi, 53. Shall we be told that this language of our Savior "is itself a figure, and not a reality to be represented by a figure." Then, we may not eat the bread and drink the wine, to represent this very thing, the feeding of the soul, by faith, on Christ. To do so is absurd if Dr. Carson's position is sound. It is true that a figure of speech *of* a figure of speech, would be nonsense. But it is equally true that it is the beauty of a metaphor,—the figure in question,—to be susceptible of physical representation. Nor is there any absurdity in the supposition that a spiritual act may be represented by two co-ordinate figures,—the one a figure of physical action, and the other a figure of speech, descriptive of that action.

Besides, the assertion that "baptism can not be either by pouring or dipping for the sake of representing the manner of the conveyance of the Holy Spirit; for

____

[12] Carson on Baptism, p. 167.

there is no such likeness," is not merely an assumption of knowledge concerning the invisible things of God which no mortal can possess. But, if the language is to be understood in any sense pertinent to the purpose of Dr. Carson, it is a plain contradiction of the testimony of God himself on the subject. True, there is no *physical* outpouring predicable of God the Spirit. It is as true of the Doctor's own word;—there is no physical "conveyance of the Holy Spirit." Does it, therefore, follow that there is *no* conveyance, *no* outpouring? He might with as good reason quibble as to the exaltation of Christ, because height and depth are mere relative terms, which change their direction, at every moment of the earth's motion on its axis and its orbit. His objection equally applies to the entire ritual of the Scriptures, robs it of all spiritual meaning and renders the whole utterly inane and worthless. And yet, if Paul's testimony be true, the tabernacle and all the vessels of ministry were "patterns of things in the heavens."—Heb. ix, 23. Are those heavenly things not spiritual? Jesus himself was "the Lamb of God," the forerunner, John, being witness. Is there any incongruity between this language, and the fact that the sacrificial lambs of the ritual law meant the same thing? If Dr. Carson is right, all this is absurd. Or, is there no spiritual truth involved in these figures? Either the physical analogies to which the Word of God constantly appeals, in figures of speech and similitudes, and upon which the whole ritual system is built, do so correspond with the spiritual realities as to assist us to true conceptions of them, however inadequate,—either the Scriptural figures, forms, and rites were selected because best adapted to convey and illustrate the spiritual ideas designed, or we are mocked by a semblance of revelation which reveals nothing. The assertion cuts us off from all knowledge of the spiritual world. Nay, it leaves us ignorant of the very existence of angel or spirit. For, what is spirit, but the *spiritus* or breath of man, the air or wind? How, then, upon the theory in question, can the word acquire or convey any idea of immaterial things? Until the portentous position of Dr. Carson shall have been established by something more conclusive than mere assertion, the contrary will stand as the truth of God. Moreover, the assertion, even if admitted, does not affect in the slightest degree, the argument against which it is directed. The fact still remains, conspicuous and unanswerable,—that, whatever be the reason, sprinkling and pouring are, in the Scriptures, constantly used, both in ritual forms, and in figures of speech, to signify the bestowal of the Holy Spirit, by the Mediator, from his throne on high.

Section XXII.—*This Ordinance meant, Life to the Dead.*—Men dead by nature. The Spirit shed down gives life to soul and body. Jesus at the grave of Lazarus

The manner of these rites, and the style of the Scriptures in connection with them are based upon the fundamental fact of man's spiritual condition as by nature dead, by reason of the apostasy and the curse,—"dead in trespasses and sins" (Eph. ii, 1, 5); "being alienated from the life of God" (Ib. iv, 18), so that they are incapable of exercising any of the activities of true spiritual life unto God, and are, therefore, outcast as were the leper and the unclean, from the camp and society of the clean; being "aliens from the commonwealth of Israel, and strangers from the covenants of promise."—Ib. ii, 12. In short, the death which by sin, through one man, entered the world was the death of the soul. With reference to it, Jesus says,—"I am the resurrection and the life: he that believeth in me though he were dead, yet shall he live: and whosoever liveth and believeth in me shall never die."—John xi, 25, 26. But inasmuch as a dead soul can not sustain life in the body, the latter too died with the soul, in the day of its death. For a little time, through the mercy of God, in order to salvation (2 Peter iii, 15), an expiring struggle is maintained; but it is with bodies ever stooping to the grave and irresistibly drawn downward into its yawning gulf. It is in view of these facts that Paul describes the old man, the carnal or inherited nature, as "the body of this death," or "this dead body;" and its works as "dead works" (Heb. vi, 1; ix, 14) which he represents to be "all manner of concupiscence," or evil desires, and consequent evil deeds. (Rom. vii, 8-24.) Hence, the seven days' uncleanness, signifying the deadness of the soul, and the offensiveness of its works. Coincident in meaning was the defilement of things by the contagion of death. For man's sake, the ground itself is cursed (Gen. iii, 17), and every product of the earth and every possession of man upon it is involved in the curse, and until delivered from it, is unsanctified to man's use. Hence, the house, the bed, the furniture and utensils, were defiled by the presence of the dead and unfitted for the use of the clean, the living.

Such were the conceptions with reference to which the rites of Levitical baptism were ordained. They were designed to answer the question: How can these dead be made alive, this defilement be cleansed, and the curse lifted from man and the earth? They announced life to the dead, and the healing of their corruption. They proclaimed Christ's atonement made to redeem us from the curse, and his Spirit given to implant in us new life and purge us from dead works to serve the living God. As the descending rain not only penetrates the soil and instils life into the clods and hardness, but washes and purges the surface, and gives freshness and beauty to the scenes of nature, cleansing the face of the impenetrable and barren rock,—so the Spirit sent down not only penetrates the heart and creates new life there, but pervades the outward life and conduct and purifies the whole. Thus, in the one figure of the sprinkling or pouring of rain, are identified the two ideas of new life and cleansing; and hence, thus taught, the cry of the psalmist, in which he identifies both with the sprinkled baptism. "Wash me thoroughly from my iniquity, and cleanse me from my sin.... Purge me with hyssop, and I shall be clean: wash me, and I shall be whiter than snow.... Create in me a clean heart, O God, and renew a right spirit within me."—Ps. li, 2-10. The same relation is recognized by Paul, who ascribes our salvation to "the *washing* of regeneration and renewing of the Holy Ghost, which he *shed* on us abundantly, through Jesus Christ our Savior."—Tit. iii, 5, 6.

In the promise of life signified in this baptism, two things were included under the one essential conception. These were, renewing to the soul, and resurrection to the body. These are as inseparably related to each other as are the death of the soul and of the body; and that, because of the essential relation between those two parts, as identified in the one person. Christ gave himself, body and soul, for us, to satisfy justice; and bought us unto himself in our whole being, body and soul. If the Spirit of life be given us, it is given both to renew our dead souls and to make our bodies his temples. And, says Paul, "If the Spirit of him that raised up Christ from the dead dwell in you, he that raised up Christ from the dead shall also quicken your mortal bodies, by his spirit that dwelleth in you."—Rom. viii, 11.

That this doctrine of the new life was the meaning of the baptismal rite, appears from many Scriptures. We have just seen the significant language of the psalmist. By Ezekiel, the Lord says to Israel: "Then will I sprinkle clean water upon you and ye shall be clean; from all your filthiness, and from all your idols will I cleanse you. A new heart also will I give you, and a new spirit will I put within you; and I will take away the stony heart out of your flesh, and I will give you a heart of flesh. And I will put my Spirit within you."—Ezek. xxxvi, 25-27.

This view of the work of the Holy Spirit is exhibited very clearly in Ezekiel's vision of the valley of dry bones, and the promises therewith addressed to Israel respecting the latter days. "Behold, O my people, I will open your graves, and cause you to come up out of your graves, and bring you into the land of Israel. And ye shall know that I am the Lord, when I have opened your graves, O my people, and brought you up out of your graves, and shall put my Spirit in you, and ye shall live."—Ezek. xxxvii, 12-15.

In the same sense Paul interprets the Levitical baptisms. Having designated the ordinances of which they formed a part as figures of the heavenly things, he says: "If the blood of bulls and of goats, and the ashes of a heifer sprinkling the unclean, sanctifieth to the purifying of the flesh, how much more shall the blood of Christ ... purge your conscience from dead works, to serve the living God."—Heb. ix, 13, 14. Here he contrasts the dead works of the unregenerate with the living works of those who, as they are alive unto God, serve in newness of life him who, being the living God, "is not the God of the dead, but of the living."—Matt. xxii, 32. Of this he recognizes the sprinklings to be a figure.

The doctrine thus involved in the water of purifying sheds a beautiful light on one of the most interesting facts in the life of our Savior. Upon the death of Lazarus, Jesus so timed his coming as to reach Bethany on the fourth day. On the previous day, or, more probably, on that very same day, the sisters and household of Lazarus had been baptized with the water of purification. And now, as He stands by the sepulcher, the resurrection, in its highest sense, as including both soul and body, and rendering both superior to death, is the theme of his discourse. "Thy brother shall rise again. Martha saith unto him, I know that he shall rise again, in the resurrection, at the last day. Jesus said unto her, I am the resurrection and the life; he that believeth in me, though he were dead, yet shall he live; and whosoever liveth and believeth in me shall never die."—John xi, 23-26.

Section XXIII.—*The Gospel in the Water of Separation.*—(1) The red heifer. (2) Without the camp. (3) Blood sprinkled, and blood and water. (4) Seven times. (5) Seven days' defilement. (6) The ashes. (7) The water. (8) The sprinkling. (9) The third day and the seventh. (10) The self-washing. (11) Things defiled and sprinkled

Much of the spiritual significance of these rites has already appeared. But in order to an adequate appreciation, they should be viewed in connection.

1. The red heifer was a sin-offering. This is denied by some, who would draw a fine distinction. Says Bishop Patrick: "Though this was not a sacrifice, it had something of that nature in it, and may be called a *piaculum*, an expiatory thing, though nothing was called *korban*, a sacrifice, but what was offered at the altar." But, (1.) *korban* does not mean a sacrifice, but a gift, a dedicated thing; and is used, not only to designate sacrifices and offerings at the altar, but even the wagons and oxen which the princes gave for transporting the tabernacle and its furniture. (Num. vii, 3.) (2.) The blood of the heifer was sprinkled by the priest toward the door of the sanctuary. It was thus brought into a relation to the altar and the mercy-seat, typically as manifest and close as though it had been actually sprinkled on the altar. (3.) The law itself expressly declares it to be a sin-offering. "It is a purification for sin,"—Num. xix, 9. The original, here, is the same that is in other places literally translated, "It is a sin-offering."—Lev. iv, 24; v, 9, 11, 12. In this, its character as a sin-offering, lay the meaning of the rite as a purification. It represented atonement for sin, at the price of blood,—the blood of Christ. Hence its use in purifying those uncleannesses which typified moral corruption in its forms of intensest malignity and deadliness. Hence the appeal to this meaning of the rite which the psalmist makes, in his penitence and sorrow for his crimes. "Behold, I was shapen in iniquity, and in sin did my mother conceive me.... Purge me with hyssop, and I shall be clean; wash me, and I shall be whiter than snow.... Hide thy face from my sins and blot out all mine iniquities."—Ps. li, 5, 7, 9. The Targum thus paraphrases this place: "Thou wilt sprinkle me, as the priest which sprinkleth the unclean with the purifying waters, with hyssop, with the ashes of an heifer, and I shall be clean." The same conception is apparent in God's language of grace to Israel, and to the nations. "Then will I sprinkle clean water upon you and ye shall be clean: from all your filthiness and from all your idols will I cleanse you." And, "So shall he sprinkle many nations." In a word, in every instance in which this rite is appointed, or figuratively alluded to, it will be found to indicate a typical impeachment of sin; and the design and effect of its use was the removal of that impeachment, the cleansing of the subject. It was *baptism unto the remission of sins.*

2. The heifer was offered without the camp. In the detailed ritual of the tabernacle and temple service, the holy of holies, the holy place, and the surrounding court, typified, respectively, God's heavenly presence chamber, the church, and the world. In a wider scheme, the whole sanctuary was representative of God's house, whilst the camp and afterward the city of Jerusalem were the figure of the church, and the outside region stood for the world at large. Hence, the unclean were excluded from the camp and the city. (Compare Rev. xxi, 27; xxii, 14, 15.) And hence, the red heifer was offered without the camp, to signify the reproach of Christ, who suffered without the gate, excommunicate and accursed. (Heb. xiii, 11-13.) The blood of the heifer, sprinkled from without toward the sanctuary, intimated in a very affecting manner, the distance to which Christ came from yonder sanctuary in the heavens, to shed his blood, and therewith to sprinkle the throne of justice on high.

3. Blood only was sprinkled toward the sanctuary, whilst it was water min-

gled with the blood or ashes, that was sprinkled on the unclean. For, his own unmingled blood, offered by Christ himself before the throne on high, and that alone, makes satisfaction to justice for sin. But the Holy Spirit is the sole channel and agent through whom Christ bestows on his people, or they can in any wise acquire, the virtue of that blood in justifying grace and holiness. Water, therefore, was the vehicle for communicating to Israel the blood of sprinkling.

4. The blood was sprinkled seven times, to show the complete and exhaustive efficacy of the sufferings of Christ to satisfy justice, sanctify the soul, and make an end of sin forever.

5. He that touched the dead was defiled seven days. This tactual defilement typified not only the guilt and depravity which *we* derive from Adam, but, especially, the contagion of man's guilt which came on the Lord Jesus, by becoming the Son of man, born in our nature. Though he knew no sin, yet was he laden with our curse. He signified this very thing, when in the days of his flesh, he defiled himself by touching the lepers and the dead, that he might restore them to soundness and life, at the price of his own life;—"That it might be fulfilled which was spoken by Esaias the prophet, saying, Himself took our infirmities and bare our sicknesses."—Matt. viii, 17. The same thing was set forth by the fact that the priest that sprinkled the heifer's blood, each assistant at the burning and gathering of the ashes, and he that sprinkled the water of separation, all became thereby unclean until the even. They, together, represented the Lord Jesus, in the exercise of his mediatorial office, which involved his taking his people's curse upon him, to free them. The seven days of this defilement have been already explained, as typical of our native condition of depravity and guilt, which, if not purged, involves continuance and condemnation in the seventh, the last day, when the sentence will be uttered, "He that is filthy let him be filthy still."—Rev. xxii, 11.

6. The ashes of the heifer were as familiar to the religious life of Israel as was the blood of sacrifice. But the significance of the blood is so much more familiar to us, that a pause is here proper, to call attention to the wonderful propriety and instructiveness of the ashes. In the blood we see the penalty of sin paid, and justice satisfied. But it is satisfied at the price of life, and leaves death in possession. But, in the ashes, Israel saw the sacrifice come forth from the exhausted fires of justice, unconsumed and unconsumable. On them, the fire could no more take hold; but, mingled with the living water, they represented Christ—the law satisfied and the curse exhausted in his blood—coming forth by the Spirit, from the expiring flames, robed in life and immortality. "Whom God hath raised up, having loosed the pains of death, because it was not possible that he should be holden of it."—Acts ii, 24.

7. The ashes were mingled with running water. Prior to the baptism of Israel at Sinai, we hear of no sacramental rite setting forth the office and work of the Holy Spirit. But the living water, then ordained in the divers baptisms of the Mosaic system, became thenceforward the standing representation and type of the Third Person of the Godhead, as the Spirit of life, shed down from heaven by the Mediator.

8. The sacrificial elements and water were *sprinkled* on the unclean. Two ideas

were thus symbolized; the *bestowment* by Christ from his throne of the virtues of his blood and Spirit; and, their effectual influence upon the heart and conscience of him to whom they are given. As the rain descends from heaven, penetrates the soil, and makes it fruitful, so Christ's Spirit shed down from him takes possession of the inmost heart, purges it from the guilt of past sins, and produces newness of life and the fruits of holiness. With reference to the mode thus employed, and its symbolical relation to Christ's administration of grace, the fact is worthy of special emphasis, that in every rite or figure by which was represented the exercise by Christ of his office as administrator in the Father's kingdom, the mode is affusion, whether it be blood, water, or oil, expressive of grace bestowed on the people of God, or indignation and fire poured down upon his enemies.

9. The water of separation was to be sprinkled on the unclean on the third day and on the seventh. "And if he purify not himself the third day, then the seventh day he shall not be clean;" for, Jesus who died under our curse, rose again the third day. And "Know ye not that so many of us as were baptized into Jesus Christ were baptized into his death? Therefore we are buried with him by baptism into death; that like as Christ was raised up from the dead by the glory of the Father, even so we also should walk in newness of life. For, if we have been planted together in the likeness of his death, we shall be also in the likeness of his resurrection." — Rom. vi, 3-5. If we do not participate in the resurrection of Christ on the third day, by rising from the death of sin to the life of holiness, we can have no part in the resurrection and life of glory. So, Paul testifies to the Ephesians, that the same mighty power which raised Christ from the dead and set him far above in the heavenly places, is at work in all his people, and by it they who were dead in sins are quickened together with him, and made to sit with him in the heavenly places. (Eph. i, 20; ii, 6.) Hence, Paul's earnest desire and labor for himself, — "That I may know him, and the power of his resurrection, ... if by any means, I might attain unto the resurrection of the dead." — Phil. iii, 10, 11. "Might know the power of his resurrection," — by realizing within, the steady vigor of the new life in Christ Jesus, working holiness and grace.

Of the resurrection of the Lord Jesus, Paul says, that "he rose again the third day, according to the Scriptures." — 1 Cor. xv, 4. But where, in the Scriptures, is the third day thus specified? The Lord Jesus makes a similar statement, which goes far to answer the question. "These are the words which I spake unto you, while I was yet with you, that all things must be fulfilled which were written in *the law of Moses*, and in the prophets and in the Psalms concerning me. Then opened he their understanding, that they might understand the Scriptures, and said unto them, Thus it is *written*, and thus it behooved Christ to suffer and to rise from the dead *the third day*." — Luke xxiv, 44-46. In another place, there is a remarkable allusion to the same thing. When Jesus, in response to the Jews demanding a sign, said, "Destroy this temple, and in three days, I will raise it up," the disciples did not understand. But "when he was risen from the dead, they remembered that he had said this unto them; and they believed *the Scripture*, and the word that Jesus had said." — John ii, 18-22. It would thus appear that the resurrection on the third day was *written* in the Scriptures, and the reference to the law of Moses, and statement as to the opening of the understanding of the apostles, as though the matter were not patent on the face of the record, both lead us to look in that direction for the prophetic anticipation of the third as the resurrection day. The other Scriptures will be searched in vain for any thing to fulfill the requirements of these statements of Christ and of Paul. The law concerning the sprinkling of the water of separation contains the only intimation on the subject; and the allusions above cited appear undoubtedly to have had this typical prophecy in view.

In the design of this ordinance, as a prophecy of the resurrection, we have the reason of its peculiar relation to that particular form of defilement which arose from contact with the dead. Although designed as has been seen for the cleansing of other defilements, also, it was ordained in immediate connection with this particular uncleanness, because that is the connection in which this distinctive meaning shines forth most clearly.

10. He that was purified with the water of separation was required to follow it with an act of self-ablution. "On the seventh day, he shall purify himself, and wash his clothes and bathe himself in water, and shall be clean at even." — Num. xix, 19. It has been asserted that this rule was meant for the administrator of the rite. But the exposition afterward given by Eleazar, the priest (Num. xxxi, 21-24), shows this to be a mistake. The propriety and beauty of the requirement, in the connection, are apparent. It was a perpetual monition to Israel that those who have been redeemed with precious blood, and raised up to new life by the Holy Spirit, should walk worthy of their calling, and keep themselves from the evil that is in the world, in the blessed assurance of being freed from all corruption and evil, and made partakers in the perfection of holiness and life, on the great Sabbath day of redemption.

This thought was more fully developed in the rites concerning the leper. Immediately upon his baptism, he was required to shave his hair, wash his garments and bathe his flesh. The hair and the defilement adhering to the garments and flesh were evident types of the outgrowth and fruits of his leprous life. Of the shaving and cleansing thus appointed, Paul may give the interpretation — "That ye put off concerning the former conversation, the old man which is corrupt according to the deceitful lusts." — Eph. iv, 22. After this, the meaning of the like shaving and washing on the seventh day is apparent. It sets forth the final and complete putting off of the old carnal nature, in the resurrection of life, when our bodies themselves also shall be transformed into the likeness of Christ's glorious body, and be reunited to our souls, perfected in holiness.

11. The defilement from the dead, and the purifying use of the water of separation were not only incident to persons; but the tent or house where the dead lay, and every thing that was in it, became defiled, and must be cleansed by the water of separation, sprinkled on the third day, and on the seventh. (Num. xix, 14, 18; xxxi, 20, 22, 23.) Thus were Israel taught that the curse of sin is on the earth, also, and all that is in it, as well as on man; that, only as sanctified to him through the atonement of Christ, can the productions and possessions of the earth be blessed, and that in the regeneration, the earth and the creatures themselves, also, shall be delivered from the bondage of corruption into the glorious liberty of the sons of

God, and *"Holiness to the Lord,"* be written on the very bells of the horses. (Zech. xiv, 20.) "For," saith the Lord, "behold I create new heavens and a new earth."—Isa. lxv, 17.

Thus, all the great truths of the Gospel, were set forth and symbolized in this ordinance, the last, the consummate and crowning sacrament of the Old Testament.

Section XXIV.—*These were the Divers Baptisms.*—The argument of Heb. ix, 8, 9. The sprinklings were the theme of Paul's argument. They were his "divers baptisms."

That the sprinkled purifyings were the theme of Paul's argument is evident:

1. He distributes the whole ritual system under two categories. His statement (Heb. ix, 8, 9), literally translated, is, that "the first tabernacle," erected by Moses, was *"(parabolē eis ton kairon enestēkota),* an illustrative similitude, unto the present time *(kath hen*[13]*) in accordance with which* (similitude), both gifts and sacrifices are offered, which, as to the conscience, can not perfect the worshipers; depending only on meats and drinks and divers baptisms,—righteousnesses of the flesh, imposed until the time of reformation." The word *(dikaiomata)* "righteousnesses" (from *dikaios,* righteous), is repeatedly so translated in our English version (Rom. ii, 26; v, 18; viii, 4), although in some other places beside the text it is rendered,—"ordinances."—Luke i, 6; Heb. ix, 1, 10. The latter rendering, however, fails to develop the true idea of the word, which is,—ordinances imposed, *in order to the attaining of righteousness by obedience.* So it should be in the first verse of this chapter. "Then, verily, the first covenant had also righteousnesses of worship," (ritual righteousnesses), "and an earthly holy place." By the phrase, "righteousnesses of the flesh," the writer indicates the contrast between the outward ritual righteousnesses of the law,—its circumcision of the flesh, its offerings of bulls and goats, and its washings and sprinklings with material elements,—and "the circumcision of the heart;" "the offering of Jesus Christ," and "the washing of regeneration and renewing of the Holy Ghost." The ritual observances fulfilled the law of carnal commandments, and were thus righteousnesses of the flesh, and figures of the true, the righteousness of Christ.

Paul distributes these observances into the two categories of offerings and purifyings. The law required each sacrifice to be accompanied with a meat offering made of fine flour mingled with oil, and a drink offering of wine. For the altar was God's table, where he as a Father fed and communed with his children. It must, therefore, be furnished with all the provisions of a table. (Num. xv, 3-5, 7, etc.) Thus, the offerings upon the altar were all comprehended under the two heads of meats *(brōmasi,* solid food), and drinks,—nourishments for *the body.* Paul's other category is, the divers baptisms. These, of necessity, are the purifying rites of the Levitical system. For, he describes the whole system as including *"only* meats and drinks and divers baptisms;" whereas all were actually comprehended under the two heads of offerings, which symbolized atonement made, and purifyings, rep-

---

[13] This reading is attested by codices Bezæ, Alexandrinus, Vaticanus, Sinaiticus, and is fully sustained by the internal evidence.

resenting its application, to the purging of sins. That it is of the purifyings that he now speaks, is evident not only from the meaning of baptism, itself, but from the whole tenor of his argument, which is directed exclusively to the two points just indicated, atonement made, and purification accomplished.

2. The baptisms of which the apostle speaks were purifyings of persons and not of things. They were righteousnesses of the flesh, upon which men in vain relied for the purging of their consciences, (vs. 9, 14.)

3. There were but two ordinances to which Paul can possibly refer. Except the sprinklings, and the self-performed washings, there was no rite in the Levitical system in which water was used, or to which the name of baptism is, or can be, attributed, with any pretense of reason or probability.

4. The self-washings will be examined presently. As compared with the sprinklings, they were of minor importance. Separately used only for superficial defilements, they purged no essential corruption. They were without sacrifice, administrator, or sacramental meaning. They symbolized no work of Christ, signified no bestowal of grace, and sealed no blessing of the covenant. In all this, they stood in eminent contrast with the sprinkled rites. To suppose that Paul, in a discussion which has respect to the cleansing efficacy of Christ's blood and Spirit, and the Levitical types of it, should refer to the minor rite of self-washing, which did *not* symbolize those things, and by an exclusive *"only"* reject from place or consideration the sprinklings which did, is absurd; as it is, moreover, to suppose that, in such an argument, the latter would not, of necessity, have a paramount place and consideration.

5. This conclusion is fully confirmed upon a critical examination of the connection of Paul's argument. The "meats and drinks and divers baptisms" he characterizes as "righteousnesses of the flesh," in confirmation of the assertion just made, that they could not "perfect," or purify the conscience of the worshiper. He then, immediately, presents in contrast the atonement of Christ. "They," says he, "depended only on meats and drinks and divers baptisms, righteousnesses of the flesh imposed until the time of reformation. But Christ being come, ... neither by the blood of goats and calves, but by his own blood he entered in once into the holy place, having obtained eternal redemption for us. *For* if the blood of *bulls* and *of goats* and the *ashes of a heifer sprinkling* the unclean, sanctifieth to the purifying of the flesh, how much more shall the blood of Christ ... purge your conscience." Thus, in immediate exposition of his statement as to divers baptisms, the apostle specifies the two most conspicuous forms of the sprinklings of Sinai, that of the whole people, upon the making of the covenant, and that administered with the water of separation — the one being the original of the ordinance, and the other its ordinary and perpetuated form. For, that there may be no mistake as to his reference, in speaking of the blood of bulls and of goats, he proceeds, a little farther on to describe particularly its use in the Sinai baptism: "For when Moses had spoken every precept to all the people according to the law, he took the blood of calves and of goats, with water, and scarlet wool and hyssop, and sprinkled both the book and all the people, saying, This is the blood of the testament (the covenant), which God hath enjoined unto you." — Vs. 19, 20. As we examine Paul's argument

throughout the chapter, we find his attention directed, from first to last, to the sprinklings of the law alone, while the self-washings are not once named nor alluded to. This, afterwards, very signally appears in that magnificent contrast of Sinai and Sion, in which he sums up the whole argument of the epistle. The crowning feature in the attractions of Sion is "the blood of sprinkling that speaketh better things than that of Abel." — Heb. xii, 24. In the presence of it the self-washings are not counted worthy to be named.

6. The manner in which, in the next chapter, self-washing is at length introduced is a singular confirmation of the view here taken. So long as the writer is occupied in the argument as to Christ's work of expiation, he makes no allusion to the self-washings. But when he proceeds to urge upon his readers the practical plea which his argument suggests, he does it by referring to the two rites, in the relation to each other which we have indicated. "Having, therefore, brethren, boldness to enter into the holiest, by the blood of Jesus, ... and having a High Priest over the house of God, let us draw near with a true heart, in full assurance of faith, having our hearts sprinkled from an evil conscience, and our own bodies washed with pure water." — Heb. x, 19-22. To an unclean person, desiring to claim the privileges of the sanctuary, the requirement of the law was, Let him be sprinkled on the third day and on the seventh, to set forth Christ's and the Spirit's grace; and then, let him wash himself, in token of the maintaining of personal holiness. From the rites which he has been discussing, Paul's exhortation takes form, and in them finds interpretation.

The conclusion is evident. Had Paul meant by the phrase in question to designate the self-washings, they were by affusion, and it would follow that that is the mode of baptism. But that his reference was distinctively and emphatically to the sprinkled rites is beyond candid contradiction. We, therefore, plant ourselves upon this impregnable position, and challenge assault. *For fifteen hundred years of the church's history, baptism was uniformly administered by sprinkling.* It was so administered down to the time of Christ. It was so administered in the time of Paul. The word does *not* then mean to dip or to immerse; for, Paul being witness, the rite was not so performed. Had we no further evidence, this should be conclusive.

PART IV.

THE RITUAL SELF-WASHINGS.

Section XXV.—*Unclean until the Even.*—From expiatory rites. From contact with the unclean. Self-washing

The clean, that is those who had been purified by sprinkling, were liable to contract certain minor defilements, which were characterized by continuing until the even. Of these there were two classes. First, were those which resulted from participation in expiatory rites. Among the most conspicuous examples of this class were the uncleanness of the priests and assistants by whom the red heifer was sacrificed, the ashes collected and the water of separation sprinkled on the unclean. These all were, by participation in those rites, rendered unclean until the even, and were required to wash their clothes, and bathe their flesh, in order to their cleansing. (Num. xix, 7, 8, 10, 21.) The meaning of this is evident. The red heifer was a sacrifice of expiation, "a purification for sin."—Ib. 9. In it, the priests and assistants and he that sprinkled the ashes, with the heifer itself, together, constituted a complex type of the Lord Jesus, offering himself a sacrifice to justice, sprinkling the altar in heaven with his own blood, and applying it with his Spirit to his people for the purifying of their uncleanness. The defilements for which the ashes of the heifer were provided were typical of our native depravity and death in sin and the curse. From these, Christ freed his people, by being himself made a curse for them (Gal. iii, 13), dying in their stead, that they might live. To represent this the priests, assistants, and administrator of the water of separation, became defiled, by participation in the cleansing rites. The same explanation applies to the defilement which the high priest and others incurred by participation in the observances of the day of atonement. (Lev. xvi, 24, 26.)

The curse under which the Lord Jesus came exhausted itself on his natural life, and expired as he rose from the dead. Of the period during which he bore its burden, and fulfilled his atoning work, he himself says: "I must work the works of him that sent me, *while it is day*; the night cometh, when no man can work."—John ix, 4. And on the night of the betrayal he said to the Father, "I have finished the work which thou gavest me to do."—Ib. xvii, 4. It thus appears that a day is a symbol of the period of man's natural life, the period during which the Lord Jesus was under the curse. Hence the typical uncleanness of the priests and assistants was limited to the even of the day on which it was incurred. It was removed by self-washing; for it was by his own power and Spirit that Christ threw off the curse and rose from the dead. (Rom. viii, 2, 11; John x, 17, 18.)

2. The other class of uncleannesses until the even arose from the more or less intimate contact of the clean with persons or things that were unclean in the higher degree; or from other causes essentially similar in meaning. Defilements resulting from expiatory rites symbolized the putative guilt incurred by the Lord Jesus, in making atonement for us; while he ever remained, in himself, "holy, harmless, undefiled, separate from sinners."—Heb. vii, 26. But the forms of uncleanness now under examination resulted from contact with things that were typical of the debasement, corruption, and depravity of the world. The uncleanness hence arising signified the spiritual defilement to which God's people are liable from contact with evil. Hence, the grades of defilement, consequent upon the closeness and fellowship of the contact, and the nature of the uncleanness with which it took place. These were designed to teach the lesson with which James crowns his definition of pure religion and undefiled. "To *keep himself* unspotted from the world."—James i, 27. The same idea is presented by the beloved John. "We know that whosoever is born of God sinneth not; but he that is begotten of God *keepeth himself*, and that wicked one" (that "unclean spirit," the representative and source of all moral evil) "toucheth him not" (to defile him, as would the touch of the leper or the unclean). "And we know that we are of God, and the whole world lieth in wickedness." Literally,—"lieth in that wicked one,"—in his bosom, and the defilement of his contact and communion. (1 John v, 18, 19.) And, again, "Beloved, now are we the sons of God, and it doth not yet appear what we shall be; but we know that when he shall appear, we shall be like him; for we shall see him as he is. And every man that hath this hope in him *purifieth* himself, even as he is pure."—1 John iii, 2, 3.

From many such Scriptures, the meaning of these uncleannesses and of the self-washings is easily gathered. The defilements which they symbolized are not of a radical nature, but extrinsic and superficial. They represented those spiritual defilements,—those soilings of heart and conscience to which God's people are subject through contact and intercourse with an ungodly world. It is postulated only of those whose hearts have already been quickened and sanctified by the blood and Spirit of Christ, "once for all" (Heb. x, 10); and who are "the habitation of God through the Spirit." They do not require a new atonement and renewing of the Spirit, but the exercise of the graces of that Spirit which is already in them. For their cleansing, therefore, no new sacrificial rites nor official administrator were appointed; but they were required to wash *themselves*. This did not prohibit the employment of any customary assistance in the washing; as, for example, that of a servant pouring water on the hands. But such assistance, if employed, was merely ministerial, and not official. The washing, however performed, was the duty and act of the subject of it, and therein lay its significance. Its language was that of the apostle; "Having, therefore, these promises, dearly beloved, let us cleanse ourselves from all filthiness of the flesh and spirit, perfecting holiness in the fear of God."—2 Cor. vii, 1.

The termination of the defilement, upon the performance of the appointed self-washing, with the going down of the sun, certified the deliverance of God's people from sin and corruption, with the end of this present life, in the coming rest of the believer's grave, awaiting the seventh day of resurrection and glory.

Section XXVI.—*Gradation of the Self-washings.*—1. The hands. 2. The hands and feet. 3. The clothes. 4. The clothes and flesh. 5. Shaving the hair

There was a noticeable gradation in the self-washings.

1. First was the washing of the hands, alone. This was required of the magistrates expiating a concealed murder. (Deut. xxi, 6.) It is also indicated in Leviticus xv, 11. It will be further examined hereafter. The figure of washing the hands, as expressive of innocence and purity, occurs repeatedly in the Scriptures; and as the hands are the ordinary instruments of the actions and labors of life, the meaning of the figure is very manifest. Says Job, in his complaint to God, "If I wash myself with snow water, and make my hands never so clean, yet shalt thou plunge me in the ditch, and mine own clothes shall abhor me."—Job ix, 30, 31. That is, "Though I give the utmost heed to conform my whole life and conduct to the requirements of thy holiness, yet, in the severity and penetration of thy judgment, thou wilt discover and reveal me to myself as utterly unclean." The psalmist has recourse to the same figure, in a happier spirit. "I will wash mine hands in innocency, so will I compass thine altar, O Lord; that I may publish with the voice of thanksgiving, and tell of all thy wondrous works."—Ps. xxvi, 6, 7.

2. Next in the order of these observances was the ordinance requiring the priests to wash their hands and feet in preparation for the duties of their ministry at the sanctuary. This will be discussed hereafter.

3. In certain milder forms of uncleanness till the even, the person was required to wash his clothes, merely. This rule applied to such as he that ate or slept in a house shut up on suspicion of leprosy (Lev. xiv, 47); and he that carried an unclean carcase, or ate unclean flesh. (Lev. xi, 25, 28, 40.) From the time when our first parents, in the conscious nakedness of guilt, made themselves aprons of fig-leaves, which the Lord replaced with coats of skins, the garments had a recognized significance, which is traceable long before the giving of the law; and, running through all the Scriptures, gives form to the imagery of the last book of all. When Jacob, on his return from Chaldea, was required by God to go to Bethel and erect an altar, he called on his household and followers to be clean and change their garments (Gen. xxxv, 2); that is, to put off their soiled garments and put on clean. So, at Sinai, in preparation for its transactions, Moses was directed to "sanctify the people to-day and to-morrow, and let them wash their clothes."—Ex. xix, 10, 14.

A few other Scriptures will develop the meaning of this symbol. In the vision of Zechariah: "He showed me Joshua the high-priest, standing before the angel of the Lord, and Satan standing at his right hand to resist him. And the Lord said unto Satan, The Lord rebuke thee, O Satan; even the Lord that hath chosen Jerusalem rebuke thee: Is not this a brand plucked out of the fire? Now Joshua, was clothed with filthy garments and stood before the angel. And he answered and spake to those that stood before him, saying, Take away the filthy garments from him. And unto him he said, Behold I have caused thine iniquity to pass from thee, and I will clothe thee with change of raiment."—Zech. iii, 1-4. "Others save with fear," says Jude, "pulling them out of the fire; hating even the garment spotted by the flesh."—Jude 23. With this compare the definition of "pure religion and undefiled,"—"to keep himself unspotted from the world."—Jas. i, 27. "Thou hast a few names even in Sardis, which have not defiled their garments; and they shall walk with me in white; for they are worthy."—Rev. iii, 4. In his visions, John saw the souls of them that were slain for the word of God, and a great multitude out of every nation, "clothed with white robes." And the angel told him, "These are they that have washed their robes, and made them white in the blood of the Lamb."—Ib. vi, 11; vii, 9, 14. "Behold I come as a thief. Blessed is he that watcheth and keepeth his garments, lest he walk naked, and they see his shame."—Ib. xvi, 15. To the bride, the Lamb's wife, it "was granted that she should be arrayed in fine linen, clean and white; for the fine linen is the righteousness of saints."—Ib. xix, 8. Literally, "is the righteousnesses of the saints."

From these Scriptures, it is evident: that clean or white garments primarily and essentially mean, the righteousness of the Lord Jesus Christ, in which his people are robed, so that the shame of their spiritual nakedness may not appear (Rev. iii, 18; vii, 14; Phil, iii, 8, 9); that keeping them clean, or unspotted, means, the maintaining of that watchful holiness of heart and life which is becoming those who have been bought and robed as are Christ's people; and that washing the garments signifies recourse to the blood and Spirit of Christ, as the only and effectual means of making and keeping them free from defilement.

4. In certain cases, the unclean until the even were required to wash their clothes and bathe their flesh. The characteristic examples of this observance, are those who had carried or touched any thing on which one defiled with an issue had sat or lain. (Lev. xv, 5, 6, etc.) A careful examination of this class, in comparison with the preceding, proves them to be essentially one in meaning, the difference being mainly if not entirely in degree. The defilement in the present case was aggravated by the fact that its cause was symbolical of man's depravity, breaking out in active corruption and transgression. On the other hand, the unclean animals, from which the milder form of this uncleanness was contracted represented the evil of man's nature, simply as native and indwelling, without the active element of outbreaking depravity and wickedness. Hence, the difference, in requiring the washing of both the flesh and the garments, was designed to give emphasis to the admonition conveyed; and to teach the additional lesson, that whilst all contact with the ungodly and the world is dangerous to the purity of Christian character, and renders necessary a continual recourse to the sanctifying power and grace of the Holy Spirit; especially is this requisite in case of intimate relations with it, in its active forms of ungodliness and corruption, dissipation and riot.

5. The only other class, to be enumerated under this head, consists of those who, in addition to other rites of purifying, were required to shave off their hair. Such were lepers, in their cleansing (Lev. xiv, 8, 9); the Levites, upon their consecration (Num. viii, 7); a Nazarite, defiled, before the completion of his vow (Num. vi, 9); and a captive woman, chosen as a bride (Deut. xxi, 12). With these may be compared the Nazarite, at the completion of his vow, although this did not belong to the category of purifying. The Scriptures contain no formal explanation of this requirement. But the nature and circumstances of the cases as compared with each

other, and the general principles of typical analogy, indicate the interpretation. The hair of the leper, for example, was the product and outgrowth of his leprous state, and must therefore be put off and repudiated, with his entrance on the the new life of the clean. The same principle applies to all the other cases, except that of the Nazarite, upon the completion of his vow. His hair was the product of the time during which, by the consecration of his vow, all belonged to God. It could not, therefore, be retained, but was shaved off and offered upon the altar, as holy. (Num. vi, 18.) In the other cases, it was cast away as unclean. Thus, as in all the preceding regulations, the same lesson is repeated, which is so needful, and to our stupidity, so hard to learn;—the lesson of putting off the old man and putting on the new.

Section XXVII.—*Mode implied in the Meaning of the Rite.*—The self-washings meant the active putting off of the sins of the flesh

The instructiveness and utility of types and symbols consist in an appreciable analogy between them and the spiritual things which they are appointed to symbolize. In the case of the Old Testament self-washings, I suppose it has never entered the imagination of any one that they were types of the burial of the Lord Jesus. Of such an interpretation there is not a trace anywhere in the Scriptures. On the contrary, such meaning is there attributed to them that, in order to a sustained analogy, the subject of the rite should, by a voluntary and active exercise of his own powers take and apply the water to his members and person, for their cleansing. In this respect, they stand in emphatic contrast with the sprinkled water of purifying. That was designed to concentrate the attention of Israel upon the active agency of the Mediator, in bestowing the baptism of his blood and Spirit, for the renewing and quickening of dead souls. In it, therefore, the subject was the passive recipient of rites dispensed by the hands of another. But the activity of the Christian life and warfare were symbolized by the self-washings. Christ's grace is given his people, not to sanction supineness and indolence; but to stimulate to activity in the pursuit of holiness. As the Spirit is now to them an opened fountain, they are to have recourse to it, to seek and obtain, day by day, more grace, for the purging of the flesh, for overcoming the world, for bringing forth the fruits of the Spirit, for fighting the good fight of faith and laying hold on eternal life.

This, which comprehends the whole matter of practical religion is urged in the Scriptures, not only by direct and continual admonitions, but in the use of every variety of figures and illustrations. It was the lesson taught, under the figure of self-washing. Pure water is alike adapted to quicken the soil, to quench the thirst, and to cleanse the garments and the person. But, as the water of life will not quench the thirst of the soul, unless we *come* and *drink*, neither will it purge away the defilements of evil, unless we take it and apply it, with diligence and labor. "Wash ye! make you clean; put away the evil of your doings from before mine eyes; cease to do evil; learn to do well; seek judgment, relieve the oppressed, judge the fatherless, plead for the widow."—Isa. i, 16, 17. The Spirit thus clearly indicates that self-washing signified an intense and life-pervasive activity,—an activity applied, in detail, to each particular relation and duty, so as to purge out every principle of evil, and conform every act to the law of holiness. To correspond with this meaning of the rite, its form should be such as to call forth the active energies of the subject, by the application of the water to the appointed parts and members of the person in detail; and by such successive manipulation as is proper to secure a thorough cleansing. The ordinary mode of washing, among Israel, as we shall presently see, perfectly met these requirements; whilst immersion would have been wholly inadequate, not to say directly contradictory to them, since it indicates a mere passive recipiency, and not an active appropriation and use of the means of cleansing.

Section XXVIII.—The Words used to designate the Washings.—1. Shātaph. 2. Kābas. 3. Rāhatz

The discriminating use of words on this subject, in the original Scriptures is very noticeable, and is susceptible of being brought within the comprehension of any intelligent reader of the English version. There are three which are worthy of special notice.

1. *Shātaph* means, to overflow, or rush over, as a swollen torrent or a beating rain. Thus,—"Behold the Lord hath a mighty and strong one, which, as a tempest of hail and a destroying storm, as a flood of mighty waters *overflowing*," shall beat down the crown of pride. (Isa. xxviii, 2.) Again,—"Say unto them which daub with untempered mortar that it shall fall; there shall be an *overflowing* shower," beating it down. (Ezek. xiii, 11-14.) From this, the radical meaning of the word, is derived its use to signify the act of washing or rinsing, by means of water dashed or flowed over the object. It is employed in application to vessels of wood and of brass (Lev. vi, 28; xv, 12), and to the hands of the unclean. (Ib. xv, 11.) In all these places it is translated, to rinse.

2. *Kābas.* The radical meaning of this verb is, to tread, to trample. The participle from it is used to designate the craft of the fuller, who fulled his goods by treading them with the feet. Hence its use to signify the thorough cleansing and whitening of clothing and stuffs. The word occurs in the Old Testament forty-six times, with this uniform meaning. It is used whenever the ritual washing of clothes is spoken of. From it a very striking figure is derived, which appears twice, to indicate the most thorough self-cleansing, under the idea of a garment scoured, with "nitre and much soap" (Jer. ii, 22; iv, 14), and twice, to indicate a like thorough cleansing wrought by the Holy Spirit. "*Wash* me thoroughly from mine iniquity, and cleanse me from my sin.... Purge me with hyssop, and I shall be clean: *wash* me, and I shall be whiter than snow" (Psa. li, 2, 7), white, as a garment is made by the fuller's art. (Mark ix, 3.) These passages indicate the essential idea of the word. It is expressive of a scouring, or washing, which searches the very texture of the fabric. It is, however, worthy of notice that in the Targum of Onkelos, on Numbers xix, 19, it is rendered, "to sprinkle." "The clean person shall sprinkle upon the unclean, on the third day and on the seventh day; and on the seventh day he shall be clean; and he *shall sprinkle* his raiment, and wash with water, and at even he shall be clean." This rendering is very noteworthy, as it indicates the manner in which the law was understood on this point. In fact, as we have already seen, sprinkling signified the

most thorough cleansing.

Rāhatz. While *kābas* indicates a purifying of the substance, *rāhatz* signifies a washing of the surface. This is the word which is invariably used to express the ritual self-washings or bathings of the hands, the feet, and the person. It is sometimes assumed that, like the English, to wash, *rāhatz* is strictly generic in its meaning—that it signifies to cleanse with, or in, water, without any regard to mode. This is an error, as a single fact shows. It is never used for the cleansing of skins, clothes, or garments. Nor is this an accidental omission. Such washings are mentioned nearly fifty times, and in nineteen places they are brought into connection with the bathing of the person. But in no one place is the word in question used either generically, as comprehensive of both the person and garments, or specifically for the latter. In every place where the two processes come in the same connection, the language is accurately discriminated. The directions are, to *wash*, or scour (*kābas*), the clothes, and to *bathe (rāhatz)* the flesh. This word occurs over seventy times. In five or six places, it applies to the washing of sacrificial flesh, before it was placed on the altar. (Lev. i, 9, 13, etc.) In every other instance it refers to the human person. It expresses cleansing with water actively applied to the surface. Thus, when Joseph "*washed* his face," to obliterate the traces of tears (Gen. xliii, 31), and when the Beloved is described, "His eyes, as the eyes of doves by the rivers [rivulets] of waters, *washed* with milk and fitly set" (Cant. v, 12), the reference is clearly to the familiar mode of washing the face with water applied. When the Lord, by Isaiah, speaks of the time when he "shall have *washed away* the filth of the daughters of Zion" (Isa. iv, 4), and when the Preacher describes "a generation that are pure in their own eyes, and yet is not *washed from* their filthiness" (Prov. xxx, 12), the idea presented is the same—that of water actively applied to the surface, so as to detach and carry off the dirt. In another place this definition is even more imperatively indicated. "Then (*rāhatz*) washed I thee with water; yea (*shātaph*), I thoroughly washed away thy blood from thee, and I anointed thee with oil."—Ezek. xvi, 9. Here three things unite to determine the meaning of *rāhatz*. 1. It is explained by *shātaph*, the signification of which we have seen. 2. The defilement from which the washing is promised, is that of *nidda*, for which expressly the sprinkled "water of *nidda*" was appointed and named. 3. The construction is precisely the same in the two clauses of the verse, "I washed thee *with* water," and "I anointed thee *with* oil." Of the mode of the latter there can be no question. In both clauses the element named is the *instrument* of the action specified. The ideas of washing and of immersion are not merely different, but sharply contrasted with each other. Where there is an immersion, there may also be a washing. But it must be by additional action. *Rāhatz* expresses the latter. It neither expresses nor implies the former.

Section XXIX.—*The Mode of Domestic Ablution.*—By water poured on. The patriarchs. Mode in Egypt. In the wilderness. Story of Susanna. Purgation of a concealed murder. Washing the feet at table

The customs of Israel as to personal ablution would, it is evident, decide the manner of these self-washings, in the absence of explicit directions. The indications in their history are very decisive on this point.

1. The patriarchs were keepers of cattle, dwelling in tents. The circumstances of such a mode of life forbid the supposition that they were accustomed to the use of the immersion bath. The possession, the transportation, and the use of the requisite vessels, are wholly foreign to that mode of life.

2. Facts in the history of the patriarchs confirm the correctness of the inference thus indicated. Although in later ages, after Palestine had been pierced with wells, water was abundant for all the uses incident to the mode of life of the people, the contrary was true, in earlier times. Surface streams are of rare occurrence. The substratum is a cavernous limestone, into the cavities of which the rains quickly percolate. Hagar and Ishmael were in danger of perishing of thirst, when sent away by Abraham. (Gen. xxi, 15.) Abraham and Isaac relied on digging for water; and the scarcity and value of the element were indicated by the violence with which the other inhabitants of the country seized wells digged by each of those patriarchs. (Gen. xxi, 25; xxvi, 19-22.) These were usually deep, and all the water used for personal washings, as well as for drinking and for culinary uses, must be laboriously drawn and carried by the maidens of the camp. We can thus see the bearing of the phraseology of Abraham in tendering his hospitality. "Let a *little water*, I pray you, be fetched, and wash your feet." —Gen. xviii, 4.

3. We may safely conclude that Jacob and his family did not take with them into Egypt the habit of bathing by immersion. But may they not have acquired it in the land of their bondage? It happens that we have very interesting evidence as to the custom of the Egyptians on this subject. Sir J. Gardner Wilkinson, in his splendid work on "The Manners and Customs of the Ancient Egyptians," gives an engraved copy of the only pictorial illustration on this subject found by him among the abundant remains of Egyptian art. It is taken from a tomb in Thebes. In it, a lady is represented with four attendants. One removes the jewelry and clothes which she has put off; another pours water from a vase over her head: the third rubs her arms and body with open hands; and a fourth, seated near her, holds a flower to her nose, and supports her, as she sits. "The same subject," says Wilkinson, "is treated nearly in the same manner on some of the Greek vases, the water being poured over the bather, who kneels or is seated on the ground."[14] The Greeks were colonists from Egypt, with which country their relations were always intimate. And the fact, which will hereafter appear, that this was the only mode of domestic or in-door bathing, in use among them, is very significant, as to the customs of Egypt on the point.

4. It is hardly necessary to insist on the utter impossibility of the Hebrew bondmen having acquired in Egypt more luxurious habits than those of their Egyptian taskmasters, —habits, too, requiring much more expensive appliances, such as would be necessary for immersion-bathing. And, when they left Egypt, "their kneading troughs being bound up in their clothes upon their shoulders" (Ex. xii, 34), the supposition that they had with them a sufficient supply of bath tubs to serve for the continual immersions which, upon the Baptist theory, the Levitical law demanded, does not need to be controverted. In fact, the customary mode of washing, among Israel, as traceable in all their history, was precisely that which

---

[14] Wilkinson, vol. iii, p. 388; Abridged edition, ii, 349.

we have seen in use among the patriarchs and the Egyptians. It was, with water poured on, and the necessary rubbing by the bather himself, or by an attendant. This custom was universal in Israel, and throughout the east, from the earliest ages. At first, the only utensil used was a pitcher or jar, out of which the water was poured. A case before referred to in the history of Abraham illustrates the circumstances and manner of this usage. As he sat in his tent door, in the heat of the day, he saw three men approach. He ran to salute them, and said, "Let a little water be fetched, and wash your feet, and rest yourselves under the tree." —Gen. xviii, 1-4. The washing was done in the open air, and the earth received the flowing water. In the same region, the Dead Sea expedition found the same custom among the tent-dwelling Arabs. On one occasion, "having as usual submitted to be stared at and their arms handed about and inspected, as if they were on muster, water was brought and poured upon their hands, from a very equivocal water jar; after which followed the repast."[15]

So long as the simplicity of tent life was maintained, this was all-sufficient. But, afterward, the convenience of a bowl or basin was added, which was so placed as to catch the water, as it flowed off, in washing, thus preventing the wetting of the floor. The water, once used, was not applied a second time, but rejected, as being defiled. The examples of Bathsheba and Susanna indicate that, in bathing the person, even in the later times, the primitive custom still so far survived that resort was sometimes had to a retired place outside the house; no doubt because of the inconvenience of flooding the floor with the water, as it was poured over the person. "The History of Susanna," (one of the Apocryphal books), dates as far back as two centuries before Christ. The heroine is described as an eminently modest and virtuous woman. Her husband, Joachim, "was a rich man, and had a fair garden adjoining his house." His house was a place of resort to the Jews, and the magistrates commonly sat there, to exercise their office. It was Susanna's custom to walk in the garden at noon, after the people had left the house. Two of the elders are described as plotting against her. "And it fell out, as they watched a fit time, she went in as before with two maids only, and she was desirous to wash herself in the garden; for it was hot. And there was nobody there save the two elders, that had hid themselves and watched her. Then she said to her maids, Bring me oil and washing balls, and shut the garden doors, that I may wash. And they did as she had bade them, and shut the garden doors, and went out themselves at private doors, to fetch the things that she had commanded them." Her purpose is prevented by the appearance of the two elders, from whose false accusation she is in the sequel rescued by the famous "judgment of Daniel." The same custom is illustrated by the case of Pharaoh's daughter at the finding of Moses, and by the Egyptian picture, from Wilkinson. A signal proof of the prevalence of the custom of washing with water poured on by an attendant, presents itself, in the fact that the designation of a body servant, or personal attendant, was derived from it. Elisha the prophet had been the minister or attendant of Elijah, before the translation of the latter. Of this relation, king Jehoshaphat was informed by the statement that it was he "which poured water on the hands of Elijah." —2 Kings iii, 11.

---

[15] Lynch's Dead Sea Expedition, p. 206.

The circumstances render it certain that this was the form of washing in the expiation of a concealed murder. The elders of the nearest city were required to take an unbroken heifer down into a rough and uncultivated valley or gorge, and there, in the presence of the priests, strike off its head, wash their hands over the carcass, and call God to witness their innocence in the matter. Thus, the water flowing from their hands upon the carcass, transferred to it and the barren spot where it lay the putative guilt of the crime. (Deut. xxi, 3-9.)

From this ordinance, the form seems to have become a familiar mode of protesting innocence of crime, and is memorable for that occasion when Pilate "took water and washed his hands before the multitude, saying, I am innocent of the blood of this just person: see ye to it."—Matt. xxvii, 24. Two primitive representations of this scene, in sculptured relief, have been found in the catacombs at Rome. They date from the first centuries of the Christian era. In them the wife of Pilate appears in the background, with averted face. An attendant holds a vase or pitcher in one hand, and in the other a bowl: while Pilate sits rubbing his hands. The position of the bowl shows it to be empty. "The mode of washing implied in the empty bowl is characteristic. In the east, the water is still poured from the vase over the hands, and caught in the bowl, so that it should not pass over them twice."[16]

The manner of washing the feet is illustrated by a fact in the life of our Savior. At dinner, in the house of Simon, the Pharisee, a woman that was a sinner "brought an alabaster box of ointment and stood at his feet, behind him, weeping, and began to wash his feet with tears, and did wipe them with the hairs of her head, and kissed his feet, and anointed them with the ointment."—Luke vii, 37, 38, 44. But how was it possible for the woman, coming behind him at table, to get access to his feet: which, according to our custom, would be concealed under the table? The ordinary mode of sitting, in the east, then as now, was, on the ground or floor, squat, cross-legged, or reclining. Chairs were not in common use, but were reserved for purposes of state, and used almost exclusively by dignitaries. In later times a bench or settee was introduced, which was without a back. Whether on it or the floor, the usual position, in eating was the same. The guests reclined on the left elbow, leaving the right hand free. The person next on the right thus leaned toward or against the breast of him who was at the head. (John xiii, 23.) The feet were drawn up behind. Persons who wore sandals, always, on entering a house, left them at the door. These were not ordinarily worn by the common people, but only upon occasions of special travel; and our Savior, therefore, forbade his disciples to take time to provide them, in the haste of the mission on which he first sent them to preach. (Matt. x, 10; Luke x, 4.) They poorly protected the feet from the soiling and roughness of the way.[17] Decency, therefore, and comfort both,—especially in the case of guests coming from a distance, required that the feet should be washed, immediately upon entrance, and the addition of oil or ointment was

---

[16] Maitland's "Church of the Catacombs," p. 261. Also, Withrow's "Catacombs," p. 333.

[17] "Several of them [Arabs of the Jordan] wore sandals, a rude invention to protect the feet. It was a thick piece of hide, confined by a thong passing under the sole at the hollow of the foot, around the heel, and between the great toe and the one which adjoins it."—Lynch's "Dead Sea Expedition," p. 282. These thongs were the "latchets" of Mark i, 7.

not only agreeable, for the perfumes commonly mixed with it, but very soothing and grateful to the weary and excoriated feet. It was one of the first obligations of hospitality to provide for this washing of the feet of guests. (Gen. xviii, 4; xix, 2; etc.) Where special respect was intended, the office was sometimes performed by the master of the house, or his wife. As the guest reclined, his feet projecting over the edge of the seat behind him, a basin was placed beneath, so as to receive the flowing water, as it was poured over them. To this mode there is an allusion in the language of our Savior, to Simon the Pharisee, upon the occasion just referred to, which is lost in our translation. "I entered thine house. Water *upon* my feet thou didst not give."—Luke vii, 44.[18] So, the night of the betrayal, Jesus took water and a towel and washed and wiped the disciples' feet, as they reclined; and thus the woman came behind him at the table, and bedewed his feet with her tears. To this customary rite of hospitality Paul refers, when he describes a widow—"if she have lodged strangers, if she have washed the saints' feet."—1 Tim. v, 10. To it, Abigail alludes, when, in response to David's offer of marriage, she replies,—"Behold, let thine handmaid be a servant, to wash the feet of the servants of my lord."—1 Sam. xxv, 41. If the ritual bathings of Israel were immersions, the mode was without precedent in the domestic habits of the people; as it was without prescription in the law.

Section XXX.—*The Facilities requisite.*—The water drawn from wells by women. No vessels for immersion. The bath of Ulysses

Not only was the rite of immersion without precedent in the domestic customs of Israel. It was wholly impracticable as an observance to be fulfilled with the frequency of the ritual washings of the law. On this point, delicacy forbids unnecessary detail. But an examination of the various requirements on the subject of uncleanness, and especially as contained in the fifteenth chapter of Leviticus, will establish the fact that recourse to those washings, was a matter of constant,—almost daily,—necessity, in every household, and for both men and women. In order to fulfil these obligations, the supposition that immersion was the mode would render two things imperatively necessary in every family,—a very large supply of water;—and a capacious bath-tub or tank in which the immersions might be performed. As to these points, but few words are necessary. The people of Israel did not usually live on their lands in the country; but, like all other populations of the east, were gathered in towns and villages, to which they resorted at night; going forth in the day-time to their labors in the field. This mode of life was rendered necessary to avoid exposure to the depredations of bands of wandering marauders; and was equally congenial to the social disposition and habits of the people. The population of each village was accustomed to depend, for the supply of water, upon a well to which all resorted, and which was usually near the gate of the village. From this source, each household was supplied; the water being carried in pitchers, or jars, on the shoulders of the females of the family.[19] It is unnecessary

---

[18] "Ὕδωρ ἐπὶ τοὺς πόδας μου οὐκ ἔδωκας." The preposition, επι, with the accusative, means *upon*, with the idea of previous or present motion,—to wit, (in this place,) of the water, poured and flowing upon the feet.

[19] Gen. xxiv, 13.—; Ex. ii, 15-19; Judges v, 11; Ruth ii, 1-4; 2 Sam. xxiii, 15; 1 Sam. ix,

to protract argument. The facts are of themselves conclusive. The washings can not have been immersions.

This conclusion is confirmed by the absence of vessels of any kind suited to the performance of such a rite. Neither in the Old Testament nor the New, neither in the Apocrypha, Philo, nor Josephus is there any mention of such facilities, or such a rite, nor allusion to them. In fact, with all the advantages and appliances of modern civilization, there is not, and there never was a people on the globe of whom one in a hundred could comply with the law of Moses, if interpreted in the Baptist sense. And it is certain that no primitive people ever adopted that mode of domestic bathing—a mode which implies a very great advance in luxury and its appliances. The Greeks themselves did not use it, except as they sometimes resorted to rivers and streams. In their arrangements for bathing, domestic and public, the immersion bath was unknown until introduced with the luxury of imperial Rome. In Homer's description of the bath of Ulysses in the palace of Circe, the hero is described as seated in a vessel which contained no water, but was designed to receive that which was poured over him; and the bathing was performed in a manner identical with that which we have seen practiced in Egypt. In the remains of antique Greek art, the bath is frequently represented. But the mode is invariably the same. The bather is placed *beside* the vessel containing the water, which is taken thence in a dipper or jar, and poured over him.[20]

Homer's description of the bath of Ulysses is thus rendered by Bryant:

> A nymph—"the fourth
> Brought water from the fountain, and beneath
> A massive tripod kindled a great fire,
> And warmed the water. When it boiled, within
> The shining brass, she led me to the bath,
> And washed me from the tripod. On my head
> And shoulders, pleasantly, she shed the streams
> That from my members took away the sense
> Of weariness, unmanning body and mind."[21]

Section XXXI.—*The Washings of the Priests.*—Symbolism of the tabernacle. The laver. Priestly washings. The laver and river of Ezekiel. No immersions here

Writers upon the types and symbols of the Scriptures too often fail to recognize or appreciate their unity, symmetry, and completeness as a system, and the just proportion and propriety of each several part in its relation to the whole. That such must have been their character was impressively intimated to Israel by the emphasis with which Moses was admonished to "look that thou make them after their pattern, which was shewed thee in the mount."—Ex. xxv, 40; xxvii, 8; Num. viii, 4. The reason of this particularity is stated by Paul. "Who serve unto the ex-

---

11; John iv, 7; Matt. xx, 1-7.

[20] See Wilkinson, above quoted, and Smith's Greek and Roman Antiquities, *article* "Balneæ;" and below pp. 200, 207.

[21] Bryant's Odyssey, Book X, 429-437.

ample and shadow of heavenly things, as Moses was admonished of God when he was about to make the tabernacle; for, See, saith he, that thou make all things according to the pattern showed to thee in the mount." — Heb. viii, 5. The tabernacle and its appurtenances were a systematic and luminous exposition of the plan of grace. Approaching it from without, the first object that presented itself was the brazen altar of burnt-offering, exhibiting the price of redemption. Between it and the door of the tabernacle stood the laver, the pure water of which symbolized the Holy Spirit, through whom is the washing of regeneration and renewing of the Holy Ghost, the essential condition precedent to admittance to the fold of Christ. Entering the tabernacle, the first apartment represented the church on earth, the fold of the covenant. In it the light always shone from the seven branched golden candlestick, the lamps of which, continually replenished with oil by the priest, symbolized the church shining as the light of the world, through the oil of grace, the unction of the Holy One, ministered by our great High Priest. The table of show bread always supplied with twelve loaves, according to the number of the twelve tribes, set forth that Bread of life ever abundant for all, which nourishes the people of God in the earthly church, in preparation for the heavenly. Immediately before the veil, and before the ark of the covenant in the holy of holies stood the altar of incense, the fire of which, kindled with coals from the altar of burnt-offering, set forth the prayers of God's people, made acceptable and fragrant before the throne, by virtue of the atonement and intercession of Christ. Within the veil, — thin curtain between the earthly and the heavenly house, — the mercy seat covering the ark, and the tables of the covenant law enclosed therein, represented the throne of God's grace resting upon the firm foundation of his eternal law, thus showing that mercy to man is conditioned upon satisfaction to that law by the blood of atonement sprinkled there. All the other features of the system, its rites and ceremonies, were constructed and ordered in a strictly symmetrical and congruous relation to these. A recollection of these points will aid in a just appreciation of the points involved in the present discussion.

Of the form and dimensions of the laver, the Scriptures give no account, except that it stood on a foot or pedestal. (Ex. xxx, 18.) It was, however, of such size and proportions as to be carried about with Israel in their journeyings, probably with bars, borne on the shoulders of the Levites, as was the altar. In preparing facilities for the purpose of immersion, our Baptist brethren invariably sink the font to such a level that the minister and the subjects of the rite may descend into it. And this arrangement is a dictate, not of convenience only, but of decency, in the performance of the service. But, to suppose the laver sufficiently large and deep to serve as an immersion font, and then place it upon a pedestal, involves an elevation which must have rendered it, practically, inaccessible for such purposes, and precludes the idea that it was intended to be so used. In fact, the laver was not a bath tub, nor ever used as such, but a containing vessel from which was drawn water for all the uses of the sanctuary. The engravings which appear on pages 107, 113 below, precisely correspond with the Mosaic description of the laver, and probably give a very closely approximate idea of its form, size, and proportions.

In the temple of Solomon, the one laver of the tabernacle was replaced by a "sea of brass," and ten lavers. The sea was appropriated to the washings of the priests, whilst the lavers were used for washing the sacrifices. That they were used as fountains of supply, and not as vessels in which the sacrifices were washed, appears from the fact that they rested on bases four cubits square, by three cubits high, and were of the same proportions. (1 Kings vii, 27, 38.) The Hebrew text gives the length, breadth, and height of the bases, but only the length and breadth of the lavers. The Septuagint and Josephus give the former dimensions, and add the height of the lavers—three cubits. Thus, the bottoms of the lavers were four and a half feet above the pavement on which they stood, and their brims, nine feet above it. They were, moreover, provided with wheels, so as to be removed from place to place, as occasion required. That the sacrifices were not immersed in them is evident. The Talmud states that they were washed upon marble tables; and this is the mode for which provision is made in the vision of Ezekiel. (Ezek. xl, 38-43.)

The sea of brass was ten cubits in diameter, and five cubits high; that is, about fifteen feet by seven and a half. It was elevated on twelve brazen oxen, the height of which is not given. But if we allow them no greater height than the bases of the lavers, the whole height was about twelve feet; a height not suggestive of convenience for immersions.

2. The brazen sea was no part of the tabernacle furniture when God directed Moses to "bring Aaron and his sons unto the door of the tabernacle of the congregation and wash them with water."—Ex. xl, 12; comp. xxix, 4. "And Moses said unto the congregation, This is the thing which the Lord commanded to be done. And Moses brought Aaron and his sons and washed them with water."—Lev. viii, 5, 6. Respecting this, the facts are so evident as to admit but one conclusion. (1.) The command given was not to immerse Aaron and his sons, but (*rāhatz*), to wash them, according to the proper meaning of that word, as already shown, and after the ordinary manner of ablution. (2.) The transaction is thrice described, in the places referred to above; but the laver is not once mentioned, nor any means of immersion. (3.) The place of the washing is so described as to exclude immersion. Thrice repeated, it is still, "*at* the door," of the tabernacle. (Lev. viii, 4.) If the priests were immersed, on this occasion, the laver was the only vessel in which it can have been done; and, not only was it so constructed as to render its use impossible, but the language of the account is such as to conceal the fact. But here was no immersion. As commanded, Moses *washed* Aaron and his sons.

3. When Moses was ordered to make the laver, its purpose was stated: "Aaron and his sons shall wash their hands and their feet thereat; when they go into the tabernacle of the congregation, they shall wash with water, that they die not; or, when they come near to the altar, to minister, to burn offering made by fire unto the Lord. So they shall wash their hands and their feet, that they die not: and it shall be a statute for ever to them, even to him and to his seed throughout their generations."—Ex. xxx, 19-21. Not only were the priests thus to wash their hands and their feet, but also certain parts of the sacrifices.—"The priests, Aaron's sons, shall lay the parts, the head and the fat in order upon the wood that is on the fire which is upon the altar; but his inwards and his legs shall he wash in water; and the priest shall burn all on the altar."—Lev. i, 8, 9, 13; viii, 21; ix, 14.

Should we set aside the arguments arising from the meaning of the word employed,—from the customs of the people as to personal ablutions,—and from the form and elevation of the laver, the present facts discover an insurmountable objection to the idea of immersion. Or, will it be insisted that the priests as they came into the sanctuary at the appointed times of service, successively, climbed to the top of the laver and, balancing on its brim, immersed their hands and feet; and, then, in fulfillment of their official duties, immersed in the water thus fouled, the inwards, or bowels and intestines, and the pieces of the sacrifices, about to be offered to God? The supposition would be indecent and profane. And yet, this is the unavoidable result of demanding immersion, in this case. For, the same language is used in requiring the washing of the priests and of the sacrifices, and there was but one laver, to supply all demands for water at the sanctuary.

4. But, again: On the day of atonement, the high priest was required, at a certain time in the order of observances for the day, being alone in the sanctuary, to "wash his flesh with water in the holy place."—Lev. xvi, 24. Here, at least, there is no room for controversy. The laver was outside the door of the tabernacle. The priest was within, "in the holy place." In it, there was no vessel in which an immersion could take place. Immersion was not merely improbable.—It was impossible. The circumstances compel us to accept the language of the place, just as it stands; and to believe that the high priest, on this occasion *washed* himself, and that he did so, as all washings of the person are performed, *"with* water," as an instrumental means; and that it was applied with his own hands to his own person.

5. Living or fresh water is the most familiar Scriptural symbol of the Holy Spirit. This is fully considered elsewhere. In the symbolism of the tabernacle and temple, the water of the lavers and sea of brass was the appointed symbol of that blessed Person, as the source of all cleansing and sanctifying influences. In this view, the fact is instructive, that, in the temple of Ezekiel's vision, (Ezek. xl-xlviii) there was no laver; but, instead, the waters of the river of life flowed from the spot on which the laver should have stood. Jewish tradition states the laver to have stood on the south side of the door of the tabernacle, which looked toward the east. That was the position of the brazen sea. "He set the sea on the right side of the house, eastward, over against the south."—1 Kings vii, 39. "On the right side of the east end, over against the south."—2 Chron. iv, 10. In Ezekiel, "the forefront of the house stood toward the east, and the waters came down from under, from the right side of the house at the south side of the altar."—Ezek. xlvii, 1. Nor is it unworthy of consideration, that, if the laver was designed as a baptistery or immersion font, the living stream described by Ezekiel was wholly inadequate to such a purpose; being, at that point, but a rivulet, not ankle deep. (Ib. 3-5.)

6. The meaning of the water, taken in connection with the relation which Moses, by divine appointment, sustained to Aaron, suggests the interpretation of the washing of the latter by Moses. Moses was to Aaron "instead of God" (Ex. iv, 16); and since Aaron's priesthood was typical of that of the Lord Jesus, it follows, that the action of Moses, in washing his brother, and then robing him in the holy garments of the priesthood, was typical of the agency of the Father, in endowing our great High Priest, through the Holy Spirit, with a sinless humanity, (Heb. x,

5-7) and in it, investing him with the eternal priesthood which he now fulfills. This washing of Aaron is to be discriminated from his official anointing. The latter signified the official gifts and qualifications of Christ, whilst the former had respect to his birth and growth in personal holiness. (Luke ii, 52.)

7. The significance of the feet, in the figurative system of the Scriptures, appears in the proverb, which, among the things that the Lord hates, enumerates "feet that be swift in running to mischief."—Prov. vi, 18. On the other hand, the Psalmist says,—"I turned my feet unto thy testimonies."—"I refrained my feet from every evil way."—Ps. cxix, 59, 101. The hands and feet, together, represent, fully, the active energies of man. And the priests washing their hands and feet, when they came to minister at the altar was typical of the active righteousness of the Lord Jesus. This is the more apparent, when associated with the other fact, that in fulfilling the office for which they thus washed themselves, they were required, as already stated, to wash the inwards and the legs of the burnt offerings, (Lev. i, 9, 13; etc.); the inwards, or bowels representing the affections, and the legs the active powers. Thus, the priests and the sacrifices together typified the essential holiness and the active obedience of the Lord Jesus, "who, through the eternal Spirit, offered himself, without spot, to God."—Heb. ix, 14. In all this, there is still nothing to demand, to suggest, or allow, the idea of immersion. The significance of the rites accords perfectly with all the other irresistible indications, which lead us to the conclusion that under no circumstances was immersion ever used in the washings of the priests, or the rites of the tabernacle and temple service.

Section XXXII.—*Like these were the Self-washings of the People.*—Designations and meaning the same. Immersion would have been without meaning

The conclusion just indicated as to the washings of the priests, carries with it a like decision respecting all the self-performed washings.

1. The word *rāhatz*, to wash, is used in the same manner, in the directions given with respect to all the various cases, of hands, feet and person,—of priests and people, and of the sacrificial pieces, alike.

2. The self-washings imposed on the people were of the same essential nature and meaning as those of the priests. In both, the idea was that of holiness and purity of heart and life, maintained by personal watchfulness and efficiency through the grace of the Holy Spirit. If this idea was properly symbolized by the priestly ablutions without immersion, the conclusion is unavoidable, that among the people immersion was unknown. To them, the mode used by the priests would be the standard of propriety.

3. It is impossible to elicit any consistent meaning out of the supposed immersions. The ritual system was characterized by congruity in all its parts, and meaning everywhere. What else upon Baptist principles, can the immersions be thought to mean, if not the burial of Christ? But how, then, are we to understand the grades of washings, of the hands, and feet, and garments, as so carefully distinguished from each other, and from that of the person? What means the fact, which is so

clearly marked, that these washings were self-performed? Did Christ entomb himself? How are we to explain the washing of Aaron by Moses? If immersion is typical of the burial of the Lord Jesus, what pertinence could it have to his birth and inauguration as priest? What mean the peculiar times at which the self-washings were to be performed,—the priests being required always to wash *before* offering sacrifice or ministering at the altar; whilst, the unclean for seven days performed the same rite at the end of the seven days, *after* they had been restored from typical death? Was Christ buried *before* he had made of himself an offering and a sacrifice? Or, again, was it *after* he had, by the Spirit, risen from the dead? On the immersion theory, the facts can not be reconciled.

Whilst all these considerations point decisively to one conclusion, there is not a fact nor a circumstance to occasion even a moment's embarrassment in its acceptance. Assume the washings to have been immersions, and confusion and perplexity invest the subject. Recognize them in their true character as ablutions and not immersions, and all is clear and congruous. The customs of the people,—the circumstances in which the rites were performed,—the words used to describe them,—the ritual relations in which they occur,—the analogies of the whole system,—the examples of the priests, and every casual incident and allusion,—all find, in this view, a center around which they cluster and shine, in perfect harmony, clearness and congruity of meaning.

The conclusion is impregnable. Immersion, as a rite of cleansing or purifying, was utterly unknown to Israel. And, particularly, there is nothing whatever to be found, in all the records of the Levitical system to which the advocates of immersion can point and say,—"Here are the ordinances of which Paul speaks, wherein divers immersions were imposed on Israel, until the time of reformation." It is therefore certain that *in the vocabulary of Paul,* BAPTIZO *did not mean, to immerse, and baptism is not so performed.*

> Section XXXIII.—*Defilements and Purifyings of Things.*—One case of immersion. Minor defilements cleansed by this immersion and by washings. The major, by sprinkling

Things, as well as persons, were liable to defilements, both the major and the minor, and the law made correspondent provision for their cleansing.

1. To the class of minor defilements belonged those of wooden vessels, and bags of cloth or skin, which had been touched by the dead carcase of an unclean animal. "It must be put into water," and be unclean until the even. (Lev. xi, 32.) Here, at last, is an immersion; the only one found in the entire law. The case is of great interest as illustrating the ease and clearness with which immersion is expressed when it was intended. We search in vain for any corresponding directions, in the case of persons:—"They must be put into water." This rule moreover is of great importance, as constituting a standard of reference by which to ascertain the divine estimation of the value of immersion as a ritual purifying. Of certain animals, the ordinance was that "whosoever doth touch them, when they be dead, shall be unclean until the even. And upon whatsoever any of them, when they are dead, doth fall, it shall be unclean; whether it be any vessel of wood, or raiment,

or skin, or sack, whatsoever vessel it be wherein any work is done, it must be put into water, and it shall be unclean until the even;—so it shall be cleansed."—Ib. 31, 32. Thus, it appears, from both examples,—of persons and of things,—that the uncleanness described was of the minor grade, which continued only till the even. In fact, it seems to have been the lightest form of this grade. For, while the law provided that he that bore such carcase must "wash his clothes," (vs. 25, 28) and be unclean until the even,—it directed, concerning the present case of mere casual and momentary contact by touching it, that he shall be "unclean until the even," without any prescription of cleansing rites. (Compare also, v. 29.) The meaning of this may be gathered from a comparison of 1 Cor. v, 9-13. In the Levitical system, unclean beasts seem to represent unregenerate men. To God's people, a certain amount of contact with them is inevitable; from which, therefore, and its defiling influences, the only remedy is to be looked for in the ending of this life, and the entrance upon heaven's rest. The emphasis of the ritual warnings was, therefore, directed, not against involuntary and casual contact with the evil, but against dalliance with it, expressed by carrying and eating the unclean. The immersion which we have found to be prescribed, was appointed, not for persons, but for things,—and for things tainted with this slightest of all the defilements known to the law. On the other hand, as we shall presently see, for major defilements of things,—by the dead and by leprosy,—the same sacrificial rites, and sprinkling of water were ordained, as in the case of persons. Such is the divine testimony as to the relative ritual value of immersion and sprinkling. I will not wrong the intelligence of the reader, by discussing the possibility of this immersion, being what Paul meant by the "divers baptisms" of the law.

Other minor defilements of things were, (1.) Brazen vessels used for cooking the flesh of the sin offerings. They were to be "scoured and rinsed in water." If the vessel was of earthenware, it was to be broken. (Lev. vi, 28. Compare 1 Cor. xi, 24.) (2.) "The vessel of earth that he toucheth, which hath an issue, shall be broken; and every vessel of wood shall be rinsed in water."—Ib. xv, 12.

2. Things defiled by the dead, were to be sprinkled with the water of separation, on the third day and on the seventh. (Num. xix, 14, 15, 18.) In the case of the spoil of Midian, there was a further purifying.—"Every thing that may abide the fire, ye shall make it go through the fire; and it shall be clean; nevertheless it shall be purified with the water of separation; and all that abideth not the fire ye shall make go through the water."—Num. xxxi, 23. The word "go through," here, is the same that is used when Jesse is said to have caused seven of his sons to "pass by," and to "pass before" Samuel, (1 Sam. xvi, 9, 10); when Jacob caused his household to "pass over" the brook, (margin, Gen. xxxii, 23); and when God promised to make all his goodness to "pass before" Moses. (Ex. xxxiii, 19.) The alternatives here of fire and water seem to have reference to the two great facts of purgation in the world's history, of which Peter speaks. (2 Pet. iii, 5-7.) The deluge was a purifying of the earth, defiled by sin, and so will the fire be, in the final day.

3. A house infected with leprosy, when cured, was treated in a manner essentially the same as was a person so afflicted. (Lev. xiv, 34-53.)

PART V.

LATER TRACES OF THE SPRINKLED BAPTISMS.

Section XXXIV.—*Old Testament Allusions.*—The rite everywhere, from
  Moses to Zechariah

The rite of purifying with the ashes of the red heifer was one of the most familiar and impressive of the Mosaic institutions. That its observance was maintained through the whole course of Israel's history, is evinced by the frequent allusions of the sacred writers. King Saul found in the ordinances on this subject an explanation of David's absence from his table.—"Something hath befallen him. He is not clean: surely he is not clean."—1 Sam. xx, 26. The words of David himself have been referred to already, as he cries,—"Purge me with hyssop, and I shall be clean."—Psa. li, 7. This was written about five hundred years after the giving of the law. Three centuries later, the Lord says to Israel by Hosea,—"Their sacrifices shall be unto them as the bread of mourners," (that is, bread made or touched by those that were defiled by the dead), "all that eat thereof shall be polluted."—Hosea ix, 4. Isaiah began his prophecy about twenty-five years later,—about B. C. 760-698. In his time a great revival took place, under the hand of King Hezekiah, in connection with which the laws of purification came into prominent notice. It began with the exhortation of Hezekiah, to the priests and Levites.—"Hear me, ye Levites; *sanctify*" (or, cleanse) "now yourselves, and sanctify the house of the Lord God of your fathers; and carry forth the filthiness out of the holy place."—2 Chron. xxix, 5. When this was done, the king appointed a service of dedication. In it "the priests were too few, so that they could not flay all the burnt offerings; wherefore, their brethren the Levites did help them, till the work was ended, and until the other priests had sanctified themselves: for the Levites were more upright in heart to sanctify themselves than the priests."—vs. 34. Immediately afterward the king kept a great passover, gathering the remnants of the ten tribes, with Judah. "And the priests and the Levites were ashamed and sanctified themselves, ... for there were many in the congregation that were not sanctified: therefore the Levites had charge of the killing of the passovers for every one that was not clean, to sanctify them unto the Lord. For a multitude of the people, even many of Ephraim and Manasseh, Issachar and Zebulun, had not cleansed themselves, yet did they eat the passover otherwise than it was written. But Hezekiah prayed for them, saying, The good Lord pardon every one that prepareth his heart to seek God, the Lord God of his fathers, though he be not cleansed according to the purification of the sanctuary. And the Lord hearkened to Hezekiah, and healed the people."—Ib. xxx,

15-20.

In Isaiah, occurs that prophecy of God's grace for the Gentiles, "Behold my servant, ... as many were astonied at thee, his visage was so marred more than any man, and his form more than the sons of men; so shall he *sprinkle* many nations."— Isa. lii, 13-15. There are two words in the original Hebrew, meaning, to sprinkle. That which here occurs is used to describe the purifying of the leper, and of those defiled by the dead. The priest, with the scarlet wool, cedar wood and hyssop, "shall *sprinkle* upon him that is to be cleansed from the leprosy, seven times."— Lev. xiv, 7. "A clean person shall take hyssop and dip it in the water, and *sprinkle* it upon the tent, and upon all the vessels, and upon the persons."—Num. xix, 18. The Jewish translators of the Septuagint, have rendered the passage, "so shall he *astonish* many nations." But this only shows how willingly those writers would have obliterated from the text the promise of salvation for the Gentiles, which it contains. We know that the Gentiles were by the law, held to be unclean—"dead in trespasses and sins."—Eph. ii, 1, 11; Acts x, 14-16, 28; xv, 9. We have seen baptism by sprinkling to have been appointed for the purifying of every kind of uncleanness, and witnessed its use in the reception of the children of Midian. Moreover, the word here found in the original is everywhere else used in the sense of sprinkling. With one exception, it is invariably employed as descriptive of the ritual purifyings. The exception describes the sprinkling or spattering of the blood of Jezebel, when she was hurled from the height of the palace. (2 Kings ix, 33.) There is no conceivable reason for making the text an exception to the meaning thus invariably indicated. Christ, the Baptizer, will sprinkle many nations. He "will pour out of his Spirit on all flesh."—Acts ii, 17; Joel ii, 28. Of this it is that Isaiah speaks in the place in question.

The same grace was promised to Israel by the prophet Ezekiel (B. C. 595-574), in language which we have already quoted, "Then will I sprinkle clean water upon you, and ye shall be clean."—Ezek. xxxvi, 24-27. In this prophet's vision of the future temple, he says of the priests: "They shall come at no dead person to defile themselves: but for father, or for mother, or for son, or for daughter, for brother, or for sister that hath had no husband, they may defile themselves. And after he is cleansed, they shall reckon unto him seven days. And in the day that he goeth into the sanctuary, unto the inner court to minister in the sanctuary he shall offer his sin-offering, saith the Lord God."—Ezek. xliv, 25-27.

About fifty years after the close of Ezekiel's prophecy Haggai was sent to Judah (B. C. 520). He inquires of the priests, respecting "bread, or pottage, or wine, or oil, or any meat," "If one that is unclean by a dead body touch any of these shall it be unclean? And the priests answered, and said, It shall be unclean."—Hag. ii, 13.

Except the brief testimony of Malachi, Zechariah was the last of the prophets. His ministry closed, about B. C. 487. In his prophecy occurs that promise of "a fountain opened to the house of David and to the inhabitants of Jerusalem, for sin and for uncleanness."—Zech. xiii, 1. The word, "fountain," in the original means a flowing spring, "opened," as was the rock in the wilderness; of which the Psalmist says, "He opened the rock and the waters gushed out; they ran in the dry places like a river."—Psa. cv, 41. The language of Zechariah seems to be an allusion to this.

We have thus traced the baptism of purifying with the water of separation through the writings of the prophets for a thousand years, from the time of its institution to within less than five hundred years of the coming of Christ. We shall presently follow it down to the time of Christ and to the destruction of Jerusalem.

Section XXXV.—*Rabbinic Traditions as to the Red Heifer.*—One heifer from Moses to Ezra. Eight thence to the end

According to Jewish tradition the burning of the red heifer took place but nine times, from the beginning, until the final dispersion of the nation. The first was by Eleazar, in the wilderness. (Num. xix, 3.) This, they say, was not repeated for more than a thousand years, when Ezra offered the second, upon the return of the captivity from Babylon. From that time, until the destruction of Jerusalem by Titus was about five hundred years, during which they report seven heifers to have been burned—two by Simon, the just, two by Johanan, the father of Matthias, one by El-ioenai, the son of Hakkoph, one by Hananeel Hammizri, and one by Ishmael, the son of Fabi. Since then, it has been impossible for them to fulfill the rite according to the law, as the altar and temple are no more. The tenth they say will be offered by the Messiah, at his coming.[22] Lightfoot finds in the increased frequency with which the heifer was burned, during the later period of Jewish history, a circumstantial illustration of the growing spirit of ritualism, which multiplied the occasions of using the ashes. It is, however, impossible to accept the account, at least, as to the earlier period, as authentic history. It is probably mere conjecture, suggested by the silence of the Scriptures, and is most improbable in itself. But the later tradition is more reliable; as, at the time when it was put upon record, the Jews were undoubtedly in possession of abundant historical materials, for the period subsequent to the return of the captivity under Ezra. According to this account, seven heifers served all the purposes of that form of purification, for five hundred years. In that time, over fifteen generations, or not less than fifty millions of Jews were consigned to the sepulcher, and the consequent sprinkling administered to the families, attendants, houses, and furniture. If we ignore all other applications of these ashes, to those defiled by the slain in battle, and to those subject to other causes of defilement, it is still evident that the sufficiency and virtue of the rite were not held to depend upon the quantity of the ashes employed, and that the amount actually used was so minute that it can not have been perceptible in the water. The manner of administration was thus true to the nature of the ordinance, as having no intrinsic virtue, in itself, but only in its significance as addressed to intelligence and faith. And it prepared the minds of the people to witness without perplexity, the change from water in which an inappreciable quantity of ashes appealed to the imagination, to that in which, while no ashes were used, the association of ideas and meaning remained the same.

---

[22] Juchasin, fol 16, in Lightfoot.

Section XXXVI.—*The Festival of the Outpouring of Water.*—Feast of tabernacles. The outpouring. The festivity. Its meaning

Not only are the Old Testament Scriptures full of the doctrine of the outpouring of the Spirit, under the figure of living water; but one of the most remarkable of the institutions observed by the Jews from the days of the prophets here last quoted, had immediate relation to the same thing. It was called "The festival of the outpouring of water." Its origin was by the Jews attributed to the prophets Haggai and Zechariah, under whose ministry the temple was rebuilt, and the ordinances restored; a tradition which is confirmed by internal evidence. The festival was incorporated with the feast of the ingathering, or tabernacles. That feast seems to have been the pre-eminent type of the prosperity, the rest and gladness of the kingdom of Messiah. By the law, the people were required to gather "the boughs" (in the margin, "the fruit") "of goodly trees, branches of palm trees, and the boughs of thick trees, and willows of the brook, and ye shall rejoice before the Lord your God seven days."—Lev. xxiii, 40. They used the fruit of the citron or lemon, with branches of the palm and the myrtle, and willows from the brook Kedron. These tied together in one bunch were called, the *lulab.* Early on the morning of the first day of the feast, the people, clothed in holiday garb, assembled at the temple, each having a lulab in one hand and a citron in the other, and each carrying a branch of willow, with which they adorned the altar round about. As soon as the morning sacrifice was placed on the altar, a priest descended to the fountain of Siloam, which flowed from the foot of the temple mount, bearing a golden vase or pitcher, which he filled with water. As he entered the court, through that gate which was hence called "the water gate," the trumpets sounded. He ascended to the great altar of burnt offering, where were placed two silver bowls, one on the east side of the altar and the other on the west, one of which contained wine. Into the other, he poured the water from the golden vessel, and then mingling the water and wine, slowly poured it on the ground, as it would seem, to the east and to the west, as the bowls were placed. (Compare Zech. xiv, 8.) In the mean time the temple choir sang the Hallel to the accompaniment of instruments of music.[23] Then, the people who thronged the court marched in procession about the altar, waving their lulabs, and setting them bending toward it, the trumpets sounding and the people shouting, "Hallelujah!" and "Hosanna!" with ejaculations of prayer, thanksgiving and praise, selected from the Psalms. In this service, even the little children, as soon as able to wave a palm branch, were encouraged to join. After this they went home to dine, and spent the afternoon reading the law or hearing the expositions of learned scribes. In the evening commenced the festive joy of the outpouring of the water. The water was drawn and poured out, at the time of the morning sacrifice and in connection with it,—a solemnity in the presence of which any hilarious demonstrations were inopportune. The festivity was therefore reserved until the evening. The multitude then assembled in the court of the women, that being the largest court, and the nearest approach that the women as a body could make to the holy house. On this occasion they occupied the galleries which surrounded the court, whilst the men thronged the open space. At suitable places, in the

---

[23] Ps. cxiii-cxviii, were known among the Jews as, the Hallel, that is, Praise, being sung at the temple on the first of each month, and at the annual feasts.

court there were great candelabra of such size and height that they overlooked the whole temple mount. A ladder stood by each, by means of which young priests from time to time ascended and replenished the oil, of which each bowl is reported by the Talmud to have held seven or eight gallons. Many of the people also carried torches, so that the whole mount was flooded with light. The festivity was begun by the temple choir of priests, who, standing in order upon the fifteen steps that led down from the court of Israel to that of the women, chanted some of the "songs of degrees," to the accompaniment of instruments; whilst such of the people as were skilled in music joined their voices and instruments. Then, the chief men of the nation, rulers of synagogues, members of the sanhedrim, scribes, doctors of the law, and all such as were of eminent rank or repute for gifts or piety laid off their outer robes, and joined in a joyous leaping and dancing, in the presence of the multitude, singing and shouting Hosannas and Hallelujahs, and ejaculating the praises of God. Thus a great part of the night was expended, each one emulating the others in imitation of the humility of David, at the bringing up of the ark (2 Sam. vi, 15, 16); for, the excitement now indulged in, the leaping and dancing, were, at other times, accounted unbecoming the dignity of the nobles of Israel. At length, two of the priests, standing in the gate of Nicanor, which was at the head of the stairway, sounded their trumpets, and descending the steps continued to sound as they traversed the court, until they came to the eastern gate. Here they turned around toward the west, so as to face the temple. They then cried, — "Our fathers who were in this place, turned their backs to the temple of the Lord, and their faces toward the east.[24] But as for us, we turn to Him, and our eyes look unto Him." The assembly then dispersed. With slight variations, the same order was observed each of the seven days of the feast.[25]

The joy of the people at the ingathering of the harvest and the prosperous end of the labors of the year, — the gay and festive appearance of the city, every housetop and open space, and even the sides and top of the mount of Olives, covered with the green booths, — the extraordinary services at the temple, where more sacrifices were offered during the week than in all the other feasts of the year together, — the green willows adorning the altar and daily renewed — the processions around it, the branches carried by the people, — the trumpets, songs, and Hosannas, — and, at night, the flaming lights, the jubliant concourse, the waving of the lulabs, the music and dancing, the shoutings, songs, and trumpets, must have presented a scene of exhilaration and gladness hard to conceive. It was a saying of the rabbins, that "He that has not witnessed the festivity of the pouring out of the water, has never seen festivity at all."

The rabbins are obscure in their explanations of the observance here described. Some would represent it as a thanksgiving for the rains by which the soil had been fertilized and the harvests matured. But with a better appreciation, Rabbi Levi is reported in the Talmud, "Why is it called the drawing of water? Says Rabbi Levi, Because of the receiving of the Holy Spirit, according to that which is written, — With joy will we draw water from the wells of salvation." — Isa. xii, 3. That

[24] See Ezek. viii, 16.

[25] Lightfoot on this Feast and that of Tabernacles. Lewis's "Origines Hebraeæ." Pool's "Synopsis," etc.

the outpouring had reference, not to the receiving of the Spirit by Israel, but to its outpouring upon the Gentiles, in the days of the Messiah, is confirmed by the tenor of the prophecies of Haggai and Zechariah, the authors of the observance, and by language of our Savior, which expositors agree in referring to this rite. Both of those prophets encouraged Judah in rebuilding the temple by the assurance that "the Desire of all nations should come" to it.—Hag. ii, 7. Said the Lord, by Zechariah, "Rejoice greatly, O daughter of Zion; Shout, O daughter of Jerusalem; behold thy King cometh unto thee: he is just and having salvation: lowly and riding upon an ass and upon a colt the foal of an ass.... It shall come to pass, in that day, that I will seek to destroy all the nations that come against Jerusalem. And I will pour upon the house of David and upon the inhabitants of Jerusalem the Spirit of grace and of supplications, and they shall look upon me whom they have pierced, and they shall mourn for him.... In that day there shall be a fountain opened to the house of David and to the inhabitants of Jerusalem, for sin and for uncleanness.... And it shall be in that day, that living waters shall go out from Jerusalem: half of them toward the former sea, and half of them toward the hinder sea. In summer and winter shall it be. And the Lord shall be king over all the earth: In that day there shall be one Lord, and his name one.... And it shall come to pass that every one that is left of all the nations which came against Jerusalem, shall even go up, from year to year, to worship the King, the Lord of hosts, and to keep the feast of tabernacles."—Zech. ix, 9; xii, 9, 10; xiii, 1; xiv, 8, 9, 16.

To all this, reference is evidently had in the incident related by the evangelist, John, as occurring at this feast.—"In the last day, that great day of the feast, Jesus stood and cried, saying, If any man thirst, let him come unto me and drink. He that believeth in me, as the Scripture hath said, out of his belly shall flow rivers of living water. But this spake he of the Spirit, which they that believe on him should receive; for the Holy Ghost was not yet given, because that Jesus was not yet glorified."—John vii, 37-39. These words of Jesus, as will hereafter appear, had distinct reference to the giving of the gospel to the Gentiles. A few additional facts will shed a clearer light upon the meaning of the festival.

The feast of tabernacles, strictly so called, was of seven days' continuance; during which the people dwelt in booths. On the eighth day, they removed the booths and re-entered their houses. They observed that day as a distinct and peculiar festival. "On the eighth day shall be a holy convocation unto you; and ye shall offer an offering made by fire unto the Lord; it is a solemn assembly." (Lev. xxiii, 36; Deut. xvi, 13-15.) During the seven days the offerings upon the altar had a very remarkable order. On the first day, they were "thirteen young bullocks, two rams, and fourteen lambs of the first year," and one kid of the goats for a sin offering. These were in addition to the ordinary daily offerings. On each successive day, the number of the bullocks was reduced by one, whilst the other offerings remained the same. But on the eighth day the offering was one bullock, one ram, and seven lambs, and one goat for a sin offering. (Num. xxix, 12-38.) On this peculiar order of sacrifices, the explanations of the scribes are various. In the Talmud, Rabbi Solomon states the bullocks, whose aggregate number for the seven days was seventy, to have represented the seventy idolatrous nations; that being, as the Jews supposed, their number. These must be continually diminished, while Israel, represented by the other offerings, remains.[26] Says Pool,—"The eighth day was the great day, not by divine appointment, but from the opinion of the Jews, who regarded the sacrifices and prayers of the other days as made, not so much for themselves as for the other nations; but the eighth, as being solely for themselves."[27] Hence the Targum,—*"The eighth day shall be holy*. Thou seest, O God, that Israel in the feast of tabernacles, offers before thee seventy bullocks, for the seventy nations, for which they ought to love us. But for our love, they are our adversaries. The holy blessed God therefore saith to Israel, Offer for yourselves on the eighth day."[28]

The gospels render us familiar with the religion of the scribes. By the help of tradition it sought to divest the law of God of its claim upon the allegiance of the heart, to obscure and set aside the spiritual meaning of its rites, and to substitute a system of minute outward observances, and a fanatical pride in the blood of Abraham, which looked scornfully down on all other nations as unclean and accursed. This system was embodied in the Talmud, and culminated in the compilation of that work, several centuries after the destruction of the temple and the downfall of the nation. When, therefore, among the idle traditions which fill the pages of that work, we come upon occasional traces of a profounder spiritual exegesis, and sentiments respecting the Gentiles more in harmony with the spirit of Old Testament prophecy, we may confidently recognize them as precious vestiges of truth, which have escaped obliteration, as they were transmitted through that uncongenial channel, from a distant and purer antiquity.

Such is the conviction which will result from a careful comparison of the traditions above cited with the accounts of the rites in question, the language of the prophets, and the words of Jesus to which reference has just been made. By the light thus concentrated, we see, in the ingathering of the harvest of the holy land and the festivities following, a type and prophecy of the ingathering of the nations into the fold of Israel, under the scepter of Messiah, and the songs and joy that hail their coming. Then the solemnity of the eighth day may have anticipated the time when, opposition withdrawn, all nations "shall go up from year to year to worship the King the Lord of hosts, and to keep the feast of tabernacles," when "the Lord shall be King over all the earth, and there shall be one Lord, and his name One." In this light, Israel appears in her lofty character and office as the priest-kingdom, standing as mediator for the nations, and making for them offerings of atonement and intercessions. Nor less significant was the drawing of the water from

> "Siloah's brook that flowed
> Fast by the oracle of God,"

and its outpouring by the priest upon the earth, mingled with wine. From that same fountain, during the same period of Israel's history, it was the rule to draw all water that was used at Jerusalem for purification with the water of separation, especially for those who came to the annual feasts. To this, Zechariah alludes in his prophecy of that day when "there shall be a fountain opened to the house of David

---

[26] Rabbi Solomon on Num. xxix, in Lightfoot on this feast.
[27] Pool's Synopsis, on John vii, 37. He refers to Grotius.
[28] Lewis's Origines Hebraeæ, p. 606.

and to the inhabitants of Jerusalem, for sin and for uncleanness."—Zech. xiii, 1. By her great High Priest, was to be dispensed to Israel and through her to all the earth, the Spirit's grace, conveying to the nations of the Gentiles the virtue of the blood of Calvary. Jerusalem and the temple were to be the source of those healing waters which were to flow to the east and to the west, "toward the former sea, and toward the hinder sea," to gladden the world. (Zech. xiv, 8.)

Section XXXVII.—*The Hellenistic Greek.*—Alexander's favor to the Jews. Alexandria. Hellenistic Greek. Its literature. *Baptizo.* Dr. Conant's definitions. *Baptisma and baptismoi*

After the close of Old Testament prophecy, the conquests of Alexander of Macedon, the consequent diffusion of the Greeks, and the favor which that prince and his successors showed to the Jews, introduced an intimate intercourse between them and the Greeks. By him Alexandria in Egypt was founded, designated by his own name, and intended to be the western capital of his empire. In this new Greek capital, its founder assigned the Jews an extensive section, and equal privileges with the Macedonians. After the death of Alexander, and the subdivision of his empire, the Ptolemies, the Greek kings of Egypt, continued to favor the Jews, treating them on terms of equality with the Greeks. During the same period, the persecutions suffered by the Jews of Palestine from the kings of Syria, drove multitudes into exile, many of whom were attracted to Egypt, so that the Jewish population of Alexandria was at one time estimated at nearly a million of souls, occupying two of the five districts of the city; and at least, for a time, governed by their own ethnarch, or superior magistrate. Among these Jews, and those elsewhere scattered in the Greek colonies, their own language was gradually superseded by the Greek, into which, at length, the Old Testament Scriptures were translated, in a version known as the Septuagint. Of the precise time and circumstances in which this version was made, there is no reliable information, except that it was done in Alexandria, within the first quarter of the third century before Christ. In the time of Christ, the Greek had become the language of literature and of commerce for the civilized world. Among the Jews dispersed everywhere, it was prevalent, and was extensively used even in Palestine itself, and thus became the divinely prepared channel for communicating the gospel to all nations.

But the language thus employed—the Greek of the Septuagint, the Apocrypha and the New Testament—was not what is known as classic Greek. The Jews did not learn it in the schools of Greece, nor from a study of her poets, orators, and philosophers. It was the product of social and business contact and intercourse of the one people with the other, in a land foreign to both.

Already the purity of the Attic had been lost, by the commingling of the Macedonians with the various tribes of Greece proper and her dependencies, in the armies from which Alexander's colonists were taken; and still further by the mixed multitude which flocked to their new settlements. In the process of adaptation to the expression of Jewish thought, it was inevitably subjected to further modifications, in definition, in syntax, in order and construction—in the very tone and spirit which pervade the whole. By these modifications, the language, which had grown up as the native and coeval expression of the idolatrous religion, the arts and philosophy of pagan Greece, was adapted to become a repository for the system of divine and saving truth, contained in the Scriptures. Those Jews who resided in Alexandria and other Greek cities, who spake this Greek language, and were more or less conformed to the manners of the Gentiles among whom they lived, were known among their brethren, as Hellenists, that is, Greek Jews, and hence, the Greek dialect used by them has acquired the designation of Hellenistic Greek.

The authors of the New Testament adopted this as the language of their writings, and, in their references to the Old Testament, their quotations are mostly made, not from the Hebrew, but from the Septuagint, or Hellenistic version. It was ordinarily used by the Lord Jesus himself in his discourses. It thus appears as the source and standard of the language of the New Testament.

Together with these Greek Scriptures of the Old Testament, there have been transmitted to us several other Jewish documents of the same period, written in the same Hellenistic Greek. They are invaluable for the light which they shed upon the history, customs, and modes of thought and language of the Jews of that time; although the attempt of the church of Rome, to exalt some of them to an equal authority with the Scriptures, has tended to fix a stigma on them, as known to us under the name of Apocrypha. Incautious recourse to the rules and definitions of classic Greek is liable to deceive and mislead us in the critical study of the New Testament. But conclusions intelligently deduced from the language of the Septuagint and of the other Jewish writers of that age, are to be respected as of the highest authority on all questions of the New Testament language. On the subject of our present investigation, these authorities shed a flood of light. In them, we first find the verb, *baptizo*, used to designate rites of religious purifying. Once in the Septuagint, and twice in the Apocrypha, it is applied to Hebrew rites of this nature.

That the use of the word to designate religious observances is peculiar to the Hellenistic, as contradistinguished from classic Greek, is indisputable; and it is worthy of consideration, how it came to be selected from the Greek vocabulary for this purpose. The Hebrews of Egypt, in their exile from the land of their fathers, had not abandoned but rather augmented their zeal for the institutions of Moses. A circumstance in their own history, which at first might have seemed to threaten a dissolution of the ties that bound them to the temple at Jerusalem, operated in fact to renovate and strengthen them. This was, the erection by some of their number, of a temple at Onias in Egypt, in imitation of that at Jerusalem. Here, the Levitical rites were punctually observed under priests of the Aaronic line and Levites of the sacred tribe. For this they claimed warrant from the prophecy of Isaiah, xix, 19. — "In that day, shall there be an altar to the Lord in the midst of the land of Egypt." The adherents of this movement do not seem to have been numerous, and its effect was rather to increase the devotion of the people to the temple at Jerusalem, and the ordinances there maintained. Among them, was developed the same disposition which was prevalent in Judea to give undue importance to multiplied rites of purifying; and hence an increased and constant necessity of finding, in the Greek language which they were now adopting, some word suitable to designate these rites. In that language was the verb, *bapto*, meaning (1) to dip; (2) to wet by dipping; (3) to wet, irrespective of the manner; (4) to dye by dipping, and thence, to dye, without respect to mode—even by sprinkling. But, as we have seen, the rites in question were not dippings, nor were they dyeings, and the word was never used by the Jews to designate them. From this root, the Greeks derived the verb *baptizo*. (1.) Its primary meaning, as used by them, was,—to bring into the state of mersion. This meaning had no respect to the mode of action, whether by putting the subject under the fluid, pouring it over him, or in whatever manner. In other words, it expressed not *im*mersion, but mersion,—not the mode of inducing the state, but the state induced,—that of being embosomed in the mersing element. From this primary signification, was derived a secondary use of the word. As any thing that is mersed is in the possession and control of the mersing element, the word was hence used to express the establishing of a complete possession and controlling influence. As we say that a man is drowned,—immersed,—overwhelmed, in business, in trouble, in drunkenness, or in sleep; having, in these expressions, no reference whatever to the mode in which the described condition was brought about; so the Greeks used the verb *baptizo*. They spoke of men as baptized with grief, with passion, with business cares. An intoxicated person was "baptized with wine," etc. In such use of the word, the essential idea is that of the action of a pervasive potency by which the subject is brought and held in a new state or condition. On this subject, no authority could be better or more conclusive than that of the Rev. Dr. T. J. Conant, a scholar of unquestioned eminence and whose researches on this subject were undertaken at the request of the American (Baptist) Bible Union. The result of his investigations he thus states. "The word, *baptizein*, during the whole existence of the Greek as a spoken language, had a perfectly defined and unvarying import. In its literal use, it meant, as has been shown,—to put entirely into or under a liquid, or other penetrable substance, generally water, so that the object was wholly covered by the enclosing element. By analogy it expressed *the coming into a new state of life or experience*, in which one was, as it were, inclosed and swallowed up, so that temporarily or permanently, he belonged wholly to it."[29] Dr. Dale has been at the trouble to list and enumerate no less than forty different words which Dr. Conant employs in his translations of this word of "perfectly defined and unvarying import." It is, however, enough for our present purpose, that this distinguished scholar here expressly admits with Italic emphasis, that "by analogy," the word "expressed the coming into *a new state of life or experience, in which one was, as it were, inclosed and swallowed up, so that temporarily or permanently he belonged wholly to it."

Now, here was the very word required to designate the Mosaic rites of purifying. Of dippings and immersions, Israel had none; and, if these had been found in their ritual, the verbs, *bapto, to dip, and kataduo, to plunge into, to immerse*, and the nouns, *baphē* and *katadusis*,—*a dipping, an immersion*, were at hand and specific in meaning. But they did want words to express that potency by which the unclean were, in the words of Dr. Conant, introduced into "a new state of life,"—a state of ritual cleanness, typical of the spiritual newness of life in Christ Jesus which God's people receive, by the baptism of the Spirit. To express the working of that change,

---

[29] "The Meaning and Use of *Baptizein*, Philologically and Historically investigated for the American Bible Union. By T. J. Conant, D. D.," p. 158. The italics are by Dr. C.

they appropriated the word *baptizo, to baptize*; that is, to cleanse, to purify. Then, to give name to the rites by which that change was accomplished, they formed from it the two sacred words, *baptisma* and *baptismos*, words wholly unknown to classic Greek literature. They are, as to etymology and meaning identical. By grammarians, the termination, *mos*, is said generally to indicate the act signified by the verb, while *ma* indicates its effect. But the rule is neither absolute nor universal; and the sacred writers do not maintain the distinction. By them *baptisma* is used alike to signify the act of baptizing, and the effect, the new state produced by it. In their writings, the distinction seems to consist in the employment of *baptismos* generically, as designating divers kinds of purifying rites; while *baptisma* is specifically applied to the baptism of John and of Christ. It is found in no other writings of that or preceding ages. Outside the Scriptures, *baptismos* occurs once, in the works of Josephus, who thus designates John's baptism.[30]

Section XXXVIII.—*The Baptism of Naaman. Tābal=baptizo.*—The law of leprosy. Office of Elijah and Elisha. Naaman was sprinkled seven times, according to the law

In the Septuagint or Greek Scriptures, *baptizo* first appears in the account of the healing of Naaman. "Elisha sent a messenger unto him saying, Go and wash in Jordan seven times, and thy flesh shall come again to thee, and thou shalt be clean.... Then went he down, and dipped himself seven times in Jordan according to the saying of the man of God."—2 Kings v, 10, 14. It is asserted that here is clearly an immersion.—"He went down and *dipped* himself seven times." Respecting the question thus raised, it is, in the first place, to be distinctly noticed, that the decision, whatever it be, can not in any way neutralize or diminish the force of the argument already developed from the divers baptisms of the epistle to the Hebrews. Were we to allow that Naaman was immersed, that fact would constitute no reply to the demonstration that no immersions were "imposed on Israel," although divers baptisms were imposed. But, that there was no immersion in this case, will appear in what follows.

1. The word upon which the immersion argument here rests, is the Hebrew *tābal*, which is translated, "he dipped." As to its meaning in this place, there are several available sources of information. First, is the manner in which the word is employed elsewhere in the Scriptures. It occurs, in all, but fifteen times. It is evident, that while these places are sufficient to establish the fact that the word was used as they illustrate, they are wholly insufficient to constitute a basis for the assumption that it was never used in a sense not there found, or in a sense not there doubly illustrated. For example, Gesenius gives, "to immerse," as one of the meanings, and appeals to the text of Naaman as the only example. Without pretending to emulate the learning of that great scholar, I venture to assert that, although the definition be not illustrated by other examples, there is abundant and various evidence that the word is here used as the equivalent of *rāhatz, to wash*, according to the proper sense of that word as already ascertained. The primary and essential idea of *tābal* appears to be contact by touch, a contact which may be of the slightest and most superficial kind, as when the priest was directed to dip the finger of his

[30] "Antiquities of the Jews," XVIII, vi, 2.

right hand in a few drops of oil held in the palm of his left hand (Lev. xiv, 15, 16), and when those who bore the ark dipped the soles of their feet in the brim or edge of Jordan and the waters instantly fled away. (Josh. iii, 13, 15.) Again, it is used to describe the staining or smearing of Joseph's coat with the blood of the kid. (Gen. xxxvii, 31.) In this case, there can have been no immersion, since the blood of a kid would have been wholly insufficient, and the uniform stain thus induced would have detected the fraud of Joseph's brothers, as the violence of a wild beast would not have produced such a result. How the word, in this place was understood by the rabbins of Alexandria, is shown by the Greek of the Septuagint, in which it is represented by *moluno*, to soil, to stain, to smear. "They stained or smeared his coat with the blood." The same is no doubt the meaning of Job, when he says to God, "Yet shalt thou *plunge me* in the ditch and mine own clothes shall abhor me." — Job ix, 31. Not the mode of action, but the soiling contact, was the thought present to Job's mind. The usage of the word in the Scriptures does not justify the belief that it is ever employed in the energy of meaning expressed by *"plunge."* "Yet shalt thou *soil* me in the ditch."

Another source of information is the direction given to Naaman by Elisha. He dipped himself seven times *"according to the saying,* of the man of God." What was that saying? Did Elisha direct him to be immersed seven times? Elisha sent to him, saying "Go, *wash* in Jordan seven times." The verb, *rāhatz*, to wash, we have examined. It means, to perform ablution *with water applied to the person.* It does not mean, to immerse, nor can the action expressed by it be accomplished by immersion. It is, moreover, observable, that, as though to emphasize the employment of this word, it is twice repeated in the narrative. Upon receiving Elisha's message, Naaman exclaims, — "Abana and Pharpar.... May I not *wash* in them and be clean?" And his servants reply, — "If he had bid thee do some great thing, ... how much rather, when he saith to thee, *Wash,* and be clean." Manifestly, the thing which the Syrian was commanded, was not, to immerse, but, to *wash* himself. And when to the meaning of that verb, we add the facts already developed as to the customs of ablution in those lands, the conclusion is manifest. Naaman was not directed to dip or immerse himself, but expressly, to wash; and if he was in fact dipped, it was not "according to the saying of the man of God," but in express contravention of it. It may be objected, that a sprinkling is not a washing. But the Psalmist gives a different testimony. *"Purge me* with hyssop, and I shall be *clean. Wash me* and I shall be whiter than snow." Here, the word, "Wash," which is made parallel and equivalent to "Purge me with hyssop," is not *rāhatz,* but the yet stronger term, *kābas, scour me.* The very designation of "the unclean," for whose "cleansing" those rites were appointed is conclusive on the point. That the sprinklings thus ordained were, in the law everywhere, viewed as washings, is undeniable; and in fact, to wash with water applied, which is the meaning of *rāhatz,* is the very action of sprinkling. Moreover, in Ezek. xvi, 9, the cleansing of the defilement of *nidda,* for which sprinkling was the ritual remedy, is described as a washing of the most vigorous and thorough nature. "Then (*rāhatz) washed* I thee with water; yea (*shātaph*), *I thoroughly washed away* thy blood from thee." How the sprinkling of water can be expressive of such thorough cleansing, we have already seen. It is very strikingly illustrated by the language of the Lord to Israel by Ezekiel. "Then will I sprinkle clean water upon you and ye shall be clean; from all your filthiness and from all your idols will I cleanse you." — Ezek. xxxvi, 25.

The usage of the Scriptures, as to words equivalent to *tābal*, will shed further light on the present question. The word is ordinarily represented in the Septuagint Greek, by *bapto*. Of this verb, we have already stated that it means to dip; to wet, by dipping; to wet in any mode; to stain or dye by dipping; to dye, even by sprinkling. In the Chaldee of the book of Daniel, the word equivalent to *tābal* is *tzeba*. It thrice occurs in the description of the calamity of Nebuchadnezzar, when he was cast out with the beasts of the field, and "his body *was wet* with the dew of heaven." — Dan. iv, 23, 25, 33. In each of these places, the Septuagint has *bapto*, an illustration of the fact that the latter word, even, does not "always mean, to dip." If *tābal* followed the analogy of these its Greek and Chaldee equivalents, we are to expect among its secondary meanings that of wetting by affusion. In the place concerning Naaman, the word by which *tābal* is translated into the Greek is *baptizo*. This fact of itself makes it certain that the Septuagint translators did not understand Naaman to have been dipped, or immersed; else they would have expressed the fact by *bapto*, or *kataduo*, instead of *baptizo*, which, in their vocabulary, as we shall presently show, was used to express purification by sprinkling with the water of separation; as we have already seen Paul to employ it in the same way.

2. While these facts, of themselves, make it certain that Naaman was not immersed, there remains evidence even more conclusive, in the relation which Elisha himself and this whole transaction sustained to the covenant law, as given to Israel at Sinai. In considering this case, there are certain fundamental facts to be held ever in view. (1.) Leprosy was, at once, a disease and a ritual uncleanness; and was distinctly recognized in these two several aspects, in the law of God; and hence the leper could not but be ritually unclean, whilst the mere healing of the disease left him still unclean. He must be purified as well as healed. (2.) The ritual law was not a scheme of arbitrary or unmeaning regulations, but a system of accordant symbols, each of which had its own distinct meaning, and all of which together constituted a complete and intelligible exposition of the doctrine of sin and redemption. Particularly had the ritual respecting leprosy a meaning at once manifest, impressive, and profound. So important was it, in the estimation of the divine Lawgiver of Israel, that the strict observance of all its requirements was enforced by a new and special admonition addressed to them on the banks of Jordan, after the forty years wandering in the wilderness. "Take heed, in the plague of leprosy, that thou observe diligently and do according to all that the priests the Levites shall teach you; as I commanded them, so ye shall observe to do. Remember what the Lord thy God did unto Miriam by the way, after that ye were come forth out of Egypt." — Deut. xxiv, 8, 9. (3.) This law had now been in operation for six hundred years, whilst its regulations were such as to arrest and fix the attention of all observers. (4.) To Naaman, a Syrian, of a country immediately contiguous to the land of Israel, and belonging to a people of kindred blood, language, traditions, and customs, the Hebrew ideas on this subject, so interesting to him, can not have been unknown or strange. Even had he been otherwise ignorant, he could not but have been informed by the Hebrew maiden at whose suggestion he undertook

his journey to the court of Israel, in quest of healing. That hers must have been a character of both intelligence and piety, is evident from the whole narrative, and especially from the fact that it inspired such confidence as led the Syrian, at her suggestion, to obtain from his king letters to the king of Israel, and to go to that court, in the hope of cure, bearing with him rich gifts, designed as tokens of gratitude. (2 Kings, v, 2-5.) (5.) The whole history shows this episode in the life of Elisha to have been any thing but a casual incident. It bears every mark of a special and extraordinary providence, designed to bring home to the Syrians and to Israel a signal testimony to the power and grace of the true God. The peculiar relation which Elijah and Elisha bore to the Syrians is illustrated by the fact that, at this very time, the latter held a commission from God through Elijah to anoint Hazael to be king of Syria, instead of the reigning king Benhadad; by Elisha's subsequent presence in Damascus, in fulfillment of that commission, and by the application which Benhadad made to him, to inquire of the Lord as to the issue of the disease which was then upon him. (1 Kings xix, 15-17; 2 Kings viii, 7-13.)

3. Elisha treats the case of Naaman as typical in its nature, and as coming under the provisions of the law for the cleansing of leprosy. This is manifest from three things which appear in the very brief narrative. (1) In his message to Naaman, he distinguishes between the physical healing, and the ritual cleansing. "Thy flesh shall *come again* unto thee; and, thou shalt *be clean.*" Thus each is separately promised. (2.) He requires Naaman to "wash *seven times.*" The meaning of this seven times we have seen. It symbolized a radical cure of the evil of heart leprosy, the native corruption of sin—a cure by which the sinner will be presented pure and sanctified in the seventh, or judgment day. The mode of this cure was represented in the law by sprinkling seven times. The priest "shall sprinkle upon him that is to be cleansed from the leprosy seven times, and shall pronounce him clean."—Lev. xiv, 7. (3.) He must wash in the river Jordan, and nowhere else. But why there? Because the cleansing of the leper, according to the law must be by sprinkling with "running water."—Lev. xiv, 5, 6, 50-52. For the self-washing, no such prescription was given. The Jordan was appointed, because healing to the leper meant life to the dead. It meant the renewing grace of the Holy Spirit, and for this none but the water of life that flows in the river of the heavenly Canaan will suffice. And inasmuch as the land of Israel was typical of that better country, no water so proper for the present occasion as that which flowed in the one river of Israel. If Palestine was made a type of heaven, the one river of Palestine at once became the proper type of that "river of God, which is full of water."

4. Naaman recognized the significance of the directions given by the prophet, and was offended at them.—"Behold, I thought, He will surely come out to me, and stand and call on the name of the Lord his God, and strike his hand over the place, and recover the leper. Are not Abana and Pharpar, rivers of Damascus, better than all the waters of Israel? May I not wash in them and be clean? So he turned and went away in a rage."—2 Kings v, 11, 12. Here (1.) Naaman sharply distinguishes between the healing and the cleansing. For the latter purpose, the waters of Abana and Pharpar were sufficient for him,—better than all those of Israel. All he wanted was, that the prophet should heal him; and for this he was

ready to reward him liberally. But, instead of being treated with the consideration due to a lordly patron, he feels himself insulted, by being expected to take the position of an unclean and humble suppliant; and that, too, at the feet of the God of Israel. For, (2.) he indicates his understanding of what was meant by the prophet's message. If Elisha had come out and healed the leprosy, as Naaman expected, it would have been perfectly consistent with the idolatrous religion of the Syrian to recognize Elisha as a great prophet, and the God of Elisha as one of the great gods; although entitled to no exclusive worship from the Syrians, whose tutelary deity was Rimmon. But, when the prophet, instead of this, sent him to *Jordan* to be *cleansed*, and that by washing seven times, the Syrian recognized that he was thus required to own allegiance to the God of Israel, and to humble himself, as utterly unclean in His sight, and look to him, as alone able to heal his leprosy, or cleanse his sins. In a word, he was, by the message of the prophet, brought face to face with the glad but humbling word of the gospel, as it spake so clearly in the rites of cleansing for leprosy. That, in the result, he accepted the good tidings thus announced, may not be asserted with confidence. But, that he professed to do so, the narrative assures us. "Behold, now, I know that there is no God in all the earth but in Israel."—vs. 15. By this profession of faith, and by his application to Elisha for two mules' burden of the earth of Canaan, with which to make an altar to the God of Israel, the Syrian showed his intelligent appreciation of the issues involved in the observances required by Elisha, and of the typical meaning of the land and river of Israel. The purpose of the earth for which he asked was to make an altar, after the manner of those appointed in the law; which appear to have been frames or boxes filled with earth on which the fire was kindled. (Ex. xx, 24.)

5. The attempt of some writers to derive countenance to the idea of immersion, in this case, from the Levitical rites of purifying for leprosy, is wholly futile. They refer to the self-washings which were required of the cleansed leper, and assume, without a pretense of proof, that they were immersions. We have seen that they were not immersions, but affusions. But, that it was not to them, but to the sprinklings of the law that the directions of Elisha refer, is unmistakably indicated by the seven times required. The self-washings were to be performed but twice. On the first day, the seven sprinklings were administered, and the person was then, by the priest, officially *proclaimed to be clean*. (Lev. xiv, 7.) It was after this, that the man thus clean, was required to perform the first self-washing. This was repeated once only,—on the eighth day. This distinction between the sprinklings which cleansed the leper, and the self-washings which were required of him as being clean, is not casual, but essential, and intimately involved in the difference of meaning between them. By no system of interpretation, therefore, can seven supposed immersions of Naaman be identified with the two self-washings required by the law. To imagine the Syrian to have been directed to seek cleansing by means of the latter, and not by the seven sprinklings, would be to suppose him instructed by the prophet to seek to his own outward righteousness as the means of purging away his sins, and not to the virtue of the blood and Spirit of Christ, penetrating to his heart and renewing the inner man. Self-washing, as dependent upon and subordinate to the sprinkling of the water and blood, is beautifully significant of that evangelical obedience and holiness which believers cultivate, whilst resting

wholly on the righteousness of Christ; and which is acceptable only thus. But a self-washing, without the sprinkling, or even magnified to equality with it, can mean nothing else than a disparagement and rejection of Christ's blood and Spirit, and a trusting to our own works of righteousness,—to a cleansing and holiness self-attained. It would be a denial of the need of the Spirit's renewing grace.

6. Israel and the ordinances given her were appointed to be a gospel beacon to the nations. In furtherance of this purpose, the rites and ordinances with which she was endowed were clothed in forms of transparent significance, selected by divine wisdom as best adapted to set forth the gospel for men's instruction. To suppose Elisha, on this occasion, to have ignored or essentially modified those respecting leprosy, would imply him to have deliberately veiled the light which God had kindled for the Gentiles. If any ritual observances were required of Naaman, the alternative was inevitable, that they be those appointed in the law, or that by neglect these be dishonored. No motive for the supposed change can be suggested that will not imply a disparagement of the neglected rite.

7. The distinctive office successively filled by Elijah and Elisha was that of prophet to the separated kingdom of Israel, to whom they were sent to vindicate the repudiated covenant of Sinai against the apostasies and sins of that people. (1 Kings, xix, 8, 10, 14-18.) They were appointed to keep alive in Israel the knowledge and faith of the covenant God and King whose worship and ordinances at Jerusalem they had wickedly abandoned. In the extraordinary circumstances of Naaman the offerings which the cleansed leper was required to make at the temple on the eighth day after his purifying, may have been omitted. But the supposition that the rites proper to the purifying, itself, were changed without necessity or apparent motive, so that instead of being *sprinkled* seven times, Naaman was seven times *immersed*, would imply that Elisha not only thus publicly repudiated the authority of the Levitical law, but at the same time and in so doing gave direct sanction to the conduct of Israel, in separating themselves from the temple at Jerusalem and the ordinances and worship which, by divine command, were there observed. The rites of purifying were part and parcel of the system of ordinances given to Israel and concentrated at the sanctuary,—a system, in all its parts, congruous and interdependent; each shedding mutual light on all the rest. If Naaman was sprinkled seven times, according to the Levitical order, that fact would of itself have referred him to the Word and ordinances of God, for light and information, as to the vastly important questions suggested to him by the nature and manner of his disease and cleansing. But, if he was immersed, the observance was without authority in the law; without example in the Word, then possessed or afterward given to Israel; without point of contact or principle of congruity or connection with the system therein unfolded; without explanation anywhere, and without conceivable motive or meaning, unless it was, to repudiate the authority of the Levitical law. Instead, therefore, of the ordinance being a guide line, to lead Naaman to the Word and worship of the true God, the natural effect of such a change as is supposed would have been to deter him from any such inquiries. The facts would have certified him that the God of Elisha was not the same that reigned at Jerusalem;—that the doctrine of the one, set forth in the rite of sprinkling, was manifestly different from

that of the other expressed by immersion,—and that, therefore, the Word and ordinances of the God who dwelt in Zion were likely to mislead him, rather than to shed a true light upon the character of the God of Elisha, by whom he had been healed. The snare thus presented to the mind of Naaman would have been the more insidious and fatal in proportion as he should still have recognized an intimate relation, or even a kind of identity, between the God of Israel and the God of Judah. It was a general characteristic of the ancient idolatries, that the same gods, as worshiped at different places, were supposed to be endowed with different attributes and affinities, and to require different rites of worship. Thus, Zeus Olympius, Jupiter Capitolinus, and Jupiter Amon, were looked upon as the same deity; but revealing one character, as on Olympus he was worshiped by the tribes of Greece; another, as, on the Capitoline hill he presided over the destinies of mighty Rome; and yet another to the dark tribes who assembled at his temple in Thebes in Upper Egypt. Such was the idolatry which the supposed rite would have tended to confirm in the mind of Naaman. To all this we are to add the fact that the very purpose of the miracle wrought by Elisha was to let the Syrian "know that there is a prophet in Israel."—2 Kings v, 8. Not, certainly, that Elisha thus proposed to glorify himself: but to announce himself a prophet and witness, for the only living and true God, the God of Israel, whose sanctuary was in Zion. (Compare Ib. 15-18.)

8. The fact that no administrator is mentioned, but Naaman is said to have "baptized himself," is no embarrassment to our position. The self-baptism implied by the phrase, in the English translation, is not required by the form of the Greek nor of the Hebrew. The same kind of expression is used, in the directions originally given as to the water of separation. "If he purify not *himself* the third day, then the seventh day he shall not be clean. Whosoever toucheth the dead body of any man that is dead, and purifieth not *himself* ... the water of separation was not *sprinkled on him*; he shall be unclean.... A clean person shall *sprinkle on the unclean* on the third day and on the seventh."—Num. xix, 12, 13, 19. The form of expression is intended to emphasize the responsibility of the person in the matter of his own cleansing, and is equivalent in meaning to the phrase,—"cause himself to be sprinkled." Although he can not cleanse himself, he is not therefore irresponsible. He must seek to the cleansing, if he would enjoy it. The same form is used by Paul, who speaks of Ananias as saying to him (*Anastas, baptisai*), "Rising, baptize thyself, and wash away thy sins."—Acts xxii, 16. In the parallel account, we are told that "he arose and was baptized."—Acts ix, 18.

It has been shown already that, in the epistle to the Hebrews, *baptismoi* means the sprinklings ordained in the law for defilements of which leprosy was one. In our next section, it will appear that the sprinkling of the water of separation, upon those defiled by the dead, was familiarly known as a *baptizing*. And as to the case of Naaman, the considerations here presented render it certain that *baptizo* is there used in the same sense. He was not immersed, but sprinkled seven times, according to the law. *Tābal* is here used, not in a modal sense, but to express a cleansing, without defining the manner of it.

Section XXXIX.—*"Baptized from the Dead."*—Ecclus. xxxi, 30. The water of separation here called baptism. *"Baptized for the dead."*—1 Cor. xv, 29

The book of Ecclesiasticus, or "The Wisdom of Jesus the son of Sirach," is one of the Apochrypha. It was written by Joshua ben Sira ben Eliezer, a priest, at Jerusalem, about two hundred years before the coming of Christ. "The original Hebrew, with the exception of a few fragments in the Gemaras and Midrashim, is no longer extant, but we have translations in Greek, Syriac, and Arabic. The work has been always held in high esteem, by both Jews and Christians, and was judged by some of the Talmudists to be worthy of a place among the canonical Scriptures."[31] In this work, the priestly author has written this proverb, "He that is baptized from the dead, and again toucheth the dead, what availeth his washing?"—Ecclus. xxxi, 30 (xxxiv, 25 of the English version). Here, it is unquestionable that reference is had to the cleansing of those who were defiled by the dead. Such persons were "baptized from the dead," that is, purged from the defilement, incurred through the touch of the dead, by the sprinkling of the water of separation. It has been said, by Baptist writers, that the author of the proverb meant to designate the self-washing which was required of those who had been thus sprinkled. But, in the first place, we must again repeat it, the self-washings were not immersions. In the second, they were not the purification from the dead. On that point, the law was express. "The man that shall be unclean, and shall not purify himself, that soul shall be cut off from among the congregation, because he hath defiled the sanctuary of the Lord: *the water of separation* hath not been *sprinkled* upon him; he is unclean."—Num. xix, 20. The self-washings are never called purifyings, nor alluded to by that name. Besides, as before remarked, on another point, the pre-eminence thus assigned to those washings, as compared with the sprinklings, is contrary to the whole spirit and tenor of the law, and would imply a preference given to our own righteousness, which the former symbolized, over the blood of sprinkling of the Lord Jesus, and his renewing Spirit, typified by the latter. Moreover, upon this view, we are to suppose that the author of the proverb, himself a priest, ignored that official sprinkling which must be performed by a clean person, acting in priestly capacity, and which, in his days, was performed almost invariably by the priests, and falsely attributed the consequent cleansing to the self-washing, which was a private personal duty of the cleansed. On the relative position of the two ordinances, the prayer of the Psalmist, in his deep sense of guilt and defilement is very significant. "Purge me with hyssop. Wash me." He does not once think of self-washing, but looks up to the great High Priest for all. It was unquestionably of the sprinkled water of separation that this writer says, "He that is baptized from the dead, and again toucheth the dead what availeth his washing?" Here again we have an impregnable demonstration. We have before seen that Paul testifies that the sprinklings of the Mosaic system were baptisms. We now have the added voice of the son of Sirach certifying the same thing. By the mouth of two or three witnesses shall every word be established. These witnesses are ignorant or false, or else *baptizo* does not here mean, to dip, to immerse.

---

[31] J. W. Etheridge, in "Jerusalem and Tiberias." P. 105.

This conclusion is yet farther confirmed by the light which the above proverb sheds upon a passage in the writings of Paul, which has greatly perplexed expositors. "Else what shall they do which are baptized for the dead, if the dead rise not at all? why are they then baptized for the dead?"—1 Cor. xv, 29. Paul is discussing the doctrine of the resurrection. As elsewhere in the epistle, so here, he assumes his readers to know the law of Moses. (Compare 1 Cor. ix, 8-10; x, 1-10.) To it, he, therefore, appeals.—"You know that there is in the law an ordinance for the ritual restoration of such as, by contact with the dead, have become ritually dead. But what means this rite? If the saints shall not really be raised up, to what intent is this ritual resurrection?" That such was the meaning of Paul, will hardly be questioned by any who consider, (1.) That the law of defilement by the dead, and of purification with the water of separation, was a statute of universal obligation to Israel, at home, and in foreign lands: (2.) That the ordinance and its observance were so familiar that, two hundred years before Christ, it was made the ground of the proverb above cited. As we shall presently see, it is mentioned by Philo and by Josephus as, in their days, universally observed: (3.) That it was known to Paul by the name of baptism: (4.) That it meant the giving of life to the dead: (5.) That, hence, whatever might be Paul's allusion, it was a fact, throughout the dwellings of Israel, that, whenever death visited a house, it involved the consequent necessity of the baptism of the family and attendants,—a baptism which signified the resurrection of the dead. It is, therefore, beyond question that Paul meant to refer to that Levitical purification. Such were the facts that his readers could not but so understand him. Moreover, his expression here, and that which we have heretofore examined concerning the divers baptisms of the law, mutually illustrate each other and confirm all our conclusions on the subject.

Thus, starting with the "divers baptisms" of the epistle to the Hebrews, we have identified them with the seal of the Sinai covenant and the water of separation. We have traced the ordinance in the historical books, the Psalms and the prophets; have found it, in the time of the son of Sirach, familiarly known as baptism, and have recognized it in the New Testament itself, referred to by the same name, by that Hebrew of the Hebrews, the apostle Paul. We may add that the same apostle again refers to imitations of this ordinance in his dissuasive against "doctrines of baptisms." (Heb. vi, 2.) Here, he alludes to those Pharisaic rites which under the same name were condemned by the Lord Jesus, who reproved them as "teaching for doctrines the commandments of men," concerning their baptizings. (Mark, vii, 7, 8.)

Section XL.—*Judith's Baptisms.*—Story of Judith. Her baptism. Mohammedan washing before prayer

Returning to the Apocrypha, the next example of baptism occurs in the book of Judith. The book dates from the period of the Maccabean kings of Judah, between one and two hundred years before Christ; is a historical fiction, and is designed to present, in the person of Judith, an ideal type of female piety, courage, and virtue, as conceived by the Jews of that age. According to the story, "Nabuchodonosor, the king of Nineveh," being incensed against the Jews, had doomed them to destruction. He therefore sent Holofernes, with a large army to execute his vengeance. This army being re-enforced by the Ammonites and the sons of Esau, the mighty host, enters on the siege of Bethulia, a frontier city of Judah. Surrounding the city and filling the whole country, they seize "the water and the fountain of waters," upon which Bethulia depended for its supply. Soon, "all the vessels of water failed all the inhabitants of Bethulia, and the cisterns were emptied, so that they had not water, to drink their fill, one day; for they gave them drink by measure." —Judith vii, 12-21.

In this extremity, the elders of the city yield to the clamor of the famished populace, and promise that if succor should not come within five days they will surrender the city to the Assyrians. It is now that the young and beautiful widow, Judith, appears on the scene. Rebuking the elders, for their lack of faith and courage, she decks herself and goes forth to beguile Holofernes, whom, in the sequel, she slays, in his drunkenness, with his own sword, and so delivers her nation. When she came to the Assyrians, "the servants of Holofernes brought her into the tent, and she slept until midnight, and she arose at the morning watch, and sent to Holofernes, saying, Let my lord now command that thy handmaid be allowed to go out for prayer. And Holofernes commanded his body-guard not to hinder her; and she remained in the tent three days, and went out nightly into the valley of Bethulia and *baptized* in the camp, at the fountain of water. And as she returned, she besought the Lord God of Israel to direct her way to the raising up the children of her people" —Jud. xii, 5-8.

Judith's *baptism*, was evidently not one of those required by the law. It was performed stately every night, as a preparation for prayer, and was, no doubt, one of those washings which Jewish tradition was, at that time, multiplying, and which were so rife in the days of our Savior. Judith's maid was with her, and this baptism was no doubt performed in the ordinary mode of washing, with water poured on her hands. As to the place of her baptism, the language is explicit. It was (*en*) *in* the camp, but (*epi*) *at* and *not in* the fountain. Not only does the language thus forbid the supposition that she was immersed in the fountain, but the circumstances were equally conclusive. She was a young and beautiful woman, in the midst of a host of rude and licentious soldiers and followers of the army. They held the fountain with jealous care, both for the convenience of their own supply, and as the sure means of bringing Bethulia to surrender. Judith could not there be private for a moment, even at midnight, and such exposure as is imagined would have been an invitation to certain violence, even though there had been no question of defiling the very fountain whence the camp drew its supply of water.

Baptist writers, to prove that Judith, nevertheless, immersed herself, cite the fact that "as she *went up* (*anebē*), she besought the Lord God of Israel to direct her way to the raising up of the children of her people." But Dr. Dale has pointed out the fact that the very same language occurs in a parallel place in the Septuagint Greek, where no one ever pretended to find an immersion. Rebekah "went down to the well, and filled her pitcher and *went up* (*anebē*)." —Gen. xxiv, 15, 16. The fountain of Bethulia was in the valley, to which Judith had to go down from the head-quarters of Holofernes, which would be in an elevated position, so as to command a view of the situation. To suppose the *going up* to be out of the water, would give her a time for prayer so brief and in circumstances so peculiar as to give the suggestion an air of ridicule.

It is well known that the impostor Mohammed was assisted in constructing his institutions by renegade Jews, who early became his proselytes. The following precept of the Koran will illustrate the practice of baptism before prayer: "O true believers, when ye prepare to pray, wash your faces and your hands unto the elbows; and rub your heads and your feet unto the ankles; and if ye be polluted ... wash yourselves (all over). But if ye be defiled, and ye find no water, take fine sand, and rub your faces and your hands therewith. God would not put a difficulty upon you. But he desireth to purify you, and to complete his favor upon you, that ye may give thanks."[32] This regulation by Mohammed is remarkable in relation to that request of Peter, — "Lord not my feet only, but also my hands and my head." — John xiii, 9. Both he and the prophet of Mecca would seem to have had in view the same custom of the scribes.

From the passages thus examined it appears that in Hellenistic Greek the word, *baptizo* was employed to designate two classes of cleansings, — the sacramental sprinklings of the law, and the self-imposed washings of tradition, the mode of which, whether performed by affusion or sprinkling, is not clear. As to the former: the proverb of the son of Sirach is clearly a reference to the sprinkled water of separation. To the same class, the arguments adduced entitle us to refer the baptism of Naaman. To the rites of self-washing the case of Judith is to be assigned, — not to those appointed by the law, but those imitations of the scribes which obscured the meaning of the ordinance, as appointed of God.

Section XLI. — *The Water of Separation in Philo and Josephus.* — Philo on
the subject. Josephus' description

Philo, commonly called Judæus, was a Jew of Alexandria, who was cotemporary with the apostles. He thus expounds the laws of purification: —

"The law requires him who brings a sacrifice to be clean in body and soul; — in his soul, from all passions, disorder and vices, whether in word or deed; and pure in body, from such things as ritually defile it.[33] And it has appointed a purification for each of these; for the soul, by animals suitable for sacrifice; — for the body, by (*loutrōn kai perirrhantēriōn*) ablutions and sprinklings.... The body is purified, as I have said by washings and sprinklings; nor does the law allow a person washed and sprinkled once to enter immediately the sacred courts; but requires him to wait without, seven days; and to be sprinkled twice, on the third day and on the seventh; and after these, having washed himself, it admits him to enter and share the sacred rites. It is to be considered what judgment and philosophy there is in this. For, nearly all other people are sprinkled with mere water, the most drawing it from the sea; some from rivers, and others again out of vessels of water replen-

---

[32] Sale's "Koran," chapter v.

[33] ἀφ' ὧν ἔθος αὐτο μιανεσθαι. — "From those things which custom causes to defile it." Ἔθος, commonly means a custom grounded in law. (Compare Acts vi, 14; xv, 1; xvi, 21; xxi, 21; xxv, 16; xxvi, 3; xxviii, 17; etc.)

ished from fountains. But Moses, providing ashes from sacrificial fire (and in what manner will be shown presently), directed that some of these should be put into a vessel, and water poured upon them; and then dipping twigs of hyssop in the mixture, to sprinkle those who were to be cleansed.

"It is now proper to explain the suitableness of these ashes. For they are not bare ashes of wood, consumed by fire, but of an animal suited to such purification. For it is required that a red heifer which has never borne the yoke be sacrificed outside the city, and that the high priest, taking some of the blood, shall seven times sprinkle with it toward the front of the temple, and shall then burn the whole animal with its hide and flesh, its viscera and dung. And when the flame declines, that these three things be cast into the midst of it;—a stick of cedar, a stick of hyssop, and a bunch of cummin. And when the fire has wholly expired, it is required, that a clean person collect the ashes and deposit them outside the city, in a clean place."[34]

Josephus was a Jewish priest, who was made prisoner by Titus, in the war which ended in the destruction of Jerusalem. He afterward, at Rome, wrote his Jewish "Antiquities," and his "History." He thus describes the manner of purifying with the ashes of the heifer. "Any persons being defiled by a dead body, they put a little of these ashes and hyssop into spring water, and *baptizing* with these ashes in water, sprinkled them on the third day and on the seventh."[35] This is a literal translation from the Greek of Josephus; but differs from the popular version of Whiston. He renders it,—"They put a little of these ashes into spring water with hyssop, and dipping part of these ashes in it, they sprinkled them with it," etc. But this is a very incorrect translation, is incongruous to the ordinance as described by Moses, and converts the account into nonsense. According to it, the ashes are in the first place put into the water, and then part of them "dipped in it!" How they were recovered from the water, in order to the dipping, and how the ashes could be *dipped* in the water at all, we need not inquire, as the translation is incorrect. "Baptizing with these ashes-in-water," truly represents the original.[36] "Baptizing," was the action; the mixture of "ashes in water," was the element; "sprinkling," the mode; and "the third and seventh days," the time. In fact, in using the water of separation, according to the law, there was no dipping of any sort, except of the hyssop bush, with which the water was sprinkled. The only action to which Josephus can refer,—that to which he does undoubtedly refer,—by the word, "baptizing," is the purifying rite, of which he immediately states the form to have been a *sprinkling*.

To get rid of the force of this passage, Baptist writers have proposed an arbitrary alteration of the text, by the erasure of the entire clause (*te kai—pēgēn*) "with these ashes in water." The change thus suggested is purely gratuitous. The reading which they propose is without the pretense of sanction from any manuscript of Josephus, and is sustained by no sound principles of criticism. Its only warrant

[34] Philonis Judæi Opera omnia, Frankofurti, 1691, De Victimas Offerentibus.

[35] Josephus, Antiquities, IV, iv, 6.

[36] "Βαπτίσαντες τε καὶ της τέφρας ταύτης εἰς πηγὴν." Τῆς τέφρας ταύτες is the partitive and instrumental Genitive, and indicates the ashes-in-water, as that with which the baptism was to be performed. (Compare John ii, 7.—"Fill the water pots *with* water.")

is the necessities of the Baptist position. On the contrary, the rendering which we have given is, in some of the manuscripts of Josephus, enforced by the preposition (*meta*) *with*, after the word, "baptizing." According to this version, the passage can be read no otherwise than as we have given it. "Baptizing *with* these ashes in water."

In the writings of Josephus there is another and very characteristic notice as to the use of the water of separation. Speaking of the funeral rites, he says, "Our law also ordains that the house and its inhabitants shall be purified after the funeral is over, that every one may thence learn to keep at a great distance from the thought of being pure, if he hath once been guilty of murder."[37] We are not to suppose that the spiritual meaning of these rites had been so utterly lost by the Jews, that Josephus, a priest, a Pharisee, a man of extensive learning and reputation, imagined this to be a true account of the nature and meaning of the ordinance. But he was speaking in defense of Judaism, against the assaults of Apion, a Greek philosopher of Alexandria, at the bar of the pagan philosophy of Greece and Rome. He affects, for himself, a profoundly philosophic style and spirit, and aims to vindicate a similar character for the laws and institutions of Moses. Knowing that the truths of God as committed to Israel would be foolishness to the wise, to whose applause he aspired, he sets them aside in favor of his own "philosophic" inventions. He seems to have taken the suggestion from certain heathen observances, of which we shall see more further on.

The foregoing extracts not only illustrate the law as to the water of separation, and the use of the word, *baptizo*, with reference to it, but indicate the place held by the ordinance among the observances of Israel, down to the time of Jerusalem's desolation.

Section XLII.—*Imitations of these Rites by the Greeks and Romans.*—Diffusive influence of Israel. The stain of crime, and purgation for it, novelties in Greece. Purifying always by sprinkled water. Ovid and Virgil. The Greek mysteries

Placed as was Israel in the very center of the civilization of the ancient world, and on the direct line of communication between its peoples and empires, her influence upon the institutions and religious rites of other nations must have been very great, and is traceable in every direction. There is reason to believe that Greece and its colonies in Italy, from which sprang the republic and empire of Rome, derived from Israel the first great impulses of their civilization, as well as continual subsequent contributions to its maintenance and growth. Israel had dwelt in the land of Canaan about three hundred years before the supposed era of the siege of Troy, and seven hundred before the reputed date of the great poems of Homer, from the silence of which it is evident that to him letters were wholly unknown. According to the earliest Greek tradition, Cadmus, "the man of the east," coming with a colony of Phœnicians settled in Greece, bringing with him the art of alphabetic writing. But at what age he lived, or whether he was not, in fact, wholly a mythical character is a matter of conjecture. The tradition, however, distinctly

---

[37] Josephus against Apion. Book ii, 27.

points to Phœnicia as the land whence the art was introduced into Greece; and the circumstances accord with this supposition. That the Greek letters were derived from those called Phœnician is an undoubted fact. The extensive commerce maintained by the ships of Phœnicia was a constant and efficient means of disseminating the seeds of her advancing civilization; and besides, the sages of Greece were accustomed to travel to Egypt, Phœnicia, and the east, in search of knowledge; and returned thence with acquisitions of which all Greece was the beneficiary. About four hundred years before Christ, Plato himself was in Egypt in search of knowledge, a student of the priests of On. At this time, Egypt was full of Jews, and it is not to be imagined that such an inquirer would wholly fail to catch some glimpses of the light which shone in the institutions and literature of Israel.

Many things concur to show that neither Egypt nor Phœnicia was the original fountain of much that was thus disseminated to Greece. In some instances, the attendant circumstances, and in others the internal evidence, unmistakably indicate an Israelite origin. Phœnicia was a strip of sea-coast, ten or twelve miles wide, lying between the northern part of the land of Israel and the Mediterranean Sea. Tyre and Sidon, its two chief cities, were the only practicable sea-ports on the coast of Palestine. They were distant, the former, about one hundred and twenty miles, and the latter, one hundred, from Jerusalem. Their supplies were derived largely from the fields, the vineyards, and the olive groves of Israel. (2 Chron. ii, 10; Acts xii, 20.) Except slight provincial differences, the language of the two people was the same; and the intimacy of the relations is seen in the fact that the drift of dialect in the two closely coincided. Hiram king of Tyre, was David's intimate friend, and Solomon's faithful and efficient ally, in the erection of the temple and his own palace, in adorning Jerusalem, and in commercial enterprises. His relation with David, and his message of salutation to Solomon (2 Chron. ii, 12) argue him a professed worshiper of the God of Israel. Thus, whilst the Phœnician territory was a mask by which Israel was concealed from the Mediterranean countries, the Phœnicians, themselves, can not but have realized a profound impression from the wonderful system of religious rites and the testimonies of religious truth which were maintained in Israel and centered around that temple on Mount Sion, which was a monument of Phœnician skill in architecture and the mechanic arts. The ideas thus communicated and the impressions thus produced must have been borne abroad by every wind that filled a Phœnician sail, and disseminated to every land that was touched by a Phœnician prow.

The art of alphabetic writing is an illustration of this. It did not originate in Phœnicia, but, as internal evidence demonstrates,—with the Arameans, of whom Israel was a branch. The Phœnician characters were the same as the Old Hebrew. Once acquired by that maritime people, the art was diffused to Greece, to Rome, and the world. The Egyptians no less than the Phœnicians were idolaters, having lords many and gods many. When, therefore, the sages of Greece returned from their explorations, prepared to whisper to their confidential disciples the sublime doctrine of the divine unity, and even to erect an altar *"To the Unknown God,"*[38] we are justified in the conviction that at some point in the course of their travels,

[38] That this altar was the expression of a blind though real groping after the true God, is distinctly attested by Paul.—"Whom therefore ye ignorantly worship, Him declare I unto

they had caught an echo of that voice which spake to the twelve tribes in the wilderness,—"Hear, O Israel: the Lord our God is one Lord."—Deut. vi, 4. To the same originals undoubtedly are to be referred many of the ceremonials of their religion. Of this, the rules of uncleanness, and rites of purifying are remarkable illustrations.

Of the various forms of purification among the Greeks, Plato makes an enumeration.—"The *purifications* (*katharmoi*) both according to medicine and vaticination, both the pharmacial *drugs*, (*pharmakois*), and the vaticinal *fumigations* (*peritheiōseis*) as also the *washings* (*loutra*) in such rites, and the *sprinklings* (*perirrhanseis*);—are not all these effectual to one end,—to render a man pure, both as to body and soul?"[39]

On this subject, the historian Grote makes some noteworthy statements.—"The names of Orpheus and Musaeus (as well as that of Pythagoras, looking at one side of his character), represent facts of importance in the history of the Grecian mind, ... the gradual influx of Thracian, Phrygian and Egyptian religious ceremonies and feelings, and the increasing diffusion of special mysteries, schemes for religious purification, and orgies (I venture to Anglicize the Greek word, which contains in its original meaning no implication of the ideas of excess to which it was afterward diverted), in honor of some particular god, distinct from the public solemnities, and from the gentile solemnities of primitive Greece.... During the interval between Hesiod and Onomakritus [B. C. 610-510], the revolution in the religious mind of Greece was such as to place both these deities [Dyonisus and Demeter, the Bacchus and Ceres of the Latins] in the front rank.... From all these countries [Egypt, Thrace, Phrygia and Lydia], novelties unknown to the Homeric men found their way into the Grecian worship; and there is one amongst them which deserves to be specially noticed, because it marks the generation of the new class of ideas in their theology. Homer mentions many guilty of private or involuntary homicide, and compelled either to go into exile, or to make pecuniary satisfaction; but he never once describes any of them to have either received or required purification for the crime. Now, in the times subsequent to Homer, purification for homicide comes to be indispensable. The guilty person is regarded as unfit for the society of men, or the worship of the gods, until he has received it; and special ceremonies are prescribed whereby it is to be administered. Herodotus tells us that the ceremony of purification was the same among the Lydians and the Greeks. We know that it formed no part of the early religion of the latter, and we may reasonably suspect that they borrowed from the former.... The purification of a murderer was originally operated not by the hands of any priest or specially sanctified man, but by those of a chief or king who goes through the appropriate ceremonies in the manner represented by Herodotus, in his pathetic narrative re-

---

you."—Acts xvii, 23. To suppose as do some that the altar was erected by one who was uncertain which of the tutelary deities he should propitiate, implies Paul to have resorted to a weak pretense, founded on the mere jingle of words, which, so far from constituting an appropriate and impressive basis for his argument and appeal, would have invited the derision and contempt of his skeptical audience. He adopted no such artifice; but appealed to a recognized and affecting fact.

[39] Plato, in Cratylo, xxii.

specting Crœsus and Adrastus.[40] The idea of a special taint of crime, and of the necessity, as well as the sufficiency of prescribed religious ceremonies, as a means of removing it, appears thus to have got footing in Grecian practice subsequent to the time of Homer."[41]

Again he says,—"Herodotus had been profoundly impressed with what he saw and heard in Egypt. The wonderful monuments, the evident antiquity, and the peculiar civilization of that country acquired such preponderance in his mind, over his own native legends, that he is disposed to trace the oldest religious names or institutions of Greece, to Egyptian or Phœnician original, setting aside, in favor of this hypothesis, the Grecian legends of Dyonisus and Pan."[42]

In these statements, the eminent historian seems studiously to avoid a recognition of the direction to which all his facts so distinctly point. All the countries mentioned by him border on the Mediterranean, and were in constant and intimate communication with Egypt and Phœnicia, the relations of which with Israel are too well known to need emphasis. They were, in fact, the channels through which Hebrew ideas must ordinarily pass, in order to gain access to Greece and the continent of Europe. To whatever source the Greeks may have been immediately indebted for the novel ideas of a special stain or defilement, resulting from crime, and of ritual purifying from it, we know that they were incorporated in the laws and ritual of Moses ages before there is a trace of them in any of the countries mentioned. The disposition of Herodotus to refer them to Egypt and Phœnicia is therefore entitled to more respectful consideration than our author gives it. That the Gentile rites in question, however grossly corrupted, were derived from divine originals, must be manifest to any one who will compare the significance and beauty of the Scriptural rites as connected with the spiritual truths of revelation, which they symbolized, with the bareness and absurdity by which they are characterized, in their distorted Gentile forms, detached from the spiritual connection to which they natively belonged.

On the matters of which it treats, no authority is higher than Dr. Wm. Smith's Dictionary of Greek and Roman Antiquities. As to the present subject, it testifies that their purifyings, "in every case of which we have any certain knowledge were *connected with sacrifices* and other religious rites, and consisted in the *sprinkling of water*, by means of a *branch of laurel or olive*; and at Rome, sometimes by means of the *aspergillum,* and in the burning of certain materials the smoke of which was thought to have a purifying effect."[43]

Of the Greek heroes the Abbe Barthelemi says,—"They shuddered at the blood they had spilt, and abandoning their throne and native land, went to implore the

---

[40] But Herodotus does not "represent" the manner of the purifying of Adrastus. Moreover, the legend of Crœsus and Adrastus, is fabulous, as appears from internal evidence (see Rawlinson's note on the place); and with it, the theory of Grote, as to the Lydian origin of the Greek purifying rites falls to the ground. See Rawlinson's Herodotus, Hist. I. 35.

[41] Grote i, 29-35.

[42] Ib. 530.

[43] Smith's Greek and Roman Antiquities, *article,* "Lustratio."

aid of expiation in some distant country. After the sacrifices enjoined them by the ceremony, a purifying water was poured upon the guilty hand, after which they again returned into society and prepared themselves for new combats."[44]

Of the Romans, Ovid says:—"Our fathers believed purifications to be effectual for blotting out every crime and every cause of penalty. Greece was the source of the custom. She believes the guilty, when purified with lustral rites, to be freed from the guilt of their evil deeds. Thus Peleus purified the grandson of Actor; and thus Acastus, with the waters of Hæmus, cleansed Peleus himself, from the blood of Phocus.—Ah credulous people! who suppose that the dreadful crime of murder can be obliterated by (*fluminea aqua*), running waters."[45]

The same poet describes the festival of Pales, the tutelary goddess of shepherds. Some days before her festival, cows were sacrificed and the unborn offspring torn from their bowels and burned with fire by the eldest of the Vestals, "that their ashes may purify the people on the day of Pales." On the festival day he sings: "I am called to the Palilia.... Often, truly, have I carried in my full hand the ashes of the calf and the bean stalks, hallowed purifiers. Truly I have leaped over the fires kindled in three rows, and the dripping branch of laurel has scattered the water.... Go, ye people, seek the fumigation from the altar of the virgin! Vesta will give it. By the grace of Vesta, you shall be purified. The blood of a horse shall be your fumigatory, with the ashes of the calf, and third the empty husk of the hard bean. Shepherd, purify your full fed flocks in the early twilight. Water should first sprinkle them, and a twig broom should sweep the ground."[46] Again, he tells of "a fountain of Mercury near the Capanian gate. If we choose to believe those who have tried it, it has a divine virtue. Hither comes the merchant with purse-girdled tunic, and being purified, draws water which he may carry away in a perfumed vase. In this, a branch of laurel is moistened, and with the wet laurel all things are sprinkled that are to have new owners. He sprinkles his own locks, also, with the dripping bush, and with a voice familiar with deceit offers his prayers. 'Wash away my past perjuries,' says he: 'Wash away the falsehoods of the past day. Whether I have called thee (Mercury), to witness, or have called upon the great majesty of Jove, wishing him *not* to hear; or, if I have been false to any other god or goddess, let the swift zephyrs carry away my dishonest words, and let my perjuries be obliterated by to-morrow. Let not the superior powers give heed to what I may say.'"[47]

In Virgil, Æneas, preparing for flight from the overthrow of Troy, says to his father,—"Do you, my father, in your hand take the consecrated things and the ancestral gods? To me, just returned from such and so recent a battle and slaughter, it were sacrilege to touch them, until I shall have washed in a living stream."[48] In another place the closing rites at the funeral pyre of Misenus are thus described,—"The same (Chorinaeus) passed thrice around his companions with water, sprinkling them with a gentle spray, and with a branch of the auspicious olive

---

[44] Travels of Anacharsis, Introduction.
[45] Ovidii Fast. ii, vs. 27-46.
[46] Ib. iv, 633-640; 731-736.
[47] Ovidii Fast. ii, v, 673-688.
[48] Æn. ii, 717.

purified the men and uttered the parting words."[49]

Of funeral lustrations at Rome, Adams in his Antiquities, gives this account: "When the remains of the dead were laid in the tomb, those present were, three times, sprinkled by a priest with pure water, from a branch of olive or laurel, to purify them.... The friends when they returned home, as a further purification, after being sprinkled with water, stepped over a fire.[50]... The house itself also was purified and swept with a certain kind of a broom." The classic writers frequently refer to similar observances among the Greeks. Thus, in Euripides, the people are perplexed as to the death of Alcestis, king Admetus' wife, because "they do not see the lustral water before the door, as is customary at the doors of the dead."[51]

The census of the population of Rome was taken every five years, and was followed by a lustration of the city. From this custom the word *lustrum* (a lustration), came to signify a period of five years. There was also a lustration for new born infants, when their names were given. For boys it was usually on the ninth day after birth; for girls, by some, on the eighth day, and by others, on the fifth, or the third day, while some performed it on the last day of the week wherein the child was born. "On the lustral day, a feast was prepared, over which the goddess Nundina was supposed to preside. The assembled women handed the child backward and forward around the fire burning on the altar of the gods; after which they sprinkled it with water, in which were mingled saliva and dust."[52]

Philo Judaeus, was a resident of the Greek colony of Alexandria. He was a man of learning, and especially versed in the religious doctrines and rites of the Gentiles, as well as of Moses, of which he wrote largely. We have seen that, in contrasting the purifying rites of other nations with those of Israel, he says that "nearly all other people are sprinkled with unmixed water, mostly drawing it from *the sea*, some from rivers and others again from vessels replenished from fountains."[53] This preference of the water of the sea, probably originated in a desire to differentiate the Gentile imitations from the divine originals as observed by Israel. Of it an illustration appears in Euripides. Iphigenia speaks of Orestes and his companions, defiled with dreadful crimes,—"First would I (*nipsai*) *imbue* them with holy purifyings."

KING THOAS. "From springs of waters? Or, from spray of the sea?"

IPHIGENIA. "The sea spray (*kluzei*[54]) washes away all the crimes of men."[55]

The rites used in the Greek *mysteries* illustrate the same subject. "The benefits which the initiated hoped to obtain were security against the vicissitudes of fortune and protection from dangers both in this life and in the life to come. The

---

[49] Ibid. vi, 229.—The (novissima verba) last or parting words, were addressed to the deceased,—"Vale! Vale! Vale!" Farewell! Farewell! Farewell!

[50] Compare above, p. 70.

[51] Euripides in Alcest. 398. See, also, Aristophanes in Eccl. 1025.

[52] Rees's Encyclopedia, article, "Lustration."

[53] Above, p. 91.

[54] Κλυζω (klyzō) to besprinkle, to water, to rinse, to dash over. "The sea, besprinkling, washes away all the crimes of men."

[55] Iphigenia in Taur. 1192-1194.

principal part of the initiation, and that which was thought to be most efficacious in producing the desired effects, were the lustrations and purifications, whence the mysteries themselves are sometimes called *katharsia* or *katharmoi.*"[56]

Those of Eleusis were a manifest imitation of the Levitical feast of ingathering or tabernacles. They were celebrated at the same season,—immediately after the bringing in of the harvest; and were in honor of Demeter, or Ceres, the patroness of agriculture. The celebration proper, continued for seven days, after which there was an additional eighth day, appropriated to the initiation of those who had been too late for the regular observances. This, again, was followed by a ninth day, which was named *plēmochoai*, from a vase called *plēmochoē*. "Two of these vessels were on this day filled with water or wine," (Should it not be "water *and* wine?") "and the contents of one thrown to the east, and those of the other to the west, while those who performed this rite uttered some mystical words."[57] From the appropriating of a ninth day to the outpouring of the water and wine, it seems probable that the mysteries were originally imitated from the Levitical feast before the festival of the outpouring was instituted; and that when the latter rite was introduced, an additional day was appropriated to it, so as to avoid any change in what had become the established and consecrated order of the preceding days.

These mysteries were of two orders. The less were celebrated at Agræ, and were essential as a preparation for the greater at Eleusis. In the preparatory rites, the candidates were required to keep themselves continent and unpolluted for nine days; and were purified with water sprinkled on them, by an officer who was thence called the *hydranos.*[58] At Eleusis they offered sacrifices and prayers, wearing garlands of flowers; and, standing on the skin of a sacrificial animal, were again purified by the sprinkling of water by the *hydranos*.

That the observances thus illustrated were corrupted forms derived from the rites and institutions of Moses, is apparent. So manifest is this, that in the third and fourth centuries it was made the ground of a specious theory by means of which the advocates of paganism sought to stay the progress of Christianity. "Among those who wished to appear wise, and to take moderate ground, many were induced to devise a kind of reconciling religion, intermediate between the old superstition and Christianity, and to imagine that Christ had enjoined the very same things which had long been represented by the pagan priests, under the envelope of their ceremonies and fables."[59]

There was, no doubt, an element of truth in this conception. The rites of Gentile idolatry were, it is evident, corrupted forms derived from divinely appointed institutions, partly, it may be, by tradition, from the parents of the race; but chiefly by imitation of the ritual of Moses.

---

[56] Smith's Dictionary, *article* "Mysteria."

[57] Smith, *article* "Eleusinia." Compare above, p. 74.

[58] "Ὑδρανος (hydranos), a waterer, a sprinkler with water; from ὑδραινο to water, to sprinkle any one with water, to pour out libations."—Liddell & Scott's Greek Lexicon.

[59] Mosheim, Eccl. Hist., Book II., Part i, § 18.

Section XLIII.—*Baptism in Egypt and among the Aztecs.*—The libation
vase of Osor-Ur. Aztec infant baptism

I am indebted to the courtesy of W. H. Ryland, F. S. A. Secretary of the (British)
Society of Biblical Archæology, for a copy of the proceedings at a meeting held
on the 4th of May, 1880. From it I make the following extract including part of a
communication read from M. Paul Pierret. It is descriptive of "the Libation Vase
of Osor-ur," preserved in the Museum of the Louvre (No. 908), an inscription on
which has been deciphered by M. Pierret.

"The vase, of the Saitic epoch, is of bronze, and of an oblong form, covered
with an inscription, finely traced with a pointed instrument. The text has been
published, by M. Pierret in the second volume of his 'Recueil d'Inscriptions du
Louvre,' in the eighth number of the 'Etudes Egyptologiques.' The goddess, Nout,
is represented standing in her sycamore, pouring the water which is received by
the deceased, on one side, and by his soul, on the other. 'Saith the Osiris, divine father and first prophet of Ammon Osor-ur, truthful;—Oh, Sycamore of Nout! give
me the water and the breath [of life] which proceed from thee. That I may have
the vigor of the goddess of vigor; that I may have the life of the goddess of life;
that I may breathe the breath of the goddess of the respiration of breaths; for I am
Toum. Saith Nout;—Oh the Osiris, divine father, etc., thou receivest the libation
from my own hands; I, thy beneficent mother, I bring thee the vase, containing the
abundant water for rejoicing thy heart by its effusion, that thou mayest breathe the
breath [of life] resulting from it, that thy flesh may live by it. For, I give water to
every mummy; I give breath to him whose throat is deprived of it, to those whose
body is hidden, to those who have no funeral chapel. I am with thee. I reunite thee
to thy soul, which will separate itself no more from thee, never.'"

The Saitic epoch, to which this vase is referred, began with the accession of
Psammetichus I, about 664, B. C., and closed with the conquest of Egypt by Cam-
byses in 525. The parallel period of Jewish history extends from the closing years of
Manasseh's reign to the time of the machinations by which the decree of Cyrus for
rebuilding the temple was suspended. But, although the date thus given is such as
might suggest the idea of derivation from the institutions of Moses, it seems highly
probable that the inscription presents a vestige, in a greatly corrupted form, of the
primitive faith touching the resurrection, as held by Noah and the patriarchs of
the old world, and transmitted to the founders of the Egyptian empire. Whatever
the view adopted on that point, the relation of the inscription to the subject of the
present treatise is manifest and very interesting. Not only does it very strikingly
illustrate the doctrine of life to the dead, as symbolized by the effusion of water,
but it brings together the two symbols of water and the breath of life, in such a
manner as presents a very remarkable analogy to the similar association of ideas
presented in the scene of Pentecost, as unfolded hereafter.

Very remarkable was the rite of infant baptism, as it was found by the Spanish
conquerors among the Aztecs of Mexico.[60]

---

[60] As this work goes into the hands of the printers, the newspapers announce that
"the Rev. Professor Campbell of Montreal has discovered that the Hittite and Aztec alpha-
bets are identical, and by applying the latter to the former, he has been enabled to read in-

"When everything necessary for the baptism had been made ready, all the relations of the child were assembled, and the midwife, who was the person that performed the rite of baptism, was summoned. At early dawn, they met together in the court-yard of the house. When the sun had risen, the midwife, taking the child in her arms, called for a little earthen vessel of water, while those about her placed the ornaments which had been prepared for the baptism in the midst of the court. To perform the rite of baptism, she placed herself with her face toward the west, and immediately began to go through certain ceremonies.... After this she sprinkled water on the head of the infant, saying, 'O, my child! take and receive the water of the Lord of the world, which is our life, and is given for the increasing and renewing of our body. It is to wash and to purify. I pray that these heavenly drops may enter into your body and dwell there: that they may destroy and re-move from you all the evil and sin which was given you before the beginning of the world; since all of us are under its power, being all the children of Chalchivit-lycue goddess She then washed the body of the child with water, and spoke in this manner: 'Whence thou comest, thou that art hurtful to this child; leave him and depart from him, for he now liveth anew, and is born anew; now is he purified and cleansed afresh and our mother, Chalchivitlycue, again bringeth him into the world.' Having thus prayed, the midwife took the child in both hands, and lifting him toward heaven, said, —'O Lord, thou seest here thy creature, whom thou hast sent into the world, this place of sorrow, suffering, and penitence. Grant him, O Lord, thy gifts, and thine inspiration, for thou art the great God, and with thee is the great goddess.' Torches of pine were kept burning during the performance of these ceremonies. When these things were ended, they gave the child the name of some one of his ancestors, in the hope that he might shed a new luster over it. The name was given by the same midwife or priestess who baptized him."[61]

How like, yet how different, the Græco-Roman, the Egyptian, and the Mexican rites, from each other, and from those of Israel and of Christ, appears at a glance.

Section XLIV.—*The Levitical Baptisms in the Christian Fathers.*—Tertul-lian on the idolatrous imitations. Other fathers on the water of separation. They recognize it as baptism

The writers of the primitive church distinctly recognize the Old Testament sprinklings, and especially the water of separation, by the name of baptism. By the same name, they designate the idolatrous imitations above described. Tertul-lian was born about fifty years after the death of the apostle John. In allusion to the renewing efficacy which he attributed to Christian baptism and the futility of the Gentile rites, he says,—"The nations, strangers to all understanding of true spiritual potencies, ascribe to their idols the self-same efficacy. But they defraud themselves with unwedded waters; for they are initiated, by washing, into certain of their sacred mysteries—as for example of Isis, or Mithras. Even their gods them-selves they honor with lavations. Moreover, everywhere, country seats, houses,

scriptions belonging to the ninth century before Christ." Should this announcement prove true, it brings the Aztecs into a relation to Israel which the reader will at once recognize.

[61] Sahagun. Hist. de Nueva Espana, vi, 37. In Prescott's "Conquest of Mexico." Vol. III, p. 385.

temples and whole cities are purified by sprinkling with water carried around. So, it is certain they are imbued (*tinguntur*) in the rituals of Apollo and Eleusis; and they imagine this to accomplish for them renewing and impunity for their perjuries. Moreover, among the ancients, whoever was polluted with murder, expiated himself with purifying waters.... We see here the diligence of the devil, emulating the things of God, since he even administers baptism to his own."[62]

Here, Tertullian expressly designates these rites of the Gentile idolatries by the name of baptism, and represents them as imitations of the divinely appointed ordinance. Some he distinctly describes as sprinklings, and among them evidently refers to Ovid's representation of the dishonest merchant, sprinkling himself to wash out his "perjuries." He does not allude to immersion, and in fact that form of rite was not found among the Greek and Roman superstitions. The only difference which Tertullian recognizes between the idolatrous rites and Christian baptism is indicated by the phrase (*viduis aquis*), "unwedded," or "widowed, waters," by which he designates the element used in the pagan rites. His meaning, here, is to be found in the doctrine of baptismal regeneration, which already prevailed in the church; according to which, it was believed that, in baptism, in response to the invocation of the officiating minister, the Holy Spirit descended upon the water, imparting to it a divine potency to produce a new birth in the recipient of the rite. Thus, the waters of Christian baptism were married waters, as being capable of generating life; whilst the others were unmarried,—unendowed with any "spiritual potency."

It is further worthy of special notice, that Tertullian here refers, among other Gentile imitations of baptism, to that purgation for murder, by affusion of water, from which evidently Josephus derived his preposterous explanation of the sprinkling of the water of separation, for defilement by the dead. The probability is great that the Greek purgation was derived from that appointed for the elders of Israel, in the case of a concealed murder.

Jerome, living between A. D. 340 and 420, comments thus upon Ezekiel xxxvi, 25-27.—"I will pour out or sprinkle (effundam sive aspergam), upon you clean water and ye shall be cleansed from all your defilements. And I will give you a new heart, and I will put a right spirit within you.... I will pour out the clean water of saving baptism.... It is to be observed that a new heart and a new spirit may be given by the pouring out or sprinkling of water." Again, he paraphrases;—"I will no more pour out on them the waters of saving baptism, but the waters of doctrine and of the word of God."—Jerome v, 341.

Ambrose, bishop of Milan from A. D. 374 to 391, thus expounds the 7th verse of Psa. li.—"He asks to be *cleansed with hyssop*, according to the law. He desires to be washed according to the gospel, and trusts that if washed he will be whiter than snow. He who would be purified by typical baptism was sprinkled with the blood of a lamb, by a hyssop bush."[63]

Again he says, "He (the priest), dipping the living sparrow, with cedar, scarlet and hyssop, into water in which had been mingled the blood of the slain spar-

[62] Tertull. de Baptisma, chapter v.
[63] Ambrosii Opera, in Psa. li.

row, sprinkled the leper seven times, and thus was he rightly purified.... By the cedar wood, the Father, by the hyssop the Son, and by the scarlet wool, having the brightness of fire, the Holy Spirit, is designated. With these three, he was sprinkled who would be rightly purified, because no one can be cleansed from the leprosy of sins, by the water of baptism, except through invocation of the Father and the Son and the Holy Spirit.... We are represented by the leper."[64]

Again, addressing the newly baptized, he says,—"You took the white garments, to indicate that you cast away the cloak of sin and put on the spotless robe of innocence; whereof the prophet said: 'Thou shalt sprinkle me with hyssop and I shall be clean, thou shalt wash me, and I shall be made whiter than snow.' For he that is baptized appears cleansed both according to the law and the gospel; according to the law, since Moses, with a bunch of hyssop sprinkled the blood of a bird; according to the gospel, because the garments of Christ were white as snow, when, in the gospel, he showed the glory of his resurrection. He whose sins are forgiven is made whiter than snow."[65]

Cyril lived in the next century. He was bishop of Alexandria, A. D. 412-444. In his exposition of Isaiah iv, 4, he says, "We have been baptized, not with bare water, nor with the ashes of a heifer,—We are sprinkled [with these] to purify the flesh, alone, as says the blessed Paul,—but with the Holy Spirit, and fire."

Thus, from the translation of the Old Testament into Greek down through the time of Christ and the apostles, and to the middle of the fifth century, the Levitical sprinklings were known and designated as baptisms. Further we need not trace them.

---

[64] Ibid., in Apocal. cap. 6.
[65] Ibid. Lit. ad initiandos. c, 7.

PART VI.

STATE OF THE OLD TESTAMENT ARGUMENT.

Section XLV.—*Points established by the foregoing Evidence.*—Twenty-one
    points of evidence enumerated

A review of the preceding pages will discover the following points to have
been established.

1. Baptism was a rite familiar among the Jews at the time of Christ's coming,
and not a new institution then first introduced.

2. Paul being witness, it was an ordinance imposed on Israel at Sinai, as part
of the Levitical system.

3. There is no trace, in the Levitical law, of an ordinance for the immersion of
the person, in any circumstances, or for any purpose whatever.

4. There is not, anywhere, in the Old Testament an allusion to immersion as a
symbolic rite, nor a figure derived from it, although those Scriptures are full of allusions and figures referring to the symbolic import of the pouring and sprinkling
of water.

5. There was an ordinance for the immersion of certain things very slightly
defiled; which at once illustrates the ritual value of immersion as compared with
sprinkling, and the plainness of the language where immersion was meant.

6. The baptisms, therefore, to which Paul refers as having been "imposed on"
Israel, could not have been immersions, and the word, *baptizo*, did not in his vocabulary mean, to immerse.

7. The only institutions to which he can have referred are comprehended under the two heads of, administered rites, and self-performed washings.

8. The self-washings were not sacraments, or seals of the covenant, but moni-
tory symbols of duty.

9. The gradation of these washings, the frequency and circumstances of their
observance, and the limited facilities available, render it impossible that they can
have been immersions.

10. Their symbolic significance, the words used to describe them, the customs
as to ablutions, and the washings of the priests in the court of the sanctuary, and
of the high priest in the holy place, concur to demonstrate that they were ablutions
performed by affusion.

11. The administered rites were sacramental seals of the covenant. They were essentially one in meaning, office, and form; and were invariably performed with a hyssop bush, by an official administrator, sprinkling the recipient with living water, in which was the blood or ashes of sacrifice.

12. In the Hellenistic Greek, the language of the Septuagint, the Apocrypha, and the New Testament, these purifications by sprinkling were called *baptisms*, and they were known and designated by that name by the primitive fathers of the Christian church.

13. These sprinklings of the law were the "divers baptisms" of Paul. So far, therefore, from *baptizo* meaning to dip, or, to immerse, and nothing else, it is an indisputable fact that for at least fifteen hundred years after the first institution of the rite, baptism was always performed by sprinkling.

14. The ordinance was first instituted to seal the covenant by which the church of God was founded in Israel; and that form of it in which the ashes of the red heifer were used was divinely appointed as the ordinary rite for the reception of applicants to the privileges of that covenant and church.

15. Its symbolism set forth all that is recognized in the Scriptures as meant by Christian baptism. Especially and distinctively was it the sacrament of the purification, or remission of sins.

16. The figure presented in the form of sprinkling or pouring is derived from the rain descending out of heaven, penetrating the earth and making it fruitful; and it signifies the Spirit of life from God imparted to the dead, entering the heart, purging its corruption, and creating new life. To the case of indwelling corruption, with reference to which this rite was appointed, no external washing, such as immersion is supposed to represent, can be of any avail.

17. Affusion is the constant form of action in the ritual law, whether with water, blood, or oil, to signify the efficient agency of the Lord Jesus, in all the functions of administration in his mediatorial office.

18. The recipients of the Levitical baptism, were, at its first institution, the whole congregation of Israel, old and young, thus purified from the defilements of Egypt, sealed unto the covenant of God, and installed as his church. Afterward, they were all, without distinction of sex, age, or nation, who having been suspended for any cause from the communion of the church of Israel, sought in the appointed way restoration; or who were received into it, as infants or proselytes.

19. While this rite was the door of admission to the privileges of the covenant, at Sinai, and so long as the Levitical system survived, it is appropriated by the Spirit, as the chosen figure by which is set forth, in prophecy, the bestowal of the grace of Christ upon the Gentiles, in the gospel day, and upon Israel, restored. "So shall he sprinkle many nations." "Then will I sprinkle clean water upon you, and ye shall be clean."

20. The figures of speech corresponding to the forms of sprinkling and pouring appear everywhere in the Old Testament. Pervading and determining the entire structure of the ritual law, they reappear continually, in the historical records,

in the devotional and penitent utterances of the Psalmist, the discourses of the Preacher, and the expostulations and warnings of the prophets, and in their glad anticipations of the grace of the coming Messiah. With one and the same spiritual meaning everywhere, these figures pervade and control the whole texture of thought and mode of expression of the sacred writers.

21. This rite of purification by sprinkling was not only thus familiar to Israel, but, under corrupted forms, it had been disseminated throughout the civilized world; so that when the apostles went forth to carry the gospel to the nations, the ideas of sin and guilt, defilement and cleansing, thus nourished, were a very important element in the providential preparation of the world to appreciate and accept the salvation of Christ. While such was the case, the fact is equally significant that among the nations contiguous to Israel there is no trace of ritual purification by immersion,—a form of observance which, had it existed in Israel, could not have failed of imitation by her idolatrous neighbors.

Thus assiduously and multifariously were the people of Israel taught, and trained—by instructions, by warnings, by promises, by rites and ceremonies, enjoined and observed at the sanctuary and at home, which laid hold upon them in every relation of their being and every function of their lives—to conceive of themselves in all their sinfulness and need, and of the coming Messiah in his offices of grace, in the light of this ordinance, and according to the similitude embodied in it. For fifteen centuries these influences were continually at work, until the very bent and tendency of their thoughts and conceptions, in so far as they yielded themselves to the divine agencies thus applied, were moulded to the forms of those rites.

In view of the facts thus developed, two questions present themselves for thoughtful consideration as we proceed with our inquiry. (1.) Is it to be imagined that John and Jesus, in coming to fulfill the prophecies of the Old Testament, which were embodied in sprinkled baptism, would ignore that ordinance, and silently substitute in its place the rite of immersion; thus bringing to naught and repudiating the products of the divine discipline so assiduously pursued through all those centuries, and dissolving every tie of association between the gospel of Christ and the hopes and expectations which the saints had been taught to cherish, by the unanimous testimony of the law, the prophets, and the Psalms, all speaking in the language of the repudiated rite? (2.) Since the name of *baptism*, was, beyond question the designation used for the Levitical sprinklings, how else can we understand John, Christ, and the apostles, than as meaning the same thing, in the similar use which they make of the same word?

The Greek Bath.—From Sir. Wm. Hamilton's vases, in Smith's Dictionary of Greek and Roman Antiquities; article "Balneæ."

BOOK II.
NEW TESTAMENT HISTORY.

PART VII.

INTRODUCTORY.

Before entering upon an examination of the New Testament, it will be well to notice distinctly what, at this stage of our inquiry, is the precise state of the question to which our attention is directed. In a word, two rites present themselves, each claiming to be the true and legitimate ordinance which Christ commanded to be dispensed to all nations.

On the one hand is the ritual sprinkling of water. In this rite, we have an ordinance instituted at Sinai by divine command, with specific directions as to the mode of observance, and abundant exemplification in the history of Israel and the writings of the Old Testament,—an ordinance by which the tribes of Israel and the Gentile children of Midian were both alike received and sealed unto the covenant of God,—its rites replete with the richest gospel meaning, as expounded by poets and prophets, and constituting in connection with the Lord's supper, a clear and symmetrical representation of the whole plan of grace. In this ordinance, the sprinkling of water for the ritual purging of sin, is a lucid symbol of the very baptizing office which is now fulfilled from the throne of heaven by Him whom John fore-announced as the Baptizer with the Holy Ghost. That the doctrine which the New Testament identifies with Christian baptism was symbolized by the ordinance, in its Old Testament form, can not be successfully questioned; nor that there was a beautiful symmetry, congruity and significance in each several part and feature of the observance. It thus stands forth, luminous with most precious gospel truth. Appointed of God at Sinai, as the most fitting form under which to figure the first act of His grace, in the bestowal of salvation on sinners,—honored as the rite by which the church was at the beginning consecrated to her exalted office, as God's witness and herald to the nations,—it comes to the New Testament church, hoary and venerable with a history of fifteen centuries,—embalmed and hallowed by commemoration in the poetic strains of the psalmist and the brightest visions of the prophets, and fragrant from association with the profoundest and most precious experiences of God's people, in all those centuries, and with every beam of hope for a better life beyond, which shone into their stricken hearts, in the times of bereavement and mourning. It comes, its image indelibly stamped on the face of God's word, and its conceptions therein transmitted to blend with the clearer visions of hope revealed to the gospel church, by Him, in whom life and immortality are brought to light.

On the other hand is that form of observance in which the person of the subject is immersed in water, as a symbol of the burial of the Lord Jesus. For this rite, no higher antiquity is claimed, by its advocates, than that involved in its supposed institution by the Lord Jesus, after his resurrection. It has no precedent in the Levitical ritual, nor place among the figures employed by the Old Testament writers. The prophets did not foreshadow it in their imagery, nor the psalmist in his strains. All other rites of divine authority, are distinctly described, both as to office and form. But, of the rite of immersion, there is neither description nor explanation anywhere in the Scriptures. Its evidence stands wholly in definitions, contrary to the unanimous testimony of lexicographers, unsustained by any broad inductions from the facts and analogy of Scripture, and at variance with the conclusions which such induction demands.

And when we examine the relations and details of the rite, we find incongruity and contradiction conspicuously displayed. If the rite be regarded as a typical seal of the covenant of grace, as are all sacraments, it follows that the administrator represents the Lord Jesus, administering the true baptism, the real seal of that covenant. But, if baptism is by immersion, to represent the burial of the body of the Lord Jesus, we are reduced to the alternative that the office of the administrator means nothing, in which case we have a burial with no one to perform it; — or, that he represents Joseph of Arimathea, and Nicodemus; by whom the body of Jesus was laid in the sepulcher.

Again, in the Scriptures everywhere, and especially, and in the most express terms, by the Lord Jesus himself (John iv, 14; vii, 37-39), living water is recognized as the divinely appointed symbol of the Holy Spirit, as the Spirit of quickening and life. How beautifully and richly appropriate to this purpose it is, we have seen. But, according to the immersion theory, the dipping of the person in this element, — that is, mersion in water of life, represents the consigning of the body of Jesus to the grave, the den of corruption and death!

Besides, the supposed resemblance of this rite to the burial of Christ's body is a transparent misconception. It results from the transfer to Palestine of ideas derived from the wholly different western method of interment. In the sense required by immersion, Jesus never was "buried." The sepulcher of Joseph, in which his body was laid was not a grave, but a spacious above-ground chamber. Such were its dimensions that, at one time, on the morning of the resurrection, there were present in it "Mary Magdalene and Joanna and Mary the mother of James and other women," at least five or six persons, and with them the two angels before whom they fell prostrate. (Luke xxiv, 1-10.) To this day, the hillsides around Jerusalem and throughout Palestine are pierced with innumerable such chambers, excavated horizontally in the rock, and frequently used as dwellings by the present inhabitants. Such was the sepulcher of Jesus, — an artificial chamber with a perpendicular door, so that Peter and John and the women could by stooping walk into it. — John xx, 5-8. The entombing of Jesus was no more a burial, in the sense required by the immersion theory, than was the laying of the body of Dorcas in an upper chamber. (Acts ix, 37.) The supposed similitude of immersion in water is a figment of the imagination, in entire disregard of the real facts.

But, even should we allow the ordinance to be a true and fitting symbol of the burial of Christ, it remains void of all spiritual significance. Study it as we may, it teaches nothing,—it means nothing. In all other sacraments the plan of salvation, in one or other of its grand features, is lucidly represented. The Lord's supper is the acknowledged symbol of Christ's atonement and death, and of the manner in which he imparts to his people the benefits of that death,—while they by faith feed upon his broken body. According to the immersion theory, baptism represents and shows forth the burial of the dead body of Jesus, contradistinguished from his death, as symbolized in the Lord's supper. But that burial is a thing wholly unimportant and insignificant, in itself, whether viewed as to the fact or the mode. No emphasis is ever in the Scriptures put upon either, nor spiritual meaning attributed to them. Thus, if we admit immersion to a place among the ordinances, it must remain a mere form, shedding no ray of divine light,—an opaque spot among the luminaries in the instructive constellation of Scripture rites. The result moreover of accepting this ordinance is, to strip the New Testament church of all sacramental knowledge of the power and glory of Christ's triumphant sceptre. In Levitical baptism, the Old Testament church had a most beautiful pledge of his triumph over death and a symbol of his grace shed down from the throne of his glory. But, upon the immersion theory, all this is utterly ignored in the New Testament ritual, and all attention directed to the humiliation, sufferings and death,—one sacrament setting forth his death, and the other his burial; whilst both are left void of meaning; since the intent of the abasement can only be found in his exaltation, and the baptizing office exercised from his throne. We are to believe that at the very moment when his exaltation became a glorious reality, and his baptizing office an active function, and when these facts had become the very crown and sum of the gospel thereupon sent forth to the world, all trace of them was obliterated from the sacramental system, to the marring of its symmetry and the utter destruction of its completeness and adequacy as a symbolical gospel.

Moreover, it is the office of the rite of baptism, to seal admission to the benefits of the covenant, in the bosom of the visible church. Appropriate to this office, the Old Testament rite was a symbol of that renewing and cleansing which the Lord Jesus by his Spirit gives, in the bestowal upon his people of the benefits of the better covenant, and the fellowship of the invisible church. The same import is attributed to baptism throughout the New Testament. But in the rite of immersion, as symbolizing the burial of the Lord Jesus, not only is this meaning excluded, but the ordinance has no conceivable congruity to the office which it fills. Dr. Carson attempts to evade this difficulty by the assumption that there are two distinct emblems in baptism,—one, of purification by washing; another of death, burial and resurrection, by immersion.[66] Then, we are to understand that in baptism, the administrator represents at once, the men by whom the body of Jesus was laid in the sepulchre, and the Lord Jesus himself, dispensing the baptism of his Spirit! The

---

[66] Carson on Baptism, pp. 265-268.

water symbolizes both the grave which is the abode of death and corruption, and the Holy Spirit of life! And the immersion of the person of the baptized represents at one and the same time, the placing of the body in the grave, and the bestowal of his Spirit by Jesus, for quickening and sanctifying his people! Manifestly, the two sets of ideas thus brought together, as involved and represented in the one form, are wholly irreconcilable. They are not merely incongruous, but mutually destructive. To assert water, in one and the same act, to signify the Spirit of life, and the corruption of the grave; or an immersion to symbolize, at once, the burial of the dead body, and the quickening of dead souls, is to deny it to have any meaning at all. The rite may be labelled with these incongruous ideas. But they can not be made to cohere in it. The theory ignores and contradicts the true nature of the rites of God's appointment; which are not mere mnemonical tokens, but representative figures, ordained as testimonies, which convey intelligible expression of their meaning by their forms; and are therefore constructed upon fixed and invariable principles, and characterized by definiteness and unity of meaning.

Are these difficulties evaded by falling back to the position of the first Baptist confession,—that baptism "being a sign, must answer the thing signified, which is, the interest the saints have in the death, burial and *resurrection* of Christ; and that as certainly as the body is buried under the water and risen again, so certainly shall the bodies of the saints be raised by the power of Christ, in the day of the resurrection?" This is, to abandon the very citadel of the cause, which consists in the position that the form and meaning of the ordinance are to be determined by a strict interpretation of the classic meaning of the word *baptizo*. That word *never* means "burial and resurrection,"—the immersion and *raising up* of the subject. It *sometimes* means a submersion; that, and nothing more. This is now distinctly admitted by the ablest representatives of the immersion theory, as we shall see abundantly evinced before we close.

Such are some of the considerations that present themselves, as, at this point in our inquiry, we view the two diverse rites which assume the name of Christian baptism. Their claims are now to be judged, by a comparison of the New Testament evidence, with what has been already concentrated from the law, the prophets, and the Psalms;—writings all of them equally authoritative and divine.

The Greek Bath.—The god, Eros, presides. From Sir. Wm. Hamilton's vases, in Smith's Dictionary of Greek and Roman Antiquities; article "Balneæ."

PART VIII.

THE PURIFYINGS OF THE JEWS.

Section XLVII.—*Accounts of them in the Gospels.*—Purifying before the
feasts. The marriage in Cana. Washings and baptisms

The fact has been referred to already that at the great passover, in the days of
Hezekiah, to which the remnant of the ten tribes were invited by the king, "a multitude of the people, even many of Ephraim and Manasseh, Issachar and Zebulun,
had not cleansed themselves, yet did they eat the passover otherwise than it was
written," not being "cleansed according to the purification of the sanctuary;" that,
thereupon, a plague was sent among them; but at the intercession of the king, the
Lord healed the people. (2 Chron. xxx, 17-20.) In the law, it appears that, at the entreaty of certain persons, who, at the regular time of the passover, were defiled by
a dead body, provision was made for a second passover, to be kept a month later,
by such as, by reason of defilement, or absence at a great distance, could not keep
it at the appointed time. (Num. ix, 6-11.) These facts illustrate the statement of John
respecting a certain occasion when the "passover was nigh at hand; and many
went out of the country up to Jerusalem before the passover, to purify themselves
."—John xi, 55. The self-washings could all be performed by the people at home.
But, in the later period of Jewish history, the ashes were kept at Jerusalem, and the
sprinkling of the unclean usually performed there by the priests alone. Hence, the
coming of these Jews to Jerusalem for purifying before the feast. It is thus evident
that at all the annual feasts, the preparatory purifying of the people must have
been a very conspicuous feature of the occasion, a fact of no little significance, as
bearing upon the observances in the Eleusinian mysteries, already referred to.

We have shown the name of *baptism* to have been used to designate both the
Levitical rite of sprinkling with the water of separation and the ritual purifyings
invented by the scribes. With the growth of ritualistic zeal, the occasions for the
latter observances were multiplied. The earliest allusion to them, in the life of our
Savior, appears in connection with his first miracle, wrought in Cana of Galilee at
the marriage feast. "There were set there six water pots of stone, after the manner
of the purifying of the Jews, containing two or three firkins apiece."—John ii, 6.
That this provision for the purposes of ritual purifying upon such an occasion was
absolutely necessary, in obedience to the traditions of the scribes, will presently
appear.

The next occasion on which these rites come into notice, is recorded by Luke.
In the course of our Lord's second tour through Galilee, after having preached the

gospel to a vast concourse, "a certain Pharisee besought him to dine with him: and he went in, and sat down to meat. And when the Pharisee saw it, he marveled that he had not first *baptized* (*ebaptisthē*), before dinner. And the Lord said unto him, Now do ye Pharisees make clean the outside of the cup and the platter; but your inward part is full of ravening and wickedness. Ye fools, did not he that made that which is without make that which is within also? But rather give alms of such things as ye have; and behold all things are clean unto you."—Luke xi, 37-41.

The next incident is mentioned very briefly by Matthew (xv, 1-9), and more fully in Mark. The apprehensions of the rulers at Jerusalem seem to have been aroused by reports of Christ's ministry, and the excitement caused by it among the people of Galilee. And as they had formerly sent messengers to challenge John, so, now, scribes and Pharisees from Jerusalem were on the watch to find occasion against Jesus. And "when they saw some of his disciples eat bread with defiled, that is to say, with unwashen hands, they found fault. For the Pharisees and all the Jews, except they wash their hands oft, eat not, holding the tradition of the elders. And when they come from the market, except they *baptize* (*ean mē baptisōntai*), they eat not, and many other things there be which they have received to hold, as the *baptisms* (*baptismous*), of cups and pots, brazen vessels and tables" (or "beds." So the margin and the Greek.)—Mark vii, 1-4.

These are the only places in which the ritual purifyings of the Pharisees are so mentioned as to shed light upon the subject of our inquiry. In them, we trace three distinct observances. These are enumerated by Mark, who represents them as common to "the Pharisees and all the Jews." They are, (1) Washing the hands, before meals; (2) Baptism, after coming from the markets; (3) The baptisms of utensils and furniture.

Section XLVIII.—*Washing the Hands before Meals.*—Origin of the rite.
    The marriage feast

It appears to have been a custom, enjoined by tradition and observed by all the Jews, always to wash the hands ritually before eating. The origin and meaning of the tradition may probably be inferred from a few Scriptural facts. (1.) Flesh was used for sacrifice, before it was given to man for food. Compare Gen. i, 29; iv, 4; viii, 20; ix, 3. It was thus transferred from the altar to the table. (2.) One essential idea in the Levitical system as to sacrifice, was communion of Israel with God at his table. Of this, the passover was but one among many illustrations which the books of Moses contain. (Deut. xii, 17, 18, 27, etc.) (3.) Hence, all eating of flesh was treated as sacrificial in its nature, and, therefore, the prohibition of blood—a prohibition perpetuated in the church by the apostles. (Gen. ix, 4; Lev. xvii, 3-14; Deut. xii, 20-27; Acts xv, 20, 29.[67]) If, to these facts be added the rule which required the priests to wash themselves before entering upon their official duties, one of which was the eating of the sacrificial flesh in the holy place, and the words of the Psalm-

---

[67] This is not the place to enlarge upon the present obligation of this law. In the above places, the reader will find it, as at first given to Noah, as expounded and perpetuated under the Levitical dispensation, and as again re-enforced upon the Gentile churches by the apostles. When and why was it abrogated?

ist,—"I will wash mine hands in innocency, so will I compass thine altar, O Lord" (Psa. xxvi, 6), we will have the probable foundation of the ritualistic structure.

As to the mode of these washings, the rules given in the ritual law are very significant. But two cases in which the washing of the hands was required are there found. One of these is the washing of the hands of the elders in expiation of a concealed murder. (Deut. xxi, 3-9.) Here the circumstances render it certain that the water was poured on the hands. The other is mentioned in Lev. xv, 11, where the English, "rinsed," represents the Hebrew, shātaph, to dash, or pour on with violence. If the Jews imitated the Levical rites they did not immerse their hands. Mark throws but little light upon the mode of the Pharisaic washing. In the expression, "except they wash their hands oft," the last word of the original (pugmē,—"oft"), probably had a technical meaning, by which the mode was designated. But if such was the case, that meaning has been lost. By some writers, it is interpreted, "to the elbows," "to the wrist," "with closed fist," etc. But all this is mere conjecture, as is the opinion of Dr. Lightfoot, that it denoted a certain form of the affusion of water upon the hands.

The account of the marriage feast affords ground for surer deductions. There were set six water pots of stone, holding two or three firkins apiece. Whatever were the rites referred to by Mark, under the two designations of "washing the hands," and "baptism," it was necessary that sufficient water should be provided for all occasions of both kinds which were likely to occur, in the large concourse of wedding guests, of whom Christ and the apostles were but a small proportion. For, whilst the guests, generally, were expected, of course, to make use of the ordinary rite, by washing their hands, there might be numbers who had incurred such exposure as to require the appointed *baptism*. What, then, are the indications as to the nature of the rites thus provided for?

The capacity of the water-pots, according to the most probable estimate, was not more than ten gallons each. The highest supposition sets them at about eighteen. They were, therefore, altogether too small to have been used as bath-tubs, for the immersion of the guests. The possibility, therefore, of such a necessity, did not enter into the calculations of those who provided for the occasion. Were the water-pots, then, used for immersing the hands? The customs of the east, then and to this day,—the fact that Jesus and his disciples evidently appear as but a small proportion of the guests,—and the quantity of wine miraculously made by Jesus for their supply, unite to certify that the great body of the community of Cana was present at the feast. The first suggestion, therefore, that presents itself is, that the supposed process must soon have rendered the water disgusting, from its use in the manner supposed, by a succession of persons. Another and conclusive fact is the use made by our Savior of these waterpots. The feast had been some time in progress, so that the guests had "well drunk," before the exhausting of the wine. All had been purified, and the pots, appropriated to that use, stood with the remaining water, as thus left. When, Jesus said to the servants,—"Fill the waterpots with water," "they filled them to the brim," and immediately carried the wine to the governor of the feast. The servants were ignorant of the purpose of Jesus, and, as the narrative shows, simply did as they were directed. There was no emptying of foul water.

There was no cleansing of the waterpots. There is no consciousness, manifested in the narrative, of occasion for it. Nor was there time. It was in the midst of the feast; and the wine was already exhausted, although the ruler of the feast and the guests were unaware of it. (V. 9.) The account of the transaction was written by John, an eye-witness, for the information of cotemporaries who were familiar with the rites of purifying, whatever they were. And had they been performed *in* the water, in any way, an explanation was necessary, or the inference became inevitable that the vessels were used just as they stood. In these circumstances, is it to be imagined that the waterpots already contained the washings of the guests; or even that they were emptied of these and then appropriated as recepticles of the wine, which was immediately served to the very persons who had just washed in them? Clearly, the facts compel the conclusion that "the purifyings of the Jews," here provided for were not done *in* the waterpots, but with water taken from them, and poured or sprinkled on the guests.

This conclusion is confirmed by the explicit testimony of the rabbins. Rabbi Akiva was a doctor of the law of the most eminent reputation, his disciples being numbered by thousands. He was president of the sanhedrim, less than one hundred years after the death of Christ. Being made prisoner by the Romans, upon the suppression of the insurrection of Bar Kokeba, of which he was an active promoter, he was thrown into prison awaiting execution. When food was brought to him, the jailer thinking the supply of water too liberal, poured the greater part on the ground. The rabbi although famishing of thirst, directed what remained to be *poured upon his hands*, saying, "It is better to die with thirst than to transgress the traditions of the elders."

Section XLIX.—*Baptism upon return from Market.*—Market defined. Jesus at the Pharisee's table

Another point in Mark's statement is, that, "When they come from the market, except they *baptize*, they eat not." Here, it would seem that Mark means something different and more important than the ordinary washing of the hands, to which he has just before referred. It is an additional statement, of other rites employed on special occasions. The word, *agora*, which is translated "the market," has a much more extensive signification than the English word. Its primary meaning is, a concourse, an assembly, of any kind. And while it was used among others, to designate the assemblies for traffic, and hence the places of such assemblies, it is not, in the text, to be understood in that limited sense; but as comprehensive of all promiscuous assemblages of the people, in which a person was liable unwittingly to come in contact with the unclean. It was upon occasion of our Savior's coming from such an assembly, that the Pharisee of whom Luke informs us was surprised that he had not first *baptized* before dinner. He had been preaching in the midst of a multitude "gathered thick together" (Luke xi, 29), when he received and accepted the invitation to dine. He had thus been exposed to a contact which the Pharisees would have carefully avoided, as liable to involve them, unaware, in the extremest defilement, and to render necessary special rites of purifying. This was undoubtedly the cause of the surprise of the Pharisee at the conduct of Jesus.

As to the mode of the baptism here referred to, the gospels are silent. In favor of the supposition that it was immersion, there is nothing whatever in the Scriptures. It rests wholly upon the assumption that that is the meaning of *baptizo*. The circumstances all very strongly favor the conclusion, that as the major defilements of the Mosaic law were all purged by sprinkling, so this, the major defilement of Pharisaic tradition was cleansed in a kindred way. Among the indications in favor of this conclusion are, the fact that the provision made for purifying at the marriage feast excludes the idea of immersion;—the entire silence of the Scriptures as to any facilities for that purpose;—the incongruity of the supposition to the circumstances of Jesus, in the act of sitting down at the Pharisee's table;—the absence from the narrative of any allusion to means provided by the Pharisee for the performance, in that mode, of a rite by him so highly esteemed, and for which special provision was necessary;—and the improbability of such a form gaining prevalence among "the Pharisees and all the Jews," involving, of necessity, both expense and labor, to an intolerable extent. If, on the contrary, as we may reasonably suppose, the house of the Pharisee was provided with appliances, "after the manner of the purifying of the Jews," they would consist of water pots set at the door, as at the marriage feast, out of which the guests, as they entered, could take water for pouring on their hands, or baptizing their persons by sprinkling, without inconvenience or delay.

We have formerly seen that the self-washings of the Mosaic law,—in which alone its advocates have ever pretended that immersion may be found in the Old Testament,—were of continual recurrence in every family. We find in the time of Christ the rites supplemented by those now in question, which were of even more frequent occasion. If they were performed by self-washing, by affusion, or by sprinkling, such provision of vessels as thus indicated was all-sufficient. But if they were immersions of the person, the almost daily necessities of every family would have required not only an extraordinary supply of water, but a capacious bath tub in every house. Without such a vessel and supply, at home, immersion of the person, with the frequency required, was not merely improbable; it was impossible. But such arrangements would have involved an amount of expense and of labor which no people could endure.

If we open the Scriptures to inquire what is their testimony on this point, on which, if the system of immersion was in operation, some hints could not fail to appear, we find that the one only statement or allusion is contained in the account of the six water pots at the marriage feast. They were set "after the manner of the purifying of the Jews." This expression, alike in itself, and in the attendant circumstances, as already considered, is exclusive of the supposition that any purifying rite was observed among the Jews, for which the water pots were not a sufficient provision. In short, all the evidence concurs to determine that "the purifying of the Jews," however performed, was not by immersion of the person.

Section L.—*A Various Reading.*—Baptizōntai and rantizōntai. Care taken in transcribing the New Testament. These two readings

There is a various reading, in the Greek manuscripts, which is full of meaning with reference to our present inquiry. Whilst many manuscripts, including the Alexandrian, which is referred to the fifth century, read *baptisōntai*,— "except they *baptize* they eat not," (Mark vii, 4); the two oldest and of the highest authority, the codices Sinaiticus and Vaticanus, both dating from the fourth century, and with them numbers of a later date, read, *rantisōntai*, "except they *sprinkle* they eat not." The presumption is very strong in favor of *rantisōntai* being the true reading. Its bearing on the logical connection of Mark's statement is worthy of note. According to it, he describes three classes of rites. He specifies, first, *self-washings* of the hands, as always used before dinner; second, certain *sprinklings*, resorted to upon supposition of more serious defilements; and third, *baptisms* of pots and cups, etc., the modes of purifying, for which, prescribed in the law, were various. The relation of these purifyings to those appointed by Moses is apparent. They coincide with the self-washings, the sprinklings, and the purifying of things prescribed by him. The various readings here involve considerations of great importance. As before stated, *rantisōntai* is the reading of the two oldest and most highly esteemed manuscripts, dating back to within about two hundred and fifty years of the death of the apostle John. These manuscripts are recognized by critical scholars as being so far independent of each other that their various readings indicate the gradual divergence which would progress from copy to copy through several generations of manuscripts; so that the reading on which they unite must have originated, if not with the evangelist, at least very soon after the first publication of his gospel. On the other hand, the reading, *baptisōntai*, first found in the Alexandrian codex, of the fifth century, appears in the great majority of extant manuscripts. We may confidently conclude that there must have been earlier copies of high authority in which this reading was found. It thus appears that at a time but little if any removed from the age of the apostles, these two readings existed side by side in the received copies of the gospel.

This fact is the more significant in view of the jealous care with which the purity of the New Testament text was guarded. So long as the last of the apostles survived, his inspired authority was an available resort on all questions of controversy, arising in the churches. (2 Cor. xi, 28; 3 John 9, 10.) During this period, the importance of an absolutely pure text of the writings of the apostles and evangelists was not fully appreciated. The work of transcription was left to the zeal of private individuals, who were often wanting in the necessary qualifications; whilst there was no system of responsible revision. It was probably during this period, closing about fifty years after the death of the apostle John, that the most important variations and errors crept in. About that time, the importance of a pure text, as an authoritative standard of appeal on questions of controversy, began to be felt; and, thereafter, great vigilance was exercised by the officers of the church in securing correct copies. The transcriptions were made from the best and most accurate manuscripts. And when a copy was made, it appears to have been subjected to a critical revision, after having been first collated usually by the scribe himself, with the copy from which it was taken, for the purpose of correcting any clerical errors, that might have occurred in the transcription. The manuscript was then handed over to "the corrector," whose business it was to revise the text by a comparison with other available manuscripts. In this office the services of the most learned and able men in the church were employed; and it was not until sanctioned by such revision that a manuscript was accepted as an authentic copy. Beside the process here described, the ancient manuscripts abound in changes made by subsequent critics. The codex Sinaiticus exhibits alterations "by at least ten different revisers, some of them systematically spread over every page, others occasional or limited to separate portions of the manuscript, many of them being cotemporaneous with the first writer; far the greater part belonging to the sixth or seventh century, a few being as recent as the twelfth."[68]

In view of the diligence of the criticism thus systematically exercised, the fact is very remarkable that the two readings, *baptisōntai*, and *rantisōntai* should have been transmitted side by side, and traceable back nearly to the apostolic age. And it is further remarkable, that no one of the ten successive critics whose revisions are traceable on the codex Sinaiticus has corrected the place in question so as to read *baptisōntai*, although it is certain that reading did extensively prevail. Nor is the variation alluded to in the writings of the fathers. It is immaterial to the present argument which is the true reading. If it was *rantisōntai*, the language of Mark explains the meaning of Luke. What the Pharisee expected was that Jesus should have *baptized* himself by *sprinkling*. And, whichever is the true reading, this fact is patent that at an age so early as to be undistinguishable from that of the apostles and evangelists, so intimate was the relation between sprinkling and baptism that the one word was inadvertently substituted for the other, in transcription; and the alteration received by the ablest men in the church, without question or protest, then or afterward, or the betrayal even of a consciousness of change; despite the watchfulness of a criticism systematic in its exercise and jealous for the purity of the text. If the primitive church understood baptism to mean immersion, if the rite was administered in that, as the only Scriptural mode, the occurrence of the case here presented would have been plainly impossible. It could only happen where the two words were identified as designating the same rite. How easily the words might be confounded will appear by a comparison of them as written in the primitive Greek, known as uncials, or capital letters:—

ΒΑΠΤΙΖΩΝΤΑΙ.

ΠΑΝΤΙΖΩΝΤΑΙ.

Were the first and third letters dimly written, or blurred, the one word might readily be taken for the other.

Section LI.—*Baptisms of Utensils and Furniture.*—Their prototypes in
    the Levitical purifyings of things

Another point in Mark's statement is the baptisms of cups and pots, brasen vessels and tables. It is unnecessary to insist upon the argument which is deducible from the practical impossibility of the immersion of these things; nor to notice

[68] Scrivener's Collation of the Codex Sinaiticus, Introduction, p. xx.

the theories which have been devised to overcome the difficulties which it interposes to the Baptist mode. The reader who has followed the course of this history will recognize, in the Levitical ordinances respecting the purifyings of things, the source whence was derived the hint of these supererogatory rites. And a comparison of the various Mosaic regulations on the subject will satisfy the candid reader that the list here given is not designed to be exhaustive, but an exemplification merely of the observances in question. This is further evident from the fact that the enumeration, as made by the Lord Jesus (v. 8), was of pots and cups, only; which Mark in his subsequent account amplifies by the other additional examples. Respecting them, the ritual of Moses provided modes of purifying varied both with respect to the nature of the things to be cleansed, and the character of the defilements; as we have formerly seen. We may well suppose that the scribes did not fail to imitate every form of the legal purifyings, in their additions to the law of God. It is not only possible, but very probable that some of these inventions were in the form of immersion. For, as we have formerly seen, that was one of the forms appointed in the law, for the purifying of things. But the evangelist speaks, not of one, but of various rites; which he designates by the plural and generic name of (*baptismous*), — baptisms. The word thus selected is the very same which is used by Paul as the comprehensive designation of the purifying rites of the Mosaic law, — the "divers baptisms," imposed at Sinai. The conclusion is therefore irresistible, that whilst Paul used the word in a generic sense, as comprehending the various forms of legal purification, among which the immersion of person is not to be found, Mark uses it in a like generic sense as comprehensive of the various forms for the purifying of things, among which immersion *may* have been one, although, if such was the fact, the proof is yet to be produced.

The result of our examination is, that among the Pharisaic rites, no trace of the immersion of the person is to be found.

PART IX.

JOHN'S BAPTISM.

Section LII.—*The History of John's Mission.*—The accounts of it. John
the herald of the Angel of the Sinai covenant

The account of John's ministry in the evangelists, is invariably introduced by
an appeal to the prophecies which foretold his coming and office. A remarkable
passage from Malachi is alluded to by the angel Gabriel, in announcing to Zacharias the birth of the forerunner (Luke i, 17), and by Mark in his introduction to the
gospel. (Mark i, 2). A prophecy of Isaiah is cited in all the gospels; as is also John's
own account of his commission and office. It will be convenient for the purposes of
the present discussion to bring these passages together. Says the Lord by Malachi,
"Behold, I will send my messenger, and he shall prepare the way before me, and
the Lord whom ye seek shall suddenly come to his temple, even the Messenger of
the covenant whom ye delight in; behold he shall come, saith the Lord of hosts. But
who may abide the day of his coming, and who shall stand when he appeareth?
For he is like a refiner's fire and like fuller's soap; and he shall sit as a refiner and
purifier of silver, and he shall purify the sons of Levi, and purge them as gold and
silver, that they may offer unto the Lord an offering in righteousness. Then shall
the offering of Judah and Jerusalem be pleasant unto the Lord, as in the days of
old, and as in former years. And I will come near to you to judgment, and I will be
a swift witness against the sorcerers.... Remember ye the law of Moses my servant
which I commanded unto him in Horeb, for all Israel, with the statutes and judgments. Behold, I will send you Elijah the prophet, before the coming of the great
and dreadful day of the Lord; and he shall turn the heart of the fathers to the children, and the heart of the children to their fathers, lest I come and smite the earth"
(the land of Israel) "with a curse."—Mal. iii, 1-5; iv, 4-6.

The citation from Isaiah (xl, 3-5), together with John's exposition of it, is thus
given by Luke. "John came into all the country about Jordan, preaching the baptism of repentance for the remission of sins; as it is written in the book of the words
of Esaias the prophet, saying, The voice of one crying in the wilderness, Prepare ye
the way of the Lord; make his paths straight. Every valley shall be filled, and every
mountain and hill shall be brought low; and the crooked shall be made straight,
and the rough ways shall be made smooth; and all flesh shall see the salvation of
God. Then said he to the multitude that came forth to be baptized of him, O generation of vipers, who hath warned you to flee from the wrath to come? Bring forth,
therefore, fruits worthy of repentance, and begin not to say within yourselves, We
have Abraham to our father; for I say unto you that God is able of these stones to

raise up children unto Abraham. And now also the axe is laid unto the root of the trees; every tree, therefore, which bringeth not forth good fruit is hewn down, and cast into the fire.... I indeed baptize you with water; but one mightier than I cometh, the latchet of whose shoes I am not worthy to unloose; he shall baptize you with the Holy Ghost and with fire; whose fan is in his hand, and he will thoroughly purge his floor, and will gather the wheat into his garner; but the chaff he will burn with fire unquenchable." — Luke iii, 3-17. In John's gospel, some additional points are given. "John seeth Jesus coming unto him, and saith, Behold the Lamb of God which taketh away the sin of the world. This is he of whom I said, After me cometh a man which is preferred before me; for he was before me. And I knew him not; but that he should be made manifest to Israel, therefore am I come baptizing with water. And John bare record, saying, I saw the Spirit descending from heaven, like a dove, and it abode upon him. And I knew him not, but He that sent me to baptize with water, the same said unto me, Upon whom thou shalt see the Spirit descending and remaining on him, the same is he which baptizeth with the Holy Ghost. And I saw, and bare record, that this is the Son of God." — John i, 29-34.

The title by which, in the prophecy of Malachi, the Lord Jesus is designated, — "the *Messenger of the covenant*," carries us back to the scene at Sinai, when the covenant was made and sealed. In the close of the prophecy, our attention is expressly directed to that occasion. "Remember the law of Moses, which I commanded unto him in Horeb, for all Israel, with the statutes and judgments." The intimations thus given lead us up to the originating occasion of John's testimony.

Immediately after the coming of Israel to Sinai, among the communications which expounded the covenant, preparatory to its sealing, the Lord said to them, "Behold I send an Angel before thee, to keep thee in the way, and to bring thee into the place which I have prepared. Beware of him and obey his voice. Provoke him not, for he will not pardon your transgressions; for my name is in him." — Ex. xxiii, 20, 21. This Angel is by the Lord elsewhere called "My Presence" (Compare Ex. xiv, 19; xxxii, 34; xxxiii, 2, 14, 15), and by Isaiah, "the Angel of His presence." — Isa. lxiii, 9. He is thus announced to Israel as sent to be God's servant in the fulfilling of the Sinai covenant, and is hence by the prophet called "the Messenger of the covenant."

Another line of facts leads in the same direction. When, at the mount, Israel was overwhelmed with the terror of the great fire and of God's audible voice, and entreated Moses, "Speak thou with us, and we will hear; but let not God speak with us lest we die" (Ex. xx, 19; Deut. v, 22-27), their proposal thus to accept Moses as Mediator between them and God was graciously approved. "They have well said, all that they have spoken." — Deut. v, 28. Moses was accepted in that office, and Israel dismissed from the assembly at the mount. (Ib. 28-31.) But, afterward, Moses revealed to them how much more richly their abasement and prayer had been answered than they had asked or imagined. "The Lord thy God will raise up unto thee a prophet from the midst of thee, of thy brethren like unto me; unto him ye shall hearken; according to all that thou desiredst of the Lord thy God in Horeb, in the day of the assembly, saying, Let me not hear again the voice of the Lord my God, neither let me see this great fire any more that I die not. And the Lord said unto me, They have well spoken that which they have spoken. I will raise them up a prophet from among their brethren, like unto thee, and will put my words in His mouth; and He shall speak unto them all that I shall command Him."—Deut. xviii, 15-18. Compare John xiv, 31; xvii, 8, 14.

We are thus brought to the relation which Moses and the Sinai covenant, sustained to the Lord Jesus, and that better covenant of which he is the Mediator. (Heb. viii, 6.) The covenant of Sinai as formally accepted by Israel and ratified through the mediation of Moses, was of unspeakable moment, as being the installation of the visible church. But it was, at the same time, an outward type, a manifestation and announcement of the covenant of grace made with the invisible church. Of the one, Moses was the Mediator;—of the other, the Lord Jesus. The one is founded upon the public professions and promises of Moses and the assembly of Israel (Ex. xxxiv, 27);—the other on the engagement of the Lord Jesus to fulfill all righteousness. The former was graven on tables of stone; the latter is written in the fleshly tables of the hearts of Christ's people. (Jer. xxxi, 33; 2 Cor. iii, 3; Heb. viii, 10.) The former was sealed with the blood which was partly sprinkled on the Sinai altar, and partly mingled with water and sprinkled on Israel; the latter, with the blood of sprinkling of Jesus Christ offered in the holy place in heaven, and the baptism of the Spirit which, through the merits of that blood, he gives his people.

We can now see the bearing of certain memorable words uttered by the Lord Jesus. When Moses sealed the covenant, he sprinkled the book and the people with the sacrificial blood and water, saying, "Behold, the blood of the covenant, which the Lord hath made with you concerning all these words." At the table, the night of the betrayal, the Lord Jesus took the cup, and having given thanks, gave it to the disciples, saying, "This is my blood of the new covenant, which is shed for many, for the remission of sins."—Matt. xxvi, 28. He thus signified the typical nature of the transaction in the wilderness, as relating to him, and announced himself about to fulfill all that it foreshadowed. Particularly did his language, by appropriating that of the Sinai baptism, recognize both it and the supper as symbols and seals of the remission of sins, of which his own blood bestows the reality.

To the same relation between the Sinai transactions and Christ's office and work, Peter bears witness. A few days after Pentecost, upon occasion of the healing of the impotent man, he reminded the wondering assembly of the promise made by Moses to the fathers.—"A prophet shall the Lord your God raise up unto you of your brethren, like unto me.... Yea and all the prophets, from Samuel and those that follow after, as many as have spoken, have likewise foretold *of these days*."—Acts iii, 22-24.

> Section LIII.—*Israel at the Time of John's Coming.*—No longer idolatrous, but apostate. Prophetic warnings. They were excommunicate from the covenant

When John came, the Jews had been for four hundred years without a prophet, or any sensible token of God's presence among them. The captivity and return from Babylon and subsequent circumstances in their history had effectually and finally cured the inveterate tendency to idolatry, which had characterized them from the days of the Egyptian bondage. But this change did not bring with it an awakening of true spiritual devotion to the service of God. Instead thereof an intense zeal of self-righteousness was cherished, under the two forms of a fanatical pride in the blood of Abraham, and an ardent devotion to the external forms and rites of religion, to tithes and offerings, to fastings and purifyings, — to "righteousnesses of the flesh," — whilst the spirituality and power of the divine law were obscured and set aside by the glosses and interpretations of the elders. Such was the religion of the scribes, who "sat in Moses' seat," as the instructors of the people. The great mass of the nation, led by these blind guides, were with them hastening to destruction; while the few who still sought after the God of their fathers were as sheep without a shepherd. In the meantime, Jerusalem and Judea had been the prey alternately of the Ptolemies of Egypt, the Seleucidæ of Syria, and factions among themselves. After the successful revolt of the Maccabees, a brief time of peace and prosperity was enjoyed under the sceptre of that family. But the rivalry and seditions of its members brought in the Romans, under whose patronage the Herodian family, of Edomite origin, had come into power.

During the progress of these events, the whole land had been polluted with crimes and atrocities of every kind, and of the deepest dye. The high priesthood was habitually subject to barter and sale, one possessor of the office giving place to another in rapid succession, as the respective aspirants were able to purchase the office from the kings of Syria, or of Judea, or to seize it by violence or the favor of the rabble. The temple itself had been desecrated by being formally set apart to the worship of Jupiter Olympius. And as though that was not enough, it had been yet more horribly defiled by fratricidal blood; an aspirant for the high priesthood having secured and held the office by the murder of his own brother, in the very precincts of the temple. The entire social system was rotten, and the nation was fast ripening for the developments about to be witnessed, in the denial and crucifixion of the Son of God, the rejection of the gospel, and the crimes which precipitated society into a chaos of anarchy and a reign of terror, ending in the destruction of the temple, the desolation of Jerusalem, and the dispersion of the nation to this day.

Thus, when John began his ministry, the land of Israel, the city, the temple, and the nation were lying under the burden of the unexpiated and unrepented crimes of many centuries. (Matt. xxiii, 29-36.) The covenant was forfeited and trampled under foot, and the land and the people were, in every sense, moral and ritual, utterly unclean. At the beginning of the declension, the prophet Haggai had been sent to the priests with a lesson out of the law. — "Ask now the priests concerning the law, saying, If one bear holy flesh in the skirt of his garment, and with his skirt do touch bread, or pottage, or wine, or oil, or any meat, shall it be holy? And the priests answered and said, No. Then said Haggai, If one that is unclean by a dead body touch any of these, shall it be unclean? And the priests answered and said, It shall be unclean. Then answered Haggai, and said, So is this people, and so is this nation before me, saith the Lord: and so is every work of their hands, and that which they offer there is unclean." — Hag. ii, 11-14. After the cotemporaneous ministries of Haggai and Zechariah, the Spirit of prophecy was withdrawn for about one hundred years. Then suddenly, a trumpet note from Malachi broke the silence, with a brief and startling call.—"If ye will not hear, and if ye will not lay it to heart, to give glory unto my name, saith the Lord of hosts, I will even send a curse upon you, and I will curse your blessings. Yea I have cursed them already.... From the days of your fathers, ye are gone away from mine ordinances and have not kept them. Return unto me, and I will return unto you, saith the Lord of hosts.—Mal. ii, 2; iii, 7. But they did not return. Thereupon, God their King withdrew from all communication with them as a people, for four centuries following.

Such was the situation of that people at the coming of John. They had the oracles of God, his ordinances, and his temple; of which Haggai had said,—"I will shake all nations; and the Desire of all nations shall come, and I will fill this house with glory, saith the Lord of hosts."—Hag. ii, 7. But all this was as a piece of holy flesh in the skirt of a garment. It did not purify the nation, while their uncleanness defiled these and all their hallowed things.

Section LIV.—*The Nature and End of John's Baptism.*—Elijah the champion of the covenant, to the ten tribes. John the same to the Jews. His baptism renewed the Sinai seal

Whilst Israel was thus apostate and excommunicate from God, the Messenger of his covenant was about to appear, in that character the aspect of which, as toward the rebellious and unbelieving, had been especially emphasized in the prophecies above cited; and the exercise of which resulted in the desolation of the land, and the dispersion of the nation a byword and a hissing in all lands. "Beware of him and obey his voice. Provoke him not; for he will not pardon your transgressions; for my Name is in him."—Ex. xxiii, 21. "Who may abide the day of his coming? And who shall stand when he appeareth?"—Mal. iii, 2. So, John announced him.—"Whose fan is in his hand, and he will thoroughly purge his floor, and gather his wheat into the garner, but he will burn up the chaff with unquenchable fire."—Matt. iii, 12. His coming was, to Israel, the great crisis in their history. Therefore the mission of John. Said the angel to Zacharias, "He shall go before Him in the Spirit and power of Elias, to turn the hearts of the fathers to the children and the disobedient to the wisdom of the just; to make ready a people prepared for the Lord."—Luke i, 17.

When the ten tribes had forsaken the worship of God on mount Zion, abandoned his covenant, and devoted themselves to the worship of Baal and Ashtoreth, Elijah was sent to them as the vindicator of the forsaken covenant, and messenger of grace, of warning and of judgment. His first work was to demonstrate the sovereignty and Godhead of Jehovah, and the imbecility of their false gods, by the famine of three years and six months, and by the fire from heaven consuming both sacrifice and altar on Carmel. He then executed judgment upon the prophets of Baal and Ashtoreth, the seducers of Israel, eight hundred and fifty in number. On this occasion, Israel professed to recognize and do homage to the God of their fathers. But Elijah saw too clearly, that it was a conviction without root in their hearts and affections. When therefore he received Jezebel's message of vengeance, his faith failed, and he fled to the wilderness, where he was fed by an angel and led forty days and forty nights "to Horeb the mount of God," the spot where the covenant was made and sealed with the twelve tribes. (1 Kings xix, 8, 9.) "And he came thither unto a cave and lodged there; and behold the word of the Lord came to him, and He said to him, What dost thou here, Elijah?" The interview held at that place exhibits the prophet as the ordained champion and avenger of the covenant. To the foregoing question twice proposed, he twice responds,—"I have been very jealous for the Lord God of hosts: for the children of Israel have *forsaken thy covenant*, thrown down thine altars; and slain thy prophets with the sword; and I, even I, only, am left; and they seek my life to take it away."—vs. 10, 14. Thereupon, he was commissioned to anoint Hazael, king over Syria; and Jehu king of Israel, and Elisha to be prophet in his stead;—"And it shall come to pass that him that escapeth the sword of Hazael shall Jehu slay; and him that escapeth from the sword of Jehu shall Elisha slay. Yet I have left seven thousand in Israel, all the knees which have not bowed unto Baal, and every mouth which hath not kissed him."—vs. 15-18.

The office thus fulfilled by Elijah, as a messenger of grace, calling Israel back to the allegiance of the abandoned covenant; and of wrath, announcing and inflicting its penalty upon the transgressors, is the key to the closing words of the book of Malachi.—"Remember ye the law of Moses my servant, which I commanded unto him in Horeb for all Israel, with the statutes and judgments. Behold, I will send you Elijah the prophet, before the coming of the great and dreadful day of the Lord;" the day, to wit, of the coming of "the Messenger of the covenant;" "and he shall turn the heart of the fathers to the children and the heart of the children to their fathers, lest I come and smite the land with a curse."—Mal. iv, 4-6. The same characteristics of John's ministry were the occasion of the statement of the angel Gabriel to Zacharias, before cited, "He shall go before Him, in the Spirit and power of Elias." In the points here noticed, we have the explanation of the scene of the transfiguration, in which Moses, the mediator of the Sinai covenant, Elijah its vindicator against apostate Israel,—and Jesus, the mediator of the new covenant, talked together "of his decease which he should accomplish at Jerusalem," on behalf of the true Israel, and in fulfillment of the terms of the new covenant, typified in that of Sinai. (Luke ix, 31.)

The same office, of warning and testimony on behalf of the forsaken covenant, which Elijah exercised toward the ten tribes, John fulfilled to the Jews. To understand the full force and significance of his mission, the fact must be distinctly appreciated that Christ's humiliation and sufferings, however momentous in themselves, and however transcendently important to us, were a mere transient incident in the work undertaken by him. His coming into the world was a coming to the throne, to which the cross was a mere stepping stone,—a means to his exaltation, and to the achievements of his sceptre, in purging the Father's floor. In those achievements, justice and judgment are as conspicuous as grace; and if the latter witnessed a first signal and glorious display in the scenes of Pentecost, the former was as signally illustrated in the destruction and desolation of the city and land that rejected their King. It was with a view to the crisis thus created in the history of Israel by the coming of Christ, that John was sent as his forerunner and herald. John did not ignore that abasement of Christ which was the antecedent condition and means of his exaltation and glory. But his distinctive theme, the subject which filled his heart and inspired his tongue, was the throne, the kingdom, the power and justice. Of it he was the official herald, and from it his preaching and baptism took their form and significance. His commission was threefold; (1) To announce the kingdom of heaven at hand, and herald the coming of the King, the Messenger of the covenant, the Baptizer with the Holy Ghost and with fire; (2) To identify and point him out in the person of Jesus; (3) To prepare the way before him. In fulfillment of the first and second of these functions, John preached the coming of "One Mightier than I," who should baptize Israel with the Holy Ghost and with fire. He pointed out and announced the Lord Jesus as that coming One,—"the Lamb of God that taketh away the sin of the world,"—"the Son of God." And by connecting this testimony with his proclamation and baptism of repentance for the remission of sins, he anticipated the preaching of the apostles, and summed and published the gospel of atonement and remission through the blood of Christ. By this preaching and by the seal of baptism to those who received his testimony he fulfilled the third function above mentioned, and "made ready a people prepared for the Lord."—Luke i, 17.

There were two termini to which John's baptism sustained peculiar and intimate relations, and from which his ministry derived all its significance. The first was that "day of the assembly" at Sinai, when Israel entered into the covenant by which she took God as her King and received the baptismal seal sprinkled by the hand of Moses. It was the office of John to announce the personal coming of the King of Israel; to warn them of the penalty of the violated covenant; announce the remission of sins and restoration of the covenant, to those who should repent and return to their allegiance; and to certify this by the renewal of the broken seal.

The second terminus to which John's baptism looked was that day when the covenant King of Israel should appear in person, assume his throne, and enter on the functions announced by John, under the figures of the baptism of the Holy Ghost, and the baptism of fire. Of the former, so conspicuous in the prophecies, the baptism of Israel by Moses, and that now administered by John, were alike typical. The grace of the Holy Spirit, administered by the enthroned Baptizer, was the end and fulfillment of both.

> Section LV.—*The Extent of John's Baptism.*—Testimony of the evange-
> lists. Other evidence. A great revival

The public ministry of John commenced about six months before the baptism of Jesus, and was terminated by his imprisonment soon after that event. (Mark i, 14; Luke iii, 20, 21.) At first, his preaching was peripatetic. "He came into all the country about Jordan, preaching."—Luke iii, 3. But as his fame extended and the throng of his hearers increased, he took his station at Bethabara (or, Bethany, as the critical editions read), on the eastern side of the Jordan, and afterward at "Enon, near to Salim," where he seems to have been, when arrested by Herod. During the brief period of his ministry, there "went out to him Jerusalem, and all Judea, and all the region round about Jordan, and were baptized of him in Jordan, confessing their sins."—Matt. iii, 5, 6. The facts as to the extent of John's ministry and baptism, are stated in terms equally strong by Mark and Luke. (Mark i, 5; Luke iii, 21.) Of these statements, we are asked to believe that they are extravagant hyperbole,—that they only mean that there were some present from every place in the regions specified. As "if I should say that in the political convention of 1840, all Tennessee was gathered at Nashville to hear Henry Clay, I would not mean that every man, woman, and child in the State was there; but only that there were some from every part. Just so, Matthew says Jerusalem came,—that a great many people from Jerusalem and Judea and the country round about Jordan came. That is to say, the country as well as the city was fully represented in the crowd. Besides, John did not baptize all who came. He positively refused the Pharisees and Sadducees, who composed a great part of the Jewish nation."[69] This explanation forgets that the language in question is not the exaggerated statement of excited and partisan newsmongers; but sober history dictated by the Spirit of God, and reported to us by "two or three witnesses," in concurrent language. As to the assertion concerning the Pharisees, every thoughtful reader of the gospels knows that in comparison with the whole body of the people, they were very few. In all their conspiracies against Jesus they were constantly embarrassed by fear of "the people."

Of the vastness of the multitude who were baptized by John we have not only the express testimony of the evangelists, but certain incidents related by them remarkably confirm it. The first is, that Herod was restrained, for some time, from the murder of John, by fear of the people, "because they counted him as a prophet."—Matt. xiv, 5. Another is, the use made of the same popular sentiment, by the Lord Jesus. A few days before his betrayal and death, upon occasion of his second purging of the temple, the rulers came to him demanding by what authority he did these things. Jesus answered, "I will also ask you one thing; and answer me: The baptism of John, Was it from heaven, or of men? And they reasoned with themselves, saying, If we shall say, From heaven; he will say, Why then believed ye him not? But and if we say, Of men; all the people will stone us: for they be persuaded that John was a prophet. And they answered, that they could not tell whence it was."—Luke xx, 3-7; Matt. xxi, 24; Mark xi, 29. Such and so strong and universal was the conviction of the people, that John's commission was from God, that neither Herod nor the whole united body of the priests, scribes and elders,—the great council of the nation,—dared to antagonize it. This, too, was three years after the close of John's ministry.

It may be said that no intimation is here given that the people spoken of had been baptized of John. But, in the first place, the evangelists had already expressly stated the universal fact, in their distinct account of his ministry, and did not, therefore, need to repeat it; and, in the second, the issue involved in his ministry was too vital and sharply defined to allow any to profess, even, to recognize his divine authority, and yet neglect his baptism. But there is yet further testimony on the point.

Jesus had been preaching about two years, when John from his prison sent two of his disciples to ask,—"Art thou he that should come, or do we look for another? On this occasion Jesus uttered a testimony concerning John, of which it

---

[69] Theodosia Ernest, Vol. I, p. 79. Published by the Baptist Publication Society.

is said that, "all the people that heard him, and the publicans, justified God, *being baptized with the baptism of John*. But the Pharisees and the lawyers rejected the counsel of God against themselves; being not baptized of him." —Luke vii, 29, 30. This occurred in Galilee, which district was not included in any of the statements of the evangelists, respecting the attendance on John's ministry. He does not seem ever to have preached in Galilee. And yet, from that comparatively distant region, the people had so flocked to his baptism, that two years afterward the evangelist could state that all the people had been baptized of him, the lawyers and Pharisees excepted, and find in this the explanation of the universal acceptance of Christ's testimony. The exception here greatly strengthens the former clause of the statement, and establishes the fact of the universal reception of John's baptism by the common people.

In fact, this conclusion is involved in the very nature of the circumstances of Israel. However viewed, the ministry of John created a most momentous crisis in the history of God's dealings with that people. John came to them, the fore-announced, —the last, —the greatest, of all the prophets. He came on the loftiest mission that had ever been entrusted to man, —to act as the immediate personal messenger and herald of the coming King. He came to Israel, excommunicate from God, to call them individually, and as a people, to repent and return to the fold of God's longsuffering mercy; and to seal the offered grace, by baptizing those who professed to obey his call. The alternative which his ministry set before them was plain and imperative. To absent themselves, or to attend on his preaching without receiving his baptism, would have been an open act of treason to the coming King, an express and aggravated rejection of his authority and of this extraordinary and final overture of grace to the nation. John's ministry thus compelled a decision by which a broad and public line was drawn among the people. On the one side, were those who professed to repent and return to the forsaken covenant and God of their fathers, and to own the authority of the promised King of Israel; and whose profession was sealed by the reception of John's baptism;—on the other, those who, in rejecting John's testimony and turning their backs upon his baptism, repudiated the coming King and spurned his overture of mercy. Of the significance and importance of all this, the evangelists were fully aware. To suppose them in such circumstances to have indulged in a loose and exaggerated style of statement, asserting that Jerusalem, and all Judea, and all the region round about Jordan were baptized, when, in fact, not one in a hundred of the people received the rite, would be a contradiction of the divine testimony, which nothing but ignorance and lack of consideration can excuse or palliate. It is further to be considered that every class of the people, and both men and women resorted to John's baptism, the lawyers or scribes, that is, the Pharisees and Sadducees, only excepted. (Matt. xxi, 31, 32; Luke vii, 29; xx, 6.)

5. His rejection of the Pharisees is adduced as proof that "though great multitudes came to John and followed Christ, yet comparatively few brought forth fruit to justify their baptism."[70] But how is it supposed that John could know any thing, ordinarily, as to the fruits manifested by those who sought his baptism? It

---

[70] Theodosia Earnest, vol. i, p. 80.

is perfectly evident that,—as at Sinai, on the day of Pentecost, and on every other occasion that is on record in the ministry of the apostles,—so, in the case of John's hearers,—a good profession was the sole ordinary condition of baptism. Is it asked,—How, then, came John to refuse the Pharisees? That he did, in fact, refuse them, is an assumption, without proof or probability. He warned them; and that is all we are told of the matter. As to the occasion of such warning,—the ruling sin of that sect was self-righteousness. The pride of it found expression in unmistakable tokens. Says Jesus, "All their works they do for to be seen of men. They make broad their phylacteries, and enlarge the borders of their garments."—Matt, xxiii, 5. The phylacteries were parchments on which portions of the law were written. They were folded in the form of a cube, and bound to the forehead or the arm, with ribbands. The borders were fringes and ribbands of blue, which God directed Israel to wear on the skirts of their garments, as a memorial of their covenant relations to him. (Num. xv, 38, 39.) These the scribes and Pharisees made broad, so as to be seen of men. The first step therefore toward a true repentance, on their part, would have been a putting off of these badges of self-righteousness. And their being worn by any of John's hearers was to him an instant and evident token of vain glory and self-righteousness unabased; whilst putting them off would have been a manifest fruit and evidence of repentance.

The facts, therefore, as set forth in the gospels, clearly indicate that the ministry of John was attended by an apparent revival of religion, but little short of that which occurred at Sinai, when the covenant was first made. And although, like the tribes in the wilderness, many of those who received John's baptism failed to profit, for lack of true repentance and faith,—many brought forth fruit out of good and honest hearts. Of such, the college of the apostles was formed; and of such, no doubt, largely consisted the firstfruits of the gospel, in Judea and Galilee,—as we see repeated traces of it in the ministry of Paul, among the far off Gentiles. (Acts xiii, 24, 25; xviii, 25; xix, 3.)

Section LVI.—*John did not Immerse.*—The circumstances forbade it. It
would have been unmeaning

As to the mode of John's baptism, there are several circumstances which interpose insuperable objections to the supposition that it was by immersion.

1. That form would have been utterly incongruous to John's office as the herald of the covenant. No rational account can be given of the origin and meaning of such a rite, in that connection. The Levitical law was, in all its ordinances, a testimony to the covenant; and of it John was a minister. But in that law there was but one *administered* baptism, and that by sprinkling, whilst there were no immersions of persons, whatever. It therefore furnishes no trace of the origin of the supposed form. On the other hand, it certainly did not originate with John. Baptism,—the rite which he administered, was in his day, no novelty among the Jews. The only remaining supposition, if we assume John to have immersed his disciples, is, that it may have been borrowed from the inventions of the scribes. But, in the first place, there is not a trace of evidence nor of probability that such a rite was *then* included in the ritual of the scribes;—and in the second, it is preposterous to suppose

that, in such circumstances and on such a mission, John would have turned his back on the ordinances of God's law, by which for fifteen centuries the covenant had been sealed, and chosen for the characteristic and seal of his ministry one of those inventions by means of which that law was made void and God's people led astray. (Mark vii, 6, 8, 13.) This too, when he in the most open and decisive manner set himself in opposition to the inventors of those rites, whom he denounced as a generation of vipers!

2. The meaning of the rite, in supposed connection with John's ministry, is as inexplicable as its origin. Neither the law nor the Old Testament Scriptures anywhere give a clue to it. John in his ministry is equally silent. Or, rather, his statements are altogether incongruous to the supposed form.—"He shall baptize you with the Holy Ghost, and with fire. Whose fan is in his hand, and he will thoroughly purge his floor, and gather his wheat into the garner, but he will burn up the chaff with unquenchable fire."—Matt. iii, 11, 12. Thus, John, announced the Lord Jesus, not in his character of humiliation and death; but in his exaltation and royalty, as he appeared at Sinai, the covenant King of Israel,—as he is now, the enthroned Baptizer, dispensing his Spirit and grace to his people, and pouring out the fire of his justice on his and his Father's enemies. In such circumstances, and in connection with such a preaching, what meaning could the disciples of John have discovered in the rite of immersion? Respecting it, they ask no questions, and John makes no explanation. If it be supposed to have meant the burial of Christ, this much at least is certain, that the resemblance was not so close as to have been self-evident to the people. And even though understood by them in that sense, it would have been so far aside from the immediate intent and end of John's ministry, and so defective in its testimony, since it knows nothing of the resurrection, that it would have been calculated to distract and perplex his hearers, rather than to serve the object of his preaching. But John was explicit as to the meaning of his baptism. *Whatever its form, it meant—not the burial of the Lord Jesus, but the baptism of the Spirit by him dispensed. "I baptize you with water, but he shall baptize you with the Holy Ghost."*

3. The great discomfort, and the gross indecency which are inevitably involved in the supposition that John immersed his followers are decisive against it. Neither had John a water-proof suit in which to officiate, nor were his auditors supplied with "immersion robes," nor change of garments, so needful, now, to obviate the discomfort and danger of the dripping attire. But this, even, is a less consideration than the indecent exposure which the supposed rite would have involved. The garments of the Jews were of two patterns. That next the person was in the form of a sleeveless shirt, descending to the knees. A second garment was of the same shape, but usually of more costly materials, which reached to the ankles. Over all were thrown one or two shawls or blankets, large enough to enwrap the entire person. Beside sandals, which were not ordinarily worn, except by those in easy circumstances,—these were the only articles of apparel. Those of the women were of nearly the same shape; the distinction of sex appearing mainly in the materials and ornaments. When at rest, the garments were left free. But in preparing for labor or for travel, they were drawn up to the knees, and fastened with a girdle at

the loins, thus leaving the lower limbs unencumbered. That, with such clothing indecent exposure must have been a constant incident to the extemporaneous and hasty immersions which the Baptist theory requires, is manifest; and the weight of the consideration needs no enforcing.

4. The number resorting to John was such as to preclude the possibility of their having been immersed. When Israel came out of Egypt, they were "about six hundred thousand on foot, that were men, beside children; and a mixed multitude went up also with them."—Ex. xii, 37, 38. When about to enter the promised land, the census was six hundred and one thousand, seven hundred and thirty men, from twenty years old and upward, beside the Levites, who numbered twenty-three thousand males from a month old. (Num. xxvi, 51, 62.) Upon this basis, the whole number of the people was between three and four millions. In the days of David, in the enumeration from which the tribes of Levi and Benjamin were omitted, the number of fighting men was one million five hundred and seventy thousand. If we make a proportional addition for the omitted tribes, it gives a total of one million, eight hundred and fifty-five thousand seven hundred and fifty-four. These would represent a population of seven or eight millions. From two independent statements occurring in Josephus, it appears that the population, just before the destruction of the nation, was at least as much as four million souls.[71] If we suppose John to have stood in the water three hours a day, during the six months of his ministry, and to have administered the rite at the rate of one per minute, during the entire time, the total results of such miraculous labors and endurance, would have been about thirty-two thousand seven hundred and sixty persons baptized, that is, one in every one hundred and twenty-two of the people. Without the intervention of miracle—and John did no miracle—even this was utterly impossible. And yet, how entirely it falls short of the statements of the evangelists, upon any candid interpretation of them, is evident.

That the theory of immersion is encumbered with difficulties of the most serious nature must be evident to every candid reader.

> Section LVII.—*John Baptized by Sprinkling with unmingled Water.*—Why
> the prophecies speak of water only. "The kingdom" John's theme.
> Hence, water only. It was sprinkled. Some may have stood in the
> water

We are now to consider an important feature in the history of this rite, which has not yet been brought into distinct notice. It has appeared how thoroughly the sprinkled baptisms of the Levitical system are identified in their meaning and office with the prophecies concerning the sprinkling of Israel and the nations, and the outpouring of the Spirit, in the days of the Messiah. The point of present interest concerning those prophecies is, that in all the expressions referred to, the figure is that of water alone,—the sacrificial elements never being alluded to in that connection. A coincident fact appears, with relation to John's ministry. In his own announcement he uses language which seems to be emphatic and exclusive,—"I indeed baptize you *with water.*"—Matt. iii, 11; Mark i, 8; Luke iii, 16; John i, 26.

---

[71] Jewish war. II. xiv, 3; and VI. x, 3.

So, Jesus says,—"John truly baptized *with water.*"—Acts i, 5. And Peter refers to it in the same terms. (Ib. xi, 16.) This form of expression constantly used, and the antithesis always stated, between his baptism and that of the Holy Spirit, to be administered by the Lord Jesus, render it certain that John baptized with water alone, without any sacrificial elements. A careful examination of the prophecies above referred to and a consideration of the subject matter of John's preaching, may furnish the explanation of these facts. The Mosaic ritual was constructed with a view to a very full and systematic exposition of the gospel, in the symmetry of its parts and proportions. In the baptisms of that ritual, therefore, provision was made for showing forth, not only the power and grace of the Lord Jesus in the bestowal of the Spirit, but, also, the virtue of his blood, which was the procuring cause of the Spirit's grace. But that blood is the token of humiliation and sufferings. On the contrary, the theme of the prophecies here referred to is, the exaltation and glory of Christ's throne, and the conquests of his saving scepter, after the days of humiliation and sorrow shall have been forever ended. This was the distinctive meaning of the water of the Sinai baptisms, and by the figure of the sprinkling or pouring of bare water, the prophets represent the same thing.

So, when John came in the spirit and power of Elias, he did not, indeed, ignore the office of Christ as the atoning Lamb of God. But his distinctive commission, and the controlling function of his ministry was to herald the coming of their covenant King, in his exaltation and power to an apostate and rebellious nation—to warn them of the office which he would fill, and the judgment which he would execute, who should baptize them, not with the Holy Ghost only, but with fire also. As appropriate, therefore, to this, his office and message, he dispensed a baptism of water alone, which spake of authority, power, and royal grace, and omitted that element which signified humiliation and death.

Whilst the rite was thus modified—its nature and significance remained the same. As already indicated, the quantity of ashes used in dispensing the Levitical baptism was so small as to be wholly inappreciable to the senses. The instruction therein conveyed was dependent upon the association of ideas, and not upon the quantity of the elements used. The bestowal of the Spirit by the Lord Jesus, of necessity, presupposes the sacrifice of himself as the condition and price of his exaltation and power, by which the Spirit is sent and salvation bestowed. What the Levitical blood and ashes of sprinkling expressed the baptism of John implied. The two rites thus conveyed the same instruction, and filled the same office. They were essentially one and the same baptism. The latter form anticipated the immediate sending forth of the gospel to the Gentiles, divested of the sacrificial system and the burdens of the ritual law. That they were the same in mode will not be questioned by any who have candidly traced the foregoing line of investigation. With an enumeration of some of the points therein involved, we will close this branch of our subject.

1. Hitherto the Baptist argument has been entrenched in the definition of *baptizo.* After the same example we now plant ourselves on the ascertained meaning and use of the word, as illustrated in the foregoing pages. We have found it to be the accepted designation for the administered rites of Levitical purifying, which,

in all their circumstantial variations, were performed always by sprinkling. The rite dispensed by John was an administered baptism. It was, therefore, administered after the example of the Levitical system, by sprinkling.

2. John was the herald and champion of the covenant, and the messenger of the Lord Jesus as its surety and king. His commission, as announced by Malachi, was, in God's name, to admonish Israel to "Remember the law of Moses, my servant, which I commanded unto him in Horeb for all Israel, with the statutes and judgments;"—Mal. iv, 4.—"The law of Moses,"—that covenant law by the acceptance of which Israel became the people of God. His ministry derived all its significance from the terms of that covenant, and from the office of its Surety, in purging his floor with the baptisms of the Holy Ghost and of fire. This was the whole theme of his ministry, as it was the whole substance of the prophetic terms of his commission. To seal such a testimony, no rite could have been so appropriate as the perpetuated and familiar form of the Sinai baptism, the original seal of the same covenant, by which its scope and intent were so luminously set forth.

3. John preached the baptism of repentance for the remission of sins, in the name of Him whom God was about to exalt "to be a Prince and a Savior, for to give repentance to Israel and forgiveness of sins."—Acts v, 31. In the Levitical baptism the administrator represented the Lord Jesus in this very function of his grace, and the sprinkled water represented the Holy Spirit shed by him upon his people, by whom that repentance is wrought, and remission conveyed. It was the "purification for sin," the symbol of remission. It was thus a visible representation to his hearers of the very things which John was commissioned to utter in their ears.

4. At the time of John's coming, all the thoughts and conceptions of Israel on the subjects involved in his ministry, except as perverted by the traditions of the scribes, had been molded by the Mosaic ritual respecting the purifying of the unclean, and by the testimonies of the prophets, uttered in the language of that ritual. John was sent, not to ignore or obliterate the impress thus made by the instructions and discipline of fifteen centuries, but to confirm and build upon it, to reiterate and seal the same testimonies. To this end, no other rite was appropriate or congruous, but the old familiar baptism by sprinkling, the interpretation of which was so abundant in the prophets, and the meaning of which was known to all Israel.

5. The baptism administered by the Lord Jesus is never known nor alluded to in the Scriptures under any other form than that of affusion. It is the antitype of the ritual sprinklings of the Old Testament, the fulfillment of all the prophecies of the sprinkling of Israel and the nations, the outpouring of the Spirit upon them; and its fulfillment is in the New Testament invariably spoken of in the same style. To symbolize this, John's baptism must have been by affusion.

6. In the use of this rite, all the difficulties which embarrass the hypothesis of immersion disappear. As, at Sinai, all Israel were baptized at once, so, under John's preaching the number to be baptized would involve no embarrassment, exposure, or exhaustion. As many as were assembled at one time could be baptized in one group, with the hyssop bush. Thus, no excessive fatigue was involved; no time was consumed in mere manual labor; no danger to the health, nor liability to

indecent exposure was incurred. The meaning of the rite was familiar to all, and in its use congruity and symmetry were maintained in every part and relation of John's ministry.

The view thus presented is not inconsistent with the supposition that many of John's disciples may have received the rite while standing in the waters of the Jordan. The law requiring the use of running water, the propriety of the one river of Palestine as a type of the river of the heavenly Canaan, and the necessities of the multitudes who waited on his ministry, united in bringing him to the river. And the rite would be performed by the baptist dipping a hyssop-bush into the stream, and therewith sprinkling those who presented themselves around him. That, in these circumstances many of the people would enter the water is beyond question. The suggestion is to be considered in the light of eastern habits and modes of dress. The people were clothed in loose garments, with no covering to the feet except sandals worn by a few. Coming, the most of them, from a distance on the rocky roads of that country, — the feet sore and lacerated, and the climate hot, — no impulse would have been more natural or more congruous to custom, than to step into the water, for the sake of its refreshing coolness. A curious illustration of this occurs in the Phædrus of Plato. He describes Socrates walking in the environs of Athens accompanied by Phædrus: —

Socrates. "Here; let us turn aside to the Illyssus, and, where you prefer, we can recline in quiet."

Phædrus. "For the occasion, as it seems, I happen to be barefoot, while you are always so. Thus it will be quite convenient for us, wetting our feet in the shallow stream, to walk not without enjoyment, especially at this season of the year and of the day."[72]

It is altogether supposable that Philip and the eunuch stepped thus into the water, as the most convenient way of access to it; and it is equally possible that such may have been the case with many of John's disciples, and that Jesus himself may have been thus baptized. Nor is this a mere fanciful conjecture. Among the remains of Christian art which have been transmitted to us from the third and fourth centuries of our era, there are several representations of the baptism of our Savior, some of them in bronze bas-relief, and some in Mosaic. In them all, John pours water on the head of Jesus. In several, Jesus stands in the Jordan, and John from the bank administers the rite. In others, both are on dry ground. In no instance does John appear in the water. At the date of these representations, immersion is supposed to have been almost universally prevalent in the church. They, therefore, the more forcibly demonstrate the strength and prevalence of the tradition which still survived, representing John to have baptized in the Jordan, by affusion. In them the idea of immersion is doubly excluded, — by the direct representation of the water poured upon the head of Jesus; and by the fact that the invariable position of John, out of the water, renders immersion physically impossible, as administered by him.

---

[72] Platonis Phæd., v.

PART X.

CHRIST'S BAPTISMS AND ANOINTING.

Section LVIII.—*The Meaning of his Baptism by John.*—Various explanations. It was part of his obedience. It sealed him Surety of the covenant, and certified to him triumph in his resurrection

"Then cometh Jesus from Galilee to Jordan unto John, to be baptized of him. But John forbade him, saying, I have need to be baptized of thee; and comest thou to me? And Jesus answering said unto him, Suffer it to be so now; for thus it becometh us to fulfill all righteousness. Then he suffered him."—Matt. iii, 13-15.

Several theories have been advanced, and much discussion had as to the nature and intent of the baptism of Jesus by John. Archbishop Thomson,[73] supposes it to have been, (1.) That the sacrament by which all were hereafter to be admitted into His kingdom might not want his example to justify its use. (2.) That John might have an assurance that his course as the herald of Christ was now completed by his appearance. (3.) That some token might be given that he was indeed the anointed of God. Dr. Dale thinks that it was a public and official announcement of his entrance upon the work of fulfilling all righteousness. He strenuously denies that Jesus was baptized with the baptism of John. "It is one thing to be baptized by John and quite another to receive the 'baptism of John.' The 'baptism of John' was for sinners, demanding 'repentance,' 'fruits meet for repentance,' and promising 'the remission of sins.' But the Lord Jesus Christ was not a sinner, could not repent of sin, could not bring forth fruit meet for repentance on account of sin, could not receive the remission of sin. Therefore, the reception of the 'baptism of John' by Jesus is impossible, untrue, and absurd." But this baptism was his inauguration into the office of fulfilling all righteousness. "No one could share in such an inauguration with a fitness comparable with that of the great Forerunner. And to this fitness of relationship, reference is had in the words—'Thus it becometh us.' 'Thus,' by baptism, 'us,' administered by thee, my Forerunner, to me the Coming One proclaimed by thee; 'now,' entering upon my covenant work, which I now declare and am ready to begin,—'to fulfill all righteousness.' Can there be, in view of the persons, the time, and the circumstances, any other satisfactory interpretation of these great words?"[74]

According to another theory, it is held that as the consecration of Aaron was by baptism, anointing, and sacrifice, so all these were realized in the priestly con-

[73] In Smith's Bib. Dict. article, "Jesus."
[74] Dale's Christic Baptism, pp. 27, 29.

secration of Jesus. First, He was baptized by John. Then, the heavens were opened unto Him, and the Spirit of God descended upon Him, and He was thus "anointed with the Holy Ghost and with power." The sacrifice was not till the end of His earthly ministry, when he offered up Himself.

This latter is perhaps the most commonly received theory on the subject. And yet, a more perplexing and unsatisfactory exposition could hardly be devised. According to it Christ's consecration to the priesthood was a confused imitation of that of Aaron, was partly ritual without meaning, and partly real, and took place, part of it in the beginning of his public ministry, and part at its close, so that until his very death his priesthood was inchoate and incomplete. Upon this explanation, the baptism of Jesus was a mere unmeaning form, in supposed imitation of something in the consecration of Aaron. But Aaron and his consecration and priesthood were, in every part and aspect of them, figures of the true, — of the realities which are in Christ. Aaron's anointing is admitted to have been a symbol of the real anointing of the Holy Spirit, shed upon Jesus. The sacrifices offered at the consecration of Aaron, although by this theory misconceived, are so far correctly spoken of as that their fulfillment was had in Christ's one offering of himself. What then could be meant by Aaron's so called baptism, if its antitype is to be found in the ritual baptism of the Lord Jesus? One rite representing and setting forth another, which is nothing but a defective imitation of the first!

In fact, the washing of Aaron by Moses was not a sacramental baptism at all — a rite, that is, by which blessings of grace are represented and sealed to the recipient. It was as we have already explained a symbolical act setting forth the endowment of the Lord Jesus by the Father with a sinless humanity.

It is not, however, to this washing of Aaron, that reference is usually made by the exponents of this theory. It is said that the priests entered upon their official duties at thirty years of age, and were then set apart by baptism, and that hence Jesus, when "he began to be about thirty years of age," came to be baptized, and enter upon his official work; and reference is made to Num. iv, 3; viii, 7. But the places thus referred to are directions respecting the Levites, the priest's servants, and not concerning the priests at all. Moreover, twenty-five years was the ordinary age of entrance upon the Levitical service. (Num. viii, 24.) The age of thirty seems to have been prescribed with reference to the special labor and responsibility incident to the carrying of the tabernacle and its furniture from place to place, during the sojourn in the wilderness. (See the whole of Num. iv.) Upon such slender foundations are theories built. The law set no limitation to the ages of the priests. The rabbins say that they could not enter on the office until twenty years old. But Aristobulus the son of Alexander was high priest when less than seventeen years old.[75] On the other hand, while the definition as to the Levites was, "from thirty years old and upward even until fifty years old," — Eli was high priest when he died at ninety-eight. (1 Sam. iv, 15.)

Christ's baptism was not his inauguration to the priesthood. His priesthood was neither Aaronic nor earthly. For "if he were on earth, He should not be a priest; seeing that there are priests that offer gifts *according to the law*; who serve

[75] Josephus' Antiquities, XV, iii, 3.

unto the *example* and *shadow* of heavenly things." — Heb. viii, 4, 5. If any part of the ceremonial of Aaron's investiture was a rule of conformity to Jesus, the whole of it was equally so. But he was made a priest, "*not* after the law of a carnal commandment, but after the power of an endless life. For he testifieth, Thou art a priest forever after the order of Melchisedec." — Heb. vii, 16, 17. Christ's consecration to the priesthood and exercise of its functions belong to that "true tabernacle which the Lord pitched and not man." — Heb. viii, 2. He was not installed by human hands. "For the law maketh men high priests which have infirmity. But the word of the oath which was since the law, maketh the Son, who is consecrated forevermore." — Heb. vii, 28.

Dr. Dale understands the Lord Jesus in the above place to mean, — Thus it becomes us, by a united and public act, to announce "my entering upon my covenant work which I now declare, and am ready to begin, 'to fulfill all righteousness.'" But, in the first place, that was not the time of Jesus' entering on the work of fulfilling righteousness. Had it been so, it was too late. He was "made of a woman, made under the law." — Gal. iv, 4, 5. From the hour of his birth, he was fulfilling righteousness, — in the obedience of his childhood, as truly as in the sufferings of the cross. The work on which he entered, after his baptism and anointing by the Spirit, was his prophetic office, in which he announced and offered himself to Israel as her promised King and Savior. So he himself testified in the synagogue in Nazareth. (Luke iv, 18-20.) But this office will not fit into the above exposition. Moreover, it would seem that if any words can express the idea of a thing done as a duty of righteousness those of Jesus do so. Dr. Dale says, — "It can not be claimed that the Lord Jesus was under obligation to undergo this baptism as a part of 'all righteousness;' (1) Because there is no righteousness in it; (2) Because what there is in it is just what he did not come to do. He did not come to repent for sinners, nor to exercise faith for sinners." The latter argument has the fatal fault that it proves too much. Upon the same ground the Lord Jesus should not have been circumcised or purified with his mother. He should not have kept the passover, nor any of the Levitical feasts and ordinances. All these implied and required in others a state of heart and mind and exercises of repentance and faith which were foreign to the holy nature of the Lord Jesus.

But is it so that there was no righteousness to be accomplished by Jesus in complying with John's baptism? The answer depends wholly upon the response to be made to the question which Jesus proposed to the Pharisees, — "The baptism of John, was it from heaven; or, of men?" If from heaven, it came with the sanction of the first clause of the Sinai covenant, — "If ye will obey;" and was entitled to obedience from every soul. John's baptism, — Is it necessary to say it? — washed away no sin. Like all ritual baptisms, of the Old Testament and the New, alike, it affected the ritual and outward status, alone, of the party, as toward the church, and the ordinances. Moreover, his ministry was not addressed to the ungodly only. But, if there were any of the people still looking and praying for the Consolation of Israel, they, as much as others, were called upon, as being defiled by the contact of the unclean nation, to receive this baptismal seal of the covenant renewed, and their acceptance in it with God. Pre-eminently was it true of the Lord Jesus, that he was defiled by contact with the sinful nation. To ritual uncleanness, he was as liable as any man, and became thereby subject to the same obligation of ritual purifying, by which others were bound. Jesus, therefore, as a true Israelite, came to John's baptism, as being an ordinance of divine authority; and in his answer to John indicates the fact that his omission of the duty thus resting on him as "made under the law," would have derogated from his perfect righteousness.

Nor is this all. John was the herald of Jesus in his distinctive character as "the Angel of the covenant," — the Mediator of that "better covenant" which was enclosed in the outward form of that of Sinai. (2 Cor. iii, 3-6.) In that better covenant, and Christ as its Surety, all the transactions relating to the Sinai covenant had their significance and end; as they were also the end of John's ministry. The repentance which he preached was a call to apostate Israel to return from transgression to the obedience required by the covenant, and his baptism was a seal to its promises, upon that indispensable condition of obedience. In coming to John's baptism, therefore, Jesus formally and publicly came under the bond of the covenant for obedience, and thus presented himself to Israel as her Surety therein. The baptism which he received from John sealed to him its promises on condition of his obedience, and the descending Spirit and the voice from heaven announced the Father's approval and acceptance of him as Surety for his people, the true Israel of God. It was with a view to this office of Christ as the Messenger and Surety of the covenant, and to his own relation as the herald of Christ in that capacity, that John says, "That he should be made manifest to Israel, therefore am I come baptizing with water;" — John i, 31 — that he should be made manifest to Israel, as her covenant Surety and King; as the Lamb of God and King of Israel.

The distinction drawn between "the baptism of John" and "baptism *by* John," overlooks the profounder aspects of the subject here indicated. It is true that John's baptism addressed to sinners a call to repentance, and announced remission, on that condition. But this special form of its message, is no more than the call to *obedience*, in terms adapted to the particular case of transgressors. And the significance and propriety of the baptism depended upon its own essential meaning as heretofore unfolded. In the Levitical institutions, the ordinary form of the rite had its primary relation, as we have seen, to a ritual uncleanness by contact with the dead, which symbolized the judicial defilement of the Lord Jesus by contact, through birth of a woman, with our dead nature, and his consequent death under the curse. The baptism symbolized the resurrection of Christ, and of his people with him, in the renewing of their souls, and the final quickening and rising of their bodies. Both of these are identified by Paul with the resurrection of Christ. (Eph. ii, 5; and i, 19-ii, 10; Rom. vi, 2-5; viii, 11, etc.) It is by virtue of union with him, by the baptism of his Spirit, bestowed upon and dwelling in us, that we are enabled to "know the power of his resurrection" (Phil. iii, 10), by our own death to sin and life to holiness. This was the signification of John's baptism. To the Lord Jesus it was a symbol and pledge of his own triumph over the exhausted power of the curse, in his resurrection; and of the deliverance of his people, in him, from the bondage of sin and death, by his Spirit bestowed and dwelling in them. Through this they receive repentance and remission of sins. The same meaning precisely was signified and sealed to the people by their believing reception of the same rite.

Thus, on the one hand, Jesus, as being the Son of man, one of the family of Israel, was as much bound to come to the baptism which, by the authority of God, John dispensed, as he was to obey or observe any part of the law, ritual or moral; as much as was any true son of Israel. On the other hand, by coming and receiving that baptism, he announced himself, the Surety of the covenant which it sealed, and was so certified and accepted by John, by the descending Spirit and by the Father's voice.

> Section LIX. — *The Anointing of the Lord Jesus.* — The Spirit given him, at his birth, — at his baptism, — and at his coronation. Meaning and purpose of his anointing

The Scriptures inform us of three distinct bestowals of the Spirit, upon the Lord Jesus, by the Father. The first, was that whereby he was begotten through the Holy Ghost, and his humanity so invested with the Spirits influences, as to be born and live in perfect holiness, so that he was designated by the angel, "that holy thing." — Luke i, 35. The second was the anointing bestowed at the time of his baptism by John. And the third was that endowment of the Spirit, which was conferred on him, at his ascension to the throne. The intimate relation of his anointing to his baptism by John, and the close analogy which is traceable between baptism and anointing, bring the latter within the purview of the present inquiry.

Immediately after his baptism, as he was praying, "the heaven was opened, and the Holy Ghost descended in a bodily shape like a dove upon him, and a voice came from heaven, which said, Thou art my beloved son: in thee I am well pleased." — Luke iii, 21, 22. The Baptist adds some facts: — "I saw the Spirit descending from heaven like a dove, and it abode upon him. And I knew him not. But he that sent me to baptize with water, the same said unto me, Upon whom thou shalt see the Spirit descending and remaining on him the same is he which baptizeth with the Holy Ghost. And I saw and bare record that this is the Son of God." — John i, 32-34. This anointing of the Lord Jesus with the Holy Spirit fulfilled a three-fold purpose.

1. It was a manifestation to Israel of the long-expected Messiah, — a confirmation from heaven of John's testimonies respecting him, and a designation of him, the coming One, as being Jesus of Nazareth. From the whole account given in the first chapter of John, it seems evident that the Baptist and his disciples had distinctly in mind the language of the second Psalm, which determined the form of their conclusions, deduced from the scene at the baptizing. "Why do the heathen rage ... against the Lord, and against his Anointed?... Yet have I set my King upon my holy hill of Zion. I will declare the decree: the Lord hath said unto me, Thou art my Son; this day have I begotten thee." The glorious personage here announced is, thus designated by three titles, — as the Lord's Anointed, his King, and his Son. It was as herald of this King that John came preaching, the kingdom of heaven. And when, with his own eyes he saw the anointing Spirit descend upon Jesus, he identified the Anointed with the Son. He saw and bare record "that this is the Son of God." So, John's disciple Andrew says to his brother Peter, "We have found the

Messias, which is, being interpreted, the Christ,"—the Anointed. Not only so, but, at the same time and by the same token, John recognized in Jesus "the Lamb of God which taketh away the sin of the world!" Thus fully, by this anointing, was Jesus certified to Israel; and therein the chief intent of John's ministry was accomplished.

2. The anointing was an attestation and seal to him of the Father's favor, in view of the spotless righteousness of his character as already proved in the life which he had lived, as a private person, the carpenter of Nazareth. Of his earlier youth, it is said that he "increased in wisdom and stature, and in favor with God and man."—Luke ii, 52. And now, in the fulness of his manhood, in connection with his anointing, a voice from heaven testifies, "This is my beloved Son, in whom I am well pleased."—Matt. iii, 17. To this, the Psalmist refers his anointing. "Thy throne, O God, is for ever and ever; the sceptre of thy kingdom is a right sceptre. Thou lovest righteousness and hatest wickedness: therefore God, thy God, hath anointed thee with the oil of gladness above thy fellows."—Psa. xlv, 6, 7. "The joy of the Lord is your strength" (Neh. viii, 10), said Nehemiah to Israel; and in the joy of his Father's favor, testified in the anointing, Jesus fulfilled his ministry to the close.

3. It was his endowment for the prophetic office, as he himself testified in the synagogue of Nazareth. "He found the place where it was written, the Spirit of the Lord is upon me, because he hath anointed me to preach the gospel to the poor; he hath sent me to heal the brokenhearted, to preach deliverance to the captives, and the recovering of sight to the blind, to set at liberty them that are bruised.... And he began to say unto them, This day is this Scripture fulfilled in your ears."—Luke iv, 18-21. From the same source he derived the miraculous powers, which attested his word. (Matt. xii, 28.) "God anointed Jesus of Nazareth with the Holy Ghost and with power."—Acts x, 38. Of the relation of his anointing to the fulfillment of his priestly office, in view of which John called him "the Lamb of God," Paul says that he "through the eternal Spirit offered himself without spot to God."—Heb. ix, 14. His anointing was not his consecration to the priesthood, but his endowment with grace, by which he was qualified to perform that priesthood, to prepare and offer an unspotted, sufficient and acceptable sacrifice on the altar of justice. And, having completed that work, by the same Spirit was he raised from the dead. (1 Pet. iii, 18; Rom. viii, 11.)

Such and so signal was the meaning and intent of that fact from which Jesus derived the name of, the Christ. Its close relation in many respects to the doctrine of baptism, is apparent. As to the question of mode, a few points may here be noted.

1. In it the Holy Spirit was given to the Lord Jesus, as an indwelling fountain of all gifts for his ministry.

2. It came by a descent from the opened heavens.

3. It was in the form of a dove,—beautiful symbol of the kindness of God, and the "meekness and gentleness," the "grace and truth" of the Lord Jesus!

4. It abode on him.

5. As the result, he was filled with the Holy Spirit (Luke iv, 1), brought under his active control and guidance, and endowed with his extraordinary gifts, for the fulfillment of his ministry.

6. The symbol which by divine appointment represented it was the pouring of oil upon the head and person. (Lev. viii, 12, 30; 1 Sam. x, 1; xvi, 1, 13; 1 Kings i, 34, 39; xix, 16; 2 Kings ix, 6.)

Section LX.—*"The Baptism that I am Baptized with."*—Matt. xx, 20-22.
    The kingdom was to be after the resurrection; and upon condition of being worthy. "The regeneration" was typified by the Levitical baptisms. The baptism was his resurrection. Luke xii, 50

It was his resurrection from the dead. We have seen that the Mosaic baptism was a symbol and seal of the imparting of life to the dead. We have seen it so referred to by Paul in his argument in proof of the resurrection. The fact has been pointed out that the Lord Jesus in receiving the baptism of John, not only fulfilled the law of righteousness as a faithful Israelite, but received, therein, a symbol and seal of his own resurrection and triumph over death and the curse, under which he was already held. Twice, in the course of his ministry as reported by the evangelists, did Jesus refer to his resurrection under this figure of baptism. Matthew thus records one of these occasions, "Then came to him the mother of Zebedee's children with her sons, worshipping him.... And he said unto her, What wilt thou? She saith unto him, Grant that these my two sons may sit, the one on thy right hand, and the other on the left, in thy kingdom. But Jesus answered and said, Ye know not what ye ask. Are ye able to drink of the cup that I shall drink of, and to be baptized with the baptism that I am baptized with? They say unto him, We are able. And he saith unto them, Ye shall drink indeed of my cup, and be baptized with the baptism that I am baptized with; but to sit on my right hand, and on my left, is not mine to give (*all' hois ētoimastai*), *save to those for whom it is prepared* of my Father."—Matt. xx, 20-23. Luke records a similar expression. "I am come to send fire on the earth; and what will I if it be already kindled? But I have a baptism to be baptized with, and how am I straitened till it be accomplished! Suppose ye that I am come to give peace on earth? I tell you, nay; but rather division. For from henceforth there shall be five in one house divided, three against two, and two against three. The father shall be divided against the son, and the son against the father; the mother against the daughter, and the daughter against the mother; the mother in law against her daughter in law, and the daughter in law against her mother in law."—Luke xii, 49-53. Of these expressions, expositors have proposed two interpretations. According to one, the cup and the baptism are equivalent figures meaning the sufferings and death of the Lord Jesus. Hence, Baptist expositors would explain it as an immersion in sorrow; but they do not show by what example or argument the word *"baptism"* can be made, thus, of itself, to signify *such* an immersion. A conclusive objection lies against this interpretation. In both the gospels the distinction between the cup and the baptism is carefully preserved, in Christ's original question, and in his rejoinder. "Are ye able to drink of the cup that I shall drink of, and to be baptized with the baptism that I am baptized with?" "Ye shall indeed drink of my cup, and be baptized with the baptism that I am baptized with." It can not be admitted that a second clause, so particular and detailed in statement, and so carefully repeated in the rejoinder, is a mere blank, adding nothing to the meaning already expressed. But it is agreed that the figure of the cup indicates all that suffering by which the Lord Jesus made atonement for our sins.

The other interpretation proposed is but a modified form of that here given. It discriminates between the cup and the baptism, by interpreting the latter of Christ's sufferings viewed as "consecrating sufferings—sufferings by which he was to be separated unto God's service as a royal priest." "That the reader may understand how Christ could use such language in the sense which we give it, let him consider such passages of Scripture as these: 'Unto him that loved us and washed us from our sins in his own blood, and hath made us *kings* and *priests* unto God and his Father, to him be glory and dominion forever and ever, Amen.'—Rev. i, 5, 6. 'And Jesus said unto them, verily I say unto you, that ye which have followed me, in the regeneration, when the Son of man shall sit on *the throne* of his glory, ye also shall sit upon *twelve thrones*, judging the twelve tribes of Israel.'"—Matt. xix, 28.[76]

The Scriptures cited by this respected author do certainly prove that the royalty and priesthood of the saints in heaven are the purchase of Christ's blood and the gifts of his love. But they do not even hint at the idea, much less prove it, in support of which they seem to be cited; to wit, that the sufferings and death of Christ were his consecration to the priesthood. On the contrary, they are in harmony with all the Scriptures, which testify that those sufferings were an offering for our sins, made by a priest already consecrated. "For every high priest is *ordained to offer* gifts and sacrifices: wherefore it is of necessity that this man have somewhat also to offer."—Heb. viii, 3. Here, it appears that, inasmuch as he was a priest, he must have an offering; the very reverse of the theory that his offering was in order to his consecration to the priesthood. This man who by the word of the oath, was consecrated a priest forevermore, needed not, like those priests to enter often into the holy place with blood. "For then must he often have suffered since the foundation of the world," the original date of his priesthood. "But now once in the end of the world hath he appeared to put away sin by the sacrifice of himself."—Heb. ix, 26. Of Christ's sufferings, in their *atoning* character, the Scriptures are full and explicit. And, of them, the cup is the undoubted symbol. But of "consecrating sufferings," and especially, of such contradistinguished from the others, as here supposed, we fail to find a trace. Is it asserted that although they are the same sufferings, yet are they viewed in a different light? Still the distinction is without warrant in the Scriptures. But, even conceding that point, can it be imagined that the Lord Jesus, in the circumstances of the case as relating to James and John, would pause upon and emphasize that distinction, by separate definitions, requiring distinct consideration and answer, by them, when at last the sufferings in question were one and the same? Nothing but an absolute necessity could justify such an interpretation.

In order to a right solution of the question here considered, let us ascertain what were the facts and conditions necessarily present in the mind of the Lord

---

[76] Armstrong on the Sacraments, pp. 48, 49.

Jesus, in making his answer to James and John.

1. Their application immediately followed, and was no doubt suggested by a statement made by our Lord, in reply to a question from Peter. Upon occasion of the sorrowful turning away of the young ruler, Peter said to Jesus, "Behold we have forsaken all, and followed thee; what shall we have therefore? And Jesus said unto them, Verily I say unto you, that ye which have followed me, in the regeneration, when the Son of man shall sit in the throne of his glory, ye also shall sit upon twelve thrones, judging the twelve tribes of Israel."—Matt. xix, 27, 28. Here are several indications of the time of enthronement. (1.) It is the time "when the Son of man shall sit on the throne of his glory." This phrase, "the throne of his glory," is not used in the Scriptures to designate the invisible throne of majesty and power in the heavens, now occupied by the Son of man; but that revelation to men of his glory, of which he said to his disciples, "the Son of man shall come in the glory of his Father, with his angels."—Matt. xvi, 27. To this time he expressly refers that throne. "When the Son of man shall come in his glory and all the holy angels with him, then shall he sit upon the throne of his glory."—Matt. xxv, 31. So Paul declares that the Lord Jesus "shall judge the quick and the dead at his *appearing* and his *kingdom*;" and in view of his own finished course, exults in the fact that, "Henceforth there is laid up for me a *crown* of righteousness, which the Lord the righteous Judge shall give me *at that day*; and not to me only, but unto all them also that love *his appearing*."—2 Tim. iv, 1, 8. (2.) It is the time of the judgment. The apostles shall sit with him, judging the tribes of Israel. (3.) It is the period of "the regeneration." Some expositors, indeed, refer this word to the preceding clause, which they read, "Ye which, in the regeneration, have followed me." According to this reading, the regeneration means, the introduction of the gospel, as being the beginning of a new life to the world. But others understand, by it, the resurrection of the saints which precedes the final judgment of the world. According to this, which I take to be the true interpretation, the resurrection is called the regeneration, because, in it, the quickening power of the Holy Spirit, first experienced, in the renewing of the souls of believers, and in making their bodies his temples, will then take full possession of the whole man, quickening and transforming our vile bodies into the likeness of Christ's glorious body, and reuniting soul and body in glory. In like manner, and at the same time, the work of "restitution of all things, which God hath spoken by the mouth of all his holy prophets since the world began" (Acts iii, 21), will be accomplished. Beginning, as it does in the spiritual world, in the preaching and triumphs of the gospel, it will be consummate in the regeneration of the physical system, in the new creation, the new heavens and the new earth. That the thrones promised to the apostles could only be possessed after the resurrection, is evident from the fact that, physical death being an element of the curse, the blessedness of the saints may, indeed, be unspeakable, even in a disembodied state; but there can be no properly royal triumph, so long as the bodies are in the bonds of corruption and the grave.

2. While the time of the kingdom of the saints is thus clearly defined, there are also certain conditions precedent, revealed with equal clearness and emphasis. "Ye which have followed me," says Jesus. Elsewhere he explains more fully.

"He that taketh not his cross, and followeth after me, is not worthy of me. He that findeth his life shall lose it; and he that loseth his life for my sake shall find it."—Matt. x, 38, 39. The following must be a bearing of the cross, with the life in the hand. A pertinent illustration appears in the life of the apostle Paul. He thus states the motives and policy which governed his course.—"I have suffered the loss of all things, ... that I may win Christ, and be found in him; ... that I may know him and the power of his resurrection and the fellowship of his sufferings, being made conformable unto his death, if by any means I might attain unto the resurrection of the dead."—Phil. iii, 8-11. Paul's meaning in the phrase to "know the power of his resurrection," elsewhere appears. He prays for his readers, that they "may know,"—that is, may realize by a blessed experience,—"what is the exceeding greatness of his power to usward who believe, according to the working of his mighty power which he wrought in Christ, when he raised him from the dead and set him at his own right hand in the heavenly places.... And you hath he quickened who were dead in trespasses and sins, ... together with Christ, ... and hath raised us up together."—Eph. i, 16-20; ii, 1, 5, 6. In another place, Paul, in view of his finished course and assured reward raises the triumphant shout,—"I have fought a good fight! I have finished my course! I have kept the faith! Henceforth there is laid up for me a crown of righteousness, which the Lord the righteous judge, shall give me at that day;"—the day, to wit, of "his appearing and kingdom."—2 Tim. iv, 1, 7, 8.

It thus appears that the time of the kingdom is the resurrection;—and that the condition of its possession is not physical sufferings and death, which are common to all men; but a conformity to Christ's sufferings and death, by being, in him, crucified and dead to the world. With this condition is inseparably identified the possession of a part in the resurrection and life of Christ. "If we be dead with Christ, we believe that we shall also live with him."—Rom. vi, 8. "I am crucified with Christ, nevertheless I live, yet not I, but Christ liveth in me."—Gal. ii, 20. We can be dead with Christ, dead to sin and the world, only by being alive to God.

Not only is the resurrection of the saints the time of their kingdom, but worthiness of part in the resurrection is stated with emphasis, as the final and conclusive condition precedent to the throne. "They," says Jesus, "which shall be accounted *worthy* to obtain that world and the resurrection of the dead."—Luke xx, 35. "If, by any means," says Paul, "I might attain unto the resurrection of the dead." Herein is the propriety of the form of the question put by Jesus to the two brethren:—"Can ye ... be baptized with the baptism that I am baptized with?" That is, "Are ye ready to endure and to do all that will be required of those who would be counted worthy of that world, and of the resurrection of the dead?"

3. The same word (*palingenesia*) *regeneration*, which Jesus employs, is used by Paul, who describes God's mercy as saving us, "by the washing of regeneration, and renewing of the Holy Ghost, which he shed on us abundantly, through Jesus Christ our Savior."—Titus iii, 5, 6. It is the very grace, therefore, of which, under the Old Testament as well as the New, baptism with water was the appointed symbol and seal. And particularly was it true of the sprinkling of the water of separation, that it symbolized the resurrection of the Lord Jesus on the third day, and of his people on the seventh, the day of the Lord. Add to these considerations the

fact that from the time of his tour in the region of Cæsarea Philippi, where he was transfigured, Jesus had been earnestly endeavoring to impress on the reluctant minds of the apostles the fact that "he must go unto Jerusalem, and suffer many things of the elders and chief priests, and scribes, and be killed and be *raised again the third day.*"—Matt. xvi, 21. We have already seen that Jesus and the apostles distinctly recognized and referred to the third day's baptism with the sprinkled water of separation as being a prophecy the fulfillment of which required his rising from the dead on the third day. "These are the words which I spake unto you, while I was yet with you, that all things must be fulfilled which were written in *the law of Moses*, and in the prophets and in the Psalms concerning me.... Thus it is written and thus it *behooved* Christ to suffer, and to *rise from the dead the third day.*"—Luke xxiv, 44-46. In the law of Moses, concerning the water of separation, and there only is the third day thus defined.[77]

The points suggested in these considerations are intimately and inseparably related to the matter involved in the petition of James and John. They are constantly so treated by the Lord Jesus himself, in his personal teachings, and by his Spirit in the writers of the New Testament. And yet, we are to suppose that, in his response to the brethren, Jesus absolutely ignored all this, which he had, just before, emphasized in his reply to Peter; and that he directed their attention solely to the sufferings which he was to endure, and in which they were to share! The alternative is, that on the contrary he referred to baptism, in the meaning in which unquestionably it was used throughout the Old Testament, as a type and figure of the resurrection, and thus, by that single word, suggested all that was involved in the vastly important considerations above mentioned, as connected with the subject.—"Ye know not what ye ask. Ye neither appreciate the true nature of the honors which ye seek, nor the time and circumstances of their enjoyment, nor consider the conditions precedent. Are ye able to drink of the cup that I shall drink of,—the cup of the crucifixion of the flesh and the world; and to be baptized with the baptism that I am baptized with, doing and enduring all that is involved in attaining to the resurrection of the dead? For it is not till the resurrection that the thrones which you seek can be possessed; and only by those who are found worthy of that world and of the resurrection."

That such was the meaning of our Savior would seem to be certain. This is confirmed by the words already cited from Luke xii, 49-53. "I have a baptism to be baptized with, and how am I straitened till it be accomplished." The matter present to the mind of Jesus, as the occasion of this utterance, was that discrimination which he was to exercise and separation which he was to make, in purging his floor and dividing between the wheat and the chaff, bringing division into families and dissolving the closest and tenderest ties. It is of this that he says, "I am come to send fire on the earth; and what will I if it be already kindled?" That is, Why should I wish to restrain it? "But I have a baptism; ... and how am I straitened!" He thus indicates a straitening of the full exercise of that function which he has just described. The cause of it is an unaccomplished baptism. What then were the facts out of which this language is to be explained? (1.) Christ was under judicial

---

[77] See above, p. 48.

condemnation for us from his birth, under the curse and sentence of death. (2.) While in that condition, a servant to the law and the curse, he could not fully exercise the prerogatives proper to his royalty. (3.) Especially must his office as personally the Baptizer with the Holy Ghost and with fire, — as the dispenser of grace to his people and wrath to his enemies, — be in abeyance, till his resurrection and assumption of the throne. Thus, he was from the beginning straitened and looking forward to his resurrection as the time and means of his enlargement. And, hence his saying, — "I have a baptism." That baptism was the bestowal upon him, by the Father, of the Spirit of life, raising him from the dead to the throne, whence he now dispenses grace and judgment to the world.

PART XI.

CHRIST THE GREAT BAPTIZER.

Section LXI.—*The Kingdom of the Son of Man.*—"The kingdom of heaven." Destined to man at creation. Satan's scheme. The kingdom in the prophets. John's proclamation. Christ's triumph and coronation

The phrases, "the kingdom," "the kingdom of heaven," etc., have primary reference to that throne and kingdom to which the Lord Jesus was exalted, when he rose from the dead, and was set at the Father's right hand. It is that militant kingdom of the Son of man, the establishment of which Daniel saw in vision; the law of which is, "conquering and to conquer" (Rev. vi, 2); and the history of which is that "he must reign, till he hath put all enemies under his feet."—1 Cor. xv, 25. The phrase is sometimes used to express the efficiency of Christ's saving sceptre in the hearts of believers, as when Jesus says,—"The kingdom of God is within you."—Luke xvii, 21. It is applied to the visible church, as being that society which by public covenant and profession owns Christ as her King and his Word as her supreme law. So, it is used to designate the millennial dispensation, when "the Lord shall be King over all the earth," when "there shall be one Lord, and his name one."—Zech. xiv, 9. Its duration is by Paul said to be, until "he shall have put down all rule, and all authority and power. For he must reign till he hath put all enemies under his feet." "Then cometh the end, when he shall have delivered up the kingdom to God, even the Father."—1 Cor. xv, 24-28. Of this end and change of administration Jesus says, "Then shall the righteous shine forth as the sun in the kingdom of their Father."—Matt. xiii, 43. Of it, he teaches us to pray,—"Thy kingdom come."

Thus, in all the variety of connection in which it occurs, the phrase in question derives its propriety and significance from that dominion with which man was endowed in his creation, that royalty which is enjoyed in the throne and sceptre of the Son of man,—its authority that of God the Father,—its extent the whole universe of God,—its object the manifestation of the glory of the divine perfections, and the rectifying of the disorders introduced by Satan,—and its end, that work accomplished and the sceptre resigned to the Father, "that God may be all in all."

His coronation and kingdom were the consummation of triumph for the Seed of the woman; toward which, from the beginning, the Spirit of prophecy ever pointed and hastened with ardent desire. Its realization begun with the ascension and the day of Pentecost,—its full meaning of grace, of wrath and of glory, will only then be fully realized in fruition, in that day when the mighty angel shall, with uplifted hand, proclaim the end of the mystery with the end of time. Of its significance, I will now attempt an indication.

Sin is, in its very existence, an insult to the holiness and sovereignty of God. Its unclean and evil aspect is a disgust and abomination in his sight, and a pollution and deformity on the fair face of his creation. In its first beginning by Satan, it was an immediate assault upon the very throne in heaven. Its introduction into the world was a Satanic device to mock God's proclaimed purpose of favor to man, and to insult His love by rendering its object unworthy of His regard, and loathsome to His holiness. At the creation of man, God had said, "Let us make man in our image, after our likeness, and let them have dominion over the fish of the sea, and over the fowl of the air, and over the cattle and over all the earth, and over every creeping thing that creepeth upon the earth."—Gen. i, 26. In the eighth Psalm, this decree is anew rehearsed. (Psa. viii, 4-8.) Again, in the epistle to the Hebrews, Paul transcribes it from the Psalmist, and expounds it. "For unto the angels hath he not put in subjection the world to come whereof we speak. But one," that is, the Psalmist, "in a certain place testified, saying, What is man, that thou art mindful of him, or the Son of man that thou visitest him? Thou madest him a little lower than the angels; thou crownedst him with glory and honor, and didst set him over the works of thy hands; thou hast put all things in subjection under his feet."—Heb. ii, 5-8. From this language of the Psalmist, Paul proceeds to argue the extent of the dominion thus given to man. He insists, (1) that the decree is unlimited. "In that he put *all* in subjection under him, he left nothing that is not put under him;" (2) that man does not now have such dominion. "*Now*, we see *not yet* all things put under him;" (3) that the decree is already fulfilled in the throne which Christ now fills. "But we see Jesus crowned with glory and honor;" (4) that to that same glory the Father is now "bringing many sons," the brethren of Christ and co-heirs with him of the kingdom. Vs. 10.

In another place, Paul completes the view, in this direction. "For he must reign, till he hath put all enemies under his feet. The last enemy that shall be destroyed is death. For he hath put all things under his feet. But when he saith, All things are put under him, it is manifest that He is excepted which did put all things under him."—1 Cor. xv, 25-27. It is a legal and common sense rule of interpretation, as to deeds of grant or conveyance, that an exception on one point proves the intention of the grant to be otherwise unlimited. So it is here. The apostle, in excepting God the Father from the grant of dominion to the Son of man, leaves all else in the universe under his subjection. It thus appears that, in the decree of man's creation, a dominion was assigned him which in the purpose of God comprehended all the power which Jesus, the Son of man, now exercises, over the whole creation of God.

How far this extent of the purpose of God was understood by Satan, we are not informed. But it is evident from the whole tenor of the Scriptures that the fulfillment of this decree was the subject on which the serpent joined issue with God, in the seduction of our first parents, and his policy toward our race. The issue thus on trial since the foundation of the world is this: Shall God fulfill his announced purpose, by exalting man to the promised throne? Shall he, thereby, vindicate his own wisdom, sovereignty, truth, and grace, and reveal and glorify all his perfections? Or, shall Satan triumph over God and man, thwarting God's decree, through man's ruin and bondage? Shall he succeed in the impious attempt to array the very attributes of God against each other, so that his justice and holiness shall forbid the performance of the purpose which his sovereign love determined and his wisdom and truth proclaimed? This has been the problem of the ages: This, the question which has roused intensest interest in all heaven's hosts, "Which things the angels desire to look into." —1 Pet. i, 12. This is the key to the fact, that, amid the scenes of human sin and ruin which fill the pages of God's word, the doctrine of the kingdom gradually dominates amid the gloom, looming up into proportions of grandeur which overshadow earth and heaven. "I beheld," says Daniel, "till the thrones were cast down, and the Ancient of days did sit; whose garment was white as snow, and the hair of his head like the pure wool; his throne was like the fiery flame, and his wheels as burning fire. A fiery stream issued and came forth from before him; thousand thousands ministered unto him, and ten thousand times ten thousand stood before Him.... I saw in the night visions, and behold one like the Son of man came with the clouds of heaven and came to the Ancient of days, and they brought him near before him. And there was given him dominion and glory and a kingdom, that all people, nations, and languages should serve him. His dominion is an everlasting dominion, which shall not pass away, and his kingdom that which shall not be destroyed." —Dan. vii, 9-14.

At length, the fullness of time drew nigh when the mystery of the ages should be disclosed, and the promised kingdom given to the Son of man. John came, the herald of its advent, crying, "The kingdom of heaven is at hand." —Matt. iii, 2. Soon, Jesus himself went forth uttering the same announcement, "Repent, for the kingdom of heaven is at hand." —Ib. iv, 17, 23. And lest his voice should fail to reach every ear, he shortly sent the twelve, and then the seventy, to fill the land with the cry. "As ye go, preach, saying, The kingdom of heaven is at hand." —Ib. x, 7; Luke x, 9.

But before the kingdom could be established, before the Son of man might assume the crown, there was a work for him to do. That crown might not be a gift of God's arbitrary grace—a mere assertion of purpose unchanged. It must be a reward of manifest and glorious merit. Nay, not even so is it to be a gratuitous endowment; but as a trophy won by battle and conquest is it to be received and worn. The Seed of the woman—the Son of man—must give proof, in presence of all intelligences, both holy and apostate, of his worthiness of that favor which God, from the beginning, so openly bestowed. He must display the mystery of a man walking in the flesh among men, in the glory of a spotless and untarnished righteousness, amid the reign of abounding sin. He must be seen—this glorious man—taking upon his mighty shoulders the vast incubus of the curse, with which Satan's malicious fraud had burdened the world, and bearing it away to a land not inhabited. He must meet the great enemy himself, whose impious challenge has raised the issue of the fitness of God's choice, and man's competence to reign—the enemy who, in insolent contempt of God's purpose, has chosen this earth as the seat of his own empire, and here usurped dominion over man. He must subdue

Satan, break his scepter and lead him captive in the train of his triumph, before he may claim and assume the kingdom and the glory.

Satan saw, with dread the coming of the champion, and proposed a compromise. — "Behold the kingdoms of the world and their glory! Do homage to me, and all shall be thine!" — Matt. iv, 8, 9. It needs not to trace the manner of the triumphs of the carpenter's son, ending in the resurrection from the guarded sepulcher, and ascension to the throne in heaven. As the time of the kingdom came to be immediately at hand, he entered Jerusalem, amid the exultant Hosannas of his followers, proclaiming him the King of Israel. He was betrayed and brought to the council. And when the high-priest adjured him whether he was the Son of God, his answer, whilst attesting that blessed fact, held up to equal prominence his royalty as the Son of man. — "Thou hast said; nevertheless, I say unto you, hereafter shall ye see the *Son* of *Man*, sitting on the right hand of power and coming in the clouds of heaven." — Matt. xxvi, 63, 64. And so, they crucified him, with the accusation written in letters of Hebrew and Greek and Latin, — "THE KING OF THE JEWS."

He had already foretold his apostles that they should live to see his kingdom established with power. On the morning of his resurrection, he said to Mary, "Touch me not, for I am not yet ascended to my Father. But go to my brethren, and say unto them, I ascend unto my Father and your Father, and to my God and your God." — John xx, 17. The word, "I ascend" (properly, "I am ascending"), indicates his immediate ascension and reception of the throne, on the very day of the resurrection. And it is worthy of notice that John who relates this does not mention that subsequent public ascension which was made in the presence of the apostles, as Christ's official witnesses. He had already recorded the essential fact. Between these two events, the first and the final ascension, on the occasion of one of his appearances to his disciples, he expressly told them that he was now already in possession of the throne. He "came and spake unto them, saying, All power is given unto me in heaven and in earth." — Matt. xxviii, 17, 18. On the day of Pentecost, Peter testified of the supreme authority now vested in Him. "Let all the house of Israel know assuredly that God hath made that same Jesus whom ye crucified, both lord and Christ." — Acts ii, 36. Paul more fully states the extent of his dominion. God "raised him from the dead and set him at his own right hand in the heavenly places, far above all principality, and power, and might, and dominion, and every name that is named, not only in this world, but also in that which is to come; and hath put all things under his feet, and gave him to be the head over all things to the church, which is his body, the fullness of him that filleth all in all." — Eph. i, 20-23.

Section LXII. — *Christ is enthroned as the Baptizer.* — His commission, — to purge the universe. Order of precedence in the Godhead. On earth, Jesus was "in the Spirit." On the throne, the Spirit is in and subject to him. "The promise of the Father,"

The announcement of the coming of the Lord Jesus as King was made to the Jews, in a very striking and impressive manner. Clothed in sackcloth of hair and subsisting on locusts and wild honey, John came in the wilderness of Judea, crying to an apostate people, — "Repent ye; for the kingdom of heaven is at hand.... He that cometh after me is mightier than I, whose shoes I am not worthy to bear. He shall baptize you with the Holy Ghost and with fire; whose fan is in his hand, and he will thoroughly purge his floor and gather his wheat into the garner, but he will burn up the chaff with unquenchable fire."—Matt. iii, 2-12. The baptizing office of Christ, as thus set forth, was the objective point toward which the Old Testament baptisms directed the faith and hopes of Israel; and the theme, as we have seen, of some of the most exultant strains of prophecy. And to it, the baptism of the Christian church ever looks up and testifies.

The intent of Christ's enthronement is here stated to be that he may "thoroughly purge his floor." So Jesus himself explains the parable of the tares. "The Son of Man shall send forth his angels, and shall gather out of his kingdom all things that offend and them which do iniquity; and shall cast them into a furnace of fire."—Matt. xiii, 41, 42. The dimensions of his kingdom, to be thus purged, we have seen to be coextensive with the universe of God; over which Paul declares that "he must reign till he hath put all enemies under his feet."—1 Cor. xv, 25. The same apostle further states that "it pleased the Father that in Him should all fullness dwell; and having made peace through the blood of his cross, by him to reconcile all things unto himself; by him, whether they be things in earth, or things in heaven."—Col. i, 19, 20.

In the execution of a work so vast and so momentous, the baptist states two means to be employed,—the baptism of the Holy Ghost; and the baptism of fire. By the one, Jesus gathers his wheat into the garner; by the other, he will burn up the chaff. We will first consider the baptism of the Holy Ghost.

In the blessed Triune Godhead there is one nature, one mind, and purpose, and will; so that all concur, equally, and freely in the eternal origination of the divine plan, and in every step of its administrative fulfillment. Yet is there an essential and native order of precedence and operation clearly traceable in the Scriptures. In this order, the Father is the first, of whom the Son is begotten, and from whom the Spirit proceeds. So, in the executive administration of the sacred scheme, there is an order of precedence in the manifestation of the Godhead, revealed with equal clearness. In it, the Son was sent by the Father to humble himself under the law, in the form of a servant; and he so performed the Father's will as to be designated by him "my righteous servant."—Isa. liii, 11. In it, the Father put the anointing Spirit upon the incarnate Son. (Isa. xlii, 1; Matt. xii, 18.) And, by the Spirit thus given, was he directed in his entire ministry, until he, "through the eternal Spirit, offered himself without spot to God," a sacrifice for sin. (Heb. ix, 14.)

But, upon the enthronement of the Lord Jesus as God's great Baptizer, there was a change in this order of administration. With the sceptre and kingdom of the Father, the dispensing of the Spirit was given to the Son of man. In this endowment, two great ends were accomplished. (1.) As the third Person of the Godhead is essentially the *spiritus*, or breath, of the Father (2 Sam. xxii, 16; Job iv, 9; xxxii, 8; xxxiii, 4; Matt. x, 20), "which proceedeth from the Father" (John xv, 26), so now, being given to the Lord Jesus, and mediatorially subject to and sent forth by him, as his Spirit, our Savior is thus constituted a likeness and revelation of the Father, in that respect also; as he is, in being robed with the Father's glory, sitting on his throne, and swaying his sceptre. This was signified by the Lord Jesus, when he came to the disciples after his resurrection, and breathed on them, saying, "Receive ye the Holy Ghost."—John xx, 22. Thus, "in him dwelleth all the fullness of the Godhead bodily."—Col. ii, 9. (2.) This investiture with the Spirit, was an essential qualification, without which it was impossible that the Lord Jesus should have fulfilled the work assigned him, of purging the Father's floor and gathering the wheat into his garner. Among the Persons of the Godhead, it is the office of the Spirit to be the author and source of life, by whom only, therefore, dead souls are quickened and dead bodies raised to life. Hence, Jesus, in announcing his prerogative respecting these things, attributes it to the gift of the Spirit of life conferred on him by the Father. "The Son can do nothing of himself, but what he seeth the Father do: for what things soever He doeth, these also doeth the Son likewise.... For as the Father raiseth up the dead and quickeneth them: even so the Son quickeneth whom he will. For the Father judgeth no man, but hath committed all judgment unto the Son; that all men should honor the Son, even as they honor the Father.... Verily, verily, I say unto you, The hour is coming and now is, when the dead shall hear the voice of the Son of God, and they that hear shall live. For as the Father hath life in himself, so hath he given to the Son to have life in himself; and hath given him authority to execute judgment also, *because* he is the *Son of man*."—John v, 19-27.

In his last discourse with his disciples, the night of the betrayal, Jesus was very explicit on this subject. Fully to appreciate his statements on that occasion, it is necessary to keep in view the general features of the divine economy which were about to culminate in Christ's exaltation. Inasmuch as Satan, in his insolent scorn of the human race, sought, through its weakness and ruin to cast contempt upon God, and to involve his government in chaos, God in the mystery of his glorious love, saw fit, in honor of the human race, to place his government upon the shoulders of the child of that very woman whose weakness Satan betrayed, and to appoint him to redeem her and her seed from the usurper's power, and avenge her wrong upon the betrayer's head; and ordained him, *because* he is the Son of man, to rectify all the evil that Satan has done,—to baptize this earth and yonder heavens from the defilement and dishonor that he has wrought, through sin, and to "reconcile all things to the Father, whether they be things in earth or things in heaven." It is manifest that in the fulfillment of such a plan, the Son of man must take actual possession of the scepter, before full entrance can be made upon its manifested execution. It is further to be remembered that the entire discourse in question was addressed to the apostles, with distinct reference to their commission and qualification to proclaim the gospel of the kingdom. The statements and promises therein contained do not, therefore, have immediate respect to the ordinary graces of the Spirit, in the hearers of the word, but to his comforting, enlightening and directing influences in the apostle-witnesses.

"I will pray the Father, and he shall give you another Comforter that he may abide with you for ever; even the Spirit of truth.... These things have I spoken unto you, being yet present with you. But the Comforter which is the Holy Ghost, whom the Father will send in my name, he shall teach you all things, and bring all things to your remembrance whatsoever I have said unto you…. When the Comforter is come, whom I will send unto you from the Father, even the Spirit of truth which proceedeth from the Father, he shall testify of me…. It is expedient for you that I go away; for if I go not away, the Comforter will not come unto you; but if I depart I will send him unto you. And when he is come, he will reprove the world of sin, and of righteousness, and of judgment. Of sin, because they believe not on me; of righteousness, because I go to my Father, and ye see me no more; of judgment, because the prince of this world is judged. I have many things to say unto you, but ye can not bear them now. Howbeit when he, the Spirit of truth, is come, he will guide you into all truth; for he shall not speak of himself; but whatsoever he shall hear, that shall he speak, and he will show you things to come. He shall glorify me; for he shall receive of mine and shall show it unto you. All things that the Father hath are mine; therefore said I, that he shall take of mine and shall show it unto you." —John xiv, 16, 17, 25, 26; xv, 26; xvi, 7-15.

In these passages, there is a very remarkable order of progress in the statements concerning the mission of the Spirit. "I will pray the Father, and *he* shall give you another Comforter." "The Holy Ghost, whom *the Father* will send *in my name.*" "The Comforter whom *I* will send unto you *from the Father.*" "If I go not away, the Comforter will not come unto you: but if I depart *I will send* him unto you." As the Spirit essentially proceeds from the Father, so, primarily, in the manifestation of the Godhead, he is sent forth by the Father, and in all his work of grace to man, is sent through the mediation of the Son. Hence the form of the first statement:—"I will pray the Father, and he shall give." In the next passage, he indicates that whilst, in the concurrence of the Godhead, the Father is the primary source of the Spirit, the mission spoken of, is in the name, and for the purposes of the Son, namely,—to remind the apostles of his words, and interpret them to their understandings and hearts. "Whom the Father will send in my name,"—that is, to do my commission,—to utter my words. In the next clause he assumes to himself and asserts the prerogative conferred on him, and says,—"When the Comforter is come, whom *I will send* unto you from the Father." And since the mission thus promised was to be a testimony on his own behalf, he goes on to mark that the testimony of the Spirit is that of the Father, also, since essentially and eternally, he proceedeth from and is the Spirit of the Father. "Even the Spirit of truth which proceedeth from the Father, he shall testify of me; and ye also shall bear witness because ye have been with me from the beginning." Compare John v, 36; Heb. ii, 4.

Next, since the triumphs of the gospel were reserved to honor the scepter of the Son of man, Jesus declares that he must ascend to heaven and assume that scepter, before the apostles could receive the gifts which would qualify them for spreading those triumphs.—"If I go not away the Comforter will not come unto you, but, if I depart, I will send him unto you." He declares the Spirit's offices, toward the world and toward them, whom he "the Spirit of truth" should "guide into all truth;" and emphasizes the fact that in fulfilling these offices, he will act strictly as an interpreter. Christ is the Word of God; and the Spirit sent by him, "shall not speak of himself; but whatsoever he shall hear, that shall he speak." — "He shall glorify me; for he shall take of mine and shall shew it unto you." And lest the unlimited purport of this declaration should not be fully appreciated, he adds, "All things that the Father hath are mine; therefore said I that he shall take of mine and shall show it unto you." As essentially the Father's, but given to the Son;—such is the aspect in which the Spirit shall reveal them to the glory of the Son.

Such were the testimonies with reference to which Jesus, after his resurrection, commanded his apostles to "wait for the promise of the Father, which ye have heard of me. For John truly baptized with water; but ye shall be baptized with the Holy Ghost not many days hence."—Acts i, 4, 5. Of it, on the day of Pentecost, Peter said, "Being by the right hand of God exalted, and having received of the Father the promise of the Holy Ghost, he hath shed forth this which ye now see and hear."—Acts ii, 33. What the promise was, Peter, here distinctly indicates. It was fulfilled in giving the Holy Spirit to the Lord Jesus, that he might of his royal prerogative shed down that Spirit upon his people.

The relation thus existing between the enthroned Mediator and the Holy Spirit, was very remarkably intimated by Jesus the night after the resurrection. He came to the assembled disciples with the salutation,—"Peace be unto you: as my Father hath sent me, even so send I you. And when he had said this, he breathed on them, and saith unto them, Receive ye the Holy Ghost."—John xx, 21, 22. Thus by anticipation, he interpreted the gift of Pentecost, as an imparting to them of the Holy Spirit, which was now given to and dwelt in him, as his Spirit, the breath of his life.

Dr. Dale, in his invaluable treatises has overlooked the distinction here pointed out, between the endowment of the Spirit which Jesus enjoyed in the performance of his earthly ministry, and that which belongs to him as Baptizer on the throne. Discussing John i, 33,—which he translates,—"This is he that baptizeth *by* the Holy Ghost," he says, "He upon whom the Holy Ghost descended and on whom he remained, 'without measure' was thus qualified for his amazing work, and qualified to be ['*o baptizōn en Pneumati Agiō*] the Baptizer who was himself *in* the Holy Ghost, and being *in* the Holy Ghost was thereby invested with power to baptize *by* the Holy Ghost.—The Lord Jesus Christ—'*o baptizōn en Pneumati Agiō*,—is 'the Divine baptizer, *being in* the Holy Ghost.'... The passage is to be understood as announcing the peculiar character of the Lord Jesus Christ as baptizer. This is done by exhibiting him in a two-fold aspect: 1. As being personally *en Pneumati Agiō*. 2. As a consequence of being *en Pneumati Agiō*, being invested with the power of baptizing by the Holy Ghost."[78]—In another place he says,—"The original author of this baptism is the Lord Jesus Christ; the executive Agent is the Holy Ghost; the giver of the Holy Ghost is the Father.... Does not the Dative and *en* announce the Agent in whom the power to baptize resides?"[79]

1. The anointing of the Lord Jesus at his baptism did not qualify him as Baptizer. Else, neither He nor the apostles need have *waited* "for the promise of the Father," which was fulfilled at the ascension, and demonstrated on Pentecost. (See Acts i, 4; ii, 33.)

2. As the water is the immediate efficient cause of the cleansing, in washing,

[78] "Christic Baptism," pp. 53, 56, 57.
[79] Ibid, p. 76.

so the Spirit is the immediate efficient cause of the grace wrought in the spiritual baptism. But to describe him as the executive Agent of that baptism, is the same error which should represent the water in that capacity, in ritual baptism.

3. Jesus was "in the Spirit," that is under the pervasive influence and control of the Spirit, during his entire earthly life. But it was precisely herein that he filled the character of being God's "righteous servant." — Isa. liii, 11. It was characteristic of his humiliation, to be thus subordinate. But upon his exaltation, the order was reversed. It is no longer Christ in the Spirit, fulfilling the service and work appointed him. But it is the Spirit in Christ, subject to his control, speaking his words and doing according to the will of Jesus, the Lord. And Jesus does not baptize *by* the Holy Ghost doing it for Him, but "*with* the Holy Ghost," as his Spirit and instrument; as he so clearly intimated, when he breathed upon his disciples and said, "Receive ye the Holy Ghost."

Section LXIII.—*Note, on the Procession of the Holy Spirit.*—History of the *filioque* clause. Objections to it

In the year 325, the council of Nice condemned the heresies of Arius concerning the Son, and formulated the orthodox doctrine on the subject in what is known as the Nicene creed. In 381, the council of Constantinople, being assembled on account of the errors of Macedonius, concerning the Spirit, inserted into the Nicene creed a statement of doctrine concerning the Third Person, in which occurred the phrase, "which proceedeth from the Father." About the year, 434, the council of Ephesus, being the third general council, as the before mentioned were the first and second, determined that no further addition should be made to this creed. Disregarding this decree, and without the sanction of any general council, the western or Latin church, about the end of the sixth century, silently interpolated the formula of Constantinople, so as to make it read, — "which proceedeth from the Father *and the Son.*" The resulting controversies became one cause of the division between the Latin and Greek churches. At the reformation, the Protestant churches generally, without discussion, accepted the Romish doctrine on the subject, and incorporated it into their doctrinal formularies.

In the foregoing discussion this theory is ignored, in favor of the primitive doctrine; for the following reasons:

1. The point in question is the essential and eternal procession of the Spirit. If there is one Scripture, referred to by any writer, or contained in the sacred volume, which even seems to describe *such* procession from the Son, it has not been my privilege to meet with it, in the course of a careful and long continued inquiry. The texts usually cited are, all of them, statements explicitly referring to the voluntary and temporal mission of the Spirit, coming into the world; and *not* to his essential procession, which is involuntary and eternal. They are John xv, 26; xvi, 7: Gal. iv, 6. "When the Comforter is come whom I will send unto you from the Father." — "If I go not away, the Comforter will not come unto you; but if I depart, I will send him unto you. "Because ye are sons, God hath sent forth the Spirit of his Son into your hearts, crying, Abba, Father." Will any one pretend that these passages refer to the eternal procession?

2. The language in which Jesus speaks of this procession as being from the Father seems designed to be adequate and exhaustive. "When the Comforter is come, whom I will send unto you from the Father, even the Spirit of truth *which proceedeth from the Father*, he shall testify of me."—John xv, 26. That the Father, specifically, is the one essential and peculiar source of the Spirit, is here doubly asserted, by the phrase, "whom I will send unto you *from the Father*;" and by the further expository statement, "which proceedeth from the Father." Should James and John unite in writing a book, any one who in speaking of James should say that he wrote it, would be justly chargeable with carelessness of statement. But if the book itself and its authorship and origin are the subject of discussion, it could not be said, with any regard to truth and accuracy that "This book was written by James." And, if the subject of the book were the life of John, and the statement were made that "This book was written by James, and gives the story of John's life," the omission, which previously might perhaps be accounted an inadvertence, assumes a character of falsehood and deceit. This, it seems to me, is a just parallel to the case which is made by the insertion of the *filioque* clause, making the procession to be from the Father *and the Son*. In the place in question, Jesus is speaking expressly of the Spirit, whom he describes with reference to his qualification to be a witness, on behalf of the Son. Had the whole thought of the passage been concerning the Father, and in describing him Jesus had said, "From him proceedeth the Spirit," the declaration would seem scarcely reconcilable with a coincident procession from the Son. But when the Spirit, himself, and his qualification to be a witness on behalf of the Son, is the distinct subject of discourse,—the statement that "He proceedeth from the Father, and will testify of me," utterly excludes a like procession from the Son. This conclusion is strengthened by the remarkable language on the same subject, uttered by the Lord Jesus upon another occasion. "If I bear witness of myself, my witness is not true. There is another that beareth witness of me, and I know that the witness which he witnesseth of me is true.... The works which the Father hath given me to finish, the same works that I do bear witness of me that the Father hath sent me."—John v, 31-36. Peter declares that "God anointed Jesus of Nazareth with the Holy Ghost and with power, who went about doing good."—Acts x, 38. Jesus here expressly certifies that the testimony thus by the Spirit given to his ministry was distinctively the Father's testimony and not that of the Son,—a statement wholly irreconcilable with the supposition that the Spirit of witness who was the efficient author of those miracles proceeded alike from the Son and the Father.

3. The phrase,—"which proceedeth from the Father,"—is explanatory of the language immediately preceding. "When the Comforter is come whom I will send unto you *from the Father*." But why "from the Father," since it is Christ that sends Him? Why not "from the Father and the Son?" Jesus gives the reason,—"Which *proceedeth* from the Father." Either this indicates something peculiar and exclusive, or words are without meaning.

4. There is undoubtedly a voluntary and temporal bestowal of the Spirit by the Father upon the incarnate Son, a bestowal in virtue of which, he, as the Spirit of the Son, is by the Mediator breathed or shed upon his people. But if the doctrine

in question is true, the Spirit, proceeding from the Father and the Son, sustains essentially and eternally the very same identical relation to each, and it would be just as impossible that he should be given by the Father to the Son, as on the contrary, by the Son to the Father. The fact that he is given to the Son shows conclusively that his relation to the Father is not only primary, but peculiar, a fact which is the express contradictory of the theory in question. In fact, by that theory the voluntary, temporal, and mediatorial mission of the Spirit, by the Son as incarnate, is necessarily and inextricably confounded with the eternal procession, which is essential and involuntary, the Scripture testimony on the subject is distorted and set at naught, and the whole subject involved in perplexity and confusion. These considerations, and especially the fact that there is not even a plausible pretense of Scriptural authority for the doctrine, lead me to its rejection.

> Section LXIV.—*The Baptism of Fire.*—The Holy Ghost, and fire, two several things. Fire means wrath. The places cited against this view. The contrasted language of the evangelists. Grace and wrath inseparably connected. John's theme and imagery are from Malachi. Arguments to identify the two baptisms in one. *Baptizo.* Mode of the baptism of fire

Christ's baptizing office is not all of grace. "He shall baptize you," says John, "with the Holy Ghost and *with fire.*" John thus, in harmony with the Old Testament writers, from Moses to Malachi, sets forth two distinct functions to be exercised by the coming One; the one, of grace, the baptism of the Holy Ghost, and the other, of justice and wrath, the baptism of fire. As this interpretation of John's language is denied, and the two baptisms interpreted as signifying essentially one and the same thing, it is necessary to consider with some care the evidence on the subject.

1. John, as the context shows, is addressing himself in terms of earnest admonition to the Pharisees and Sadducees, and to the Jews, as infected with their leaven. (Compare Matt. iii, 7, and Luke iii, 7.) He warns them of the discrimination which the Lord Jesus was about to use, in the purging of his floor. He begins with the expostulation, "O generation of vipers, who hath warned you to flee from *the wrath to come?*" He proceeds to indicate that the time then current was one of threatening portent. "And now also the axe is laid unto the root of the trees." The safety of the righteous he leaves to silent implication; but emphasizes the doom of the wicked,—"Every tree which bringeth not forth good fruit is hewn down and cast into the fire." He then modifies the figure, with reference to his own baptizing office. "I indeed baptize you with water.... But he shall baptize you with the Holy Ghost and with fire;" and lest there should be any doubt, as to his meaning, he completes the sentence with an expository detail,—"whose fan is in his hand, and he will thoroughly purge his floor, and gather his wheat into the garner; but he will burn up the chaff with unquenchable fire." It is certainly very improbable that in a Scripture so closely knit together and consecutive, so pervaded with one spirit and intent, the baptist should have used the word, fire, at the beginning and end, as a vivid figure of the judicial wrath of Christ, and in the middle, change it, without notice or explanation, into a figure of his grace; and this, too, when the first and

third clauses present every appearance of being parallel to, and expository of the second. The supposition that the baptism of fire, means an exercise of grace is, in fact, irreconcilable with the purpose of John's whole announcement, and renders the passage contradictory to the context, and false to John's mission and Christ's office and work. This is the only clause in the connection in which John states in direct terms, to the Pharisees and Sadducees whom he is addressing, the office of Christ, as toward them distinctively. And if, while proclaiming in general terms, His judicial and executive functions, consuming the evil trees and burning up the chaff, he is to be understood as saying,—"He shall baptize you with the Holy Ghost and with his gracious influences," the only justifiable conclusion would be that those self-righteous sectaries were the favorites of heaven, and had no reason to fear that day that should burn as an oven.

2. It is a mistake to suppose the figure of fire to be, in the Scriptures, arbitrary and variable in its signification. On the contrary, while constantly resorted to, as a figure of speech, and as a symbol, both real and ritual, it stands out with a meaning, fixed and invariable,—a meaning which springs out of its essential nature and its familiar phenomena and effects, and is incorporated in the language and institutions of the Word, by express divine sanctions. The two most conspicuous phenomena of fire are its consuming power, and the torture which its contact inflicts upon sentient beings. Hence, with constant reference to the final fiery day, it is everywhere employed as the appointed symbol of the divine wrath, arrayed against sin. In this character, it appears in such real symbols as the flaming sword of the cherubim, at Eden's gate,—the fire of God which was rained down upon the cities of the plain, thus "set forth for an example, suffering the vengeance of eternal fire" (Jude 7), and the fire in which God descended on Mount Sinai. In the same sense was the ritual use of fire which continually burned on the altars of the Old Testament, from the beginning of man's history, to the desolation of Jerusalem. Thus, as conspicuous as were the temple, and the altar, and incorporated in the very heart of the ritual system, was this symbol of God's avenging wrath, the fierceness of fire. As a figure of speech, it is constantly used to express the inflicted wrath of God. And, in fact, it is never employed in any sense incongruous to this. It is true, that processes which are dependent on the use of fire are sometimes employed as symbols of the manner in which the divine grace is exercised. Says Malachi,—"He is like a refiner's fire, and like fuller's soap; and he shall sit as a refiner and purifier of silver; and he shall purify the sons of Levi, and purge them as gold and silver."—Mal. iii, 2, 3. But, even here, the fire is not the Spirit, but the inflictions which the Savior employs and which by the Spirit he sanctifies to his people. Of this we have the divine certificate. "I have refined thee; but not with silver; I have chosen thee in the furnace of affliction."—Isa. xlviii, 10. But, while the figure is thus used, and while it is further true, that phenomena of fire, such as light, and heat, are used as figures of particular graces, it may with confidence be asserted that fire, itself, is never employed to represent the Spirit or his fruits.

3. It is impossible, here to examine all of the multitude of passages in which the figure occurs. It will be sufficient to notice those which are most commonly appealed to in proof of such use as is here denied. On the words of John, Dr.

Addison Alexander thus remarks:—"*With fire*,—not the fire of divine wrath, as in verse 10; but the powerful and purifying influences of the Spirit; so described elsewhere. (See Isa. iv, 4; lxiv, 2; Jer. v, 14; Mal. iii, 2; Acts ii, 3.)[80] Other writers add Isa. vi, 6; Zech. xiii, 9; 1 Cor. iii, 13, 15. These are the most pertinent passages referred to, in support of the exegesis given by Dr. Alexander. How entirely perfunctory and really inapposite these references are, appears in the fact that of the places cited by Dr. Alexander two occur in the prophecy of Isaiah, and one in the Acts of the Apostles, on which books the church is enriched with commentaries from the pen of that distinguished divine; and that in those commentaries he, in every instance, ignores and excludes the interpretation implied in his above-cited references. Thus; Isa. iv, 4,—"the spirit of judgment and the spirit of burning," he explains as "the judgment and burning of the Holy Spirit, with a twofold allusion to the purifying and destroying energy of fire; or rather, to its purifying by destroying; purging the whole by the destruction of a part, and thereby manifesting the divine *justice*[81] as an active principle." In Isa. lxiv, 2, the figure of the ebullition of water, represents the agitation of the ungodly nations in the presence of God's justice, delivering and avenging Israel; and so it is expounded by Alexander. "O that thou wouldst rend the heavens, that thou wouldst come down, that the mountains might flow down at thy presence; as when the melting fire burneth, the fire causeth the waters to boil, to make thy name known to thine adversaries, that the nations may tremble at thy presence." In Isa. vi, 6, the cherub takes a coal of fire from off the altar, and applies it to the lips of the prophet, saying, "Lo! this hath touched thy lips, and thine iniquity is taken away, and thy sin purged." It would seem evident, that, by the coal from off the altar, is meant the atoning merits of the Lord Jesus, of whose sufferings the fire of the altar was the appointed symbol. Or, if the language be interpreted of the golden altar of incense, the fire of which was kindled from the altar of burnt offering, the meaning is the sweet savor of Christ's intercession grounded on the merit of his sufferings. By no legitimate exegesis can it be made to mean, the Spirit of God. Jer. v, 14 needs only to be recited. "Behold I will make my words in thy mouth, fire, and this people, wood; and it shall devour them." The destruction of Jerusalem by Nebuchadnezzar, and the captivity of the land, in fulfillment of Jeremiah's prophecy, sufficiently expound this language. Remarks already made are sufficient as to the next citation:—Zech. xiii, 9. "I will bring the third part through the fire and will refine them, as silver is refined, and will try them as gold is tried." With this, the interpretation of Mal. iii, 2, is identical. The reference to Acts ii, 3, looks to the "cloven tongues like as of fire," of the day of Pentecost. But, we shall presently see that not burning but brightness,—illumination as of a lamp was the phenomenon of that day. Says the Psalmist, "The entrance of thy word giveth light." The day of Pentecost was, to the nations, the entrance of God's word,—the beginning of the gospel; and its appropriate symbols were tongues of light and voices of praise in many languages. As little pertinent is the next passage: 1 Cor. iii, 13-15.—"Every man's work shall be made manifest, for the day shall declare it; because it [the day], shall be revealed by fire; and the fire shall try every man's work, of what sort it is.... If any man's

---

[80] Alexander on Matthew.
[81] The italics are his own.

work shall be burned, he shall suffer loss; but he himself shall be saved; yet so as by (*dia, through*) fire;" —that is, —"so as passing through the fire, with a bare escape." That fire here means the judicial and punitive agencies of the last great day, in the discovery and punishment of sin, is clear.

Such are the most pertinent Scriptures to which I find reference made, to prove that, by fire, John meant, the Holy Spirit, or his gracious influences. That they wholly fail to establish the point, is evident; and a further independent examination induces the conviction that no others more pertinent are to be found.

4. A comparison of the four evangelists on the language of the baptist strongly confirms the interpretation here maintained. Mark and John, in giving account of the baptist's preaching, direct attention more particularly to the gospel aspect of his mission; as he was the herald of the atoning Lamb of God. Neither of them, therefore, mentions his impressive warnings to the Pharisees and Sadducees, respecting the trees cast into the fire and the threshing floor purged by burning. And, while they both record the testimony of John concerning Jesus, as he that should baptize with the Holy Ghost, they are both silent as to the baptism of fire. (Mark i, 8; John i, 33.) But Matthew and Luke enter more into the sterner aspects of John's office, as coming in the spirit and power of Elias, to announce judgment as well as mercy. They both, therefore, report his words of warning to a generation of vipers, words which the others omit. They both tell of the axe laid to the roots of the trees, and the threshing floor purged with fire; and both of them interpose between these passages the announcement of the two baptisms, "with the Holy Ghost, and *with fire*." The omissions of Mark and John, and the harmony of Matthew and Luke show that the baptism of fire belonged to the judicial and avenging aspect of Christ's mission, as emphasized by the latter evangelists, but only lightly touched by the others.

5. The inseparable relation of these two functions of Christ's office as the enthroned Son of man is certified in all the Scriptures. It is prominent in those which had immediate relation to the coming of John, and the purposes of his ministry. We have seen this, as to the first announcement made of the Angel of the covenant, to Israel at Sinai. On the one hand, he was described as the Guide and Deliverer, who should bring them into the promised land. On the other, they were warned to "Beware of him.... Provoke him not; for he will not pardon." —Ex. xxiii, 20, 21. In the second Psalm, the terrors of the Son are almost exclusively signalized, in warning to the rebellious nations. "Thou shalt break them with a rod of iron; thou shalt dash them in pieces like a potter's vessel. Be wise now therefore, O ye kings; be instructed, O ye judges of the earth. Serve the Lord with fear and rejoice with trembling. Kiss the Son, lest he be angry, and ye perish from the way when his wrath is kindled but a little. Blessed are all they that put their trust in him." Especially does Malachi emphasize Christ's two contrasted functions. A careful examination of the third and fourth chapters of that prophecy, particularly the latter, will satisfy the intelligent reader that not only do they contain John's commission, as the forerunner of Christ, but give the keynote and substance of his preaching. He is there announced as the Lord's herald, to go before the face of the Messenger of the covenant, who is described as coming to execute two opposite but inseparable func-

tions. On the one hand, he is to be the refiner and purifier of the sons of Levi; on the other, a swift witness and avenger against the wicked. (Mal. iii, 2-5.) Particularly did John have in his mind the fourth chapter, the first verses of which are thus given in the admirable translation of Dr. T. V. Moore. "For behold! the day comes! burning like a furnace! and all the proud, and all the doers of evil are chaff! and the day that comes burns them, saith Jehovah of hosts, who will not leave them root nor branch. And then shall rise on you the sun of righteousness, and healing in his wings; and ye shall go forth and leap as calves of the stall. And ye shall trample down the ungodly; for they shall be ashes under the soles of your feet, in the day which I make, saith Jehovah of hosts."[82] The "stubble" of Malachi and the "chaff" of John refer to the same thing. The threshing floor was a spot in the field which was beaten hard and smooth. The grain was threshed by the treading of cattle, or by dragging over it "a sharp threshing instrument with teeth." The process of winnowing with the fan separated the grain into one heap, and the broken straw or "stubble" and "chaff" into another. To clear the floor, the latter were burned. From this custom was derived the vividness and beauty of the prophet's imagery. He represents the wicked as thus separated and consumed, and the righteous, like calves let forth from the stalls in the brightness of the morning, skipping over the fields where the threshing floor lay, and thus treading among and trampling under foot the ashes of the wicked. Compare Rev. vi, 10; xi, 18; xv, 3, 4. It was with a view to the portentous character of the day thus described, that Malachi announces the commission of John to preach repentance to Israel. "Behold I will send you Elijah the prophet, before the coming of that great and dreadful day of the Lord." From the prophecy, which sets forth in such vivid colors, the tremendous issues depending on his ministry, John derived the imagery of his own warning, which is, in fact, a running paraphrase of Malachi.

"Behold," says Malachi, "the day cometh." "It is now immediately at hand," says John. "It shall burn as an oven," says the prophet, "and all the proud and all that do wickedly ... the day that cometh shall burn them up, saith the Lord of hosts, that it shall leave them neither root nor branch." John responds: "The axe is laid at the root of the trees. Therefore every tree which bringeth not forth good fruit is hewn down and cast into the fire." Says Malachi, "All the proud and all that do wickedly shall be chaff, and the day that cometh shall burn them up." John repeats and develops the figure. "Whose fan is in his hand, and he will thoroughly purge his floor, and gather his wheat into the garner; but will burn up the chaff with unquenchable fire."

Thus thoroughly are the thought and language of John imbued with the conceptions and imagery of the prophet, concerning "that great and dreadful day of the Lord," the description of which derives all its vividness and terror from the manifest and accepted meaning of fire, as an intense figure of God's consuming wrath. In the presence of these facts, the supposition is at once incredible and revolting that, into the very midst of the prophet's tremendous portraiture of that fiery day, with the awe and dread of which he had so successfully striven to fill the imaginations and the hearts of his hearers,—John should have injected, abruptly,

---

[82] The Prophets of the Restoration, by Rev. T. V. Moore, D. D.

and without the shadow of explanation or reason, a phrase, in which the same figure is employed in a sense wholly foreign to that in which it is used by Malachi, — foreign to its ordinary meaning in the Scriptures, and to the whole spirit and tenor of the connection alike of the prophet, and of the baptist.

The words of John are, in themselves incapable of being forced into coincidence of meaning. "He shall baptize you with the Holy Ghost and with fire." Here are two distinct affirmations connected by the copulative, "and." The latter, uttered through the inspiration of the Holy Spirit, purports, upon the face of it, to be additional to the former. And the more critically it is examined, the more thoroughly it will be found to vindicate that character. It can not be a mere repetition. It can not be explained as interpreting the first clause. What then does it mean, but to announce a baptism of fire, in addition to the baptism of the Holy Ghost? — a baptism of justice and wrath, as well as one of renewing and grace?

Appeal is sometimes made to phraseology employed by the Lord Jesus, in his interview with Nicodemus, as being similar in construction. — "Except a man be born of water and of the Spirit, he can not enter into the kingdom of God." — John iii, 5. But the resemblance disappears, upon a moment's examination. With Nicodemus, our Savior first employs the ritual figure of water, which was or should have been familiar to the Jewish ruler. But then, to avoid the possibility of mistake on a point so vital, he explains himself literally by naming the Holy Spirit, of whom water was the symbol. But, in the words of the baptist, the Spirit is first named, in literal terms, which neither needed explanation, nor could be made clearer by it. But the second clause is a supposed explanation of that which needs none; an explanation less intelligible than the words to be explained, — an illustration by a figure, used in a sense directly the reverse of its familiar meaning in the Scriptures, the meaning in which it is used in the same immediate connection, both before and after the clause in question, — an illustration, therefore, at once obscure and embarrassing, shedding no ray of light upon the subject, but involving it in darkness, and turning to weakness, not to say, platitude, the stern energy of the baptist's warning cry. "He shall baptize you with the Holy Ghost, *and* with his gracious influences."

Whilst the interpretation in question is without precedent or authority in the Scriptures, the arguments in its behalf are of no appreciable force. First, it is said to be "harsh" to understand the baptism of fire to mean Christ's judicial administration as toward the wicked. As I must confess myself unable to understand the meaning and force of this argument, if argument it be, I leave it without note or comment. Another plea assumes the form of assertion that "the idea of baptism does not admit of any reference to punishment."[83]

It may be allowed that *baptizo* would not admit of such interpretation, if found alone and disconnected from any modifying or explanatory word or expression. But, that, in such connection and with such modifying words and statements as occur in the text of John, it can not be so interpreted, is by no means self-evident, and is supported by no sufficient or probable argument. The fact has already been indicated that the Hellenistic use of the word was predicated upon its employment

---

[83] Ebrard, in Olshausen, on the place.

among the Greeks to express a condition changed by a pervasive and controlling influence. It remains to be proved that the Jews had entirely forgotten this, which was to them the radical meaning of the word; so that, in their vocabulary, it could never have been used in that sense. In fact, however, a remarkable proof remains to us that the reverse of this is the truth. Says Isaiah, the prophet, — "My heart panted; fearfulness affrighted me: the night of my pleasure hath he turned into fear unto me. — Isa. xxi, 4. Alexander, with the later Germans, understands this as a personification of Belshazzar, the king of Babylon, on that night when the handwriting on the wall proclaimed his judgment and doom. This, however, is unessential to the present purpose. Whether the prophet spoke of himself or of some other man, the fact of present interest is, that in the Septuagint Greek, the phrase, "Fearfulness affrighted me," is rendered, "My iniquity baptizes me." By this language, the Jewish translators express the agonies of remorse seizing and controlling the speaker, and turning the pleasure of the night into fear. Thus he was *baptized*, by sudden terrors by which he was controlled and brought into a new state of anguish and despair. So will the judgment of the final day seize upon the wicked and control and bring them into a like new condition by the baptism of fire.

Moreover, the connection in which John uses the expression in question, is such as to constitute abundant ground for the vindication of his language, even though baptism were restricted to the sense of purification. The purpose of Christ's mission, as set forth by John, was, to "thoroughly purge his floor;" by "his floor," meaning, primarily the people and land of Israel; but, in its ultimate intent, the world and the universe. In order to accomplish this object, not only must the wheat be garnered, but the chaff must be burned. And, as washing with water is none the less a purifying, because it does not cleanse or transform the filthiness, itself, but only removes it, — so, none the less is the baptism of fire a baptism, because it does not cleanse, but punishes the wicked. In so doing, it will purge the race, and cleanse the world, which it inhabits. That the baptism with the Holy Ghost is a real baptism, and that to it in the strictest and most peculiar sense the word belongs, can not be denied. But in that baptism we see the separating of the righteous and the wicked. It is as much the exclusion of the latter as it is the reception of the former. If the one is taken, it means, separation; it means that the other is left. Neither in conception nor in realization, is it possible to separate these two things, nor to eliminate the rejection and punishment of the wicked from that function by which the righteous are called and saved. By both alike, and by the one as much as the other, is the commission of the great Baptizer fulfilled and his floor purged.

Not without a significant bearing upon the present question is the language in which the Lord Jesus himself speaks of the discrimination which he is to exercise and the judgments which he is to inflict in the exercise of his royal authority. "I am come *to send fire* on the earth; and what will I if it be already kindled?... Suppose ye that I am come to give peace on earth? I tell you, Nay, but rather division." — Luke xii, 49, 51. That fire, here, is no symbol of grace, is manifest; as it is, also, that the theme of Malachi and John is the subject of these words of Jesus. Nor is the fact to be forgotten that, in the Levitical system, fire was distinctly recognized, along with water, as a purifying element. See Num. xxxi, 10; and compare Isa. xlviii, 10, and Mal. iii, 2, 3.

From all this it is evident that the baptism of fire is the exercise by the Lord Jesus of his judicial function, in the separation and punishment of the wicked.

Whilst it may be admitted that no absolute conclusion concerning ritual baptism, is to be deduced from the facts set forth in the Scriptures, as to the manner of this baptism, yet are they not unworthy of consideration as one element in the mass of evidence. (1.) The diluvial purgation of the world, in the days of Noah, was by means of rain. "The fountains of the great deep were broken up, and the windows of heaven were opened; and the rain was upon the earth forty days and forty nights."—Gen. vii, 11, 12. (2.) Sodom and Gomorrah suffered a destruction, typical in its intent, and "are set forth for an example suffering the vengeance of eternal fire."—Jude 7, and 2 Pet. ii, 6. Its manner is thus recorded. "Then the Lord rained upon Sodom and upon Gomorrah brimstone and fire from the Lord out of heaven."—Gen. xix, 24. (3.) The final destruction of the wicked is predicted under the same form. "Upon the wicked he shall rain snares, fire and brimstone, and a horrible tempest: this shall be the portion of their cup."—Psa. xi, 6. (4.) More than thirty times the figure of outpouring is used in the Scriptures to indicate the infliction of God's wrath. It is a pouring out, of wrath, of indignation, of vengeance, of anger and fury. Thus, in the Revelation, the seven last plagues are inflicted by the outpouring of cups or bowls (*phialas*) of wrath from heaven upon the earth. (Rev. xvi.) (5.) The final destruction of Gog and Magog, is described as being by fire which "came down from God out of heaven and devoured them."—Rev. xx, 9.

The analogy of all these facts and expressions with those concerning the baptism of the Spirit, as designed to indicate the exaltation of the Son of Man, and point to his throne as the source of the indignation poured out, is apparent. On the other hand, the fact is to be observed, that the eternal state of those wicked is represented under the figure of dwelling in the lake of fire,—a figure which corresponds with the primary classic meaning of *baptizo*, in that there is no resurrection.

    Section LXV.—*The Baptism of Pentecost.*—The apostles must "wait for the promise." The Spirit poured out

Before his crucifixion, Jesus had assured his disciples that they should see the kingdom of God come with power. After his resurrection, in visits manifestly preternatural, "he was seen of them forty days, speaking of the things pertaining to the kingdom of God; and being assembled together with them, he commanded them that they should not depart from Jerusalem, but wait for the promise of the Father, which saith he, ye have heard of me. For John truly baptized with water; but ye shall be baptized with the Holy Ghost, not many days hence."—Acts i, 3, 4. He moreover told them, "Ye shall receive power, after that the Holy Ghost is come upon you; and ye shall be witnesses unto me, both in Jerusalem, and in all Judea, and in Samaria, and unto the uttermost parts of the earth."—Ib. 8. For ten days after his public ascension they awaited the promised baptism. "And when the day of Pentecost was fully come, they were all with one accord in one place. And suddenly there came a sound from heaven as of a rushing mighty wind, and it filled all the house where they were sitting. And there appeared unto them cloven tongues, like as of fire, and it sat upon each of them, and they were all filled with the Holy Ghost, and began to speak with other tongues, as the Spirit gave them utterance." — Acts i, 1-4. They were inspired with divine courage, zeal, and power, and in presence of those who had cried, "Away with him!" and of the rulers, who had condemned him to the cross, proclaimed the kingdom and glory of the man of Nazareth. And, on that day, three thousand, a few days afterward, five thousand, and daily multitudes of believers added to the church, were the trophies of the power of Christ's baptizing scepter, — the firstfruits and pledge of the baptism of his Spirit which still continues to pour from on high its floods of salvation upon the world.

Such was our Savior's entrance on his office, as the royal Baptizer, — such the first administration of his baptism of grace. There are four things concerning it which demand attention. These are, — the manner in which the baptism was dispensed, — the new spirit then given to the church, — the accompanying signs, — and, the baptism of repentance, which then and thenceforth accompanied the preaching of the gospel.

Section LXVI. — *The Manner of the Pentecost Baptism. — Pnoë, —* a breath. *Pheromenē,* — borne forward, — impelled. "He breathed on them." It was affusion, signalizing the height where Jesus sits

In all the expressions and statements concerning the baptism of Pentecost, there is a prominence given to the manner of it which can not be casual, nor devoid of special significance. The attendant phenomena are described as "a sound *from heaven,* as of a rushing mighty wind," which "filled all the place where they were sitting." "Cloven tongues, like as of fire, sat upon each of them." "And they were all *filled* with the Holy Ghost." The facts are by Peter described as a fulfillment of the prophecy, — "I will *pour out* of my Spirit *upon* all flesh." — vs. 17. He further tells the assembly, that Jesus "*shed forth* this which ye now see and hear." — vs. 33. Of the similar scene in the house of Cornelius, it is stated that "the Holy Ghost *fell on* all them which heard the word," and that "*on* the Gentiles was *poured out* the gift of the Holy Ghost." — Acts x, 44, 45. Peter also, in giving account of this scene to the church at Jerusalem, stated, with reference to these facts, that as he began to speak, "the Holy Ghost *fell on them, as on us* at the beginning. Then remembered I the word of the Lord, how he said, ... Ye shall be *baptized* with the Holy Ghost." — Acts xi, 15, 16.

After the same conception is the language of Paul. — "According to his mercy he saved us, by the washing of regeneration, and renewing of the Holy Ghost, which he *shed on us* abundantly through Jesus Christ our Savior. — Tit. iii, 5, 6. "Hope maketh not ashamed, because the love of God (*ekkechutai en*) *is poured* out on our hearts (*dia*) *through* the Holy Ghost given us." — Rom. v, 5. In these places, the words, "shed," and, "poured," which are interchangeably used in the translation, represent one in the original.

The first point, here, is the manner in which the phenomena of the occasion were introduced. "Suddenly there came a sound from heaven as of a rushing mighty wind, and it filled all the house where they were sitting." That this was designed to be a significant sign, would seem certain in the presence of all the other significant features of the occasion. And its meaning is not obscure. From the Greek verb, *pneo*, to blow, are derived two nouns, *pneuma* and *pnoē*. These words are nearly identical in meaning, except that *pneuma* is by the sacred writers appropriated to designate the Holy Spirit. It, and the Hebrew *ruagh*, which is appropriated in a like manner, both mean, primarily, the air, the wind; and hence, the breath, the soul of man, a spirit, the Spirit of God. In all these significations, they are found, the one in the Hebrew Scriptures of the Old Testament, and the other in the Greek of the Septuagint version. We have seen how largely the figure of water is used as a symbol of the Spirit. Its chief propriety as thus employed appears in its effects upon the earth and the creatures, penetrating and fertilizing the soil, washing away defilement, and refreshing the thirsty; while as rain from heaven, it traces the descent of the Spirit from the throne of God. In wind, or air in motion, or the breath, we have another symbol, familiar in the Scriptures, and equally interesting and significant. Its peculiar fitness consists in its relation to its source, as representing the Third Person as the *Spiritus* or breath, "which proceedeth from the Father;" and in its nature, as essential to sustain life in the animate creation. Says the Psalmist, "By the Word of the Lord were the heavens made, and all the host of them by the breath (*tō pneumati*, by the Spirit) of his mouth."—Ps. xxxiii, 6. The word, *pnoē*, is that which designates the "rushing, mighty *wind*" of Pentecost. It is used in the Septuagint in the sense of wind, stormy or violent wind, the breath, the soul, the spirit. Its relation to *pneuma* may be seen in such places as follow.—"He that giveth *breath* (*pnoē*) to the people upon it and *spirit* (*pneuma*) to them that walk therein."—Isa. xlii, 5. "The *spirit* (*pneuma*) should fail before me, and the souls (*pnoēn*) which I have made."—Ibid. lvii, 16. "At the *blast* (*pnoēs*) of the *breath* (*pneumatos*) of His nostrils."—2 Sam. xxii, 16. "All the time my *breath* (*pnoēs*) is in me, and the *Spirit* (*pneuma*) of God is in my nostrils."—Job xxvii, 3. "The *Spirit* (*pneuma*) of God hath made me, and the *breath* (*pnoē*) of the Almighty hath given me life."—Job. xxxiii, 4. In the New Testament, we have the words of Jesus to Nicodemus,—"The *wind bloweth* (*pneuma pnei, the Spirit breatheth*), where it listeth."—John iii, 8. And in this same book of the Acts, is the testimony of Paul to the Athenians that—"He giveth to all, life and *breath* (*pnoēn*), and all things."—Acts xvii, 25. Significant to the same purpose is the word, *theo-pneustos* (*God breathed*), which describes the Scriptures as the dictate of the Spirit in the prophets. (2 Tim. iii, 16.) Turning now to another word,—says Dr. Alexander, "The word (*pheromenē*) translated rushing, is a passive participle, meaning *borne*, or *carried*, and is properly descriptive of involuntary motion, caused by a superior power; an idea not suggested by the active participles, *rushing, driving,* or the like; which seem to make the wind itself the operative agent."[84] Compare 1 Peter i, 13,—"The grace that is to *be brought* (*pheromenēn*) unto you;" and 2 Peter i, 21.—"Holy men spake as they (*pheromenoi*) *were moved* by the Holy Ghost." With these notes, let us compare that action of Jesus, in which he *breathed* on his disciples, and said to them, "Receive ye the Holy Ghost."—John xx, 22. This we must understand as designed by him for an interpretation of Pentecost. It can mean nothing else. For not till then was the Spirit to be given.

---

[84] Alexander on the Acts, *in loco.*

The same figure is fully developed in the prophecy of Ezekiel (xxxvii, 1-14), of the valley of dry bones. "There were very many in the open valley; and lo, they were very dry." At the divine command, Ezekiel prophesied to them, — "O ye dry bones, hear the word of the Lord. Thus saith the Lord God unto these bones, Behold, I will cause breath to enter into you, and ye shall live.... And as I prophesied, there was a noise, and behold a shaking, and the bones came together, bone to his bone. And when I beheld, lo, the sinews and the flesh came up upon them, and the skin covered them above; but there was no breath in them. Then said he unto me, Prophesy unto the wind.... Come from the four winds, O breath, and breathe upon these slain, that they may live. So I prophesied as he commanded me, and the breath came into them and they stood up upon their feet, an exceeding great army." The vision is interpreted to the prophet. "These bones are the whole house of Israel.... Thus saith the Lord God; Behold, O my people, I will open your graves and cause you to come up out of your graves, and bring you into the land of Israel. And ye shall know that I am the Lord, when I have opened your graves, O my people, and brought you up out of your graves, and shall put my Spirit in you and ye shall live." Ezek. xxxvii, 1-14. Throughout this passage, the words, "wind," "breath" and "Spirit," are in the original the same (Hebrew, *ruāgh*, Greek, *pneuma*), and the word, "breathe," — "Come from the four winds, O breath, and *breathe* upon these slain," — is the same that describes the action of the Lord Jesus, just referred to. If now, in the light of these illustrations, we return to the account of the Pentecostal scene, we read that "suddenly there came a sound from heaven as of an outbreathed, mighty breath, and it filled all the house where they were sitting.... And they were all filled with the Holy Spirit." Thus was signified the Spirit of Christ, as the breath of His life, by Him breathed into His disciples. So distinctly and profoundly was this idea impressed on the mind of the primitive church, that it became the occasion of one of the unwarranted forms which were at an early age added to the Scriptural rite of baptism. After the interrogation and immediately before the baptism, there was an exorcism, with an insufflation or breathing in the face of the person baptized; which Augustine calls a most ancient tradition of the church.[85] It was meant to signify the expelling of the evil spirit, and the breathing in of the good Spirit of God.

In the outbreathing of Pentecost we have the only phenomenon of the day, that was expressive of the actual performance of the baptism by the Lord Jesus. It was the specific symbol of the manner of it. Comparing it with the various other statements above quoted, it appears that of that baptism, the element was the Spirit of life in Christ Jesus; the administrator was Jesus seated on the throne of glory; the manner of it was an outbreathing from him; its coming was by descent, — a shedding down from the height of his throne to his disciples in Jerusalem; in its reception, it was a falling upon them; and the result was that they were all filled with the Holy Spirit, as the breath of their lives. For, in the symbol as described, they were surrounded as it were with an atmosphere of the Spirit. "It filled all the house where they were sitting;" so that they could breathe no other breath.

In this account, the chief interest centers on the source of the outpouring.

---

[85] Augustinus de Nupt. et Concup. II, 29.

And, in fact, the very purpose of the forms of expression used and of the sensible phenomena which they describe was to direct the attention of all, upward to that source. To the same effect, was the whole argument of Peter's discourse to the multitude. Each position in it, has this as the end.— "Ye men of Israel, Jesus of Nazareth ye know, for him ye crucified. Him God raised from the dead and exalted to his own right hand, and gave the Spirit in all fullness to him. That Spirit hath he shed down upon us, as ye now see and hear, and thus is shown his exaltation and power. Therefore let all the house of Israel know, assuredly, that God hath made that same Jesus whom ye crucified both Lord and Christ,—both sovereign over all and that Anointed One who was promised to David, and heralded by all the prophets, as he that should sit on David's conquering throne."

We have seen how Paul labors to exalt our imaginations to some proportionate conceptions of the unapproachable height of the throne of Christ's glory. And now, in our times, from the day of Pentecost unto the end, it is signalized in the exercise by him of that highest prerogative of God, the sending forth of the infinite Spirit. It is shed down by him from yonder height to this low earth,—down to us worms in the abyss where we lay, strown in the upas valley of death, to breathe life into the dead and give salvation to the lost. And to signalize that height of his exaltation, the depth of his condescension, and the measureless immensity of his matchless love, the Baptism of Pentecost was given, its miracles were wrought, and its myriad trophies of salvation gathered. All these point upward and cry,— "Behold! on high! Far above all powers and dominions, Jesus fills the throne! Thence he breathes forth the Spirit of God! Thence he sheds down salvation!"

Section LXVII.—*The New Spirit Imparted on Pentecost.*—The Spirit no novelty. Peter's explanation. Hitherto, the church's office was conservative. Now the aggressive Spirit of missions given

The previous announcements which heralded the baptism of Pentecost, and all the attendant facts and statements unite to indicate that in the very nature of the gift then conferred there was something essentially new and different from any previous endowments bestowed on the church,—something by which peculiar honor was reflected on the baptizing office of the Lord Jesus, upon this its first assumption and exercise. It is a question to be considered,—What were the new characteristics of grace now first imparted to the church?

The Holy Spirit was no novelty, now first bestowed. At the coming of Christ, the Jews were familiar with the doctrine of the personality and offices of the Third Person of the Godhead. Of this the evidence is conclusive,—in the story of John's birth,—in the theme and style of John's preaching,—in the facts stated as to the birth, anointing, and ministry of Christ,—in His manner of reference to the subject in his teaching,—and especially in his warning as to the sin against the Holy Ghost, which is only explicable upon the supposition that the doctrine of the Spirit was familiar to the Jews. The knowledge thus evinced had its source in the Scriptures of the Old Testament. So full are they on the subject that there is scarcely an aspect in which it appears in the New Testament which has not its counterpart in the Old. In them his agency is distinctly and fully recognized, both in the inspiration of the prophets, and in the gifts and graces which have been common to God's people in all ages. See for example, Psa. li, 11-13; cxliii, 10; Isa. lxiii, 10, etc. The graces which Paul testifies to be the fruits of the Spirit (Gal. v, 22; Eph. v, 9), and which are in the above cited places, by the Old Testament writers referred to the same source, were abundantly displayed in the saints of the former dispensation, insomuch that Paul holds them up as ensamples to us. (Heb. xi and xii, 1.) The Psalms, which gave expression and nourishment to their graces, are never exhausted by the profoundest attainments of Christian experience. And with all the lamentable facts of unfaithfulness and apostasy which darken the pages of Israel's history, there were periods of fidelity, in which the church shone in the beauty of holiness, fair and comely in the eyes of God. In fact, with all the disposition which we sometimes realize to dwell on the unbelief and apostasies of the twelve tribes, and lamentable as they were, it is certain that the New Testament church is in no condition to boast herself against Israel. If we survey the nominally Christian church, in its various sections—the communions of Rome and of the east, and of the various Protestant churches in Europe and America—a just judgment will pronounce them, on the whole, scarcely less unfaithful and surely more inexcusable than was Israel. Assuredly, there is no such difference in our favor as to indicate the absence of the Spirit from the latter, and his peculiar presence with the former.

In what then did the peculiarity of the day of Pentecost consist? To this question, Peter in his discourse on the occasion, gave an explicit answer. "This is that which is spoken by the prophet Joel:—And it shall come to pass, in the last days, saith God, I will pour out of my Spirit upon all flesh."—Acts ii, 16, 17. In this citation of prophecy, and in the discourse which followed, Peter defined the peculiarities of the occasion as consisting in three things: First, that the outpouring of that day was made by the Lord Jesus in person. Second, that the miraculous phenomena attending it were designed to attest the fact that He, being risen from the dead and exalted to God's right hand, was endowed with supreme and universal authority. Third, that the gifts of salvation by him dispensed were adapted and designed not for Israel only but for "all flesh,"—for the world. Thus was implied a change in the whole aspect of grace, in the hearts of God's people.

We have formerly seen that God's entrance into covenant with Israel, at Sinai, implied a temporary withdrawal of his overtures from the nations,—"suffering them to walk in their own ways," (Acts xiv, 16), but with a distinct assertion of a reserved right, inserted in the covenant itself,—"For, all the earth is mine." So long as God "winked at" the wickedness of the Gentiles, the church had neither commission nor call to labor for their salvation, nor impulse of grace to look for it. The doors of salvation and of the church were held open to all, and the word and ordinances maintained in Zion were an invitation to the world to enter freely. But, beyond that Israel was not called to go. On the contrary, she was discouraged from all active or intimate contact or intercourse with the apostate nations. Her primary and paramount office and obligation it was to keep her own self pure, and to preserve and transmit the oracles and ordinances of God faithfully, until the time of the Messiah. In the meantime, since the operations and graces of the Spirit can not but be in harmony with the will and purpose of God, his influences in the hearts of Israel, corresponded with the purpose thus indicated concerning the nations. For, grace is nothing but harmony of affections and will with the character and will of God. Grace, in Israel, was therefore without disseminating zeal or power, as toward the Gentiles. It contained no impulse to seek their salvation. But, knowing them as apostate and enemies to God and to his people, and as the objects of his indignation and wrath, it concurred in that indignation, and at times gave expression to it, in forms which offend a shallow and unsanctified criticism. Yet are they no more incongruous to the active enjoyment and exercise of the profoundest and most abundant measure of the Spirit's graces, than is the absence in heaven's blest inhabitants of zeal for the welfare of Satan, and their adoring approval of God's justice in his doom. All this was rather confirmed than modified by the fact that the Spirit of prophecy constantly indicated that a day was coming when all the ends of the earth should see and share in the salvation of God. The more distinctly it was revealed as the purpose of God for the future, the more clearly was it seen to be not of the present.

But, now, the time had come. The Son of man, the Prince Messiah, to whom was reserved the ingathering of the Gentiles (Gen. xlix, 10), had assumed the scepter and received the Spirit of life for the nations. The sanctifying grace of that Spirit must be essentially the same in all ages and times. But there was now a change in its aspect to the Gentiles, coincident with the change of the divine attitude toward them. Instead of the old passive sentiment concerning the world's ruin, — instead of the former ardor of indignation against its ungodliness, — the apostles and the church were now inspired with a divine pity and beneficent love, — with an active and aggressive zeal for the conversion of men. While the enclosed water of the laver at the tabernacle was the symbol of the Spirit's influences, under the former dispensation, the increasing river of Ezekiel's vision is their representative in the New Testament times. Flowing forth out of Zion, with a widening and deepening current, it pours its living waters into the dead sea of our apostate humanity, to the healing of the waters. This difference in the nature of the Spirit's influences, now, and of old, is beautifully exhibited in two figures employed by our Savior, the distinctive features of which should not be overlooked because of the points of analogy. Speaking to the woman of Samaria of the personal blessings which the Spirit bestows, he tells her, — "Whosoever drinketh of the water that I shall give him shall never thirst; but the water that I shall give him shall be in him a well of water springing up into everlasting life." — John iv, 14. A well, within; living, active, but confined. But, at Jerusalem, at the festival of the pouring of water, which anticipated the giving of salvation to the Gentiles, — "In the last day, that great day of the feast, Jesus stood and cried, saying, If any man thirst, let him come unto me and drink. He that believeth on me, as the Scripture hath said, out of his belly shall flow rivers of living water." — John vii, 37, 38. "*Out* of his belly shall *flow*." Here is grace, not enclosed and restricted in its sphere, but outflowing and aggressive, disseminating itself without stint or limit. Hence the explanation which the evangelist adds: — "This spake he of the Spirit which they that believe on him should receive; for the Holy Ghost was not yet given, because that Jesus was not yet glorified." — Ib. vs. 39. Hence, also, the selection made by Peter, in explanation of the Pentecostal scene. Among the prophecies, there are many in which the outpouring of the Spirit is spoken of. But of them all the apostle selected that which, in the briefest and completest manner, indicates the breaking down of the wall of partition. "I will pour out of my Spirit *upon all flesh.*" This he afterward explains. "For the promise is unto you, and to your children, and to *all that are afar off,* even as many as the Lord our God shall call."—vs. 39.

But there was another point, equally important, in the endowments bestowed on that memorable day. Heretofore, not only had commission to the Gentiles been withheld from the church, but gratuitous labors by her in that behalf would have been necessarily futile, for lack of power accompanying the word. But, said Jesus to the apostles, "Ye shall receive *power,* after that the Holy Ghost is come upon you; and ye shall be witnesses unto me both in Jerusalem, and in all Judea, and in Samaria, and unto the uttermost part of the earth."—Acts i, 8. What was the nature of the power thus given, Paul tells the church of Corinth. "God who commanded the light to shine out of darkness, hath shined in our hearts, to give the light of the knowledge of the glory of God, in the face of Jesus Christ. But we have this treasure in earthen vessels, that the excellency of the power may be of God, and not of us."—"And my speech and my preaching were not with enticing words of man's wisdom, but in demonstration of the Spirit and of power, that your faith should not stand in the wisdom of men, but in the power of God."—2 Cor. iv, 6, 7; 1 Cor. ii, 4, 5. This illuminating, convincing, and converting power of the Spirit of God attending the word, remains the perpetual endowment and authentication of the Christian ministry. In addition to the zeal and power thus conferred, the apostles were by this baptism invested with those gifts of courage, wisdom, inspiration, and miracles, which had been promised by the Savior, and were requisite to qualify them for their special office and to attest their ministry. (Mark xvi, 17, 18; Luke xxi, 15-19; John xiv, 26; xvi, 13-15.)

Such was the change wrought by the baptism of Pentecost; such the new gifts by it conferred. With the coming of God's set time of mercy to the world, it awakened in the hearts of his people a zeal for souls of every class and nation. And it imparted to the word of the gospel a demonstration and power of converting grace, correspondent to the breadth of the new commission, and to the saving purposes of our blessed God, toward an apostate race. In proportion as we, in these latter days, have part in the baptism and Spirit of Pentecost, will we share in the same ardor of zeal for the spread of the gospel and the conquest of the nations to the banner of Christ.

> Section LXVIII.—*The Tongues like as of Fire.*—Not "cloven," but "distributed." Like the flame of a lamp. The candlestick. The seven stars. "Arise! shine!"

Jesus had foretold his disciples that miraculous signs and wonders should accompany and attest the word of the gospel published by them (Mark xvi, 17, 18), and the subsequent history gives abundant illustration of the fulfillment of this promise, in the healing of the sick, raising the dead and other miracles of power. But the only signs mentioned on the day of Pentecost are the "rushing mighty wind," the "cloven tongues like as of fire," and the gift of "other tongues." The first of these has been already considered. We will now inquire into the "tongues like as of fire." "There appeared unto them cloven tongues, like as of fire; and it sat upon each of them." Says Alexander, "*Cloven* should rather be, *distributed*, so that one sat on each of them. (Vulg. *linguæ dispertitæ*.) The common version, which implies that each tongue was divided into two or more, is at variance with the usage of the Greek verb (*diamerizomenai*), which sometimes denotes moral separation or estrangement (Luke xi, 17, 18; xii, 52, 53), but never, physical division. Its usual sense of distribution, or allotment, may be seen by a comparison of Matt, xxvii, 35; Mark xv, 24; Luke xxii, 17; xxiii, 34; and Acts ii, 45."[86] "There appeared unto them distributed tongues like as of fire, and one sat on each of them." Such is the literal meaning of the evangelist. These tongues *"appeared," "like as* of fire." Not burning, but brightness or illumination was their characteristic. They had thus the appearance of burning lamps, and seem evidently to have been symbols of that divine illumination which through the ministry of the gospel was about to be given to the Gentiles. In the tabernacle and temple stood the seven branched golden candlestick, with its seven lamps, which were by the priests daily replenished with oil, and kept burning continually. In the opening of the vision of the Apocalypse, John saw seven golden candlesticks, or lampstands, in the midst of which was one like the Son of man, in whose right hand were seven stars. These stars were the burning lamps of the lampstands. (Compare Rev. i, 12, 13, 16, 20; iii, 1; and iv, 5.) They were explained to him. The candlesticks were the seven churches of Asia, and the stars were the angels of the seven churches. There has been some question among expositors, as to the form of church government contemplated in this vision. But the most are agreed that, whatever was the form, the angels were the ministry, conceived as lamps of light upborne by the churches. By this interpretation, we are led to the same understanding as to the golden candlestick in the tabernacle and temple, since the scenery of the Revelation is a recognized transcript from the temple, which was a pattern of the heavenly things. The seven lamps shining as stars in the darkness of the sanctuary, through the continual supply of oil ministered by the priests, were a beautiful type of the ministry and ordinances of the church of God, shining amid the moral darkness of the world, through the gifts and graces of the Spirit poured upon them by Jesus, the great high Priest. The day of Pentecost had been predicted of old, as the time of the shedding of light upon the Gentiles by the awakened church. "Arise, shine; for thy light is come and the glory of the Lord is risen upon thee. For behold the darkness shall cover the earth and gross darkness the people; but the Lord shall arise upon thee, and his glory shall be seen upon thee. And the Gentiles shall come to thy light, and kings to the brightness of thy rising."—Isa. lx, 1-3. By Zacharias, at the birth of John, and by Simeon, at the presentation of Jesus in the temple, He had been described in this character,—"The dayspring from on high hath visited us, to give light to them that sit in darkness and in the shadow of death; to guide our feet into the way of peace."—Luke i, 78, 79. Says Simeon, "Mine eyes have seen thy salvation, which thou hast prepared before the face of all people,—a *Light* to lighten the *Gentiles,* and *the glory* of thy people Israel."—Ib. ii, 30-32. John, in the beginning of his gospel speaks in the same manner,—"In him was life and the life was the Light of

---

[86] Alexander on the Acts.

men, and the Light shineth in darkness."—John i, 4, 5. Jesus had described the ministry of John, under this figure. "He was a burning and a shining light."—John v, 35. He had distinctly foretold his disciples that they were ordained to be the light of the Gentiles. "Ye are the light of the world. A city that is set on a hill can not be hid. Neither do men light a candle (*luchnon*, a lamp), and put it under a bushel, but on a candlestick; and it giveth light unto all that are in the house. Let your light so shine before men that they may see your good works and glorify your Father which is in heaven."—Matt. v, 14-16. And now, upon them waiting and expectant, He sheds down the oil of the Spirit's grace, kindles a light upon every brow, and inspires them to utter God's praises in the tongues of every land; thus, to them signifying that the time was come to "Arise and shine," and to others announcing that the Light of the Gentiles had risen upon the world.

Section LXIX.—*The Gift of Other Tongues.*—Signified the union of all people in God's worship. The phrasing of the historian. History of the sign

The nature of this gift, and all the circumstances attending it unite in investing it with a character of peculiar impressiveness, significance and propriety among the miracles which attested the gospel. Devotional in its nature, and exercised in celebrating "the wonderful works of God," it was an indication of the reception and enjoyment by those on whom it fell of a large measure of the sanctifying graces of the Spirit. The report of it, spreading over Jerusalem, was the attraction which assembled together that vast company, of whom three thousand were converted that day. The prophetic nature of the sign demonstrated the identity of the occasion with that predicted by Joel. And the significance of the scene,—God's praises uttered in many languages,—as the anticipation of a world-wide acceptance of the gospel,—brings this sign into intimate accord with the new spirit of missionary zeal, and the tongues as of fire, which were the other principal phenomena of the day. It exhibited, in a figure, all the tribes and tongues of men, till then immersed in idolatry and darkness, uniting with sudden harmony in a glad burst of praise to God for the wonderful works of his grace.

The conspicuous position occupied by this gift amid the scenes of Pentecost and the relation which it sustained to the outpouring of the Spirit, as being the most observable gift thereby bestowed, occasioned a manner of expression on the subject in the book of the Acts, which has led to some misconception and error. It consists in the use of the name of the Holy Spirit, and of phrases respecting his falling on the disciples, being received by them, etc., when the subject spoken of is, not his renewing and invisible graces, but the sensible phenomena which attested the preaching of the apostles. Thus, Peter, on the day of Pentecost, having assured the multitude that what they saw and heard was the fulfillment of the promise, "I will pour out of my Spirit on all flesh; and your sons and your daughters shall prophecy," and explained that Jesus having received of the Father the promised Spirit, had shed forth this "which ye now *see* and *hear;*" exhorted his hearers to repent and be baptized, "and ye shall receive the Holy Ghost. For the promise (by Joel), is to you and to your children ('your sons and your daughters'), and to all that are afar off ('all flesh')." Here, the assurance of receiving the Holy Ghost, upon condition of repentance and baptism, as well as the quotation from Joel, shows that Peter did not speak of the renewing gift of the Spirit; which precedes and gives repentance, but of the miraculous gifts which followed, and which they saw and heard.

Again, upon the mission of Peter and John to Samaria, it is stated that they prayed for the Samaritans, "that they might receive the Holy Ghost. For as yet he was fallen upon none of them; only they were baptized in the name of the Lord Jesus. Then laid they their hands on them, and they received the Holy Ghost." — Acts viii, 14-17. Here, no distinct mention is made of miraculous endowments. But the manner in which the gift was imparted, the fact that they were already believers, and especially the proposal of Simon magus, on the occasion, show that it was miraculous gifts that were conferred. The sorcerer would have offered no money for the invisible renewing and sanctifying graces of the Spirit. "Simon *saw* that through the laying on of the apostles' hands the IIoly Ghost was given." And what he saw was what he sought to purchase. These perceptible and miraculous signs were therefore the things intended in the expressions used, as to the receiving of the Holy Ghost, and his falling upon the disciples.

The same manner of expression is seen in the account of Paul's interview with certain disciples of John at Ephesus. (Acts xix, 1-7.) Paul asked them, "Have ye received the Holy Ghost, since ye believed?" So reads the common version. But it should be, — "(*Elabete, pisteusantes*), Did ye, upon believing receive the Holy Ghost?" The question had reference to the time of their first reception of the gospel. The apostle predicates his question upon the assumption that these men were believers; and he elsewhere testifies that faith is one of the fruits of the Spirit. It is thus evident, as the sequel also shows, that it was not the ordinary graces of the Spirit of which Paul inquired, but his extraordinary gifts. Such being the purport of his question, the answer is to be interpreted in accordance with it. "They said unto him, We have not so much as heard whether there be any Holy Ghost." That is, We have not heard of the miraculous gifts. "And he said unto them, Unto what then were ye baptized? And they said unto him, Unto John's baptism." So intimately was Christian baptism related to the baptism and miracles of Pentecost, that Paul could not imagine any one to have received the former, and yet remain ignorant of the latter. To suppose, as do some, that these disciples of John meant to declare themselves ignorant of the existence of the Third Person of the Godhead, is little short of a contradiction in terms, in view of the essential place which was given to the Spirit in John's teachings, — even were we to ignore the Old Testament testimonies, of which John's disciples can not have been ignorant. What they meant, is manifest from the whole tenor of the narrative. In the result, the Holy Ghost was bestowed on them by the laying on of Paul's hands, "and they spake with tongues, and prophesied." That was the subject of Paul's inquiry, — the subject on which they were ignorant. And the form of expression is another example of the style of language which we have seen running through the pages of the Acts on the subject.

In striking coincidence with the relation of this sign, as representing the dissemination of the gospel to the nations of the Gentiles was the order of its manifestation. The command of Jesus was that the gospel should be preached "in Jerusalem, and in all Judea, and in Samaria, and unto the uttermost parts of the earth." Precisely this was the order of manifestation of the gift of tongues. First, it was given to the disciples assembled in Jerusalem and representing all Judea, on the day of Pentecost. Then Philip having preached in Samaria, to the conversion of many, Peter and John were sent thither; and by the laying on of their hands, the gift was conferred upon the Samaritans. (Acts viii, 12-17.) Afterward, Peter was called to the house of the Gentile, Cornelius, and upon his preaching, "the Holy Ghost fell on all them that heard the word," and they spake with tongues and magnified God. (Acts x, 44-47.) Beside these, there is but one other account, in which the manner of the gift is indicated. It is the case already mentioned, of the disciples of John in Ephesus. Respecting this sign, the following points are to be noticed.

1. As to its nature, it came under the general designation of prophecy, being an inspired utterance of the praises of God (Luke i, 67, 68), in which in the beginning at least, all the assembly, men and women united. (Acts i, 14; ii, 1, 4, 11; 1 Cor. xi, 5.) As such, Peter declared it to be a fulfillment of the prophecy of Joel. "Your sons and your daughters shall prophesy.... And on my servants and on my handmaidens I will pour out of my Spirit, and they shall prophesy."—vs. 17, 18. In this exercise, while the hearts and affections of the speakers were edified by the Spirit, in connection with the utterances thus inspired, their understandings did not ordinarily apprehend the meaning. (1 Cor. xiv, 2, 4, 13, 14, 18, 19, 28. Compare Rom. viii, 26, 27.) It was in "another tongue" than that which was native to the speaker, and usually to him an "unknown tongue."

2. It was not, therefore, designed to facilitate the labors of the apostles, by enabling them to preach in foreign languages; and there is no reason to believe that it was ever so used. The Scriptures are silent on the subject, and the traditions of the primitive church to that effect are worthless. Its design seems to have been two-fold,—the edifying of those upon whom the gift was bestowed;—and, for a sign to the hearers. (1 Cor. xiv, 22.) Of what it was a sign, intimation has been, already, given. It was a token that henceforth the Spirit of all grace would be bestowed as freely, and work as effectually, in the hearts of Gentiles, as of the Jews; and that God's praises thus inspired would be equally acceptable to him in every tongue and from every people.

3. Being intended as a sign of the ingathering of the Gentiles, it seems at first, and until the minds of the disciples had become fully imbued with that idea, to have been very abundantly bestowed, and especially at Jerusalem, the centre whence the healing waters, were to flow. In fact, its value as a great public sign depended materially upon the abundance of the gift, whereby, as on the first occasion, it presented a figure of all nations uniting in the worship of the true God and our Savior. But as the idea became familiar to the mind of the church, and the churches of the Gentiles multiplied, this gift seems to have fallen gradually into a subordinate place, among the many with which the church was endowed. (1 Cor. xii, 1-10.) The occasion of its importance as a public sign having passed away, its chief value now consisted in the spiritual edification which was ministered to the

possessors themselves, in its exercise (Ib. xiv); and it gradually disappeared from the church.

4. As the apostles were the official witnesses, appointed by the Lord Jesus to testify of his resurrection and exaltation to the baptizing throne, this sign was at first given in immediate connection with, and confirmation of, their personal testimony. It was also, with a like intimate relation to their witnessing office, conferred by the laying on of their hands, upon disciples who had been gathered in by the ministry of others. Apart from the personal presence and ministry of the apostles, in one or other of these forms, there is no Scriptural intimation, nor reason to believe, that it was ever bestowed.

> Section LXX. — *The Baptism of Repentance for the Remission of Sins.* — The firstfruits. John's "baptism of repentance." Jesus gives repentance and remission. His baptism unites to him and the Father. Its manner. The Spirit's relation to it

We have yet to contemplate the chief and crowning glory of Pentecost. The endowments conferred on the apostles, and the new spirit infused into the church, were but subsidiary means; glorious indeed; but only as they ministered to a more glorious end. The signs and wonders of the day were but an index hand which pointed away from themselves, and directed all interest and attention to that end. It appears, in the baptism of repentance, then first administered by the ascended Savior from his throne; the first fruits of which were the three thousand converts of that day, and the harvest of which still coming in, will only then be complete, when all his redeemed shall have been gathered from every nation and kindred and people and tongue.

The baptism of John is called "the baptism of repentance." — Acts xix, 4. But it was so, only as the rock in the wilderness was Christ; only as the bread and cup of the supper are the body and blood of the Lord. "The baptism of repentance, for the remission of sins" which he preached (Mark i, 4), was not his own. He preached "saying that they should believe on him that should come after him, that is, on Christ Jesus." — Acts xix, 4. He confessed his own weakness, and the emptiness and futility of his own baptism, which was only a symbol, calling men to repentance, but without power to confer it. "I, indeed baptize you with water, unto repentance; but he that cometh after me is mightier than I, whose shoes I am not worthy to bear; he shall baptize you with the Holy Ghost." — Matt. iii, 11. Jesus, after his resurrection, told his disciples, — "Thus it is written and thus it behooved Christ to suffer, and to rise from the dead the third day; and that *repentance and remission* of sins should be preached in *his* name, among all nations." — Luke xxiv, 46, 47. A few days after the baptism of Pentecost had been received, Peter, in the presence of the rulers of Israel, testified. — "Him hath God exalted with his right hand; a Prince and Savior, for to *give repentance* to Israel, and the *forgiveness of sins.*" Acts v, 31. "The forgiveness of sins," here, is the same in the original, as "the remission of sins," in the other places, and especially in the statement concerning John's preaching. This identity of language is undoubtedly designed to indicate identity of subject. The baptism which John preached, — that of which his own was the figure, — was the true baptism of repentance and remission, which Jesus was enthroned to dispense, — the baptism which, on the day of Pentecost, he bestowed, by the outpouring of the Spirit, whose office it is to work repentance and to seal remission. The doctrine concerning this baptism, may be thus briefly summed. By it, as given by the Lord Jesus, the Spirit is breathed into the subjects of grace, entering them as a Spirit of life. This is regeneration, the immediate effect of which is a new nature formed after the image of God in righteousness and true holiness. The indwelling Spirit and the new nature, inspired by him, lust against the flesh and loathe sin; and by consequence induce a true repentance and turning from it, and a pursuit after holiness. At the same time, the Spirit with which they are baptized, being in Christ as the head and source of life to all the body, and in them as members, unites them to Him by such a tie, — the tie of the one infinite Spirit common to both; so that they are, with him, one body, and therefore, in him, partake in the merits of his righteousness, and in it are justified.

In that last discourse of our Savior, to which we have already so fully referred, — that discourse which was an immediate anticipation and prophecy of Pentecost, — this subject is presented in a form of great interest and prominence. In fact, the thoughtful reader will find that entire discourse to center upon the two correlative ideas of the unity of the Persons in the Godhead, and the unity of believers, in Christ. Moreover, these two doctrines are presented as sustaining the most intimate relation to each other. In answer to Philip's request, "Lord show us the Father," Jesus emphasizes with reiteration his own unity with the Father, and exhorts the disciples, "Believe me that I am in the Father and the Father in me." Then, having promised to secure for them the presence and illumination of the Comforter, he says, "Yet a little while and the world seeth me no more, but ye see me; because I live, ye shall live also. At that day, *ye shall know* that *I am in my Father*, and *ye in me and I in you*." — John xiv, 8-11, 19, 20. This he illustrates by a parable. "I am the vine, ye are the branches. He that abideth in me, and I in him, the same bringeth forth much fruit, for without me (severed from me) ye can do nothing." — Ib. xv, 1-8. In the wonderful prayer which closed that discourse, Jesus recurs to this theme, in language which from any other lips would have seemed profane, so closely does he identify us with the glory of the Godhead. "Neither pray I for these alone, but for them also which shall believe on me through their word, that they all may be one; as thou Father art in me, and I in thee, that they also may be one in us; that the world may believe that thou hast sent me. And the glory which thou gavest me I have given them; that they may be one, even as we are one; I in them, and thou in me, that they may be made perfect in one; and that the world may know that thou hast sent me, and hast loved them as thou hast loved me." — Ib. xvii, 20-23. The "glory" which the Father gave the Son and Jesus gives his people, "that they may be one," is the Holy Spirit, who is called "the Spirit of glory and of God," who rests on his people (1 Peter iv, 14), and "the glory of the Father," by whom Christ was raised from the dead. (Rom. vi, 4. Compare viii, 11; and 1 Peter iii, 18.)

Such is the relation which by the baptism of the Spirit is established between Christ and the Father and believers. Touching the manner and process of it, the following are the most important points.

1. Each Person of the Godhead severally co-operates in this work of grace. The Father is its Author and source, by whom the Son was commissioned for its execution and the Spirit given him to that end. Hence, this gift of the Spirit to the people of God, whilst made through the Son, is constantly referred to the Father, as being primarily and essentially his gift. The Son, having purchased salvation through the blood of his cross, is commissioned as sovereign administrator, to dispense it to the redeemed, — "to give eternal life to as many as the Father hath given him." — John xvii, 2. In fulfilling this office, he, as the Father's representative and likeness, "can do nothing of himself, but what he seeth the Father do." And as the Father, having life in himself, has given to the Son to have life in himself, and to quicken whom he will (John v, 19-30), he bestows his salvation and quickens his people, by shedding on them that Spirit of life which the Father shed on him. The Spirit, thus given, dwells in the believer in his own proper character, as being the efficient cause of life and holiness.

2. All is postulated upon the fact that the Spirit, as given to and dwelling in all fullness in the Lord Jesus, is the principle and spirit of his life; by which he was born of the virgin; by which he lived in holiness, and offered himself a spotless victim to justice; by which he was quickened and rose from the dead, and which, as his Spirit, the breath of his nostrils, he now breathes into whom he will.

3. In baptizing his people, he imparts to them the same Spirit which is thus in him, to be in them the Spirit of life, making their bodies his temples and instruments (1 Cor. vi, 19; Rom. vi, 13); and their souls the subjects of his pervasive and transforming power. (Rom. viii, 4, 5.)

4. In this baptism, the Holy Spirit is not sent as an outside messenger or agent, — a third party coming *from* Jesus to the objects of his grace. To impress us with the height of his throne and the exaltation of his majesty, he says, "I will *send* him unto you." But, in the same discourse, he also says, "At that day ye shall know that I am in my Father, and ye in me and I in you;" and moreover promises, that "If a man love me, he will keep my words, and my Father will love him, and *we* will come unto him and make our abode with him." — John xiv, 20, 23. The Father and the Son are just as nigh the believer as is the Holy Spirit, whose office it is to attest their presence and interpret their communications to the soul. Since the Spirit is "the Spirit of Christ," — is given to him and remains in him in all fullness, it follows, that only in him, can any one receive or enjoy the indwelling and graces of the Spirit. Hence, the style in which, in the narrative of Pentecost, the baptism is spoken of, not as the sending of a person, but the shedding down of an element. "He hath shed forth *this*."[87] Hence the manner in which, in Peter's quotation from Joel, it is repeatedly said, "I will pour out *of* my Spirit." — Acts ii, 17, 18. And hence the interpretation which Jesus, by anticipation, gave to the Pentecostal baptism; when he breathed on the disciples and said, "Receive ye the Holy Ghost;" and the sign of the outbreathed mighty breath. Hence Paul's testimony, — "Your life is hid with Christ in God;" and his declaration as to himself, — "I live; yet not I, but Christ liveth in me." Christ and his people breathe one Spirit and live one life. Baptized by that one Spirit into one body, and all made to drink of that one Spirit, they are

---

[87] Τουτο, in the neuter gender.

thus one with him, "members of his body, of his flesh and of his bones."—Eph. v, 30. This union is only less close and intimate than that of the Father and the Son. (John xvii, 21.) On it depends the whole process of justification and grace.

Section LXXI.—*Paul's Doctrine of this Baptism.*—Titus iii, 4-7. Meaning of *loutron*. 1 Cor. xii, 12-14. Eph. iv, 4-16. Gal. iii, 27-29. Rom. vi, 2-6. Col. ii, 9-11. The doctrine of these places

Paul, in one brief sentence gives a comprehensive view of the manner and results of this Baptism. "After that the kindness and love of God our Savior toward man appeared, not by works of righteousness which we have done, but according to his mercy he saved us, by the washing of regeneration, and renewing of the Holy Ghost, which he shed on us abundantly, through Jesus Christ our Savior; that being justified by his grace, we should be made heirs, according to the hope of eternal life."—Titus iii, 4-7.

Here, an amendment is proposed, in the fifth verse, so as to read,—"the *laver* (*loutrou*) of regeneration. Bishop Ellicott declares this rendering to be "indisputable."[88] Other expositors favor it, and the Committees of revision of the New Testament have honored it by inserting the word, in the margin of the Revised Version, here, and in Eph. v, 26. A rendering thus importunate and intrusive, necessitates a critical examination. The first point to be noticed is that the word, laver, is ambiguous; and in the sense which is assumed in its insertion in the text, is without warrant in the Greek language or customs. "We know very little of the baths of the Athenians during the republican period; for the account of Lucian, in his Hippias, relates to baths constructed after the Roman model. On ancient vases, on which persons are represented bathing, we never find any thing corresponding to a modern bath, in which persons can stand or sit; but there is always a round or oval basin (*loutēr* or *loutērion*), resting on a stand, by the side of which those who are bathing are represented standing undressed and washing themselves, as seen in the following wood-cut, taken from Sir. W. Hamilton's vases."[89] The vessels used by the Greeks in bathing were, (1) the *asaminthos*, in which, sometimes, the bather sat, while the water was poured over him, as we have seen in the bath of Ulysses; (2) the *loutēr*, the *laver*, a vessel neither in size nor proportions adapted to the purposes of immersion, nor ever so employed, but designed and used as a containing vessel for the water; (3) the pitcher or dipper (*arutaina*), with which

[88] Ellicott's Commentary, on Eph. v, 26. On the mode of baptism, circumstances detract greatly from the authority of divines of the English church. The doctrine of that body on the prerogative of the church to ordain rites and ceremonies has a double effect. On the one hand, it takes away the motive to a thorough study of the Scriptural evidence on the subject. On the other, it induces a sense of satisfaction in admitting that the apostolic mode of baptism was by immersion, and then pointing to the contrary form now in use, as an illustration of the exercise of the church's authority over the matter. When to this is added the veneration cherished for "the primitive church" of the third and fourth centuries, in which immersion had gained extensive footing, and the recognition of that form in the rubric for baptism, hereafter quoted (below, p. 199), we will be justified in looking farther before accepting, as conclusive, the judgment, however pronounced, of divines of that church.

[89] Smith's Dictionary of Greek and Roman Antiquities, *article*, "Balneæ." The engravings referred to, will be found on pages 107, 113, above.

water was taken from the laver, and poured over the bather. There was no bath tub, nor provision of any kind for immersion. The mode of bathing appears in the story, in Theophrastus, of one who entered the bathroom (*balaneion*), and not being promptly waited on, dipping the ladle, (*arutaina*), poured it over his own person, and declared himself bathed, "no thanks to you."[90]

The word *loutron* was used, (1) for the *water* of the bath. In Athenæus, the question is asked, why *hot springs* (*therma loutra*), appearing out of the ground, are by all declared sacred to Hercules, if warm bathing was an unmanly luxury, as some asserted.[91] To the same point, in Aristophanes, the question occurs, — "Where did you ever see cold Heracleian *baths* (*loutra*)?"[92] In Sophocles, Œdipus directs his daughters "to bring a *bath* (*loutra*) of running waters."[93] Homer represents the curly headed Hecameda heating a warm *bath* (*loetra*).[94] And Euripides describes Antigone pleading to be allowed "to pour *waters* (*loutra*) over the corpse" of Polynices;[95] that is, to bathe it for burial. In this use of the word, together with the mode of bathing by the pouring of successive dippers, or waters, over the person, is explained the fact that the word is very rarely found in the singular number, and in Homer, the oldest of the classics, never; although in its plural form (*loetra*, contract, *loutra*), it frequently occurs in his poems. This fact is very strongly against the supposition that the word contained any allusion to the bathing vessel, which would demand the singular number.

The word designated (2.) the *washing* which was accomplished by the water. In the comedies of Aristophanes, the women in revolt, warn the men who threaten to assail them, — "If you happen to have soap, we will give you a *bath* (*loutron*);" which they do, by dashing buckets of water over them. Thereupon, the men run to the police, complaining, — "Do you not know what a *washing* (*loutron*) these have washed us, just now, and that in our clothes, and without soap?"[96] The idiomatic expression here ("to wash a washing"), indicates how very close is the relation between the verb *louo*, to wash, and its derivative, *loutron*, a washing. The one expresses the action, or doing; the other, the thing done. The same idiom presents itself in Antigone's account of the obsequies of her slain brother Polynices. "Washing it a pure washing (*lousantes agnon loutron*)," they gathered leaves, and burned "the poor remains."[97]

As bathing was performed by the outpouring of water on the person, the word was thence used (3.) to designate libations, performed by a like outpouring of water, in honor of gods or heroes. Thus, Agamemnon having been murdered at the instigation of his wife Clytemnestra, Orestes pours (*loutra*) *libations* at his father's

---

[90] Βάψας ἀρύταιναν, αὐτος ἑαυτον καταχέασθαι, καὶ ειπεν ὂτι λέλουται. Theophrastus, Char. 16 (9).

[91] Athenæus, Deipnosoph. xii, 6 (512).

[92] Aristophanes, Nub. 1051.

[93] Ἡνώγει ῥυτῶν ὑδάτων ἐνεγκεῖν λουτρὰ. Soph., Œd. Col. 1598.

[94] Εἰσόκε θερμὰ λοετρὰ ἐϋπλόκαμος Ἑκαμήδη θερμήνη.—Iliad xiv, 6.

[95] Σὺ δ' ἀλλὰ νεκρῷ λουτρὰ περιβαλεῖν μ' ἔα.—Eurip., Phoen. 1667.

[96] Οὐκ οἶσθα λουτρὸν οἶον αἵδ' ἡμᾶς ἔλουσαν ἄρτι.—Aristophanes, Lysist. 377, 469.

[97] Sophocles, Antigone, 1201.

tomb;[98] and Electra dissuades her sister Chrysothemis from fulfilling her mother's commission, to offer (*loutra*) *libations* at the same place, as a means of averting coming vengeance.[99]

The word designates (4.) a bathing place. Plutarch describes Alexander as speaking of "having washed off the sweat of battle (*loutrō*) *with the bath* of Darius."[100] In such passages, the controlling idea is not a supposed bathing vessel, but the cleansing water of the bath; as is here indicated by the form of the participle "(*apolousamenoi*), having washed off;" and by the instrumental dative "(*loutrō*), *with the bath*;" which show that, whatever the construction of the bathing place of Darius, the Greek mode was present in the mind of Alexander. The idea of *loutron* is further illustrated by its compounds. At Athens, before a marriage, the bride was bathed with water brought from the fountain of Callirhoe, by a young girl, who was hence called (*hē loutrophoros*), "the bath-water carrier." So, the fee for the privilege of the bath, was, *epiloutron,—for the bath*.

The voice of the classics is clearly against the rendering in question. The fact that the Greeks are entirely silent as to a washing by immersion, or any vessel for the purpose,—the distinct name of *loutēr* given to the only vessel that contained water,—the bathing performed by pouring,—the use of *loutron* to express such bathing, and to designate the water itself, where there was no vessel, and libations, in which there was water poured out, but no laver, nor bathing,—the primitive and peculiar employment of the word in the plural number,—and the derivatives formed from it, all inure to the one conclusion. At least, in classic Greek, *loutron* does not mean, a *laver*, but *water* for washing, and the *washing* accomplished by it; and that, with intimate reference to its affusion on the person.

Nor does the Hellenistic Greek utter a different testimony. In the Song of Songs, it is said,—"Thy teeth are like a flock, shorn, which came up *from the washing* (*apo tou loutrou*)." So reads the Septuagint. From Ecclesiasticus (above, p. 88) we have the proverb, "He that is baptized from the dead, and again toucheth the dead, what availeth his *washing* (*loutrō*)?" Here, cleansing by the sprinkled water of separation is called *loutron*, a washing. So Philo (above, p. 91) describes the purifying rites, the *washings* (*loutra*) and the sprinklings, of the Jews. Josephus says of the two springs of Machærus, near the Dead Sea, the one hot, and the other cold, that "when mingled together they make a most pleasant *bath* (*loutron*)."[101] And Paul, himself, writes that Christ gave himself for the church, "that he might cleanse it, purifying it with *the washing* (*tō loutrō*) of water." Here the new version must either make nonsense of the passage, or do violence to the Greek. Either it must read, "purifying it *with* the laver," that is, with the bath tub, not the washing; or, "*in* the laver," a rendering forbidden by the instrumental dative (*tō loutrō*.)

On the other hand, in more than a dozen places,—wherever the lavers of the tabernacle and the temple are mentioned, the Septuagint is *loutēr*,—the same word,

---

[98] Πατρὸς χέοντες λουτρά. Sophocles. Elect. 84.

[99] Οὐδε λουτρὰ προσφέρειν πατρί. Ib. 434.

[100] Ἴωμεν, ἀπολουσάμενοι τόν ἀπο τῆς μαχῆς ἰδρώτα τῷ Δαρειοῦ λουτρῷ. Plutarch, Alexand. 20.

[101] Jewish War. VII, vi, 3.

in the same sense in which it was used by the Greeks to designate the containing vessel. In a word, neither in the classics, nor in Hellenistic Greek, is *loutron* ever found in the sense of a laver, or bathing vessel. Or, if it is so used, the Lexicons ignore it; Stephanus, in his great Thesaurus, knows nothing of it; and the advocates of that rendering do not adduce it. And were such example found, it would be wholly insignificant as to the interpretation of Paul, in presence of all these facts.

If now, we ask for the evidence in favor of the new version, the answer presents two points, —first, that certain versions of the New Testament, —the Vulgate, Claromontanus, Syriac, and Gothic, —have so translated loutron; and second, that in accordance with Greek usage, the termination, on (loutron), justifies the assumption that the word designates an instrumental object. As to the first consideration, —it may be asserted with confidence that we are as fully possessed of the means of determining the question as were the unknown authors of those versions; and the growing prevalence at that time, of a ritualistic spirit in the church, and the consequent introduction of the form of immersion, sufficiently account for the rendering, apart from any critical considerations. Respecting the termination, on, the number of examples in which it is found in words that designate instrumental objects is too few to establish a rule. But were it accepted as decisive, the whole weight of its authority is against, instead of being in favor of the proposed amendment. A laver, and especially a Greek laver, is no instrument of bathing. Perhaps the arutaina, the dipper, might be so called. But the water and the washing, each are instrumental causes of the cleansing, the salvation; of which, in the text, the apostle says, — "he saved us (dia loutrō) by means of the washing." Nor do the classics ignore this relation. Plato (above, p. 95) asks concerning "the washings (loutra) and sprinklings," — "Are they not effectual to one end, to render a man pure, both as to body and soul?"

In the text, *loutron* means, the washing, but with intimate reference to the water as the means, —a sense which we have just seen illustrated from the classics. Strictly, the regeneration is the washing, of which the water is the instrument. The figure thus used, the apostle immediately explains. "The washing of regeneration, even the renewing of the Holy Ghost." As water is the instrument of washing, so the Spirit shed down by Jesus Christ is the instrument of that spiritual work which is indicated alike by the two identical words, regeneration, and renewing. Paul then proceeds with the pronoun "which," —equally appropriate, in the construction of the original, to the water (*loutrou*), or to the Holy Spirit, as its antecedent; and, in fact, referring to both, as identified in one, — "which water, even the Spirit, he shed on us abundantly (*dia*) by the hand of Jesus Christ." Orestes speaks of himself and companions "(*cheontes loutra*) pouring water" of libation at the tomb. So Paul speaks of "(*loutrou hon execheen*) the water of cleansing which He shed forth on us." In the latter case, the prefix, *ex*, emphasizes the source of the outpouring, but otherwise the conception and action of the two passages is the same. By the hand of his Son, God the Father from on high sheds his Spirit, and baptizes us with his renewing power. Thereby united to the Lord Jesus, we are thus invested with his righteousness, and so, says the text, "are justified by his grace." And since by the same union we share his relation as Son; — "if sons, then heirs," "according to the hope of eternal life."

This baptism of the Spirit is the theme of frequent discussion in Paul's writings. He particularly dwells on it as being the instrumental cause of that intimate unity which exists in the body of Christ, and of equality in privilege among all the members, Jews and Gentiles. "As the body is one, and hath many members, and all the members of that one body, being many are one body, so also is Christ. For, by one Spirit are we all baptized into one body, whether we be Jews or Gentiles, whether we be bond or free; and have been all made to drink one Spirit.... Now ye are the body of Christ, and members in particular." — 1 Cor. xii, 12-14, 27. Here, the figure of baptism is followed up by the expression, "have been all made to drink one Spirit;" — literally, "have been all watered with one Spirit." The preposition, (*eis*) "*into* one Spirit," is rejected by the critical editors as spurious; and the verb (*potizo*) means, to *apply* water, either externally or internally, — to water, to cause to drink. Compare in the same epistle, 1 Cor. iii, 2, "I have *fed you* (*epotisa*) with milk;" and 6-8, — "Apollos *watered* (*epotisen*)."

The same point is set forth in another epistle — "Endeavoring to keep the unity of the Spirit in the bond of peace. There is one body, and one Spirit; even as ye are called in one hope of your calling; one Lord, one faith, one baptism, one God and Father of all, who is above all, and through all, and in you all. But unto every one of us is given grace, according to the measure of the gift of Christ.... That we henceforth be no more children, ... but speaking the truth in love, may grow up into him in all things, which is the Head, even Christ, from whom the whole body, fitly joined together and compacted by that which every joint supplieth, according to the effectual working in the measure of every part, maketh increase of the body, unto the edifying of itself in love." — Eph. iv, 3-16.

That the "one baptism" here spoken of is that wherein, "by one Spirit we are all baptized into one body," is manifest from the connection and the analogy of the other passages here presented above and below. To suppose it to be water baptism, would be to make the apostle exclude that spiritual and real baptism of which water baptism is the shadow, and to which, in all his writings, he constantly gives so much importance as the means of the union which he here discusses.

In another place, the apostle represents this baptism as merging all other relations in the one tie of identity with Christ. "As many of you as have been baptized into Christ, have put on Christ. There is neither Jew nor Greek; there is neither bond nor free; there is neither male nor female; for ye are all one in Christ Jesus. And if ye be Christ's then are ye Abraham's seed, and heirs according to the promise." — Gal. iii, 27-29. Here, again, it is clear that the baptism spoken of is that of the Spirit. The oneness with Christ, thus complete by this baptism, Paul uses as a powerful argument of the duty of his people to be dead to the world that crucified him, dead to sin and all the works of the old man, and alive only to God. (Rom. vi, 3-6; Col. ii, 9-11.) These passages will receive special consideration hereafter.

The unity of conception which pervades these Scriptures is manifest, and makes it evident that they all contemplate one and the same baptism, that in which by one Spirit all Christ's people are baptized into one body, the spiritual body of

Christ.

Touching the nature of this baptism, the following are the chief particulars:

1. The entrance of the Spirit shed down by Jesus is regeneration, or the new birth. It is the imparting of new life to the soul,—the introduction of a principle of grace, "the new man," which, like its source, the eternal Spirit, is immortal and supreme wherever it exists; and which, sustained and nourished by the indwelling Spirit, will grow and expand until it gains full and exclusive possession of all the faculties and powers, making the soul its seat, the body its temple, and the members its instruments.

2. Coincident with this is the death of the old man, the destruction of the controlling principle and power of evil in the soul. Hitherto, it reigned supreme. But now, slain; and, cast out, it remains, a "body of death" in the members; offensive in its corruption, and by its loathsomeness acting as a stimulus to the opposing principle of grace. (Rom. vii, 24.)

3. The result is, that whereas, formerly, the sinful affections "did work in our members to bring forth fruit unto death," "now, being made free from sin and become servants to God," his people have "their fruit unto holiness."—Rom. vii, 5; vi, 22.

4. The Spirit thus given is not a transient influence; but is within the believer, a well of living water, springing up unto everlasting life;—a well, from which it is his privilege at all times to drink of that one Spirit. Thereby, "to every one of us is given grace according to the measure of the gift of Christ;" so that we "grow up into him in all things which is the Head, even Christ."—Eph. iv, 7, 15. Thus grace is nourished, in preparation for glory.

5. While such are the effects of this baptism on the spiritual condition of the redeemed, equally important are its influences on their external relations. The first is their justification. United to the Lord Jesus, as members of his body, the consequence is that their sins are laid to the charge of their Head, and satisfaction for them credited to the blood of his cross. On the other hand, his righteousness is recognized as theirs, and in it they stand, not only pardoned, but justified; approved, and entitled to the inheritance of glory. They are "accepted *in* the Beloved; *in* whom we have redemption through his blood, the forgiveness of sins according to the riches of his grace."—Eph. i, 6, 7.

6. Another result is their reception to the relation and privileges of children of God. Born of the Spirit,—born of God, they are thus by inheritance children. Members of Christ,—the first-born, the eternal Son,—they share in his relation, and are in him sons; and if sons then heirs;—heirs of God, and joint heirs with Christ.

7. The final result is the resurrection unto glory. "If the Spirit of him that raised up Jesus from the dead dwell in you, he that raised up Christ from the dead shall also quicken your mortal bodies, by his Spirit that dwelleth in you."—Rom. viii, 11.

Such is the one baptism, of which all ritual baptisms are mere shadowy symbols,—the baptism which Paul proclaims,—"One Lord, one faith, one baptism"

(Eph. iv, 5), a baptism, one and alone from its very nature, as dispensed by the one only Mediator, in the bestowal of that one Spirit, which belongs to and is therefore imparted by him alone. Thus have we the perfect antitype of the baptisms of the Old Testament,—the administrator, Jesus the great High Priest; the element, that living water, the Holy Spirit; the mode, his outpouring upon us from heaven; the effect, washing to the corrupt,—life to the dead. By this means, does our Baptizer bestow on his people all grace for the present time, and the resurrection and glory in the end.

Section LXXII.—*Noah "saved by Water."*—1 Pet. iii, 17-22. Peter and Paul. The theme,—the saints persecuted with impunity. Noah persecuted, and saved by means of the flood. Christ's people saved by antitype baptism

Beside the places before cited, one remains to be noticed. It is 1 Peter iii, 17-22. There are some various readings in the MSS., although none that materially affect the interpretation. Adopting what seem the best, the passage is as follows:—"It is better, if the will of God be so, that ye suffer for well doing, than for evil doing. For Christ, also, once suffered for sins, the just for the unjust, that he might bring us to God, being put to death as to the flesh, but quickened as to the Spirit. By which also he went and preached to the spirits in prison, formerly disobedient, when the longsuffering of God waited in the days of Noah, while the ark was preparing, in which few, that is, eight, souls were saved by water. You also now antitype baptism saves (not the putting away of the filth of the flesh, but [conformity to] the demand of a good conscience toward God); by the resurrection of Jesus Christ from the dead; who is at the right hand of God, having gone into heaven, angels and authorities and powers being subjected to him."

Both Peter and those to whom his epistles were addressed, were familiar with Paul's writings. (2 Peter iii, 15, 16.) In the passage here cited, the preacher of the day of Pentecost speaks of that Spirit baptism the beginning of which he had then witnessed, in a style which constantly reminds us of the language and manner of Paul, on the same subject. If Peter speaks of Christ as having been "quickened by the Spirit," or rather "quickened as to the spirit," Paul tells us that thus he became, "a quickening spirit."—1 Cor. xv, 45. If Peter states that "antitype baptism now saves us," the baptism, that is, of the Spirit, of which water baptism is the type,— Paul says that "He saves us by the washing of regeneration and renewing of the Holy Ghost, which he shed on us abundantly through Jesus Christ."—Tit. iii, 5. Peter represents this baptism as saving us "by the resurrection of Jesus Christ from the dead;" and Paul, to the same effect, testifies that "even when we were dead in sins God hath quickened us together with him and hath raised us up together" (Eph. ii, 1, 4-6); and that we are "buried with him in the baptism, wherein also ye are risen with him, through the faith of the operation of God who hath raised him from the dead."—Col. ii, 12. To the account which, on the day of Pentecost, Peter gave of the exaltation of the Lord Jesus to God's right hand, he here adds,—"angels and authorities and powers being subject to him,"—language in which we recognize the style of Paul's repeated descants on the same theme. (Eph. i, 20, 21;

Col. i, 16; ii, 10.) As Peter's language is so thoroughly imbued with the style of thought and expression of Paul, we need not hesitate to interpret the passage by the doctrine of the great apostle of the Gentiles.

The design of Peter is, to encourage the people of God in the endurance of injustice and persecution for righteousness sake. His first argument is the example of Christ, who suffered patiently the just for the unjust, "being put to death as to the flesh," that is, "as to his natural life," "but quickened as to the Spirit," inasmuch as his death was to him the exhausting of the curse under which he died, and was, therefore, the release of the Spirit of life which was in him, from all restraint upon his quickening energies, by which, therefore, he rose from the dead. Thus, the very sufferings of his death were his door of entrance into life. Unexpressed, but latent in the apostles' argument is the fact which, on the same subject, he states, in his second epistle, that "the longsuffering of the Lord is salvation" (2 Peter iii, 15), that having so pitied the ungodly as to die for them, praying for his enemies on the very cross, he now spares the persecutors of his people, if possibly they may repent (2 Peter iii, 9), and that, in the end, "the Lord knoweth how to deliver the godly out of temptations" (or persecutions), "and to reserve the unjust unto the day of judgment to be punished." — Ib. ii, 9. This, he illustrates by the case of Noah and the old world. The question as to "the spirits in prison" (Vs. 19), does not belong to the present inquiry. The point of interest is the eight souls "saved by water." — Vs. 20. To understand this, it is necessary to keep it distinctly in mind that the point to which the apostle's argument is directed is, — the righteous suffering persecution, and the persecutors spared. He assumes what can not but have been the fact, that during the one hundred and twenty years of the building of the ark, Noah, "a preacher of righteousness" (2 Peter ii, 5), was exposed to bitter persecution. If we consider that "the earth was filled with violence" (Gen. vi, 11-13), that Noah's preaching could not but be exceedingly offensive to those whose wickedness he reproved, and that his holy life, as "he walked with God," and his building of the ark, by which he "condemned the world" (Heb. xi, 7), combined to intensify the hostility, it must be evident that nothing but the almighty protection under which he was sheltered could have saved him and all his from speedy destruction. It also seems to be implied by the language here, and by the connection in which Peter elsewhere introduces the same matter (2 Peter ii, 5-9), that when the flood came, the enmity and hatred had reached a crisis; so that the call to enter the ark was like the bringing of Lot out of Sodom, a rescue from present destruction by the wicked. Thus, the very waters which purged the world by sweeping away the ungodly, were the salvation of the eight persons, who shut up in the ark, were upborne upon their bosom. They were "saved by water," while, as it rose, the world ready to perish would, in mad and impotent despair, have wreaked a blind vengeance upon the prophet and his family, for the terrible judgment of God; like Ahab with Elijah, in the days of the famine. But "the Lord shut him in" (Gen. vii, 16), and the waters bore them up, safe amid their perishing enemies.

Peter next points out that analogous to this is the salvation of Christ's people, — that as the waters of the deluge were the destruction of the old world, but life to the new, to Noah, and his house, — so the baptism of the Spirit is death to the old man, but life to the new, through union with the Lord Jesus and participation in his life. "You also, now, antitype baptism saves, by the resurrection of Jesus Christ from the dead. Forasmuch then as Christ hath suffered for us in the flesh, arm yourselves with the same mind; for he that hath suffered in the flesh" (that is, as stated immediately after, he that hath become "partaker of Christ's sufferings"), "hath ceased from sin."—Ch. iv, 1, 13. Here we recognize perfect identity of thought and argument with what has already appeared in Paul's writings. "So many of us as were baptized into Jesus Christ, were baptized into his death. Therefore, we are buried with him by the baptism into his death, that like as Christ was raised up from the dead by the glory of the Father, even so we also should walk in newness of life."—Rom. vi, 3, 4.

The conclusion of Peter's argument is found, a little farther on,—"Beloved, think it not strange concerning the fiery trial which is to try you, as though some strange thing happened unto you. But rejoice, inasmuch as ye are partakers of Christ's sufferings, that when his glory shall be revealed, ye may be glad also with exceeding joy."—1 Peter iv, 12, 13. So Paul says, "If so be that we suffer with him, that we may be also glorified together."—Rom. viii, 17. It is evident that the two great apostles are perfectly united in their testimony concerning this baptism and its relations to the plan of salvation.

In the foregoing exegesis, I have regarded both forms of the pronoun in the beginning of the twenty-first verse, as alike spurious; at the same time that the language of that verse is understood as containing a reflex allusion to Noah and his family "saved by water." The phrase "antitype baptism" does not, it is true, necessitate the previous mention of a type baptism. But it certainly does invite us to look for, and expect such mention, an expectation confirmed by the presence of the particles, "*also, now.*" "You, *also, now*, antitype baptism saves." Here seems to to be an allusion to something in the past, corresponding to the antitype baptism of the present. And when we find the immediately preceding mention of the salvation by water of Noah and his family, we can not be mistaken in recognizing this as the type to which, in the phrase "antitype baptism," Peter refers. The salvation, therefore, of Noah by the waters of the deluge was a baptism. Dr. Dale asserts the ark and not the water, to have been the instrument of the salvation, and quotes examples to justify the translation of *dia hudatos*, by "*through* the water," as a medium and not an instrument. But (1.) it is, of course, true that this is one meaning of *dia*. (2.) One of his examples, "faith tried by fire" (1 Peter i, 7), shows that it may also express instrumental relations. (3.) More pertinent would have been a citation of the parallel clause which immediately follows the phrase in question. As Noah is stated to have been saved "by water" (*dia hudatos*), in the typical baptism, so "antitype baptism saves us *by the resurrection* (*dia anastaseōs*), of Jesus Christ." The parallel, here, between type and antitype, requires that in both clauses, the preposition should be understood in the same sense; and, as in the antitype, *dia* certainly points out the resurrection of Christ, as being the instrument or means of our salvation, so in the type, must we understand it to designate the waters of the flood as the means of Noah's deliverance.

Section LXXIII.—*Christ's Baptizing Administration.*—It covers his whole work on the throne. In the end, triumph complete, physical and moral. When he shall have purged earth and heaven, then will his baptizing office cease

Thus Jesus fills the throne in the heavens, and possesses all power and prerogative for accomplishing the purposes of the Godhead, concerning the human race—the redeemed and the lost; concerning Satan and his angels, and the whole universe of God, moral and physical, as inseparably connected with the moral history and destinies of these. And thus, in every aspect of his work, as it progresses, from the day of Pentecost to the final consummation and glory, he is in the exercise of that office wherein he was announced by his herald John, as he that should baptize with the Holy Ghost, and with fire,—that office of the gracious aspects of which as toward his people, the baptism of water has been, for all ages, the symbol and seal. For, on Pentecost, Jesus only began to fulfill the prophecy and promise,—"I will pour out of my Spirit on all flesh." Not even yet is the breadth of its meaning accomplished. He will continue to breathe his Spirit into his people, till all are gathered in. So, of them, individually, the purifying, although assured by the first baptism which they respectively receive, is brought to fruition only through the daily breathings of Christ's life in them, the influences of his Spirit quickening them continually; as the leper was not cleansed by one affusion, but was sprinkled seven times. And while the idea of baptism has special reference to the first act of grace in bestowing the Spirit, it views that act as comprehensive of the whole process of grace, which is potentially involved in, and secured by it.

It is not for us to know the times and seasons "which the Father hath put in his own power."—Acts i, 7. But, respecting some things of vital interest as to the order and issue of coming events, in the history of Christ's baptizing office, we do know by the testimony of God.

1. Whatever, to our limited and carnal apprehensions, may be the mysteries of the past history of the gospel in the world, there has been no lack of power in the baptizing scepter of Christ, nor mistake in its exercise. The Baptizer is that Son of man in whom dwelleth all the fulness of the Godhead bodily, and who is the personal Wisdom of God, and the Power of God. His blood paid the price of salvation. His arm overcame and his heel crushed the serpent, during the days of his humiliation in the flesh. And now, enthroned in power, he doeth in his wisdom according to his pleasure. If the heathen of old could say, "The mills of the gods grind slow, but they grind exceeding fine," well may we confide in our King, that he need not make haste, in the fulfillment of his purposes. "Beloved, be not ignorant of this one thing, that one day is with the Lord as a thousand years, and a thousand years as one day."—2 Pet. iii, 8. Four thousand years rolled by, before the promise made to the fallen woman in the garden was fulfilled, in the virgin birth of the babe of Bethlehem. And now, "the vision is yet for an appointed time; but at the end it shall speak and not lie; though the promise tarry wait for it; because it will surely come; it will not tarry."—Hab. ii, 3.

It does not fall in with the purposes of the present discussion to enter into the prophetic question, as to the time and manner of the future developments and glory of the Redeemer's kingdom. Respecting it, one thing is certain. The past has been a time of the hiding of his power; but the light of the knowledge of the glory of the Lord will yet cover the earth as the waters cover the sea. The Branch of Jesse "shall stand for an ensign of the people; to it shall the Gentiles seek; and his rest shall be glorious." — Isa. xi, 10.

2. Every soul to whom the grace of God has come, from the day of Pentecost to this hour, has received it from the immediate hand of Jesus, baptizing him with the Holy Ghost. And so it will be to the end. Thus, each one so redeemed is a new proof and pledge that Jesus fills the throne, — that Satan and all the powers of darkness are under his feet; and that the hearts of men are in his hands, to give eternal life to as many as the Father hath given him.

3. When the end shall come, and the mystery of God shall be finished, it will appear that in every aspect of the issues joined with Satan, triumph and glory crown the head of the Son of man. Nor will it be the mere force of physical omnipotence crushing the feebler powers of Satan. But the glory of perfect righteousness, of wisdom and understanding, of counsel and might, of knowledge and fear of the Lord, in the Head and leader of the salvation, — a perfection, not merely of moral excellence but of all gifts and endowments, tried and proved, first, in the form of a servant under the law, in obedience and sufferings, amid the temptations of the world and the flesh, the wiles of the devil, and the inflictions of God, — a perfection then shown upon the throne of glory, in administering with perfect wisdom and perfect skill the vast and various affairs of God's boundless empire, thwarting and turning to confusion the plots and policies of Satan and his angels, rectifying the disorders wrought by the enemy, and vindicating God's glory impeached through man.

It will be a moral triumph revealed in each one of the redeemed, once a prostrate slave of Satan and sin, baptized and quickened, and aroused to struggle for liberty, and made more than conqueror, in the conflict, through the grace and Spirit of Christ, over Satan and all his powers without, and indwelling sin and corruption, — each one scarred with the wounds of battle, but all — the crushed serpent writhing beneath their feet, — wearing the white robes of triumph and waving the palms of victory; — all clothed in the righteousness of One, and each grown to the stature of Christ, in the perfection of holiness and beauty, after the image of God.

It will be the moral triumph of the whole ransomed host, by one Spirit baptized into one body, her garments of wrought gold and needle-work, received and revealed, spotless and complete in all divine perfections, — the bride of the Lamb, the glory of her husband, as he is the image and glory of God. (1 Cor. xi, 7.) In them shall the principalities and powers in the heavenly places behold and study and admire the reflected likeness of the unapproachable glory of the infinite Invisible.

It will be the triumph involved in all this revelation of glory and blessedness in contrast with the spectacle of Satan and his followers and work, exposed before all intelligences, in shame and everlasting contempt; — his achievements seen in discord and darkness, in sin and suffering and sorrow, in lamentation and woe, in the loss to him and to his of all the divine perfections in which they were created, and in distortion, deformity and discord, possessing and pervading them all; his confident wisdom and power turned to imbecile folly, and his conspiracies and wiles made the occasions and means of fulfilling God's plan which he opposed, and crowning the Son of man with glory.

The true dignity and significance of the rite of baptism can only then be adequately realized when we appreciate this comprehensive extent and grandeur of the baptizing office of Christ, signified by it. In the fulfillment of that office he now orders all things; and its exercise must be continuous to the end. The Great Baptizer must breathe the Spirit of life into all that mighty multitude, out of every generation and race, whom the Father has given Him. He must send fire upon the earth, and divide between his people and his enemies, and vindicate the Father's sovereignty and grace in all his dealings with the wicked. He must, at last, by the quickening virtue of the baptism of His Spirit, raise up his saints,—their bodies glorious as his own glorious body, and their souls perfect in holiness,—and place them on the throne of judgment with himself; judge and cast the wicked out of his kingdom; confirm the holy angels in rectitude and blessedness, and cast Satan,— thwarted, defeated and bound in chains of darkness,—into the gulf of fire,—him and his angels and followers. He must purge the earth and heavens with fire, from the defilement which Satan and sin have wrought, and out of them create and adorn the new heavens and the new earth, the abode of righteousness, the home of the holy and the blessed,—where the many sons shall dwell with God and the Lamb. He must make all things new.

Then may the triumphant Son of man proclaim his work accomplished, and his office ended. Then may he,—not now from the cross, but from the throne,— cry, "It is finished!" "The former things are passed away, and behold I have made all things new." Sin and the curse are abolished;—tears, and death, and sorrow, and crying, and pain are no more; and in life and immortality the earth-born sons of God possess the glory.

"It is done!" The floor is purged; the garner filled; and the chaff burned. The baptism is accomplished. Then shall the Son, his commission fulfilled, deliver up the kingdom to God even the Father, and shall himself also be subject to Him that put all things under him, that God may be all in all. (1 Cor. xv, 24, 28.)

> Section LXXIV.—*Argument from the Real to Ritual Baptism.*—The real baptism has to do, not with abasement and the grave, but with exaltation and power. But immersion looks only to the grave. It is incongruous to all the phenomena of Pentecost. Immersed in "the sound from heaven,"

Thus is Jesus revealed in characters of unspeakable grandeur, as the true and only Baptizer,—his the real baptism, of which all others are mere shadows. His baptizing office is the very end of his exaltation, the peculiar and distinguishing characteristic of his throne and scepter. As the cross of Christ is the symbol of the whole doctrine of his humiliation, sorrow and death, so his baptizing scepter represents the whole doctrine of his exaltation his kingdom and glory. And, as the sacrament of the supper shows forth his abasement and atonement for sin;

so, that of baptism proclaims the glory and power of his exaltation, and the riches of salvation and grace which he sheds on his people from on high. The ritual ordinance therefore if true to its office, must be true to the similitude of the real baptism,—must represent and proclaim those very things which are realized in the office and work of the great Baptizer. But what has the real baptism to do with the humiliation of Christ, in any of its aspects? And, especially, what has it to do with the burial of his dead body? With the throne of his power, the prerogatives of his scepter, the grace, the grandeur and the glory of his achievements to the end, its relations are intimate and from them inseparable. But with humiliation and shame, with death and the grave, it holds no relations but those of boundless distance and infinite contrast.

Here then, at the culminating point in the history of baptism and the plan of God's grace, as identified with it, the divergence of the immersion theory from the statements, conceptions and principles of the Scriptures on the subject interposes between them a widening and deepening gulf, broad, profound and impassable. Whilst the Scriptural rite points exultingly upward to Christ's high throne, and calls us to lift up our heads and admire and adore the height of his majesty and the grace and grandeur of his baptizing work,—the immersion theory constrains its votaries, with bowed heads and stooping forms, to grope among the graves, in the vain endeavor to trace some fanciful resemblance between the rite which they espouse and the form and manner of the burial of the dead,—a burial, too, which, as thus imagined, the crucified One never received!

The doctrine of the real baptism is thus utterly incongruous to that of immersion. Equally irreconcilable with that form are all the phenomena and expressions used in connection with the administering of Christ's baptism. The sound from heaven as of an outbreathed mighty breath poured down, and filling all the place, was the only phenomenon of Pentecost indicative of form or mode. And its mode was affusion, or outpouring, and descent from above. The language in which the transaction is everywhere described and referred to is equally specific and invariable. It was a shedding down—a pouring down—a falling upon—a filling of the disciples;—a style of expression used, not on the occasion, only, but in every subsequent allusion to the subject. So, the prophecy cited by Peter is an express definition of this as the mode. "I will pour out of my Spirit." But, more than this, it identifies the outpouring of Pentecost with all those Old Testament prophecies, in which the gift of the Spirit is spoken of in terms of pouring and sprinkling. All these, again, as we have formerly seen, are intimately associated with the baptisms of the Levitical system. Those baptisms represented in ritual form the things which the prophets set forth in analogous figures. If Christian baptism departs from the Old Testament mode, it to the same degree departs from the form in which the grace of Pentecost is uniformly predicted, represented, described, and referred to.

The attempt is made to evade the force of these facts by the assertion that the "sound from heaven as of a rushing mighty wind," "filled all the place where they were sitting;" and that the disciples were immersed in it. But (1.) the immersion thus imagined is, an inversion of the Baptist theory. The result of an admitted affusion, it is an application of the element to the person, and by a sustained analogy, on Baptist principles, would require that the grave should have been brought and put about the body of Jesus, and that, in water baptism, the element should be poured over the subject, until he is covered, although drowning would be the inevitable result. (2.) There is, in fact, no analogy, except in the jingle of words, between an immersion in water, which is immediately and inevitably fatal to life, and an immersion in the vital air, which is the very breath of life, the withdrawal of which is fatal. (3.) If Christian baptism sustains any real relation at all to the baptism of the Holy Spirit, which Christ administers—as it assuredly does—it is that of type to antitype—of a similitude to the reality. Both the form and the meaning of the rite must be derived from the nature of the reality, of which it is the symbol. If then the immersion of the disciples in the wind or breath of Pentecost is the antitype symbolized in the outward form of baptism, the ordinance means, not the burial of Christ's dead body, but the imparting of his Spirit of life to his people. Thus the Baptist theory of the form and meaning of the ordinance is exploded, since the two ideas can not stand together. They are mutually destructive and the incongruity is fatal to the whole scheme, which can not stand without an immersion on Pentecost; and can not endure the crucial test of the only immersion which they can pretend to discover there.

The alternative is inexorable. If that which Christ dispenses is the normal, the antitype, baptism, then by it the ritual baptisms of both economies are to be interpreted; and their signification is to be found, not in the sepulchre, but on the throne—in the Spirit thence poured out, and the life and salvation thence dispensed;—and the form of the ordinance must needs correspond to its meaning. If, on the other hand, immersion in water is the normal baptism, and the burial of the body of Jesus, its meaning, then the baptism of Pentecost with all its phenomena and doctrine is to be struck from the record, as no baptism at all. *If that which Christ dispenses is baptism, immersion is not.*

PART XII.

THE BAPTIST ARGUMENT.

Section LXXV.—*Baptizo and the Resurrection.*—Elements of the Baptist argument. Dr. Conant on baptizo. It leaves its subjects in the water. Dr. Kendrick's admissions. A second meaning in baptizo

The argument in proof that the disciples of John and of Christ were immersed comprehends four essential propositions. (1) That *baptizo* means, to dip, to plunge, to immerse, to submerge,—one or other of these, and *nothing else*; (2) That the prepositions, *eis, en, ek*, and *apo*, as used in the New Testament, in connection with *baptizo*, require and enforce that meaning; (3) That the resort of John to the Jordan, and to Enon, "because there was much water there," is conclusive to the same effect; (4) That Paul, in saying that we are "buried with Christ in baptism," refers to the form of immersion; (5) It is, moreover, held that the account of the baptism of the Ethiopian eunuch shows it to have been by immersion. The last point will be considered further on.

As to *baptizo*, enough has already appeared to render it certain that the definition heretofore insisted on by Baptists is untenable, and that the word, in itself, determines nothing as to form. It was formerly maintained as unquestionable, that *bapto* and *baptizo* are strictly equivalent; and that the meaning is, "to dip, and nothing but dip." This assumption may now be considered obsolete. It is definitely abandoned by the ablest representatives of immersion. Dr. Conant having been appointed thereto by the American (Baptist) Bible Union entered into an elaborate investigation of "The Meaning and Use of *Baptizo*." In a treatise published under that title, he thus states the result. "The word, *immerse*, as well as its synonyms, *immerge*, etc., expresses the full import of the Greek word, *baptizein*. The idea of emersion is not included in it. It means simply to put into or under water; without determining whether the object immersed sinks to the bottom, or floats in the liquid, or is immediately taken out. This is determined, not by the word, itself, but by the design of the act, in each particular case. A living being, put under water without intending to drown him, is of course to be immediately withdrawn from it; and this is to be understood, whenever the word is used with reference to such a case. But the Greek word is also used where a living being is put under the water for the purpose of drowning, and of course is left to perish in the immersing element."[102] It is of the primary meaning of the word that Dr. Conant here speaks. As we have already seen, he also recognizes a secondary meaning, the importance

---

[102] The Meaning and Use of Baptizein, p. 88.

of which he entirely ignores. As to the former, the admission here transcribed is conclusive, although obscured by ambiguous and impertinent explanations. No verb can "determine" any thing subsequent to the completion of its own proper action. The healed paralytic, "*departed* to his own house." "Paul *arose* and was baptized." "John *came* baptizing." He that should explain that "departed" does not of necessity imply that he never returned, that Paul may have sat down again; and that for all the meaning of "came" John may afterward have gone away, would be held guilty of puerile trifling. Of course, *baptizo* determines nothing but its own action. The explanation of Dr. C. that the word does not determine whether the object sinks to the bottom or is immediately taken out, is not trifling, because open to a more serious charge. It is a diligent, although undoubtedly unconscious obscuring of the subject, induced by the instinctive recoil of the author's own mind from the picture drawn by his definition. He is therefore impelled to retire it into the background and veil its nakedness in the drapery of explanations, by which he is as much confounded as are his readers,—explanations wholly impertinent to the question in hand, which is the meaning of *baptizo*. That word, in its primary classic sense, as here defined, expresses a definite and *completed* act. When by one continuous process a person or thing is put into the water and withdrawn, it is not a *baptizing*, in the classic meaning, but a *bapting*, a dipping. It is true the word does not determine "whether the object immersed sinks to the bottom or floats in the liquid, or is immediately taken out," provided that by "immediately," is not to be understood, instantaneously,—provided that by the baptism, the object is deposited in the water and left there. The emersion, if it take place at all, must be a distinct and subsequent act, and can not be performed as *a part of the baptizing*. This, Dr. Kendrick, professor of Greek in the Rochester University, and a member of the American Committee of Revision on the New Testament, in his review of Dr. Dale, most emphatically concedes, with italics and emphasis none the less significant because of the intense irritation which breathes in his article. "Granting that *bapto, always* engages to take its subject from the water (which we do not believe), and that *baptizo never* does (which we readily admit), we have Mr. Dale's reluctant concession that it interposes no obstacle to his coming out." *Baptizo* "lays its subject under the water; it does not hold him there a single moment. Its whole function is fulfilled with the act of submersion. It offers no shadow of an obstacle to his instant emergence from his watery entombment. We have the utmost confidence in the kindly purpose of *baptizo*, and of Him who has made its liquid grave the external portal to his kingdom. Neither it nor He intends to drown us. We let *baptizo* take us into the water, and can trust to men's instinctive love of life, their common sense, their power of volition and normal muscular action, to bring them safely out." "The law of God in revelation sends the Baptist down into the waters of immersion; when it is accomplished, the equally imperative law of God in nature brings him safely out." "As between the two [*baptizo* and *bapto*], *baptizo* is the appropriate word, partly from its greater length, weight and dignity of form, and still more from its distinctive import. It is not a dipping that our Lord instituted, but an immersion. He did not command *to put people into the water* and *take them out again;* but *to put them under the water*, to *submerge* them, to *bury* them, symbolically, in the grave of their buried Redeemer; like him indeed, not to remain there, but with him to arise to newness of life. This arising, though essential to the completeness of the transaction, could not be included in the designation of the rite, any more than the rising of the Redeemer could be included in the words denoting his crucifixion and burial." "We repeat with emphasis, for the consideration of our Baptist brethren; Christian baptism is no mere literal and senseless 'dipping,' assuring the frightened candidate of a safe exit from the water; it is a symbolical immersion, in which the believer goes, in a sublime and solemn trust, into a figurative burial, dying to sin for a life with Christ; and just as far as Mr. Dale's distinction holds good (which even thus far *he* has not established), *baptizo*, and not *bapto* is the only suitable designation of the baptismal ordinance. The early Israelites were baptized to Moses in the cloud and in the sea. They emerged indeed, and were intended to emerge at last. But it was in their wondrous march, through that long and fearful night, with the double wall of water rolled up on each side, and the column of fiery cloud stretching its enshrouding folds above them,—it was in this, and not in the closing emersion that they were baptized into their allegiance to their great Lawgiver and Leader."[103]

Of the baptism of Israel, we shall take notice hereafter. In these passages, it is evident that the distinguished professor 1869, pp. 142, 143. is as much disturbed at the apparition of his own raising as is Dr. Conant. At first he seems determined to face it squarely, and calls upon his Baptist brethren to look and see that it is nothing dangerous. But suddenly, he crosses himself, and starts back in a hurried talk of the resurrection of Christ and the rising of his people to newness of life; all of which is very true and precious, but, has no more to do with the question in hand, himself being witness, than has the doctrine of original sin. The question is, the meaning of *baptizo*, and the professor admits that it has no part in the resurrection. The very perplexing position in which he found himself, is some apology for the confusion of ideas and the incongruities which appear in his statements. He is discussing the relative merits of the two words *bapto* and *baptizo*. The former, in its primary and ordinary meaning, he can but acknowledge, engages both to put its subject into the water and take him out again; while *baptizo* only puts him in. The latter, says the professor, was chosen because of this its distinctive import, because the command was, *not* "to put the people into the water and take them out again; but to put them under the water,—to submerge them." But before he is done, we are told that the coming out, "though essential to the completeness of the transaction *could* not be included in the designation of the rite." Does "the transaction," here mean the life saving operation which he confides to the "instinctive love of life, common sense," etc? Or, are we correct in supposing it to mean that baptismal rite which he is discussing? And if the latter be the design, how is the statement to be reconciled with the reason just before given for the employment of *baptizo*, because it does *not* take the subject out of the water, while *bapto* does? Waiving this difficulty, the question occurs,—Why the rising "could not be included in the designation of the rite," seeing *bapto* was ready to add that very idea to the meaning of *baptizo*? The question is anticipated by the professor, and the answer given. It is because the latter word has "greater *length*, *weight*, and *dignity* of form!" The meaning of the words was a secondary consideration! *Bapto*

[103] Review of Dale's Classic Baptism, in the *Baptist Quarterly,*

has but two syllables, while *baptizo* has three. It has the advantage, therefore, in a greater length, and a buzzing zeta, to add to its "weight and dignity of form!" Or, perhaps, the superior "weight" of the one word over the other consists in the fact that while *bapto* accurately expresses the hasty resurrection which the instinct of life and other influences specified so happily, though not invariably, connect with the administration of the rite, *baptizo* maintains a dignified silence on that part of the subject. But the professor drifts back again to his first position. He insists that the baptism of Israel into Moses was received in their "wondrous march" enclosed between the walls of water, and enshrouded in the cloud, "and *not* in the closing emersion." And yet, even here, his protest that *bapto* itself would not have given absolute assurance of exit, looks like a disposition to weaken the force of "the distinctive import" of *baptizo*.

However these "dark sayings of the wise" are to be interpreted, the facts remain, that, confessedly, the word chosen by the Savior to designate the rite of baptism does not include in it the idea of emersion, typical of resurrection,—that it was chosen in preference to a kindred word which does distinctly express that idea,—and that the best reasons suggested by Baptist scholarship for this remarkable fact are, that *burial* and *not* resurrection was the doctrine symbolized; and that *baptizo* sounds best! Such are the results of the elaborate researches of the scholarly Conant, confirmed by the eminent learning of Kendrick, divines than whom the Baptist churches have had none more zealous or more competent. Essentially the same is the definition reached through the exhaustive studies of our own departed Dale.

Thus, according to the Baptist rendering of the gospel commission, we are to go into all the world and *submerge* every creature,—a command which neither contains nor implies authority in any one to neutralize it by a systematic rescue of its subjects from the "liquid grave." A result of the most serious import to our Baptist brethren follows from these facts. The definition, to dip, for the sake of which they have so long separated themselves, in translating the Scriptures into the languages of the heathen, is demonstrably and confessedly false, and the result is a corrupting of the word of God.

The force of these facts against the very foundations of the immersion fabric is utterly destructive. But the matter does not rest even here. Dr. Conant recognizes in *baptizo* a second meaning. The word does not even limit itself to "submerge and nothing but submerge." It also "expressed the coming into a new state of life or experience, in which one was, as it were enclosed or swallowed up, so that temporarily or permanently he belonged wholly to it."[104] Thus, the man who is brought under the control of a passion of anger, fear, or love, or who is overcome with wine or sleep, was by the Greeks said to be baptized with these things. So, in the Scriptures, he who is under such control that he is "led of the Spirit," is said to be "baptized with the Spirit." This meaning of *baptizo* no candid scholar can deny; and in it we have already seen abundant relief from all the perplexities of the immersion theory. Respecting it, however, a caution is necessary. A mere momentary impulse or influence by which one is seized, but, instantly, released, is not a baptism, in

---

[104] "Meaning and Use of Baptizein," p. 158.

the classic sense. The word expressed a control which not only seizes but *holds* its object. It brings him "into a new *state* of life or experience." This use of the word flows from the primary meaning, to *submerge*, as expressive not of comprehensive control, only, but of continuance. Nothing analogous to a momentary dipping was known to the Greeks as a baptism.

Section LXXVI.—*The Prepositions.—En. Eis. Ek. Apo.* They indicate, not the mode, but the place of the baptisms

In the common English version of the New Testament, the translations which occur in connection with baptism are such as to show an evident bias on the part of the translators in favor of immersion. In fact they were, all of them, immersionists, if not by personal conviction, then, by constraint of law. They were members, and with a few exceptions clergymen of the church of England, by law established. That church had originally incorporated among its ordinances, baptism by trine immersion. By the parliamentary revision during the reign of Edward VI, the book of prayer was so altered as to require but one immersion. The rubric for baptism was and is to this day in these words:—"Then the priest shall take the child in his hands, and ask the name; and naming the child, shall dip it in the water, so it be discreetly and warily done, saying, 'N., I baptize thee in the name of the Father and of the Son, and of the Holy Ghost. Amen.' And, if the child be weak, it shall suffice to pour water upon it, saying the aforesaid words."[105]

As to the bearing of the prepositions on the present argument, a brief illustration may make it clear to the English reader. In the following citations, the words in italics answer to the Greek prepositions under which respectively they are cited.

1. *En.* "And were all baptized of him (*en*) *in* Jordan."—Matt. iii, 6. "John did baptize *in* the wilderness."—Mark i, 4. "John was baptizing *in* Enon."—John iii, 23. "These things were done *in* Bethabara, beyond Jordan, where John was baptizing."—John i, 28. "The tower *in* Siloam."—Luke xiii, 4. "Elias is come, and they have done *unto* him whatsoever they listed."—Matt. xvii, 12. "Turn the disobedient *to* the wisdom of the just."—Luke i, 17. "Lest they trample them *with* their feet."—Matt. vii, 6. "Sanctify them *through* thy truth, thy word is truth."—John xvii, 17. "They that take the sword shall perish *with* the sword."—Matt. xxvi, 52. "There is none other name ... *by* which we must be saved."—Acts iv, 12. "He will judge the world ... *by* that man whom he hath ordained."—Ib. xvii, 31. "Now revealed *by* the Spirit"—Eph. iii, 5. "That *at* the name of Jesus every knee should bow."—Phil. ii, 10. From these illustrations two deductions are manifest (1.) *En* does not always mean *in*. It may mean *with* or *by*, instrumentally. "*With* the sword." "The name *by* which," etc. It may mean *by* a mediate agent. "Revealed *by* the Spirit." "He will judge the world *by* that man." It may mean *at*, *by*, or *in*, locally. "*In* Enon." "*At* Siloam." It may be used in a yet more general signification, as, "*At* the name." Other meanings might be stated, but these are sufficient (2.) If, by reason of the phrase "*in* Jordan," we must understand that John immersed his disciples *into* the

---

[105] "The Two Books of Common Prayer," set forth by authority of Parliament, in the reign of King Edward VI, edited by Edward Cardwell, D.D., Principal of St. Alban's Hall, Oxford, 1852.

Jordan, it of necessity follows that he also immersed them *"into* Enon," and *"into* the wilderness." In short, the expression indicates that the Jordan was the place *at* which the baptizing was done:—this, and this only. Why it was done there, we shall presently see.

2. *Eis.* "Jesus came from Nazareth of Galilee and was baptized of John (*eis*) *in* Jordan."—Mark i, 9. "They went down both *into* the water, both Philip and the eunuch and he baptized him."—Acts viii, 38. These passages mutually illustrate each other and show that the going *into* the water was not the baptizing. "He came and dwelt *in* a city called Nazareth."—Mat. ii, 23. "He cometh *to* a city of Samaria," but he remained outside, at the well, while the apostles went *"into* the city," whence the Samaritans "went out of the city and came to him."—John iv, 5, 8, 28, 30. "He loved them *to* the end."—Ib. xiii, 1. "I speak *to* the world." Ib. viii, 26. "If thy brother trespass *against* thee."—Matt, xviii, 15. "*Therefore*" (Literally, *to* this) "came I forth."—Mark i, 38. "What are they *among* so many."—John vi, 9. "The Son which is *in* (on) the bosom of the Father."—John i, 18. "He went up *into* (*to*, or, *on*,) a mountain."—Matt., v, 1. "Depart *unto* the other side."—Ib. viii, 18. "Fell down *at* his feet."—Ib. xviii, 29. *Eis* is even used in express contrast with entrance into. "The other disciple did outrun Peter, and first (*ēlthen eis*) *came to* the sepulchre, ... yet went he not *in.* Then cometh Simon Peter following him and (*eis-ēlthen eis*) *entered into* the sepulchre."—John xx, 4-6. This illustrates a usage concerning *eis.* When entrance *into* is to be expressed by the mere force of the word, it must be doubled. See Matt. vi, 6; x, 5, 12; Luke ix, 34, etc. The same remark applies to *ek*, in the sense of *out of.* But neither of these words is ever used in duplicated form, with reference to baptism. It is evident that the word of itself determines no more as to the mode of the baptism of Jesus than does *en.* The ordinary office of *eis* is to point to the terminus of a preceding verb of motion. When it is said that Jesus came and dwelt (*eis*) *in* a city called Nazareth, *en* would have been the proper preposition to express the in-dwelling; but *eis* is preferred because the city was the terminus of the coming "He came (*eis*) *to* a city." So Mark above uses the same word, not because of its appropriateness to the baptizing, which is always elsewhere expressed by *en*, but because the Jordan was the terminus (*eis*) to which he came from Galilee.

3. *Ek.* "And when they were come up (*ek*) *out of* the water."—Acts viii, 39. In his gospel, Luke the author of this account thus uses the preposition. "Saved *from* our enemies."—Luke i, 71. "Every tree is known *by* its own fruit, for *of* thorns men do not gather figs; nor *of* a bramble-bush gather they grapes."—Ib. vi, 44. "He cometh *from* the wedding."—Ib. xii, 36. "All these have I kept *from* my youth up."—Ib. xviii, 21. So far as this word determines, Philip and the eunuch may have come up *from* the water, without having been *in* it, at all.

4. *Apo.* "Jesus when he was baptized, went up straightway (*apo*) *out of* the water."—Matt. iii, 16. *Apo never* means, "out of," as here translated; but, "from," "away from." "When Jesus was come down *from* the mountain."—Matt. viii, 1. "*From* whom do kings take tribute?"—Ib. xvii, 25. "Cast them *from* thee."—Ib. xviii, 8. "Beginning *from* the last unto the first."—Ib. xx, 8.

From these illustrations, which might be multiplied indefinitely, it is evident that the prepositions will not bear the stress put upon them by the Baptist argument. Not only are they, in themselves, insufficient to constitute a reliable basis for the conclusions sought; but the statements to which they belong have respect, *not* to the *mode* of the baptism, but to the places of it. They are defined by the phrases, "*in* Jordan," — "*in* Enon," — "*in* Bethabara." Recent Baptist writers have had the courage to follow their principles to the result of translating John's words, — "I immerse you *in* water, but he shall immerse you *in* the Holy Ghost and *in* fire," — a rendering from which the better taste, if not the better scholarship, of the translators of King James's version revolted. The thorough consideration already given in these pages to the baptism of the Spirit justifies an imperative denial of the correctness of this translation. If any thing in the Bible is clear, it is that the baptism administered by the Lord Jesus is not an immersion, but an outpouring.

On the question of the prepositions in this connection, light is shed by an expression of the apostle Paul. "By one Spirit are we all baptized into one body, ... and have been all made to drink one Spirit." — 1 Cor. xii, 13. Of this passage we have already indicated that "into," as found in the last clause, in the common version ("to drink *into* one Spirit"), is spurious, and that *potizo* ("made to drink"), properly signifies, to *apply* water or other fluid, whether externally or internally, to water, to cause to drink. In this passage, we have both the prepositions, *en* and *eis*, each dependent on the one verb, *baptizo*, but each having its own distinctive subject. "Baptized (*en*), in one Spirit (*eis*), into one body." Into which of these media does the immersion take place? Shall we follow the Baptist interpretation of the words of John, "He shall immerse you *in* the Holy Ghost?" But in the first place, we have seen that this is false to the real manner of the baptism in question; which consists in a shedding down of the Spirit. In the second, how then, in harmony with Baptist principles, are we to understand the other clause of the passage, — "Immersed *in* one Spirit, *into* one body?" Are there here two immersions by one act? the one subject put at one and the same time into two different media? Moreover, the language with which the apostle closes the passage, while it is in perfect accord with the true mode of the baptism of the Spirit, is altogether incongruous to the Baptist interpretation. If we are baptized with or by the Spirit, shed upon us, we may consistently be said to drink (or, to be watered with) the Spirit. For, the earth and its vegetation drink the rain that falls upon them. But if we must be immersed in the Spirit, Paul's language implies that in order that men be caused to drink they are to be immersed in the water. "Immersed in one Spirit, and all made to drink one Spirit."

But the phrase, *en heni Pneumati*, does not mean "*in* one Spirit." As we have seen, the preposition may and often does mean "*with*," or "*by*," the Spirit, as the agent or instrument. Especially by Paul, the writer of the passage in question, is the phrase so used, — "Through Him we both have access (*en heni Pneumati*), *by* one Spirit unto the Father." — Eph. ii, 18. Here is the very phrase in question. Through the Lord Jesus, the Mediator, *by* his Spirit as the instrument, who, being sent by him helpeth our infirmities, in prayer (Rom. viii, 26), we have access to the Father's presence. Again, — "On whom," as the chief corner stone, "we are builded together, for an habitation of God (*en Pneumati*), *by* the Spirit," who is the efficient builder of the spiritual temple. Again, the apostle tells of the mystery which is "now revealed unto His holy apostles and prophets (*en Pneumati*), *by* the Spirit" (Eph. iii, 5), and exhorts us, "Be not drunk with wine, wherein is excess, but be filled (*en*) *with* the Spirit" (Ib. v, 18), and to "pray with all prayer and supplication (*en*) *by* the Spirit."—Ib. vi, 18. So in the text,—"*With*, or, *by* one Spirit," the instrument and agent of grace shed on us abundantly by Jesus Christ "are we all baptized"— brought into a new state of incorporation "into one body," which he pervades and controls as the Spirit of life. Into it we are not immersed; but, united by his common in-dwelling power, are made daily "to drink of that one Spirit," which is in us, "a well of water springing up into everlasting life."—John iv, 14.

It is not necessary to the present purpose to dwell further on the signification and bearing of the prepositions. The moment *baptizo* ceases to mean, to dip, and nothing else, the prepositions lose all determining force upon the questions at issue. If John's disciples were dipped or submerged in Jordan all is plain, and discussion is at an end. But if John *baptized* in Jordan, the question still remains,—*How did he baptize?* This is very clearly illustrated by the case of the Ethiopian eunuch, if we accept the immersion rendering of the prepositions. "They went down both into the water, both Philip and the eunuch." They have now reached the place, *in* the water, if you will. But the baptism is yet to be performed.—"*And* he baptized him." But *how* did he do it? The baptism is now ended; but both are still in position "*in* the water;" out of which they are then stated to have come. (Acts viii, 38, 39.)

Section LXXVII.—"*There was much Water there.*"—Aenon=The Springs.
Many waters. Why Jesus and John resorted to waters

Appeal is made to the fact that John baptized "in Enon, near to Salim, because there was much water there."—John iii, 23. Enon (*Aenōn*), is the plural form, a word which means a spring or fountain. In a few places it is translated, a well of water. But it signifies a flowing spring. The name, therefore, means, The Springs near to Salim. All attempts to trace a town or city of that name have failed; and the whole manner of John's ministry and statements of the evangelists indicate him to have selected a retired spot, rather than a town or city, as the place of his preaching and baptism.

The phrase, "much water," is not a correct translation of the original (*polla hudata*), which means, many waters,—that is, many springs, or streams. The phrase occurs nine times in the Greek of the Old Testament, and four times in the New, beside the place in question. It is never used in the sense of unity,—"much water,"—but invariably expresses the conception of plurality. In several places, it designates the waves of the sea in a tumult. Thus, Psa. xciii, 3, 4,—"The floods have lifted up, O Lord, the floods have lifted up their voice; the floods lift up their waves. The Lord on high is mightier than the noise of *many waters*; yea, than *the mighty waves* of the sea." See, also, 2 Sam. xxii, 17; Psa. xviii, 16; xxix, 3; Isa. xvii, 12, 13; Ezek. xliii, 2; Rev. i, 15; xiv, 2; xix, 6. In these places the noise of many waters, is the sound of the waves, as they toss in the fury of a storm, or thunder upon the shore. Again, it is used to designate many streams, and even the rivulets which for the purposes of irrigation were carried through vineyards and gardens. Thus, "Thy mother was as a vine, and as a shoot planted by a stream, by waters; the fruit of which, and its sprouts were from *many waters*." —Ezek. xix, 10. See, also, Num. xxiv, 7, and Jer. li, 13. In the last of these passages, Babylon is described as dwelling "upon many waters," meaning, not the Euphrates, only; but the four rivers, Euphrates, Tigris, Chaboras and Ulai, and the many canals of irrigation, vestiges of which continue to this day, to which Babylonia was indebted for its fertility, and the city for its wealth and power. Compare Psalm cxxxvii, 1, "By the rivers of Babylon, there we sat down, yea we wept, when we remembered Zion." In the text of John, the phrase coincides with the name of Enon, to indicate that the peculiarity of the place was a number of flowing springs. The bearing of these upon the question as to the mode of John's Baptism is inappreciable; as, for the purposes of immersion, he did not need more than one.

But, we recur to the challenge, so confidently urged. If John did not immerse, why his resort to the Jordan, and to the "much water" of Enon? We reply by another question. Why did the Lord Jesus concentrate his ministry upon the shore of the Sea of Galilee? Why did he, after the close of his labors in that part of the land, take up his abode at that very "place where John at first baptized?" —John x, 40. A comparison of the evangelists shows that, as did John (Luke iii, 3), so Jesus began his ministry by journeying through the country and villages preaching the gospel. But, as his fame spread abroad and the concourse of his hearers increased, he was accustomed to resort to the shores of the Sea of Galilee and the slopes of the mountains which enclose it on the west. A comparison of the evangelists shows the sermon on the mount to have been uttered from one of those mountains. (Matt. v, 1; Mark iii, 7-13.) In the brief narrative of Mark, that sea is six times spoken of as the scene of his labors; and these are evidently mere illustrations of the habit of his ministry. Thus, the first such mention states that "he went forth *again* by the sea side, and all the multitude resorted unto him and he taught them." —Mark ii, 13, and see iii, 7; iv, 1; v, 21; vi, 31-33; vii, 31; viii, 10. Here, he fed the five thousand men, beside women and children, with five barley loaves and two small fishes; and here, the four thousand, with seven barley loaves and a few small fishes. Afterward, when his ministry in Galilee was finished and he would preach in Judea, he found himself beset, before his time, by the machinations of the scribes and rulers. He therefore withdrew beyond Jordan, to "the place where John at first baptized, and there he abode, and many resorted to him, ... and many believed on him there." —John x, 39-42, and Mark x, 1. It is evident that the facts here referred to were not casual nor fortuitous. They constitute one of the most prominent features of the story of our Lord's ministry. It is also manifest that these and the facts concerning the places of John's ministry belong to the same category; so that no explanation can be sufficient which does not account for all alike.

The Baptist theory is not thus adequate. They will not pretend that it was to immerse his disciples, that Jesus resorted to the lake and to Bethabara. We may, therefore, conclude that the explanation of John's places of baptism is to be sought upon some other principle. A candid consideration of the circumstances will discover it; and customs peculiar to this country may confirm the solution. The assemblies that attended on the ministry of John and of Jesus were essentially similar to our camp-meetings, with the only difference, that the simpler habits of the people of Judea and Galilee rendered any preparation of tents or booths unnecessary. On one occasion we casually learn that the people remained together three days (Mark viii, 2); and the circumstances indicate that generally they were "protracted meetings." For example, at one time, Mark states that "Jesus withdrew himself with his disciples to the sea; and a great multitude from Galilee, followed him, and from Judea, and from Jerusalem, and from Idumea, and from beyond Jordan, and they about Tyre and Sidon, a great multitude, when they had heard what great things he did, came unto him."—Mark iii, 7, 8. Luke in one place speaks of "an innumerable multitude of people (*tōn muriadōn tou ochlou*, the tens of thousands of the throng) insomuch that they trode one upon another."—Luke xii, 1. See, also, the descriptions of John's audiences. In choosing the place for a camp-meeting, three things are recognized as of the first necessity. These are, retirement, accessibility, and abundance of water. Why these are essential, needs no explanation. As to the last, food may be brought from a distance; but if abundance of water, for the supply of man and beast, is not found on the spot, its use for such a purpose is manifestly and utterly impracticable.

The argument applies with double force to the thirsty climate of Judea. As heretofore stated, there are very few running streams in the land. The requisite supplies for the people in the towns and villages in which the population was concentrated were obtained from wells. There is scarcely a single perennial stream flowing from the west into the Jordan, in its whole course from the sea of Galilee to the Dead Sea. Its affluents are "mere winter torrents, rushing and foaming during the continuance of rain, and quickly drying up after the commencement of summer. For fully half the year, these 'rivers,' or 'brooks,' are often dry lanes of hot white or gray stones; or, tiny rills, working their way through heaps of parched boulders."[106] In a word, the banks of the Jordan, the shores of the sea of Tiberias, and some such exceptional spots as The Springs near Salim, presented the only sites in Palestine in which the three requisites above indicated were to be found united. Suppose the multitudes that were gathered to our Savior's ministry,—four and five thousand men, beside women, children and cattle; and those of John's preaching were, without doubt, as numerous,—to have been assembled with an improvident forgetfulness of the prime necessity of water! The alternative would have been a vast amount of suffering and the dispersion of the assembly, or miraculous interposition. But this does not meet the case of John's congregations; for "John did no miracle."

It is plain that we need no immersion theory, to account for the places chosen by John and Jesus for fulfilling their ministry. The necessities of their numerous audiences were decisive, and were in harmony with the requirement of the law that the sprinkled water of purifying should be living or running water.

Section LXXVIII.—*"Buried with him by Baptism into Death."*—Rom. vi, 2-7.—"Buried with him by *the* baptism into the death." Analysis of the passage. Spiritual baptism alone referred to. Immersion incongruous to Paul's conception

---

[106] Mr. George Grove, in Smith's Bible Dictionary, *article*, "Palestine."

The principal remaining Baptist argument is derived from two expressions of the apostle Paul which are supposed to show by implication that baptism was administered by immersion. These are;—Rom. vi, 4,—"Buried with him by baptism into death;" and Col. ii, 12,—"Buried with him in baptism." In our common English version as here quoted, there is a repeated neglect of the definite article, where it occurs in the original, which obscures the meaning. This defect being rectified, the first passage reads thus:—Rom. vi, 1-11. "What shall we say then? Shall we continue in sin that grace may abound? God forbid. How shall we that are dead by sin live any longer therein? Know ye not that so many of us as were baptized into Jesus Christ were baptized into his death? Therefore, we are buried with him by the baptism into the death; that like as Christ was raised up from the dead by the glory of the Father, even so we also should walk in newness of life. For, if we have been planted together in the likeness of his death, we shall be also in the likeness of his resurrection: knowing this, that our old man (sunestaurōthē) was crucified with him, that the body of sin might be destroyed, that henceforth we should not serve sin. For (ho apōthanōn) he that died is freed (dedikoiatai, is justified) from sin. Now, if we died with Christ, we believe that we will also live with him.... For in that he died (tē hamartia) by sin he died once: but in that he liveth he liveth (tō theō) by God" (that is, "by the power of God."—2 Cor. xiii, 4.) "Likewise reckon ye also yourselves to be dead indeed by sin, but alive by the power of God, through Jesus Christ our Lord."

In the present state of our argument, it might seem almost needless to discuss this passage. But this and the parallel text sustain relations to the subject, which clothe them with an importance in the discussion, such as attaches to no other Scriptures whatever. In them is contained and exhausted the entire evidence in behalf of the assumption that the form of baptism represents the burial of the Lord Jesus. Confessedly, that supposition, if not established by these two phrases of Paul, is without warrant anywhere in the Bible. But to prove the *interpretation* of the rite, they must of necessity, first, establish its very existence, which as yet is more than problematical. That they are not likely to prove adequate to the task thus laid upon them, will be apparent to the reader upon a moment's consideration. It is evident, and admitted by all, that the immediate subject of discussion in them is the baptism of the Spirit, and not ritual baptism, in any form. If the latter is referred to, at all, it is by mere allusion. That, this is true, as to the text to the Romans, is indicated alike by the form of expression, "baptized into Jesus Christ," and by the phenomena and results which are attributed to that baptism. It will hereafter appear that the two phrases, "baptized into Jesus Christ," and "baptized into the name of Christ," are those by which, in the Scriptures, the real baptism, and the ritual, are discriminated from each other. The one unites to the very body of Christ, the true, invisible church. The other unites to the *name* of Christ, and to that visible body which is named with his name. That it is of spiritual phenomena, and not of ritual forms, that Paul speaks, is moreover evident, from the purpose and tenor of his argument. His object is to repel the suggestion that free grace gives liberty to sin. His fundamental point in reply to this is, that God's people "are dead *by* sin," in such a sense that it is impossible they should "live any longer therein." To prove this, is the whole intent of his argument. First, in designating the subjects of his statements, he uses phraseology which emphasizes the difference between a mere outward relation to Christ and the church, and that which is established by the baptism of the spirit. "Know ye not that *so many* of us as were baptized *into Jesus Christ*." It is those who are truly one with Christ by a real spiritual union, and only those, whom he describes, and of whom he predicates what follows.

"Baptized into Jesus Christ." This is the one only baptism of the passage, the effects and consequences of which the apostle proceeds to set forth. Or, are we here to recognize three baptisms,—into Jesus Christ,—into his death,—and into his burial? The first effect of the baptism into Christ Paul indicates by the phrase, "baptized into his death." In the baptism into Christ, "by one Spirit are we all baptized into one body," the body of Christ, "and are all made to drink one Spirit." But it was by that Spirit that he offered himself without spot to God, and "died by sin," it being the meritorious cause of his death; and that Spirit being in us by virtue of the baptism, will cause the same hatred of sin, and induce in us a sense of its demerit and condemnation, so that we can no longer live in it. Such is the meaning of the apostle's expression, "baptized into his death,"—so united by the baptism into Christ, that as he died for sin to destroy it in us, so we will be dead to it in the same hatred and zeal for its destruction, inspired by the same Spirit. To intensify this conception, the apostle pursues the figure yet farther.—"Therefore, we are buried with him."—How? By immersion in water? or, By any thing of which such immersion is a symbol? No. But (*dia*) through, or, by means of the baptism just spoken of; "the baptism into the death" of Christ. That the expression can not possibly mean any ritual form of baptism is certain every way. The illative, "Therefore," forbids it. It shows the burial to be, not a physical phenomenon, real or ritual, but a consequence which, by virtue of the relation of cause and effect, logically results from something which either precedes or follows. But the boundaries in both directions are the same.—"*Baptized into his death.* Therefore buried with him, by the *baptism into the death.*" The baptism into Christ, by which we are baptized into his death, is thus the instrumental cause of the burial; a fact which utterly excludes any form of ritual baptism from the purview of the passage. But what is here meant by being buried with him? In order to an answer, it will be necessary to ascertain precisely who it is that dies and is buried with Christ. The answer comes promptly. "*We* are buried." True; but the words are to be taken in the light of the apostle's own interpretation. It is not we, in the entirety of our persons, but our old man, of which this is said. "Knowing this, that our old man is crucified with him, that the body of sin might be destroyed, that henceforth we should not serve sin."—Vs. 6. It is, to signify the utterness of this death and destruction of the old man,—its obliteration out of our lives, so that we can not "live any longer therein," nor "serve sin," that the apostle represents it as buried, and hidden away in a resurrectionless grave. The old man buried, so that the new man may unimpeded "walk in newness of life." In this doctrine and these words of the apostle, we have the very baptism which Dr. Conant admits to be expressed, "by analogy," by the word *baptizo;—"the coming into a new state of life or experience."* Into the conception of the passage, when critically appreciated, it is impossible to introduce the idea of immersion, in any congruous or intelligible relation.

The apostle illustrates his subject with another figure, which has been some-times pressed into the service of immersion. "For if we have been planted together in the likeness of his death, we shall be also in the likeness of his resurrection." It has been assumed that the planting of a tree is here associated with immersion in water ("buried by baptism"), as representing the burial of the dead. Thus, "the likeness of his *death*," which was by crucifixion, is confounded with the form of *burial* of the dead. This is recognized by Dr. Carson, whose exposition of the figure is essentially correct. Of *sumphutoi* ("planted together") he says, — "It might, I think, be applied to express the growing together of the graft and the tree; but this would be the effect or consequence of grafting, and not the operation itself. It denotes, in short, the closest union, with respect to things indiscriminately. There is no need, then, to bring either planting or grafting into the passage; and as neither of them resembles a resurrection, they should be rejected. When we translate the passage, — 'For, if we have become one with him,' or, 'have been joined with him, in the likeness of his death,' — we not only suit the connexion, to both death and resurrection, but we take the word *sumphutoi*, in its most common acceptation."[107] This witness is true. The phrase has no reference to the form of ritual baptism, but to the intimacy of the union which that of the Spirit establishes. The two expressions, — "Baptized into his death," and "Coplanted with him in the likeness of his death," are coincident, meaning essentially the same thing. It is, however, a fundamental defect in Carson's conception, that while he earnestly insists on the closeness of the union, by which Christ and his people are one, he fails to recognize the essential fact that it is effected by the baptism of the Spirit. In his conception and vocabulary, it is a "*constituted* union." A ray of light entering his mind on this point would have transfigured his whole system.

But what means our being joined with Christ in the likeness of his death? Here and elsewhere, Paul explains abundantly. "He died by sin," our sin, as being the meritorious cause of his death. "He was crucified through weakness," — the weakness of his humiliation, under the law and the curse. (2 Cor. xiii, 4.) He died by the cross, the agonies of which he voluntarily assumed. And he lives again, by the power of God who raised him from the dead. So we also, if truly baptized into him, "are weak (*en autō*) in him, but we shall live with him by the power of God toward us." — 2 Cor. xiii, 4. We are weak in him, in a realizing sense imparted by his Spirit in us, of the desert and condemnation of sin, and of its prevailing power, which renders our emancipation from it a crucifixion of the flesh, the agonies of which we voluntarily incur. And we live with him, in the present life of the new man after his image, created by the baptism of his Spirit in us, as we shall finally live with him in the life of glory. Thus we are joined with him in the likeness of his death, and also of his resurrection.

From this analysis, it is evident that the assumption of allusion to a supposed ritual burial is wholly unnecessary to the exegesis of the passage. In fact, the supposition of such allusion is altogether incongruous and confusing to the argument of the place. (1.) The real baptism and its effects are the alone subjects of the discussion; and any exegesis which ignores this must lead to error. (2.) The burial of

---

[107] Carson on Baptism, p. 251.

which the apostle speaks is spiritual, as well as is the baptism. The two are in no sense identical; but the one is, by the apostle distinctly and sharply discriminated from the other. The baptism is the primary cause, of which the burial is *one*, and but one, of the results. The baptism is the shedding upon us of the Holy Spirit of life in Christ Jesus. The burial is the putting away, and obliterating of the old man out of our lives. It follows, that in any parallel figurative or ritual system, each one of these spiritual realities must have its own analogue, as distinctly defined and discriminated, each from the other, as are the realities which they are designed to represent. And, in fact, such is the figurative system of the Scriptures, which represent the one by the figure of the outpouring of water, and the other by the burial of the dead. To interpret, therefore, a ritual *baptism* as symbolic of the spiritual *burial*, is as incongruous to the Scriptural conception, as would be the employment of the burial of the dead to represent the outpouring upon us of the Spirit of life. And to understand the apostle, by the expression, "buried by the baptism" to mean directly the spiritual phenomenon which the phrase designates, and at the same time to convey an allusion to a ritual *baptism* as being a symbol of the *burial*, is an absurdity which does violence to the whole conception, to the destruction of its propriety and significance. For, not only are the two thus sharply discriminated by Paul, but he attributes to each its own relations and predicates, and assigns to each its own place in the scheme of grace and in the argument which he states. To neglect, therefore, the distinction, and confound them together, as is done by the Baptist interpretation, destroys the whole logical force and sequence of the argument, and dissolves the connection between the premises and the conclusions.

Moreover, were it even allowable, as it is not, thus to confound things that differ, there still remains a point of difficulty in the way of the immersion exegesis which, for its removal, demands something more than the mere assumption which has heretofore been put in the place of proof. The apostle speaks, not of immersion, but of burial. "Buried with him." That the two ideas are not identical does not need to be proved. Nor is the difference so slight that the one would readily suggest itself as a figure of the other. But in order to sustain the Baptist conclusions which depend on this language, it would be necessary to demonstrate that the rites of sepulture with which the writers of the Scriptures were familiar, and in conformity to which the body of Jesus was entombed, bore a resemblance to immersion in water, so close and manifest, that the one was a recognized symbol of the other. But there is certainly no such resemblance as to justify the gratuitous assumption that such a figure was employed; and of its actual use, the Scriptures contain not a trace.

Is it still insisted that, nevertheless, there is an allusion to the rite of immersion? Such an allusion must be supposed to shed light or beauty upon the presentation of the spiritual theme of the passage; or, it is an arbitrary impertinence. Let us then view the suggestion squarely, in the light of the realized observance, thus forced into critical notice. The theme of the apostle is the calm majesty and power of the Savior's three days' rest in the sepulcher, and of the silent and unseen mystery of his rising on the third day; and the tranquil energy of the same mighty power in the believer (Eph. i, 19, 20; ii, 1), by which he is quickened and raised up to the life of holiness. The figure which is intruded, to illuminate and adorn this conception, calls up before us the apprehension and haste of the ritual observance, and the agitation, the gasping and sputter of the dripping subjects of the rite, as they struggle up out of the "watery grave." Is it possible to conceive that master of rhetoric, the apostle Paul, to have called up these, the essential and inseparable features of the rite of immersion, as a means of shedding light or beauty on his exalted theme?

> Section LXXIX.—"*Buried with Him in Baptism.*"—Col. ii, 9-13. The doctrine the same as the preceding. Union with the Lord Jesus the controlling idea. "Buried with him in (or, by) the baptism." The idea of immersion perplexes the exegesis

Col. ii, 9-13.—"In Him dwelleth all the fullness of the Godhead bodily. And ye are complete in him, which is the head of all principality and power. In whom, also, ye are circumcised with the circumcision made without hands, in putting off the body of the flesh by the circumcision of Christ (*suntaphentes autō en to baptismati*), *having been buried with him by the baptism*, wherein also ye were raised up with him, through the faith of the operation of God, who raised him from the dead. And you, being dead in your sins and the uncircumcision of your flesh, did he quicken together with him, having forgiven you all trespasses." Here, in the phrase,—"the body *of the sins* of the flesh," which is the reading of the common version, the critical editors unite in rejecting (*hamartiōn*) "of the sins," which was undoubtedly a gloss inserted from the margin, in careless transcription.

It is evident that the doctrine and argument of the passage just examined from the epistle to the Romans, and this to the Colossians are essentially the same. In the former, Paul shows that the child of God can not live in sin;—in the latter that he ought to walk in Christ. The controlling motive of the apostle's argument, here, is, to free his readers from the bondage of ritual ordinances and human devices of religion. He begins with the admonition,—"Beware lest any man spoil you through philosophy and vain deceit, after the tradition of men, after the rudiments of the world, and not after Christ."—vs. 8. To this, he again recurs as the conclusion of his argument.—"Therefore, if ye *be dead* with Christ, from the rudiments of the world, why as though *living* in the world are ye subject to ordinances, ... after the commandments and doctrines of men?"—vs. 20, 21. It is with a view to these things that the exhortation is written,—"As ye have *received* Christ Jesus the Lord, so, walk ye in *him*, rooted and built up in *him*, and established in *the faith*," as contrasted with these traditions of men. Thus, as in the parallel plea to the Romans, so here, the determining idea is union with the Lord Jesus,—that spiritual union of which the baptism of the Spirit is the efficient and only cause. The dignity and glory conferred by it are emphasized by the declaration that "in Him dwelleth all, (*plērōma*) *the fullness* of the Godhead bodily." In the person of Jesus, the Son is incarnate; the Father's glory and power invest him, and the Spirit is his and dwells in him. "And ye are (*peplērōmenoi*) *made full* in him." "Made full in him" by virtue of that mutual relation which Jesus describes;—"You in me, and I in you."—John xiv, 20. Thus, made full, with all the graces of his indwelling Spirit, and so needing no recourse to the rudiments of the world. With this fullness of grace, the apostle then contrasts the coincident emptying of the old man. "In whom ye are circumcised with the circumcision made without hands, in putting off the body of the flesh, by the circumcision of Christ." Circumcision signified the cutting off and destruction of the corrupt nature derived by generation, the old man, through the blood and sufferings of the promised Seed of Abraham. This operation is here called "the circumcision of Christ," as it is that spiritual reality of which ritual circumcision was the type. The apostle holds it up to view, as the substance, in contrast with the emptiness of the ritual shadow, against dependence on which he dissuades his Colossian readers. This circumcision of Christ he proceeds to explain farther. "Putting off the body of the flesh, by the circumcision of Christ, (*suntaphentes autō*) *having been buried with him* in the baptism." In the conception and argument of the apostle, emphasis rests on the definite article, which here, and in the parallel place, already examined, is ignored in the common English version, and in the Revised version. Paul's aim in this place is to hold up the spiritual realities of the gospel in contrast with the emptiness of ritual forms. He coordinates "*the* baptism" with "the circumcision of Christ," in producing the spiritual phenomena of which he is speaking. Or, rather, he postulates the baptism as the ultimate cause of the circumcision and its results. That, by the phrase, "the baptism," he designates the same thing as in Romans vi, 4, is evident, as it is also that as in that place, so here, the baptism is not the burial, but is related to it, as the cause to the effect.—"Buried with him *by* the baptism." How the baptism effects the burial, has been shown in that place. The distinction between the two, which is there so strongly marked, is in this passage equally clear and important; and the consequences there traced are here as legitimate and pertinent. The supposition of an allusion to immersion in water, in either place, is utterly groundless, and in both alike incongruous and destructive to the apostle's conception and argument. Certainly, this place no more than the other necessitates recourse to the supposed rite of immersion, in order to a rational interpretation. And it is equally certain that at the touch of a discriminating exegesis the supposed allusion to such a rite vanishes utterly away.

> Section LXXX.—*End of the Baptist Argument.*—Baptist scholars concede that *baptizo* does not mean, to dip, only. It can not then decide the mode. They admit that it leaves its subject in the water. It knows then nothing of the resurrection. The prepositions and waters of Enon do not help the cause. Paul's burial "in *the* baptism," does not allude to the ritual ordinance. In all its parts, the argument fails

The Baptist position rests on two assumptions. The *first* is, that *baptizo* means, to dip, to immerse, to submerge,—one or other of these, as the different advocates of the cause may select,—*and nothing else.* The *second* is, that on account of its resemblance to the laying of the body of Jesus in the sepulchre, the rite of dipping, immersion, or submersion in water was appointed as a symbol of his entombing. The first of these assumptions is essential to vindicate the mode in question, and the second to establish its typical significance. If *baptizo* does not mean as defined, or if that is not the only meaning, the whole immersion fabric falls to the ground. And if the second proposition is not established, the rite becomes an unmeaning absurdity.—On these vital points, the following are the results of the evidence thus far developed in these pages.

1. While the Scriptures everywhere, in the Old Testament and the New, are full of the doctrine of the baptism of the Spirit,—while the divers baptisms of the Mosaic ritual were unquestionably typical of it, and the prophecies abound in references to it under the figure of affusion—the sprinkling of water, and the outpouring of rain,—the rite of immersion does not pretend to any better evidence than is found in a definition of *baptizo*, which is now admitted to be erroneous, and a few expressions in the New Testament which are at best of questionable interpretation. Aside from these, it is foreign and uncongenial to the whole tenor of conception and language of the New Testament as well as of the Old.

2. Not to insist on the special conclusions of Dale,—the admissions of Dr. Conant, confirmed by the authority of Prof. Kendrick, prove that the word does not mean, to dip, to put in the water and take out again; but to put under the water, to submerge. The rite, then, consists in submerging the subjects. In that action the baptism is completed. There is therefore in it no symbol nor suggestion of the resurrection.

3. The elaborate researches of Dr. Dale, and the results established by the investigations of this volume, are confirmed by the distinct admission of Dr. Conant, that the primary is *not* the *only* meaning of the word. It not only means, to submerge, but also, "the coming into a new state of life or experience." Thus, the citadel of the immersion position is definitely abandoned. The word is *not* limited to one meaning. The mere fact, therefore, that it occurs, in any given place, decides nothing as to the form of action expressed by it; since the question always arises,— In what sense is the word here used? a question which, in every instance, must be decided by evidence outside the word. Until so decided, any inference from the word is mere assumption.

4. To re-establish the crumbling structure of immersion, the prepositions avail nothing; since they are as congruous to the supposition that the rite was performed by affusion.

5. The many waters of Enon prove nothing to the purpose; since abundance of water was necessary to John's congregations, had he made no ritual use of it whatever.

6. Equally futile is appeal to Paul's "buried by the baptism," as the imagined allusion is unnecessary to the interpretation, incongruous to the argument, and destructive of the distinctions which the apostle draws, and the conclusions which he deduces.

7. As to the remaining argument, from the baptism of the eunuch, we shall see hereafter, that while the facts recorded decide nothing, they create a presumption which distinctly indicates affusion.

Thus, the rite in question,—foreign to the whole style of the Old Testament, its ritual and prophecies, and equally so to the language and doctrines of the New,— is left without a vestige of evidence, anywhere, whether as to mode or meaning, even in those particular words and passages which have been the reliance of its advocates.

PART XIII.

BAPTISMAL REGENERATION.

Section LXXXI.—*The Doctrine is Contrary to the Whole Tenor of the Gospel.*—The mystery of iniquity early developed. The gospel church viewed as the antitype of the Levitical. The Scriptures are not so. Treatment of baptism by the evangelists. Paul's testimony

Paul was yet in the meridian of his strength, and the most active period of his ministry, when he wrote to the Thessalonians that "the mystery of iniquity doth already work,"—the mystery out of which was to be developed "that Wicked, whom the Lord shall consume with the spirit of his mouth, and shall destroy with the brightness of his coming."—2 Thes. ii, 7, 8. There is nothing more remarkable, nor more humiliating, in the history of the church than the rapid defection from the simplicity of the gospel which is apparent in the early remains of patristic literature. The transition from the apostles and evangelists in the New Testament, to the writings of the fathers, is like that from the splendor of the noonday sun to the deepening twilight of the evening. It was the precursor of "the black and dark night," by which the gospel was obscured for so many ages, and which still enshrouds the churches of Rome and the East in a mantle of gloom. Of this defection, the all-powerful cause was a false and mischievous interpretation of the Scriptures concerning the relation of the covenant of Sinai to the new covenant. They were interpreted as teaching that the visible church and its ordinances under the New Testament economy, was the antitype of the Levitical church and institutions,—that the rites and ceremonies of the latter were the shadow, of which the ordinances of the Christian church are the substance. Hence the Christian ministry became a priesthood, ministering better sacrifices and more effectual purifyings than those of the Mosaic ritual; for in their hands and by virtue of their consecrating prayers, the Lord's supper became a propitiatory sacrifice of the very body and blood of the Lord Jesus, and baptism administered by them became a spiritual regeneration,—a purging of the conscience,—the true baptism foreshadowed by the "type baptism" of the Old Testament. Thus, Didymus Alexandrinus, having quoted Ezek. xxxvi, 22,—"I will sprinkle clean water upon you, and ye shall be clean from all your sins;" and Psa. li, 7,—"Sprinkle me with hyssop, and I shall be clean; wash me, and I shall be whiter than snow;" says,—"For the sprinkling with hyssop was Judaic purification; which is continued by them to the present time; but 'whiter than snow,' denotes Christian illumination, which is baptism. And Peter, that he may show in his first epistle, that if baptism, which was formerly, *in shadow (en skia*) saved, much more that which was *in reality* (*en alētheia*) immortalizes and deifies us, wrote thus;—'Antitype baptism now saves us.'"[108] So Ambrose, as already quoted, says of the Psalmist,—"He asks to be cleansed by hyssop, according to the law. He desires to be washed, according to the gospel. He who would be cleansed by typical baptism was sprinkled with the blood of a lamb, by means of a bunch of hyssop." Of the doctrine of baptism, as thus conceived, Tertullian says,—"All waters in virtue of the pristine privilege of their origin,[109] do, after invocation of God accomplish sanctification; for the Spirit immediately comes from heaven and rests upon the waters, sanctifying them by his own power; and they being thus sanctified, therewith acquire the power of sanctifying."[110] Derived from this is the modern doctrine of baptismal regeneration, according to which, it is only in and through the baptism of water that the renewing grace of the Spirit is imparted to men.

It is manifest that if this doctrine be true, baptism is the "one thing needful;" and the church of Rome, and ritualists everywhere are right in the unanimity with which they reduce the preaching of the word to a secondary place, and count the progress of the gospel by the numbers who have been subjected to the life-giving rite. If it be true, then water baptism should be the theme of the New Testament; and the apostles and Christian ministry must have been commissioned and sent forth, *not* to preach the gospel; but *to baptize*. What says the Word of God on these points?

1. As to the gospel commission, and the instructions connected therewith, we have accounts from each of the four evangelists. John confines himself almost entirely to those, of such supreme interest, which Jesus uttered at the table, the night of the betrayal. Matthew, Mark, and Luke record the essential facts which occurred after the resurrection. The first thing that presents itself in examining these accounts is, that of baptism, as connected with the last instructions given the apostles, neither Luke nor John say one word. Thus, if the doctrine in question be true, these two evangelists are guilty of leaving out of their record the very heart and essence of the whole matter. This is the more remarkable, if we consider the character of the writers who are thus chargeable. Did we forget the Spirit which guided their pens, it is yet impossible to imagine that Luke, "the beloved physician," disciple, and companion of Paul, can have been unaware of the just proportion to be preserved in his narrative; so as to ignore a matter important as this. Or, John, the kinsman of Jesus, the beloved disciple, who in the privilege of a perfect confidence and love, lay on his bosom, and who received from the cross the legacy of the stricken mother,—John was not ignorant of the mind of his Master, on a subject like this, upon which depend the whole results of the work of redemption. The silence of these writers was not inadvertent, and it is fatal to the theory in question. What they do not report can have no place among the essentials of the plan of salvation. It still, however, remains to account for their silence respecting the ritual ordinance of baptism; which, apart from the unwarranted theory in question, all agree to be of divine authority. To this point we will return hereafter.

[108] Did. Alex. xxxix, 716. In Dale's Christ. Bapt. p. 342.

[109] He alludes to a relation to the Spirit, supposed to be indicated in Gen. i, 2.

[110] Tertullianus, De Bapt., ch. iv.

If, now, we turn to the other evangelists, the record of Matthew is as follows: Matt. xxviii, 16-20. "Then the eleven disciples went away into Galilee, into a mountain where Jesus had appointed them. And when they saw him, they worshiped him; but some doubted. And Jesus came and spake unto them, saying, All power is given unto me in heaven and in earth. Go ye therefore, and teach all nations, baptizing them (*eis to honoma*), *into the name* of the Father, and of the Son and of the Holy Ghost; teaching them to observe all things whatsoever I have commanded you: and lo! I am with you alway even unto the end of the world." Here, it can not be pretended that there is any thing to countenance the idea of baptismal regeneration. The administering of the rite is enjoined on the apostles. But no hint is given of its being necessary to salvation; and no such stress is laid upon it as to imply such necessity.

Mark records the language of Jesus on another occasion. Mark xvi, 14-16,— "He appeared to the eleven, as they sat at meat, and upbraided them with their unbelief and hardness of heart, because they believed not them which had seen him after he was risen. And he said unto them, Go ye into all the world, and preach the gospel to every creature. He that believeth and is baptized shall be saved; but he that believeth not shall he damned." Here, is no more of baptismal regeneration than we have found in Matthew. Emphasis is, indeed, given to baptism, by the connection in which it is introduced. But at the very point on which all depends the evidence gives way. "He that believeth and is baptized shall be saved; but he that believeth not—shall be damned." Thus explicitly Jesus utters sentence of perdition against unbelief. But he as explicitly omits baptism from mention on that side of the alternative, and thus expressly limits the condemning sentence to unbelief. Either this language is designed to represent baptism as important but *not* essential; or, it is a snare which must take men at unawares, and involve them in danger of destruction from ignorance of the necessity of the rite. Here then is no baptismal regeneration. The same inference follows from the silence of the other evangelists on this point. The eleven were all present and heard these words. If they were meant to imply baptismal regeneration, they were of the very highest moment. They could not, therefore, be ignored, but must have been the very center and controlling principle of all their writings and teachings. And yet, the other gospels ignore them; and the epistles are equally silent. It is, therefore, certain that the apostles did not understand the expressions, in the supposed sense. The true principle of harmony for the interpretation of all these facts will be presented in another place.

2. If now we examine the position of the great apostle of the Gentiles, we shall find him give place by subjection to this doctrine,—no, not for an hour. His is an independent testimony; for he was not with the eleven under the personal ministry of Christ. It is also fuller than any other; running through his thirteen epistles. First, we find that it was not his habit to baptize the converts of his own ministry; and that, upon principle. He says to the Corinthians,—"I thank God that I baptized none of you but Crispus and Gaius; lest any should say that I had baptized in my own name. And I baptized also the household of Stephanas. Besides, I know not whether I baptized any other. For Christ sent me, not to baptize, but to preach

the gospel."—1 Cor. i, 14-17. He moreover states the reason of his special devotion thus to the preaching of the gospel,—because "it pleased God by the foolishness of *preaching* to save them that *believe*."—v. 21. Here be it observed, the apostle speaks of preaching, not abstractly considered, but in immediate contrast with baptism. He does not baptize; but preaches, because *preaching* is the means which God has chosen for the salvation of men *through faith*. Thus, baptism is, in the plainest terms denied the place assigned it by the theory in question. But the evidence is even more direct and conclusive. To these same Corinthians whom Paul thus reminded that he had not baptized them, he addressed a second epistle, in which he distinctly asserts that through his personal ministry the Spirit of God had been given them and new life wrought within them. "Ye are our epistle written in *your* hearts,[111] known and read of all men; forasmuch as ye are manifestly declared to be the epistle of Christ ministered by us, written not with ink, but with the Spirit of the living God; not in tables of stone, but in the fleshly tables of the heart." He goes on to assert his ministry to be "of the new covenant; not of the letter, but of the spirit; for the letter killeth; but the spirit giveth life."—2 Cor. iii, 2, 3, 6. It needs no words, here, to show that thus the apostle overturns the very foundations of the theory of baptismal regeneration. Paul did not baptize the Corinthians. But he ministered to them the Holy Spirit of life and grace,—the true baptism of which he speaks so largely in his epistles.

It is not necessary to go farther in tracing the doctrine of Paul on the subject. He is everywhere consistent with himself as thus presented. It is however worthy of express notice that in his three epistles to Timothy and Titus, in which he sets forth the qualifications and duties of "the man of God," he does not once name or allude to the ordinance of baptism. Had the apostle believed the doctrine of baptismal regeneration, it is not possible that he could have been thus silent. But what need is there of thus inferring the sentiments of Paul? His favorite doctrine, excludes and condemns this theory as an intrusive heresy. "Being justified *by faith*, we have peace with God, through our Lord Jesus Christ."—Rom. v, 1. "By grace ye are saved, *through faith*, and that not of yourselves, it is the gift of God."—Eph. ii, 8. "O foolish Galatians, who hath bewitched you?... This only would I learn of you, Received ye the Spirit by the works of the law or by the *hearing of faith*?"—Gal. iii, 1, 2. How is it that by no accident does he ever say,—"by the hearing of faith, and *by baptism*?" It is almost needless to add that the other apostles in their writings are in perfect accord with Paul. In fact, ritual or water baptism is not once named in their epistles. The word, itself, occurs in them all only once,—in the statement of Peter respecting "antitype baptism," which has been already examined. If the apostles and evangelists are true witnesses as to the mind of Christ, the doctrine of baptismal regeneration is contrary to his teachings and subversive of the gospel.

This heresy is to be regarded with peculiar detestation and abhorrence because of the disparagement which it does to the sovereignty and glory of Christ's baptizing scepter. In any and every form of it, it divides the work of grace between Christ and the human administrators of the empty sign. It subordinates and limits

---

[111] That ἡμῶν, the reading of the Textus Receptus, should be ὑμῶν, "*your* hearts," is testified by a number of MSS., among which is the Sinaiticus, and is imperatively demanded by the connection.

the sovereign exercise of his saving power to the discretion of their wisdom and will, to the measure of their fidelity and ardor of their zeal. Whom they baptize,—upon them his grace may be bestowed, and upon them only.

We shall not examine in detail all the Scriptures which are appealed to in support of this theory. There are two which are the chief reliance of its advocates, an examination of which will be sufficient. If not in them, the doctrine is not to be found in the Bible. They are, John iii, 5, and Eph. v, 25-27.

> Section LXXXII.—*"Born of Water and of the Spirit."*—John iii, 4-8. Metaphor of water. "Water *even* the Spirit." John had already stated the way of the new birth

Said Jesus to Nicodemus,—"Except a man be born of water and of the Spirit, he can not enter into the kingdom of God."—John iii, 5. Dr. Pusey asserts that "The Christian church uniformly for fifteen centuries interpreted these words of baptism; on the ground of this text alone, they urged the necessity of baptism; upon it they identified regeneration with baptism." If the position thus maintained by the churches of Rome and the east for so many centuries be the truth, it presents the Savior, the apostles and evangelists, and the Scriptures written by them, in a most extraordinary light. In the very beginning of his ministry, in a private interview with the Jewish ruler, Jesus imparts to him this doctrine, on which confessedly the salvation of every man depends. But, from that hour, neither he nor his apostles ever name it. In his public instructions to the people,—in his private interviews with his disciples,—in those particular and assiduous teachings by which, as his own ministry drew to a close, he put them in possession of his whole mind concerning their ministry and the world's salvation (John xv, 15), he is persistently and entirely silent on this vital point. "Still," says Dr. Pusey, "the truth in holy Scripture is not less God's truth, because contained in one passage only." The principle is sound; but its application here is a mere begging of the question. That question is, What mean these words? And the above axiom is no more true, and much less pertinent to the present occasion than is the rule of interpretation laid down by Paul. "Having then gifts differing according to the grace that is given to us, whether prophecy, let us prophesy according to the proportion of faith."—Rom. xii, 6. An *interpretation* which takes a passage out of all congruous relation to the rest of the Scriptures, and overturns the very foundations of the faith therein set forth, is false. And such is the interpretation in question. The circumstances and connection indicate the true meaning of the passage.

That Nicodemus, although perhaps lacking in courage, was an honest inquirer after the truth, is evinced by the circumstances of this interview and by his subsequent history. He came by night, for fear of the Jews. He came not to cavil but to be taught, as appears alike from his own language and the manner of Christ's dealing with him. John had been for some time causing the land to ring with his warning cry; and men's hearts were in expectation because of it and his baptism. After this interview of Nicodemus with Jesus, we incidentally learn that in connection with Christ's preaching his disciples also baptized. And their baptism was assuredly of the same intent as that of John,—to prefigure the office of the Baptizer with the Holy Ghost. We may, therefore, conclude that their baptism was from the beginning associated with Christ's ministry. Of these facts, a man of the rank and intelligence of Nicodemus, and in his state of mind, could not be ignorant. He therefore comes for instruction as to the way of salvation. At the beginning of the interview, he places himself definitely at the feet of Jesus, as a disciple to be taught of him. "Rabbi, we *know* that thou art a *teacher* come from God; for no man can do these miracles that thou doest except God be with him." To an application thus so precisely in accord with Christ's own testimonies as to himself and his miracles (John v, 36; x, 25; xiv, 10, 11), he responds by entering directly upon the question which was agitating the ruler's heart,—that great question,—How to be saved? "Jesus answered and said unto him, Verily, verily, I say unto thee, Except a man be born again, he can not see the kingdom of God,"—that kingdom of which the cry then was, "The kingdom of heaven is at hand." The figure of the new birth was strange to Nicodemus; for, while the doctrine of renewing by the Holy Spirit is familiar to the Old Testament writers,—the figure of a new birth is not found in them. He therefore asks,—"How can a man be born when he is old" Here evidently the ruler views the matter as of practical and present interest to him personally. "How can I, Nicodemus, at my age, be born again?" The purpose of Jesus, in using this new illustration was thus accomplished. Old truths in new forms often develop a power which otherwise they lack. Jesus therefore, now answers, by a figure, familiar to his hearer, in the Old Testament Scriptures, and in the baptisms of John and of Christ's disciples, "Except a man be born of water and of the Spirit, he can not enter into the kingdom of God."

From this view of the connection and circumstances, it is evident that the passage is to be interpreted in the light of the Old Testament, and of the baptisms administered at the time of this interview, several years before the ascension and day of Pentecost; and not by any thing peculiar to the time subsequent to that event. But it is an essential feature of the theory of baptismal regeneration, that it holds the New Testament church to have this eminent advantage over that of the Old Testament, that the grace of regeneration is peculiar to the former, and to the ordinance of baptism as administered subsequent to the ascension of Christ. But the words of Christ to Nicodemus were no abstract setting forth of phenomena of grace to be enjoyed by the church in a coming time, but an explanation of the way in which the ruler must be saved, then and there, under the old economy. Viewing it in this light the following are the facts essential to the exposition of the passage.

1. The figure of metaphor was especially congenial to the Hebrew mind. To its abundant use, the Scriptures are largely indebted for the energy and clearness with which the profoundest thoughts are there presented. "Lord, thou hast been our *dwelling place* in all generations."—Ps. xc, 1. "Moab is my *wash pot*."—Ps. lx, 8. "In the hand of the Lord, there is *a cup*, and the *wine* is *red*; it is full of *mixture*; and he poureth out of the same; but the *dregs* thereof, all the wicked of the earth shall wring them out and drink them."—Ps. lxxv, 8. "Unto you that fear my name shall *the sun of righteousness* arise with healing in his wings."—Mal. iv, 2. Who would imagine the necessity of pausing to explain that these expressions are not to be understood literally?

2. Among these metaphors, no one was more familiar to the Jews than that of water, signifying the Holy Spirit. "I will *pour water* upon him that is thirsty and floods upon the dry ground. I will pour my Spirit upon thy seed and my blessing upon thine offspring."—Isa. xliv, 3. This figure has been already illustrated abundantly in these pages. It is only here important to emphasize the fact that upon it the whole significance of John's and the Old Testament baptisms depended,—which were, at that precise time, so earnestly pressed upon the attention of the Jews.

3. This very figure was repeatedly used by our Saviour in the course of his ministry. To the woman of Samaria he says, "thou wouldst have asked of him, and he would have given thee *living water*.... Whosoever drinketh of *the water* that I shall give him, shall never thirst; but *the water* that I shall give him, shall be in him *a well of water* springing up into everlasting life."—John iv, 10, 14. Again, "In the last day, that great day of the feast, Jesus stood and cried, saying, If any man thirst, let him come unto me and drink. He that believeth on me, as the Scripture hath said, out of his belly shall flow rivers of *living water*."—Ib. vii, 37, 38. It is, moreover, to be remarked that both of these places occur in the same gospel of John in which is found the interview with Nicodemus. Nor is it without significant bearing on the present point, that in the Revelation, by the pen of this same writer, the metaphor of water is conspicuous, in this same sense. "The Lamb ... shall lead them unto living fountains of waters."—Rev. vii, 17. The Lord Jesus says,—"I will give to him that is athirst of the fountain of the water of life freely;"—Ib. xxi, 6. John sees the "pure river of water of life clear as crystal proceeding out of the throne of God and the Lamb;"—Ib. xxii, 1. And the volume of revelation closes with the invitation,—"Let him that is athirst come, and whosoever will, let him take of the water of life, freely."—Ib. 17.

4. The Greek conjunction, *kai*, ("and,") does not always express addition; but sometimes indicates an expository relation between two members of a sentence, and is equivalent to, *even, to wit, namely*. Thus,—"For blasphemy, *even* because that thou being a man makest thyself God."—John x, 33. "Hath made us kings and priests unto God, *even* his Father."—Rev. i, 6. "A golden cup, full of abominations, *even* the filthiness of her fornications."—Ib. xvii, 4. "But ourselves, *even* we ourselves, groan."—Rom. viii, 23. "God, *even* our Father."—Phil. iv, 20. Three of these examples being from the writings of John again illustrate his style. It is evident that the phrase in question may be translated thus;—"Except a man be born of water, *even* of the Spirit." In fact, such must have been the sense in which it was understood by Nicodemus. (1.) The phrase is professedly *explanatory*. It is in reply to the perplexity of Nicodemus, at the primary statement of Jesus,—"Except a man be born again,"—an expression the meaning of which is abundantly illustrated, in all parts of the New Testament. (2.) The explanatory clause thus introduced, having performed its office, immediately drops out of the discourse, which subsequently dwells upon the new birth of the Spirit alone. "Except a man be born of water, even of the Spirit, he can not enter into the kingdom of God. That which is born of the flesh is flesh, and that which is born *of the Spirit* is spirit. The wind bloweth where it listeth, ... so is every one that is born *of the Spirit*." It is impossible

to account for the manner in which, after the one explanatory phrase, the water is thus ignored and excluded, upon any other supposition than that by which it is viewed as an interpretation of the previous expression, a metaphor for the Spirit. (3.) The fact that in the circumstances, it was impossible for the ruler to have understood the language in question as referring to a water baptism, which, upon the theory of baptismal regeneration, was not to be administered until after the day of Pentecost; and that he was therefore shut up to regard it as a metaphor, rendered explanation necessary, if that theory is true. The absence of any explanation makes it certain that such was not the meaning of Jesus.

5. The author of this narrative had, already, in the beginning of his gospel given an account of the manner of regeneration, which must be accepted as governing the whole of his subsequent record on the subject. "As many as received Him to them gave He power to become" (*exousian genesthai*, "gave He *the prerogative of being*") "the sons of God, even to them that believe on His name; which were born, not of blood, nor of the will of the flesh, nor of the will of man, but of God."—John i, 12, 13. Here, it is not sufficient to say that baptismal regeneration is ignored. It is absolutely excluded. The born of God are described in terms both exclusive and inclusive, by the phrase, "*As many as* received him, ... that believed on his name." These, all of these, and none but these, were born of God. The addition of baptism makes this no more sure; nor does its absence affect the result. As many as receive Christ,—As many as believe on his name, to them it is given to be the sons of God.

It is evident that the record of the interview with Nicodemus, all of which may be read in two or three minutes, is a mere abstract of leading points of our Savior's discourse. The intent of the words in question may be thus expressed. "You do not understand how a man can be born again. But you are familiar with the rite of baptism, and you are acquainted with the Scriptures of the prophets, and the interpretation which they give to that rite as a symbol of the renewing work of the Holy Spirit. It is that of which I speak. Except a man be born of water, even of the Holy Spirit, who is the true water of life, he can not enter into the kingdom of God."

Section LXXXIII.—"*The Washing of Water by the Word.*"—The bridal
   bath. No formula of baptism. "Sanctify them through thy truth,"

To the Ephesians, Paul thus writes. Eph. v, 25-27. "Husbands love your wives, even as Christ also loved the church and gave himself for it; that he might sanctify and cleanse it with the washing of water by the word; that he might present it to himself, a glorious church, not having spot, or wrinkle, or any such thing; but that it should be holy and without blemish." It is asserted that here baptism with water, and its effects are described. The "washing of water" is the baptism, "the word," is the formula of the ordinance and unblemished holiness, the effect. But

1. The subject of Paul's discussion is the relation of husband and wife, and the reference to the church is incidental, and by reason of the analogy of the subjects. The conception which runs through and controls the passage is that of a bridal, and each particular of the language is suggested by this conception. Thus, in the phrase, "a glorious church," rather "a church gloriously adorned" (compare Luke vii, 25, "gorgeously apparelled,") the apostle seems to have had in his mind (Psa.

xlv, 3),—"The king's daughter is all glorious, within; her clothing is of wrought gold." So, the washing of water is expressly stated to be in order to his presenting her to himself "not having spot or wrinkle." The immediate reference, therefore, of the language is to the washing and decking of the bride, before marriage; and the original of the whole conception is to be found in Ezekiel xvi, 9-14. "Then washed I thee with water; yea, I thoroughly washed away thy blood from thee, and I anointed thee with oil. I clothed thee also with broidered work, and shod thee with badger's skin, and I girded thee about with fine linen, and I covered thee with silk. I decked thee also with ornaments, and I put bracelets on thy hands and a chain on thy neck." It will hardly be pretended that in this language of the prophet, the washing with water implies any mixture of the natural element with that process of grace which is there described. And that the prophet and the apostle refer to the same thing is manifest. There is no direct allusion in the passage to ritual baptism. The water is the familiar metaphor of the Spirit, and the washing is the expression for his renewing and sanctifying influences on the soul.

2. The assertion that (*rēma*) "the word," here means the formula of baptism, is an assumption, wholly indefensible. In the first place, there is no formula of baptism ordained by Jesus, or recognized or used by the sacred writers. Of this, the evidence will hereafter appear. Moreover, in the New Testament, and especially in the writings of Paul, the word in question, *rēma,* is invariably used in the sense of the testimonies,—the doctrines,—*the word* of God,—the gospel. Thus, the angel said to the apostles,—"Go, stand and speak in the temple, to the people, all (*ta rēmata*) *the words* of this life."—Acts v, 20. Peter tells the house of Cornelius,—"That *word* (*rēma*) ye know ... how God anointed Jesus of Nazareth with the Holy Ghost and with power," etc.—Ib. x, 37, 38. Paul, in this very same epistle, tells the Ephesians (vi, 17) that "the sword of the Spirit" "is the *word* (*rēma*) of God." And Peter declares that "the *word* (*rēma*) of the Lord endureth forever; and this is the *word* (*rēma*) which by the gospel is preached unto you."—1 Peter i, 25. No word in the Scriptures is of a more unequivocal meaning than this.

3. The interpretation of *rēma* as meaning the baptismal formula, is a recognition of the unquestionable fact that "the word" is made by the apostle the instrumental cause of the sanctifying. Literally translated the passage reads,—"That he might sanctify it,—having purified it by the washing of water,—by the word." Thus, the word is the instrument of the sanctifying, and the parenthetic clause states the figure by which the analogy of the bride is sustained. The sanctifying and the purifying are the same spiritual phenomenon, the one phrase being conformed to the idea of the church, the other to that of the bride. And, whether the common English version be accepted, or the construction of the original be literally followed, as above, the result remains the same, that "the word" is distinctly stated to be the instrument of the process described by the two words, "sanctify" and "cleanse." In what sense the word is sanctifying, let Jesus testify. "The words (*ta rēmata*) that I speak unto you" (*literally,* "that I have spoken unto you," that is, in his preceding discourse), "they are spirit, and they are life."—John vi, 63. "Now ye are clean, through (*tou logou*) *the word* that I have spoken unto you."—Ib. xv, 3. "Sanctify them through thy truth, thy word (*logos*) is truth.... And for their sakes I

sanctify myself, that they also may be sanctified through the truth."—Ib. xvii, 17, 19. "Chosen unto salvation, through sanctification of the Spirit and belief of the truth."—2 Thes. ii, 13. The word is the means and the Spirit the efficient author of grace.

PART XIV.

THE NEW TESTAMENT CHURCH.

Section LXXXIV.—*The Ritual Law was unrepealed.*—Christ so left it. The apostles were zealous for it. The council of Jerusalem exempted the Gentiles only. James and Paul unite to show it still in force. Paul's practice. He obeyed the law, but repudiated its righteousness. This view alone harmonizes the history

In the entrance of the church upon her new commission, her constitution was unchanged. But the ordinances of testimony with which she was entrusted received an essential modification. The nature and the manner of this were alike remarkable; and as the subject has not received the attention due to its importance, it requires here the more careful consideration. In the course thereof, it will appear that the Hebrew Christian church remained with its institutions all unaltered, as they were received from Moses, and the ceremonial law in full authority and operation, down to the close of the New Testament canon. But the Gentile element, which was by the preaching of the gospel gathered in and incorporated with the church, was, by express statute, exempted from the obligation of that law.

1. The Lord Jesus was "a minister of the circumcision for the truth of God, to confirm the promises made unto the fathers; and that the Gentiles might glorify God for his mercy."—Rom. xv, 8, 9. He lived and died in the full communion of the church of Israel, in so far as his own action or will was concerned; although he was in the end excommunicated and betrayed by the rulers of that church. He assured his disciples that he came not to destroy the law but to fulfill. (Matt. v, 17.) Neither by example nor by precept did he set aside or abrogate it; but, on the contrary, having himself obeyed every precept and observed every ordinance, he left it, at his ascension, in full and unimpaired authority.

2. The apostles and the church over which they presided in Jerusalem were not only zealous in their observance of the law; but were not altogether exempt from the influence of some of the most obnoxious of the traditions of the elders. Of this, the case of Peter's visit to the house of Cornelius presents a signal illustration. To prepare him to listen to the message from the Roman centurion, a miraculous vision was shown him. And, when the disciples in Jerusalem heard of the matter, they accused him, for having gone in to men uncircumcised and eaten with them. And yet there was not a syllable in the laws of Moses to justify such extreme reserve. It was wholly based upon the traditions of the elders. So powerful and prevalent was the sentiment among Jewish Christians, on this subject, that

it subsequently became the occasion of a very singular dereliction on the part of Peter. Says Paul,—"When Peter was come to Antioch, I withstood him to the face, because he was to be blamed. For before that certain came from James, he did eat with the Gentiles; but when they were come, he withdrew, and separated himself, fearing them which were of the circumcision. And the other Jews dissembled likewise with him, insomuch that Barnabas also was carried away with their dissimulation."—Gal. ii, 11-13. Respecting this it is not enough to say that Peter and the Judaizers were all wrong. True. But such a state of things could not have existed, had the church or the apostles understood the law of Moses to be, in any manner, abrogated or set aside.

3. The calling and decree of the council of Jerusalem are very important facts, as bearing on this subject. The occasion of the council was the attempt of Judaizing teachers to impose circumcision and the ritual law upon the Gentile converts. (Acts xv, 1-5.) Hereupon, "the apostles and elders came together to consider of this matter."—v. 6. Here, at once, it is impossible that such a question could have arisen, had the abrogation of the Mosaic law been a fact known to the church in Jerusalem; and assuredly in that case, there would have been no room for the apostles and elders to "consider" such a question, the very raising of which would have been the erection of a standard of open rebellion against Christ. The discussions and decree of the council were equally conclusive. No doubt was suggested, in any quarter as to the continued authority of the law. No one hinted at the idea of its repeal. The discussion turned entirely on the privilege of the Gentiles to be specially exempt from its requirements. The evidence of such exemption was found in the fact that God had, in a special manner, shown his acceptance of them, outside the law. Upon this point, the whole issue turned; and the proof respecting it was formally given by Peter, in a rehearsal of the facts concerning the house of Cornelius (vs. 7, 8); and by Paul and Barnabas, in an account of "the miracles and wonders which God had wrought among the Gentiles by them."—vs. 12. Moreover, the conclusion reached (vs. 14-19), and the decree issued, had express relation, to the Gentiles, only, and not to the whole body of the church. In a word, it was a decree recognizing and proclaiming the exemption of the Gentiles from the obligation of the existing law.—"The apostles and elders and brethren send greeting unto the brethren which are *of the Gentiles*, in Antioch, and Syria, and Cilicia. Forasmuch as we have heard, that certain which went out from us, have troubled you with words, subverting your souls, saying, Ye must be circumcised and keep the law, to whom we gave no such commandment.... It seemed good to the Holy Ghost, and to us, to lay upon you no greater burden than these necessary things; that ye abstain from meats offered to idols, and from blood, and from things strangled, and from fornication; from which, if ye keep yourselves ye shall do well. Fare ye well."—vs. 23-29. Such is the only rule or decree found in the New Testament, respecting the ritual law. It exempts the Gentiles from its obligations; but otherwise leaves it in unimpaired authority.

4. With this view, the whole subsequent history of the apostolic church agrees. Paul was the great apostle of the Gentiles. He was prompt and decided in asserting and vindicating their liberty from the obligations of the law; but was himself

conscientious in the observance of all its requirements, and fully recognized their obligation upon himself and his brethren of Israel. These facts were brought into question, and publicly established in the most signal manner. When he came to Jerusalem after his third missionary tour, in an interview with James and the elders of the church, they said to him "Thou seest, brother, how many thousands (*muriades*, how many tens of thousands,) of Jews there are which believe; and they are all zealous of the law. And they are informed of thee that thou teachest all the Jews which are among the Gentiles to forsake Moses, saying that they ought not to circumcise their children, neither to walk after the customs. What is it therefore? The multitude must needs come together; for they will hear that thou art come. Do, therefore, this that we say to thee. We have four men which have a vow on them. Them take and purify thyself with them, and be at charges with them, that they may shave their heads: and all may know that those things whereof they have been informed concerning thee are nothing, but that thou thyself also walkest orderly and keepest the law. As touching the Gentiles which believe, we have written and concluded that they observe no such thing, save only that they keep themselves from things offered to idols, and from blood, and from strangled, and from fornication." —Acts xxi, 20-25. To this suggestion Paul agreed, and was in the temple in fulfillment of it, awaiting the time when "an offering should be offered for every one of them," when a tumult was raised by the unbelieving Jews, and his imprisonment took place, which resulted in his being sent, in chains, to Cesarea, and to Rome. (Acts xxi, 26, 27.)

Respecting this matter, the first point to be noticed is the fact that the myriads of Jewish Christians were unanimous.—They "were all zealous of the law." The imagination of Conybeare and Howson and others that the proceeding was the work of a Judaizing faction and was consented to for the sake of peace, is not only without warrant in the record, but is in contradiction to its whole tenor, and spirit. In fact the entire conception of the first named writers on the subject is characterized by a strained and perverse ingenuity, rather than by the simplicity of a sound criticism. And yet they have to admit that the law continued in unimpaired authority over all Jewish believers. Why then labor to stigmatize the church in Jerusalem or an imaginary faction therein for being zealous in its maintenance?

The purpose and intent of this transaction as expressly avowed by James and the elders was to draw a broad line of distinction between Jews and Gentiles in relation to the law. In their very suggestion to Paul, they refer to the former council and decree.—"As touching the Gentiles which believe, we have written and concluded that they observe no such thing." Thus, avowedly, the course proposed was designed to interpret that decree, and to limit its purview to the Gentiles. It was, moreover, a transaction taking place in circumstances which imparted to it the very highest moment. It was in Jerusalem, the center whence Jesus had commanded his apostles that the gospel should go forth. They were to preach in all the world, "beginning at Jerusalem." There, consequently the first labors of the twelve were expended; there, some of them were almost always found; and to that church the Gentile churches looked as the fountain of their faith and authoritative exponent to them of the will of Christ. Such had been the prophetic anticipation long before respecting this very time. — "Out of Zion shall go forth the law; and the word of the Lord from Jerusalem." — Isa. ii, 3. Already had that church sent forth the law concerning the relation of the Gentiles to the Mosaic institutions. And now the question to be decided was equally important, and the action proposed, although different in form, was equally responsible and decisive. A decree of confirmation of the law, which had stood unimpeached for fifteen centuries would have been inappropriate and calculated rather to awaken doubts than to strengthen conviction. The course proposed and adopted was more appropriate and effective. Paul was the great apostle of the Gentiles, the recognized and world-renowned champion, not only of the freedom of the Gentiles, but of the liberty of the gospel, the liberty of all Christ's people. The spectacle, therefore, of this great apostle, performing Levitical rites of purifying and publicly appearing at the temple, in order to the offering of sacrifices, in completion of a Nazarite vow, would constitute a most decisive demonstration and announcement of the continued obligation of the law, over all Israel. It was not a case, therefore, in which a privilege might be waived for the sake of peace. Submission to these proposals, if they were unwarranted, would have been treason, at once to Christ and to the liberties of the apostle's own people. How likely it was that Paul, having already vindicated with firmness and success the freedom of the Gentiles from the bondage of the law, should have conspired to betray the liberties of his own beloved Israel, on the very same point, in the interest of a time-serving policy, may be judged from his whole history and writings. The alternative presented by the facts is of itself conclusive. Either the law remained in unimpaired authority, over Israel, — or, Paul and James, the elders, and all the myriads of believing Jews, were united, without dissent or exception, in a conspiracy to repudiate the authority of the Lord Jesus, and re-establish a law repealed by him.

5. The action of Paul upon this occasion was not an instance of mere occasional conformity, but was expressly designed by the apostle as a testimony to the Jews that he did not repudiate the law, but "walked orderly and kept it." And an examination of his manner of life and ministry will show that this testimony was true, — that he was constant and conscientious in his own observance of the law, and recognition of its authority. Wherever he went, his first recourse was to the worshiping assemblies of the Jews, to which he joined himself as one of them, withdrawing only when rejected from their company. (Acts xvii, 2; xix, 8, 9, etc.) One incident in the story of his ministry affords us a glimpse into the inner chamber of his sentiments and the spirit of his personal life, as toward the law. On his second missionary tour, leaving Corinth, he sailed into Syria, "and with him Priscilla and Aquila; having shorn his head in Cenchrea: for he had a vow." — Acts xviii, 18. Some expositors have explained this vow as taken by Aquila and not by Paul. Olshausen, who, however, rejects this theory, says that "those learned men who deny the reference of the words to Paul, suppose that the statement can not be applied to him, because it would have been inconsistent with his principles regarding the abrogation of the ceremonial law of Moses, to have taken upon him a vow." Conybeare and Howson, who hesitate between the two views, say that "the difficulty lies not so much in supposing that Paul took a Jewish vow (see Acts xxi, 26) as in supposing that he made himself conspicuous for Jewish peculiarities

while he was forming a mixed church at Corinth." But all admit that the Greek in this place points as distinctly to Paul as does the common English version. We already know enough, certainly, to caution us against forcing an interpretation, on the ground that the ceremonial law was abrogated. We have seen the apostle take upon him such a vow, in the most public and demonstrative manner. And, as to the difficulty made by Conybeare and Howson, it is founded in a palpable mistake of the facts. The vow may have been made in Corinth. Of that we know nothing. But the shaving of his head, to which alone the suggestion as to "making himself conspicuous" could apply, took place in Cenchrea, after leaving Corinth and when in the act of sailing for Syria. So that the facts as recorded look rather to the avoidance of notoriety than seeking it. So far as the record indicates, the vow being connected with Paul's own private religious life, was only known to his personal attendants, in connection with the fact of his shaving his head, and the diligence with which he sought to reach Jerusalem in time for the feast. (Vs. 21, 22.) This was no doubt connected with the fulfillment of his vow, which of necessity required offerings at the temple. It thus appears that not only did the apostle maintain an outward and formal observance of the law; but that his private devotional life and experience took its form from the ordinances of that law, and found expression in them; a fact utterly irreconcilable, as was his whole life and teachings, with the assumption that he looked upon them as being abrogated or obsolete.

On this and other occasions, there are intimations that as often as was consistent with the duties of his ministry, he was accustomed to resort to Jerusalem, in observance of the annual feasts, and for the purpose of making offerings at the temple. "I came," says he to Felix, "to bring alms to my nation, *and offerings.* Whereupon certain Jews from Asia found me *purified* in the temple." — Acts xxiv, 17, 18; comp. xx, 16.

Another important fact appears in the record. With a significant discrimination, Paul circumcised Timothy the son of a Jewess; although, his father being a Greek, he might have claimed exemption as a Gentile (Acts xvi, 1-3); "But, neither Titus, who was with me, being a Greek was compelled to be circumcised; and that because of false brethren, unawares brought in, who came in privily to spy out our liberty which we have in Christ Jesus, that they might bring us into bondage: to whom we gave place, by subjection, no, not for an hour; that the truth of the gospel might continue with you." — Gal. ii, 3-5. Thus, in Timothy and Titus, Paul's favorite disciples and constant attendants and helpers in his later ministry, he carried with him exemplars and representatives of the opposite relations to the law, which he recognized in the Jews and the Gentiles.

Moreover during his imprisonment, in reply to the charge of being a contemner of the law, the apostle repeatedly and unqualifiedly asserted that he had been constant and faithful in observance of it. In the presence of the council of Israel, he announced himself a Pharisee. Of the same thing he writes to the Philippians, that he had "no confidence in the flesh, Though I might also have confidence in the flesh. If any other man thinketh that he hath whereof he might trust in the flesh, I more: Circumcised the eighth day, of the stock of Israel, of the tribe of Benjamin, a Hebrew of the Hebrews; as touching the law, a Pharisee; concerning zeal, persecuting the church; touching the righteousness which is in the law blameless."—Phil. iii, 3-6. It is true that the description here given by the apostle has especial reference to the past time of his unconverted zeal. But it is also true, that his introductory comparison with others, as to grounds of self-righteous confidence, is in the present tense, and indicates a conscious fidelity to the law down to the time of his writing. When accused before Festus, "he answered for himself,—Neither against the law of the Jews, neither against the temple, nor yet against Cæsar, have I offended any thing at all."—Acts xxv, 8. And when at last he was taken to Rome, he there called the chief of the Jews together, and said to them, "Men and brethren, though I have committed nothing against the people or customs of our fathers, yet was I delivered prisoner from Jerusalem into the hands of the Romans."—Acts xxviii, 17.

Is it asked, how all this is to be reconciled with the doctrine of the epistle to the Galatians, and other testimonies of Paul respecting circumcision and the law? I answer,—Paul nowhere utters a syllable in disapproval of the observance of the law by the Jews, as a rule of life. What he assails is, a trusting in it, for themselves, or imposing it on others, as a rule of righteousness unto salvation. While he proclaimed salvation by grace, through faith alone, without the works of the law, moral or ritual, he with perfect consistency not only himself kept the law, but enjoined it on his brethren after the flesh. His principle of action in this respect, he states explicitly, "Is any man called, being circumcised? Let him not become uncircumcised. Is any called in uncircumcision? Let him not be circumcised. Circumcision is nothing, and uncircumcision is nothing, *but the keeping of the commandments of God*. Let every man abide in the same calling wherein he was called. Art thou called being a servant? care not for it; but if thou mayest be made free use it rather."—1 Cor. vii, 18-21. Thus distinctly does Paul recognize circumcision as still being, to the Jews, a commandment of God; as exemption from it was to the Gentiles. And it need scarcely be said, that circumcision here stands for the whole law. It is to be considered, moreover, that this language of Paul is not a mere recognition of circumcision as still existing by the providence of God; but it is an express and unreserved re-enforcement of the law, by his whole authority, as an apostle of Jesus Christ,—a re-enforcement broad and unlimited as to time or circumstances as was the law itself. This unlimited character of the apostle's decree, is emphasized and strengthened by the exception which he appends to the general form of his enunciation;—"Let every man abide in the calling wherein he was called." Lest any should interpret this rule as designed to apply to cases outside the theme in hand, he adds,—"Art thou called being a servant? Care not for it; but if thou mayest be made free, use it rather." So far from moderating or weakening the force of the apostle's previous language, this adds greatly to it; showing as it does, that the question of exceptions and limitations was present to his mind. Then was the time, if ever, for him to have intimated the doing away of the ritual law; or, at least, to so guard his language as to harmonize it with its ultimate abrogation, had such been the purpose of God. The fact, therefore, that neither here nor elsewhere does he allude to such a purpose, but on the contrary gives the above unreserved injunction as a permanent part of the written word of God, leaves us but one alternative,—to reject the authority of Paul, as an inspired apostle, or to recognize circumcision and the law as being, to the Jew, the commandment of God, unrepealed.

If, we further examine the epistles, we shall find that while they all are unanimous in repudiating the *righteousness* of the law; they do not, anywhere assert or imply its repeal, as toward Israel. It will moreover be found that any inference as to the abrogation of the law, which may be deduced from the doctrine of grace, as taught by all the apostles, applies as directly to the moral as to the ritual code; both of which are by them commonly comprehended together under the designation of, "the law." Upon their principles, reliance on a righteousness of works is just as much to be reprobated in the one form as in the other; and the doctrine of salvation by grace is as consistent with the continued obligation and observance of the ritual, as, of the moral law.

6. It is no slight argument in proof of the view here presented, that it alone exhibits the apostolic history as consistent and harmonious, based upon definite and inflexible principles, unanimously recognized and obeyed by the apostles and elders. That such must have been the case, is involved in the manner in which the apostles were appointed to preside over the transition period in the history of the church, and the Spirit given for their guidance therein. Many writers have assumed without the trouble of proof, that the ritual law could not any longer possess legitimate authority—that the coming of Christ, and his one offering of himself, of necessity, superseded and set it aside. They are, at once, involved in the necessity of treating the whole history of the apostolic church as one of compromising policies and timeserving expedients. We are told of the extreme Judaism of James, the more moderate conservatism of Peter, and the free evangelical spirit of Paul. Their principles and parties are represented as maintaining a continual struggle, and the various facts of the history are explained as the prevalence of one or the other set of opinions, or the result of compromise. On the contrary, there is not a trace of the least diversity of sentiment on these questions between the parties named, or any of the apostles or leaders of the church. Some "false brethren, unawares brought in" (Gal. ii, 4), attempted to create division; but only developed harmony. The decree of the council of Jerusalem was no compromise, but the expression of unanimous sentiments (*'omothumadon*, "with one heart," —Acts xv, 25), and was, moreover, dictated by the Holy Spirit. "It seemed good *to the Holy Ghost and to us.*" The so-called partisans of James, the Judaizing zealots, who troubled Paul's ministry, were expressly repudiated in that decree, which was moved in the council by Peter and James, and apparently drafted by the hand of the latter.[112] The reason why the labors of James and Peter were mainly confined to the circumcision in Judea, while Paul preached among the far off Gentiles, was precisely the same in both cases,—the will of Christ. Says Paul,—"When they saw that the gospel of the uncircumcision was committed unto me, as the gospel of the circumcision was unto Peter; (for He that wrought effectually in Peter to the apostleship of the circumcision, the same was mighty in me toward the Gentiles;) and when James, Cephas and John, who seemed to be pillars, perceived the grace that was given unto me, they gave to me and Barnabas the right hands of fellowship; that we should go unto the heathen, and they unto the circumcision."—Gal. ii, 7-9. No.

[112] The *"Greeting"* (*Chairein*) Acts xv, 23; is found nowhere else in the New Testament, save in James i, 1.

The blood-bought church of Christ, was not left, at this critical time, to the mercies of the passions and prejudices, the narrowness and factions of fallible men. It was under the direction of the Lord Jesus, and the inspiration of the Holy Spirit. The prayer "that they all may be one," was not unheard, nor unanswered of the Father; and the promise that the Spirit should guide them into all truth was fulfilled.

From this careful survey, it appears, that the New Testament contains no evidence of the abrogation or passing away of the ceremonial law,—that its unimpaired authority over Israel was fully and universally acknowledged and asserted by the apostles and the churches over which they presided; while the exemption of the Gentiles from its requirements was recognized as exceptional, and secured by formal consultation and decree;—that this condition of things continued unchanged to the close of the New Testament canon;—and that as a necessary consequence, that law never has been repealed, to this day. As once before, during the seventy years of the Babylonian captivity, Israel was providentially precluded from its observance, so at present, it is one of the most afflictive features of the divine dealings with them, that the law, which they idolized and so grievously perverted, still binds them; while the destruction of the temple, the disorganization of the nation and the obliterating of the priesthood renders its fulfillment by them impossible.

Section LXXXV.—*Why the Gentiles were Exempt from the Law.* —Not because the law expired. But, unsuited to a world wide extension. Its chief end accomplished. What its survival implied

The exemption of the Gentile Christian church from the authority of the ceremonial law must be accounted for upon some principle which will harmonize with all the facts. The common theory assumes it to be of the very nature of a type to perish and be abrogated by its realization in the antitype. Thus, it is supposed, that the sacrificial system of necessity expired with its fulfillment by Christ's one offering of himself. But, as we have seen, the law was not in fact abrogated, but continues in unimpaired authority over Israel. Why, then, are the Gentiles exempt from its obligations?

The reason was briefly intimated by Peter. "Why tempt ye God, to put a yoke upon the neck of the disciples, which neither our fathers nor we were able to bear;"—literally, "neither (*ischusamen*) *were strong* to bear."—Acts xv, 10. This verb means, *to be strong*, and is sometimes used with a negative particle, as here, to indicate a labor of great difficulty, not amounting to an impracticability. Thus, in John xxi, 6, it is said of the net of fishes,—"They *were not able*" (were not *strong*) "to draw it, for the multitude of fishes." And yet, immediately after, when their force had been reduced by Peter casting himself into the sea and swimming to land, they came "dragging the net with fishes," and Peter himself drew it to land. (vs. 8, 11.) The ritual law was a burdensome, although not impossible institution, for Israel, when dwelling in their own land. But, as a system of worship for a world-religion, it was unsuitable. Essential to it was the one temple, altar and priest, at Jerusalem, typical of the one sanctuary and service in heaven. Hither must all males repair statedly, three times a year, and both men and women upon many special occasions beside, of a personal nature. To a population of four or five millions, dwelling in the narrow limits of Palestine, — a territory the extreme dimensions of which were about 100 miles by 150, — this was possible, although burdensome. But, to the distant millions of the world's inhabitants, manifestly it would have been utterly impracticable.

Moreover, to the race at large, the ceremonial law had already fulfilled its most important and essential offices. Undoubtedly, it could still have been used by the grace of God, as it had been for ages before, as a mode for the effectual transmission and dissemination of the gospel testimony, kept in unimpaired purity by the agency of unchanging forms. Nor is the fact to be everlooked, or lightly regarded, that representations to the eye and the physical senses have a peculiar power over the affections and the heart, a power often greater and more influential than any appeal to the intellect through the organs of hearing. Had such been the will of God, the ritual system was certainly susceptible of being made a powerful auxiliary to the dissemination of the gospel, by its relation to these principles of man's nature.

But, when the gospel was given to the Gentiles, the system of elementary ideas which were embodied and exhibited in the Mosaic ceremonial possessed a world-wide diffusion. The art of writing had been developed and disseminated. The Old Testament Scriptures were already written and widely distributed, and the gospels and epistles were soon to follow. Thus the cardinal importance of the ritual ordinances as a mode for the recording and perpetuation of the gospel was obsolete, — replaced by means more appropriate to a religion now destined for the world. And the "demonstration of the Spirit and of power," which now accompanies the preaching of the gospel among the Gentiles, is abundant compensation for the ritual system, as an appeal to the affections, through the senses.

It is thus apparent that the discrimination, in the beginning made between Jew and Gentile respecting the ceremonial law, — its obligation on the one, and the exemption of the other, — was neither arbitrary nor unmeaning, but alike reasonable and susceptible of full and beautiful realization in practice. It implied the continuance of Israel as a priest-kingdom among the nations, maintaining at Jerusalem, as a standard of faith to the world, that system of rites which so beautifully, so clearly and impressively set forth the gospel to the eyes and senses of men; whilst, the world over, the same gospel should have been published, by the written and printed word, by the living voice, and by the simple ritual of Gentile Christianity, practicable everywhere. But such was not the purpose of God. At the beginning, our first parents by sin forfeited the Eden which might have been theirs. So, Israel forfeited her offered privilege. Jerusalem was destroyed, and the gospel and the church were given to the Gentiles, — "until the fullness of the Gentiles be come in; and so all Israel shall be saved." — Rom. xi, 25, 26.

Section LXXXVI. — *The Christian Passover.* — Wine, and blood. The passover a type of Christ's atonement. It is perpetuated in the Supper

To the church among the Gentiles, two simple ordinances remain, an inheritance from the ancient church, — a memorial and link of connection and identity between the two; and a continuous sealing of the same covenant, transmitted from the one to the other. That the Supper is thus derived from the paschal feast, can not be denied. As early as Jacob's prophecy of Shiloh, "the blood of the grape" was appropriated as a type of Christ's sufferings. (Gen. xlix, 9-12.) Afterward, in the Levitical system, a meat or bread offering made of fine flour mixed with oil, and a drink offering of wine, were made essential parts of all sacrificial offerings. (See Num. xv, and xviii.) Of the festival offerings, to which the passover belonged, a part only was offered upon the altar; the rest being appropriated to the worshippers. They thus enjoyed communion with God, at his table; and hence the proverbial description of "wine which cheereth God and man."—Judg. ix, 13. Thus, in the passover and all the Levitical sacrifices, two distinct elements were typical of Christ's sufferings; but in wholly different aspects. The blood signified the satisfaction demanded by justice; and it was, therefore, utterly prohibited that men should eat of it. (Lev. xvii, 10-14.) It was poured upon the altar. But the wine expressed the virtue of that satisfaction, imparted to believers and received by them, to their spiritual nourishment. Thus, the wine of the supper is not a substitute for the blood of sacrifice, but is a distinct and co-ordinate type, transmitted from the passover, and other sacrificial rites, and unchanged in its meaning. The unleavened bread always symbolized the Bread of life that came down from heaven; and the cup always represented the blood of the new covenant.

That the passover was from the beginning a type of the atonement of the Lord Jesus, is certain. (1.) The ordinance was a feast upon a sacrifice. From the foundation of the world, sacrifice signified one thing,—the satisfaction to be made to justice by the Lord Jesus. Such being the case, the feast of Israel upon the pascal lamb could have but one meaning. That meaning was set forth by Jesus, who having been announced by John as the Lamb of God, himself says, "If any man eat of this bread (*artou*, "of this food"), he shall live forever, and the food that I will give, is my flesh, which I will give for the life of the world."—John vi, 51. (2.) The deliverance of Israel from the bondage of Egypt, was an exercise of the same redeeming function, which is displayed in the salvation of men; and was a type of that salvation. Hence the preface to the ten commandments.—"I am the Lord *thy God* which have brought thee *out of the land of Egypt, out of the house of bondage*" (Ex. xx, 2); which the Westminster catechism explains that "because God is the Lord and our God and Redeemer, therefore, we are bound to keep all his commandments." (3.) Jesus himself at the very time when he eliminated the Lord's supper out of the passover, declared the latter to be a type of his sufferings and death. "With desire I have desired to eat this passover with you before I suffer. For I say unto you, I will not any more eat thereof, until *it be fulfilled* in the kingdom of God."—Luke xxii, 15, 16.

How plainly the Lord's supper was an epitome and perpetuation of the passover, will be understood, by reference to the manner of observance of the latter in the time of Christ. It was required of those who partook of the feast, that they should not sit, but recline at the table, as expressing liberty and rest. When they were thus disposed, wine was distributed, and after thanks given by the presiding person, each one drank a cup. The master then explained the nature and occasion of the feast, and distributed a second cup. He then brake the unleavened bread, gave thanks, and gave it to the company, with the bitter herbs and other provisions that were on the table, and afterward the flesh of the lamb. When all had eaten and the supper was ended, he that presided took another cup of wine, and, after blessing God, all drank of it. This was called "the cup of blessing," because of the blessing on it, which ended the feast. Thus the order of the feast was, (1) Thanksgiving; (2) A cup of wine; (3) The commemorative discourse; (4) A second cup; (5) A second thanksgiving; (6) The broken bread; (7) The flesh of the lamb; (8) The closing blessing; (9) The cup of blessing. So, at the beginning of the supper, Jesus took the cup, and gave thanks and said, "Take this, and divide it among yourselves." After discourse, and washing the disciples' feet, "he took bread, and gave thanks and brake it and gave unto them, saying, This is my body which is given for you; this do in remembrance of me. Likewise, also, the cup after supper, saying, this cup is the new testament in my blood, which is shed for you." — Luke xxii, 17-20.

The Lord's supper was not, therefore, a distinct ordinance, instituted after the passover was ended, by the use of remaining elements. But it was a perpetuation of the passover, itself, by appropriating and interpreting portions of the elements, from time to time, during the progress of the feast; the bread being that which was broken and eaten before the paschal flesh, and the wine that which closed the feast; which was known to the Jews and described in the Talmud, as the cup of blessing, and which is designated by that name by the apostle Paul, in speaking of the Lord's supper. (1 Cor. x, 16.) The particular number and order of the cups of wine and of the thanksgivings were regulations of the scribes, promotive of order and propriety in the observance; but not included in the divine requirements of the institution, and therefore not essential to it. This fact being taken into account, it will appear that the paschal feast remains to us entire, except only the sacrificial flesh of the lamb. Of it Paul says, "Christ our passover is sacrificed for us; therefore, let us keep the feast, not with old leaven, neither with the leaven of malice and wickedness, but with the unleavened bread of sincerity and truth." — 1 Cor. v, 7, 8.

> Section LXXXVII. — *The Hebrew Christian Church.* — The synagogue system. The sects of Pharisees, Sadducees and Nazarenes. The number and diffusion of the Nazarenes. The Hebrew church after the destruction of Jerusalem

We proceed to trace the order and process of the development of the Christian church, as it took place under the Sinai constitution, with the ordinances modified as we have seen. The synagogue system had grown up long before the time of Christ. In it provision was made for fulfilling those injunctions of the law which insisted so much on instruction and study in the word of God, and which set apart the Sabbaths as days of holy convocation. (Lev. xxiii, 3, etc.) In the organization of these societies, respect was undoubtedly had, at first, to the ties of consanguinity; so that the members of a given cluster of families, living in the same vicinity and originally descended from one head, were constituted a synagogue, under the direction and government of those who by the right of primogeniture were the family elders. But, in the time of Christ, the whole system of the distribution and inheritance of the land, and of the family organization, as appointed by the law of Moses, had been broken up by the repeated captivities, the dispersion of the ten tribes, and the vicissitudes of war and peace. The synagogue system was therefore more artificial in its structure, and more characterized by the voluntary principle. Indications of voluntary association and elective affinity are plainly seen in the names of the synagogues members of which were active in the persecution of Stephen.—"The synagogue of the Libertines, and Cyrenians, and Alexandrians."— Acts vi, 9. It is indeed evident that in the general circumstances of the Jews at that time, in Judea and elsewhere, the worshiping assemblies must usually have been the products of voluntary association, more or less influenced by congeniality of sentiments among the members. Pharisees and Sadducees severally would seek the worshiping assemblies in which their respective views were favored. Those of the same foreign nationality would naturally gravitate toward each other. And, in general, congeniality, from whatever cause, would be potential in these associations.

The existence, at this time, in the bosom of the Jewish church of the two sects, or parties, of the Sadducees and the Pharisees, was a very important fact in preparing the way for the gospel. These parties are, in the original Greek, designated by the generic word, *hairesis*, which is commonly translated, "sect," as "the *sect* of the Sadducees" (Acts v, 17), "the *sect* of the Pharisees" (Ib. xv, 5), "the *sect* of the Nazarenes," (Ib. xxiv, 5). In one place, it is, "the way which they call *heresy*."—Ib. xxiv, 14. Neither of these words, however, is a happy rendering of the original; which has nothing of the idea of doctrinal error, now attached to the word, heresy; and nothing of the odium involved in the designation of "sects;" nor, of the denominational separations which are expressed by it. The word, as used in Luke's history signifies, a party, or rather, a society having a distinctive organization more or less complete, for certain special purposes; but continuing in the enjoyment of all the rights and privileges of the Jewish church and the temple worship. Such was the position at once assumed, by the apostles and the converts of their ministry. They were organized in separate synagogues. They observed the first day of the week, as a day of assembling for worship and the breaking of bread. They received their converts by the familiar rite of baptism. But they were all zealous of the law, and faithful, therefore, even above others in the observance of its requirements. Thus, despite all the odium which Pharisees and Sadducees might seek to cast upon them, it was impossible to impeach them of apostasy from Judaism, or unfaithfulness to Moses. Hence, the result recorded by Luke. "They, continuing daily with one accord in the temple, and breaking bread from house to house, did eat their meat with gladness and singleness of heart; praising God, and having favor with all the people."—Acts ii, 46, 47.

Such was the aspect of things in Jerusalem and Judea for a quarter of a century; from the first dissemination of the gospel to the times of anarchy which preceded the desolation of the land. In the bosom of the Jewish church, beside the great body of the people, were the three societies just mentioned. The Sadducees were comparatively few in number, but influential, by reason of their social position and wealth, the party being composed almost exclusively of the priests and aristocracy. The Pharisees were more numerous, and in greater favor with the people; for, while the Sadducees were chargeable with lax opinions, the Pharisees were "the straitest sect of the Jews' religion," including all those who hoped to secure the favor of God through the righteousness of the law. Beside these was "the sect of the Nazarenes," far greater in numbers than either of the others; and, at first, more in favor with the mass of the people,—a favor which they seem to have retained till the growing corruption and disorder which heralded the catastrophe of the nation, rendered them odious, alike by the contrast of their lives with the prevailing licentiousness, and by the rebukes and warnings which they could not fail to utter.

Whilst the number of the Christians, as compared with the whole nation was, no doubt, small, the mistake is to be avoided of regarding it as insignificant. A comparison of the various statements on the subject will lead to the conclusion that the company of the believers must have been so large as to constitute one of the most conspicuous features in the aspect of the nation. On the day of Pentecost "there were added unto them about three thousand souls."—Acts ii, 41. A few days afterward, "many of them which heard the word believed, and the number of the men was about five thousand."—Ib. iv, 4. Soon after, it is again recorded that "the people magnified them. And believers were the more added to the Lord, multitudes both of men and women."—Ib. v, 13, 14. Again, it is stated that the high-priest demanded of the apostles,—"Did not we straitly command you that ye should not teach in this name? And behold, ye have filled Jerusalem with your *teaching* (*didachēs*), and intend to bring this man's blood upon us."—Ib. v, 28. Such was the progress of the gospel that these rulers were alarmed lest they should be called by the people to account for the death of Jesus. Soon, again, we read that "the word of God increased; and the number of the disciples multiplied in Jerusalem greatly; and a great company of the priests were obedient to the faith."—Ib. vi, 7. Immediately after this Stephen was martyred, and "there was a great persecution against the church which was at Jerusalem; and they were all scattered abroad throughout the regions of Judea and Samaria, except the apostles."—Ib. viii, 1. By the dispersed believers, the gospel was carried through the land and to the Gentiles. (Ib. xi, 19.) And in Jerusalem itself the word of the Lord was not bound. The persecution, in its active form, soon ceased, and when the converted Saul retired from Jerusalem to Tarsus, we read that "then had the churches rest throughout all Judea and Galilee and Samaria, and were edified; and walking in the fear of the Lord, and in the comfort of the Holy Ghost were multiplied."—Ib. ix, 31. Such was the new growth of the church in Jerusalem that when Paul made his last visit to that city, James could say to him,—"Thou seest, brother, how many (*muriades*) ten thousands of Jews there are which believe."—Ib. xxi, 20. To the inference which naturally follows from these representations, the objection has been raised, that there is no accounting for such numbers, in the after history. Alexander suggests, that many were false professors, who "afterward apostatized or separated from the church, as Ebionites, or Judaizing heretics."[113] So dark a view, however, is not required by the facts. Doubtless there were some defections. But there is no reason to suppose them to have been of the extent here implied. The circumstances in

[113] Alexander on Acts, xxi, 20.

which they united with the persecuted followers of the man of Nazareth, were not such as to present attractions to false professors. The patristic tradition that none of the Christians perished in the siege of Jerusalem, they having all retired to Pella, whilst it may possibly be true, concerning those who lived in Jerusalem, is by no means probable. And so far from Jesus having taught the disciples to expect such a result, the reverse is the case. That the churches of believers which had been flourishing for a quarter of a century in Judea, Galilee and Samaria must have suffered greatly, from the disorders and anarchy which preceded the final catastrophe, is certain, and of it Jesus expressly forewarned them. — "Ye shall be betrayed both by parents and brethren and kinsfolks, and friends; and some of you shall they cause to be *put to death*. And ye shall be hated of all men for my name's sake. But there shall not an hair of your head perish" (even though ye be put to death). "In your patience possess ye your souls. And when ye shall see Jerusalem compassed with armies, then know that the desolation thereof is nigh." — Luke xxi, 16-20. See, also, Matt. xxiv, 9-13; Mark xiii, 9-13. As to what afterward became of the Christians of Judea, — in view of the scanty remaining records of the time, and of the manner in which they were identified with their brethren of Israel as being none the less Jews because they were Christians, — it is not surprising that we can not distinctly trace their subsequent history. One fact, however, is patent on the face of the scanty record, and is sufficient to satisfy all the demands of the occasion. It is, that as the Christian churches, at a later period, emerge into the light of history they everywhere bear the broad and indelible impress of Hebrew Christian influences.

The subsequent history of the Hebrew church in Jerusalem itself very signally confirms the view here presented. As soon as the city began to be repeopled, a church was re-established, under the presidency, as Eusebius reports, of Simeon the son of Cleopas. Of his successors, that historian says, — "We have not ascertained, in any way, that the times of the bishops of Jerusalem have been regularly preserved on record. For tradition says that they all lived but a very short time. So much, however, have I learned from writers, that down to the invasion of the Jews under Adrian there were fifteen successions of bishops in that church, all which, they declare to have been Hebrews from the first, and received the knowledge of Christ pure and unadulterated, so that in the estimation of those who were able to judge, they were well approved and worthy of the episcopal office. For, at that time, the whole church under them consisted of believing Hebrews who continued from the time of the apostles until the siege that then took place." The historian gives a list of the succession of fifteen bishops. "These are all the bishops of Jerusalem that filled up the time from the apostles until the above mentioned date, — all being of the circumcision."[114] The list ends with the name of Judah, who perished by the sword of the impostor, Simon, surnamed Bar Kokeba, "the Son of the Star." This adventurer, originally a robber chieftain, had announced himself as the expected Messiah of Israel. The Jews, groaning under the oppressions of the Romans, rushed to arms and rallied to his standard, to the number of more than 200,000 men. He would brook no neutrality. The Gentiles of Palestine had to choose between his service and the sword. His demands, repelled by the Hebrew Christians, brought on them his exterminating vengeance, and Judah, the last of

[114] Eusebius iii, 11; iv, 5, 6.

the Hebrew succession of the bishops of Jerusalem, perished, with a multitude of his church, under the swords of the Jews.[115] Thus closed in blood the history of the Hebrew church in Jerusalem, in the year 132. As for Simon, — after successfully defying for two years, the whole power of Rome, he and his forces were finally cooped up in the town of Bethar, which was taken by storm. The impostor perished, with a multitude of his followers, and the remnant glutted the slave markets of the world. "The numbers of persons who perished by sword, flame, and hunger, have been stated as high as 700,000, by others, 580,000. As to Judaism and the Jewish people, the land might be said, for some time, to be a solitude. The native inhabitants who had escaped the butchery of the war were expatriated either by banishment or flight, or sold into bondage. No Jew was now permitted to come within sight of Jerusalem, and Gentile colonists were sent to take possession of the soil. Jerusalem in fact became a Gentile city."[116]

Says Mosheim, — "When the emperor (Adrian) had wholly destroyed Jerusalem, a second time, and had enacted severe laws against the Jews, the greater part of the Christians living in Palestine, that they might not be confounded with Jews as they had been, laid aside the Mosaic ceremonies, and chose one Mark who was a foreigner and not a Jew, for their bishop. This procedure was very offensive to those among them whose attachment to the Mosaic rites was too strong to be eradicated. They therefore separated from their brethren, and formed a distinct society, in Perea, a part of Palestine, and in the neighboring regions; and among them the Mosaic law retained all its dignity unimpaired."[117] These Jewish Christians, known as Nazarenes, are traceable for several centuries, orthodox in their faith and embraced in the fellowship of the Catholic church, but strict in the observance of circumcision and the law of Moses, as far as practicable in the circumstances of the Jews.

Section LXXXVIII. — *The Gentiles Graffed in.* — Mixed churches. Gentile
    churches. "Out of Zion the law." The Gentiles graffed in

While such as we have described was the constitution of the church in Jerusalem and Judea, in the days of the apostles, it elsewhere presented a different aspect. At Antioch, Ephesus, Philippi, Thessalonica, Corinth, Rome and other places, Jews and Gentiles were associated together in the churches. Where such was the case, the Jewish members, like their brethren in Judea, maintained the ordinances of both the Levitical and Christian liturgies. They kept sacred alike the Jewish Sabbath and the Lord's day. They were circumcised, and observed all the requirements of the law of Moses, and maintained all the services of the synagogue system. At the same time, they on the Lord's day, united with their believing Gentile brethren, in observing the ordinances of the gospel church, and the sacraments of baptism and the Lord's supper.

On the other hand, the Gentile members of these churches were uncircumcised and free from the bondage of the ritual law. They kept holy the Lord's day

[115] Etheridge's Jerusalem and Tiberias, p. 71.
[116] Etheridge, Ibid. p. 72.
[117] Mosheim, Eccl. Hist., Cent. II., Part II., Ch. v, 1, 2.

only; on which they united with their Jewish brethren in the ordinances of Christian worship and religion. At the same time these Gentile converts were more or less in the habit of frequenting the synagogue services, to hear the reading of the Scriptures and join in the worship of the God of Israel. In these services their position was similar to that held by the class of persons who were known as "devout persons," or "proselytes of the gate." In fact, it was usually from these that the first Gentile converts to Christ were gathered. The strong tendency, which the circumstances were calculated to induce in them, to embrace the entire system of Judaism as it was maintained by their Jewish Christian brethren, elicited from Paul those expostulations which have been misunderstood as implying the absolute abrogation of the law. His earnestness therein was induced by the fact, that the voluntary assumption of the yoke of the ritual law, by those upon whom God had not laid it, was a manifest apostasy from the doctrine of grace,—an attempt to fulfill a righteousness of works.

Of the mixed state of these churches, the first epistle to the Corinthians presents constant illustrations. In it, Paul indulges in a frequency of allusion to Old Testament facts which presupposes his readers to be familiar with the sacred books of the Jews. In one place, he addresses them as being of the stock of Israel, "Brethren, I would not that ye should be ignorant, how that all our fathers were under the cloud, and all passed through the sea, and were all baptized unto Moses in the cloud and in the sea."—Ch. x, 1-11. On the other hand, the apostle alludes to disorders and offenses, in the church, which were evidently committed by the Gentile members (vi, 9-11; xi, 20-22), and moreover, says expressly,—"Ye know that ye were Gentiles, carried away unto these dumb idols, even as ye were led."—xii, 2. He also, as we have already seen, gives express instructions for continuing the distinction between Jew and Gentile, in the church. "Is any man called being circumcised? Let him not become uncircumcised. Is any called in uncircumcision? Let him not be circumcised."—vii, 18.

But there was yet another class of churches, which may be exemplified in Lystra, Derbe, and Galatia,—churches where there were no Jews, or in which their number was so small as to constitute an unappreciable element. In them, the Christian Sabbath and ordinances were alone observed, the assemblies and services on the Lord's day being precisely the same in their nature and manner as those maintained where Jews and Gentiles were united.

Of all these churches, whether of Jewish, mixed, or Gentile elements, the local constitution and form of government was the same; being that of the synagogue. This the circumstances rendered inevitable; and to it all the statements and intimations of the Scriptures testify. In fact, in the epistle of James they are expressly designated by that name.—"If there come unto your *synagogue, (sunagogēn)* a man with a gold ring."—Ja. ii, 2. It is true the epistle is inscribed, "to *the twelve tribes* which are scattered abroad."—Ib. i, 1. But it is to the Christians of those scattered tribes, that he addresses himself. With them Gentile believers were always to be found united; and no one will pretend that there were two forms of organization; one for the Jews, and another for the Gentiles. These churches were self-governed, so far as internal order and discipline were concerned. But with relation to the fundamental laws of their existence and rule of their faith they were in a state of recognized and entire dependence on the church in Jerusalem. This relation was indicated and expressed in a very peculiar and conclusive manner. The vital question concerning the relation of the Gentiles to the law of Moses arose in the church in Antioch, in which there were not only certain prophets (Acts xiii, 1, 2), but Paul the great apostle of the Gentiles. Naturally, we should have expected such a question to be brought to an immediate decision, by prophetic revelation, or by the authority of the apostle, confirmed by signs following. And, in fact, there *was* an immediate divine interposition. But it was an interposition by which the question was remanded to Jerusalem to be decided there. Paul says to the Galatians, — "I went up to Jerusalem, with Barnabas, and took Titus with me also. And I went up (*kata apokalupsin*) in accordance with a revelation." — Gal. ii, 1, 2. Again, when he came to Jerusalem, there were present John, the beloved of Jesus, and Peter, the chief of the apostles; beside James, the brother of the Lord and head of the church in Jerusalem. (Ib. ii, 9.) But not by either or all of them was the question decided, but referred to the council of the church, and, under the direction of the Holy Spirit, was there determined by deliberative consultation and vote; and the decree was drawn up and sent forth in the name of "the apostles, and elders and brethren." — Acts xv, 22, 23, 25. The relation of that council to the Jerusalem eldership and church is indicated by the manner in which at a later date those elders referred to it, in conference with Paul. "As touching the Gentiles which believe, *we* have written and concluded." — Acts xxi, 25, 18. Upon Paul's return to Antioch, and resumption of his missionary labors, after the council, he and his attendants, "as they went through the cities, delivered them the decrees for to keep, that were ordained of the apostles *and elders* which were at Jerusalem." — Ib. xvi, 4. It would thus appear beyond question, that this business was so ordered by the Head of the church, as to demonstrate the fact of the organic dependence of the Gentile churches everywhere, — not upon the authority of the apostles, as such, but upon the ancient church of Israel, in the councils of which the apostles sat as elders, with the elders. (1 Peter v, 1.) It was an indication to the Gentile churches that their privilege was that of *partakers* with Israel in *her* spiritual things. (Rom. xv, 27.) Believing Israel was thus presented, as not only the source whence the gospel flowed to the Gentiles, but as ordained to be to them the authorized exponent of that gospel. The principle here involved, is appealed to by Paul, when in repressing the arrogant assumptions of some in the Corinthian church, he demands of them, — "What! came the word of God out from you? or, came it unto you, only?" — 1 Cor. xiv, 36. In this relation of the Jewish church to those of the Gentiles, there was a fulfilment of the prophecy of Isaiah (ii, 3) reechoed by Micah: — "In the last days ... many nations shall come, and say, Come, and let us go up to the mountain of the Lord, and to the house of the God of Jacob; and he will teach us of his ways, and we will walk in his paths: for the law shall go forth of Zion, and the word of the Lord from Jerusalem." — Micah iv, 1, 2.

Thus, while the great body of Israel after the flesh rejected the Angel of the covenant, who was promised at Sinai to their fathers (Ex. xxiii, 20), and in so doing forfeited and were cut off from its fold, their believing brethren remained in full possession of its rights, and privileges; and the Gentiles, receiving Christ, became with them partakers therein, according to the proviso which from the beginning reserved room for them;—"For all the earth is mine."—Ex. xix, 5.

It was at a time when the condition of things here described, in Judea and among the Gentiles had attained to its completest realization, that Paul addressed the Romans in a figure which is in beautiful accord with the literal facts; as they had been already realized. "If some of the branches be broken off, and thou being a wild olive tree, wert graffed in among them, and with them partakest of the root and fatness of the olive tree,—boast not against the branches. But, if thou boast, thou bearest not the root; but the root, thee. Thou wilt say, then,... The branches were broken off, that I might be graffed in. Well: because of unbelief they were broken off, and thou standest by faith. Be not highminded but fear. For if God spared not the natural branches, take heed lest he also spare not thee.... And they also if they abide not still in unbelief, shall be graffed in: for God is able to graff them in again. For if thou wert cut out of the olive tree, which is wild by nature, and wert graffed contrary to nature into a good olive tree; how much more shall these which be the natural branches, be graffed into their own olive tree."—Rom. xi, 17-24.

The Christian church is not a new institution, nor its constitution a new organic law. But it is, in the strictest and most absolute sense, lineally and organically one with that of Israel, founded and perpetuated upon the covenant of Sinai.

PART XV.

CHRISTIAN BAPTISM.

Section LXXXIX.—*History of the Rite.*—The cotemporaneous baptisms of John and Jesus. Both were the same Christian baptism. Christ did not *institute* baptism, but gave it to the Gentiles. Rebaptism at Ephesus. Note on rebaptism

But two of the evangelists, Matthew and Mark, mention baptism in connection with the last instructions of Jesus; and of these, Mark introduces it in an incidental way, as though it had been a matter already understood. (Matt, xxviii, 19, 20; Mark xvi, 15, 16.) The reason was that the apostles were not then first commissioned to baptize. On this point, Calvin speaking with reference to the arguments of the Anabaptists says, "It is a mistake worse than childish to consider that commission as the original institution of baptism,—which Christ had commanded his apostles to administer, from the commencement of his preaching. They have no reason to contend, therefore, that the law and rule of baptism ought to be derived from those two passages, as if they contained the first institution of it."[118] Upon this, Dr. Dale says,—"Calvin is right in dating Christian ritual baptism from the ministry and authority of Christ, and not from that of John, even if they were entirely identical, which they are not. The baptism of John is Christian baptism, *as far as it goes*; but it is Christian baptism undeveloped in the blood shedding of an atoning Redeemer, in which shedding of blood, 'for the remission of sins,' ritual baptism has its exclusive ground." Again, speaking of the words of Peter, on the day of Pentecost,—"Repent and be baptized,"—he asks,—"What was this baptism? Was it a Jewish baptism, a ceremonial cleansing of the body, merely? Was it John's baptism, a spiritual baptism (*baptisma metanoias*) in which no Holy Ghost was yet 'poured out,' no *crucified* Redeemer was yet revealed? Was it Christian baptism, the baptism of Christ, the crucified, the Risen, the Ascended, the Pourer out of the Holy Ghost?"[119] In these passages we have a statement of differentia upon which the lamented author insists earnestly, as distinguishing the baptisms named, from each other. As to the Jewish baptisms,—those which were appointed by the divine law, they were, as we have seen, spiritual in the same sense precisely as were the baptisms of John and of Christ; and the latter were and are "a ceremonial cleansing of the body, merely," in the same sense as were the baptisms of the Jews. To this day, "the letter," or outward form of Christian baptism is a ceremonial cleansing of those who are ritually unclean. No otherwise could it show forth "the spirit" of

[118] Institutes, Book IV, chap, xvi, §37.
[119] Dale's "Christic Baptism," pp. 430, 431.

the ordinance, which is the real purging, by the Spirit, of those who are spiritually defiled. From the beginning to the present day, the ritual baptisms always signified the very same spiritual truths. And they were all alike devoid of any spiritual power in themselves.

But let us trace the line of connection between them. Very early in the ministry of Jesus, before the imprisonment of John, while the latter was baptizing in Enon, "Jesus and his disciples came into the land of Judea; and there he tarried with them and baptized." But "when the Lord knew how the Pharisees had heard that Jesus made and baptized more disciples than John, (though Jesus himself baptized not, but his disciples), he left Judea, and departed again into Galilee." — John iii, 22; iv, 1-3. Here, be it observed, (1.) that John was the intelligent, faithful and inspired forerunner and herald of the Lord Jesus. The gospel which he preached was that which the Spirit of Christ gave him, and the baptism which he administered set forth that gospel in ritual figure. His preaching was summed in one word. "Repent, for the kingdom of heaven is at hand." (2.) The Lord Jesus preached the very same word, and gave it to the apostles and the seventy to proclaim, when he sent them abroad through the land. "Repent, for the kingdom of heaven is at hand." (3.) There is not an intimation in the Scriptures, nor suggestion to justify the idea, of the least difference in the form and nature of the baptisms at this stage of the history, administered by them respectively. Certainly if there were differences, they must have been characterized by a minuteness and subtlety, fit rather to exercise the ingenuity of hair-splitting schoolmen, than to instruct the common people of Judea; who, upon the supposition of diversity, were called to *choose between the rival baptisms*. John's baptism was at first into the name of "the coming One," "the Baptizer with the Holy Ghost and with fire." Of that baptism his was proclaimed to be a symbol. When Jesus came, John at once identified him as the coming One, and thenceforth his baptism was into the name of Jesus of Nazareth. I do not mean that John made use of those phrases. To this point we shall come presently. But "John verily baptized with the baptism of repentance, saying unto the people that they should believe on him which should come after him; that is, on Christ Jesus." — Acts xix, 4. The rite which he dispensed sealed upon the recipients their profession of repentance and faith in Jesus, the Son of God, the atoning Lamb, the King Baptizer. In a report of one of his discourses, which occupies seven verses of the gospel of John, each of these titles and the things implied in them is brought out with perfect distinctness. (John i, 29-36.) That John was ignorant of the precise form of crucifixion, as that in which atonement was to be made, is possible; although even there the facts do not warrant the confidence of Dr. Dale's assertions. But that he was not ignorant of Christ's atoning office, his own words distinctly testify. "Behold the *Lamb of God*, which taketh away the sin of the world." — John i, 29. (4.) The whole manner of the narrative from which we learn the fact that Christ's disciples baptized, indicates the identity of the ordinance as administered by them with that of John. The fact is not mentioned for its own sake, but as introductory and explanatory of the testimony of John respecting Jesus. (John iii, 22-30.) In fact, we have no information whatever of the nature and meaning of Christ's baptism, as thus originated, except in its justly assumed identity with that of John. This, the language of John's interlocutors implies (Ib. 26), and upon the basis of this assumption the whole narrative rests. This remark applies also to the subsequent statement,—that "the Lord knew how the Pharisees had heard that Jesus made and baptized more disciples than John; though Jesus himself baptized not, but his disciples."—John iv, 1, 2. Here the one word, "baptized," without qualification or differentiating phrase, is applied to both Christ's disciples and John, and plainly identifies the rite administered by them as one and the same. That such was the case can not be successfully questioned.

And now, what have we, in the ordinance thus dispensed by the disciples under the eye, and as a seal to the preaching, of Christ, but Christian baptism? True, the disciples were ignorant at that time, of the doctrine of the cross, which in fact they refused to believe, till their Master was crucified before their eyes. But while the baptism was administered by their hands, it was in Christ's immediate presence, by his authority, and as a seal to the gospel which he preached. How then could their ignorance and hardness, or that of John, if he be so impeached, change the nature of the rite which by Christ's authority they both administered? And, especially, how could this be, when in fact that baptism, while it presupposed Christ's atoning sufferings, yet had no immediate relation to them, but to his kingdom and glory,—the theme of John's preaching,—the one thing in Christ's instructions which the apostles gladly received?

To what extent this baptizing function of the apostles continued in exercise during the subsequent ministry of Christ, we are not informed. But, the manner in which, first and last, the subject is treated by the evangelists implies that it never was in abeyance. Hence, in his final interviews with them, Jesus does not speak of the ordinance as a novelty, nor as a rite to be reintroduced; but alludes to it as to a familiar subject. In fact, his only recorded references to it, have in view, not the ordinance, in itself considered, but *its bestowal on the Gentiles.* "Go ye, disciple *all nations, baptizing them.*"—Matt. xxviii, 19. "Go ye into *all the world* and preach the gospel to every creature. *He that believeth and is baptized* shall be saved, but he that believeth not shall be damned."—Mark xvi, 15, 16. By this decree, the ordinance, which, as we have seen, was already divested of its sacrificial elements, was released from its peculiar and restricted relation to the Jewish people. Heretofore, only the circumcised could be admitted to baptism; and the rite, when administered to them, was received as a certificate of title to the privileges of the covenant, in connection with the Mosaic ritual and the temple service. But, by this decree of Christ, it was appropriated to the use of the Gentiles, also; as certifying to them a part in the same covenant, relieved of the encumbrance of the ritual law. That its administration to the converts of Christ's ministry is not mentioned, presents no just occasion of surprise, in view of the familiarity of the ordinance and the emphasis already given to it in connection with John's ministry. That Christ's disciples baptized at all is only known to us by the incidental mention in the last of the evangelists.

The facts here developed are of immense importance in their bearing upon our present inquiry. The Lord Jesus did not *institute* baptism, at any time. He recognized it as an ordinance of God given to Israel ages before,—accepted it personally from the hands of John,—immediately appointed his disciples to administer it to the Jews in conjunction with John, and then, after his resurrection and assumption of the sceptre, commanded them to dispense it to the Gentiles also. — "All power is given unto me in heaven and earth. Go ye therefore and teach all nations baptizing them."

The rebaptism of the twelve disciples of John, by Paul at Ephesus (Acts xix, 1-7), may be thought inconsistent with the assertion of the identity of the baptisms of John and of the Christian church. But when the facts are considered in their true relations, they will appear in perfect harmony with all that have been heretofore adduced, and entirely consistent with the conclusions thence derived. John was the herald of Christ. His preaching and baptism had neither significance nor value, except as they directed the attention and faith of his disciples to the coming of Christ and the baptism of the Holy Spirit, which He should administer. To the great mass of those who received his baptism, no profit resulted, because it was not followed up by a waiting for Christ's coming, and a devotion to him when he was revealed. It effected no actual separation of such disciples from the unbelieving mass of the nation. When, therefore, the crisis came and the Saviour was crucified, they sustained no relation of identity with him and his cause; but were an undistinguishable part of the nation, whose rulers betrayed and crucified Him. The baptism which they had received was no magical rite, leaving an indelible impress on the recipients; but a rational ordinance, designed to mark and seal a separation and consecration unto Christ. Precisely here, was the point of Paul's testimony to these men. — "John verily baptized with the baptism of repentance, saying unto the people that they should *believe on him which should come after him*, that is, *on Christ Jesus*." Where this intent of John's baptism did not follow, — where no separation unto Christ was actually effected, the parties remained unclean, with the unclean nation. In them was fulfilled the proverb of the son of Sirach. — "He that is baptized from the dead, and again toucheth the dead, what availeth his washing?" — Ecclus. xxxi, 30. Such was the case with any of the converts of Pentecost, who had been John's disciples. And such evidently were the Ephesian disciples. They were believers in the Messiah of prophecy, as heralded by John. But their faith was weak and supineness prevalent. They had not followed up the line of John's testimony, with the zeal of a living consecration. The baptism which they had received had effected no separation unto Christ. When, therefore, under the ministry of Paul, they were prepared to begin a new life, their consecration was sealed by a new administration of the same baptism.[120]

That this is a just view of the case in question farther appears from the manner in which it is presented in immediate connection and contrast with that of Apollos, whose story closes the eighteenth chapter of the Acts, as that of the twelve opens the nineteenth. Of him it is stated that he was "an eloquent man, and mighty in the Scriptures, instructed in the way of the Lord, and being fervent in the spirit, he spake and taught diligently the things of the Lord, knowing only the baptism of John. And he began to speak boldly in the synagogue; whom, when Aquila and Priscilla had heard, they took him unto them, and expounded unto him the way of God more perfectly." — Acts xviii, 24-26. The silence, here, on the subject of bap-

---

[120] See Alexander on Acts xiv, 5.

tism, and the emphasis given to its statement immediately after, in the case of the twelve, is pregnant. For, all occurred in the same city of Ephesus, where Apollos was instructed and preaching just before Paul's coming, and the baptism of the twelve.

> NOTE.—How can we consistently restore excommunicated persons without rebaptism? Is not the prevalent practice a relic of the *opus operatum* heresy? "If any one assert that in the three sacraments, baptism, confirmation, and orders, there is not a mark imprinted on the soul,—that is a certain spiritual and indelible token, whence, it may not be repeated,—let him be anathema."—*Council of Trent, Sess.* vii. *Canon* 9. Is this the faith which we hold?

Section XC.—*"Baptizing them into the Name."*—1. Into the name. *En; epi; eis.* "Into Christ." "Into the name of Christ." 2. "The name of the Father and of the Son, and of the Holy Ghost."—"The name of the Lord Jesus,"

"And Jesus came and spake unto them and said, All power is given unto me, in heaven and in earth. Go ye, therefore, and (mathēteusate) disciple all nations, baptizing them (eis) into the name of the Father, and of the Son, and of the Holy Ghost; teaching them to observe all things whatsoever I have commanded you; and lo, I am with you alway even unto the end of the world."—Matt. xxviii, 18-20.

Here are two things to be considered:—(1) The phrase, "into the name;" (2) "The name of the Father, and of the Son, and of the Holy Ghost."

1. "Into the name." The phrase, "in the name," as found in the common English version, represents three distinct forms of expression, in the original, which are essentially different in their meaning, and should, therefore, be carefully discriminated. They are "(en) in the name;" "(epi) for the name," and "(eis) into the name." The essential idea expressed by the first of these is, representative union, as a person who speaks or acts "in the name" of another, identifies himself with that other. Thus,—"Whatsoever ye shall ask *in my name.*"—John xiv, 13, 14, 26; xv, 16, etc. "Ye are justified *in the name* of the Lord Jesus."—1 Cor. vi, 11. "Giving thanks *in the name* of the Lord Jesus."—Eph. v, 20. "Do all *in the name* of the Lord Jesus."—Col. iii, 17. Hence the use of the expression, as signifying, "by the authority of." Thus, "I am come *in my Father's name,* and ye receive me not; if another shall come *in his own name,* him ye will receive."—John v, 43. "*In the name* of Jesus Christ of Nazareth, rise up and walk."—Acts iii, 6. "I command thee, *in the name* of Jesus Christ, come out of her."—Ib. xvi, 18. There is but one passage in which this form of expression is used in connection with *baptizo.* Acts x, 48,—"He commanded them to be baptized, *in the name* of the Lord." The analogy of the phrase elsewhere, would require us to understand it here as meaning, "by the authority of the Lord." The codex Sinaiticus reads,—"He commanded them (*en to 'onomati Ju Xu baptisthēnai*), *in the name of Jesus Christ to be baptized.*" Cyril of Jerusalem quotes the passage in the same order.[121] Not only does the form of the phrase in itself call for this rendering, but the connection is equally clear, in the same direction. The

[121] In Dale, Christic Baptism, p. 205.

case was the baptism of the house of Cornelius. Peter demands,—"Can any man forbid the water, that these should not be baptized, which have received the Holy Ghost, as well as we?" The point at issue was the admission of the Gentile world to a part in the salvation of Christ. Peter had on the day of Pentecost testified that it was the Lord Jesus by whom the Holy Ghost had been poured out. He had been admonished by Jesus in a vision that the Gentiles were not to be excluded from the blessings of the gospel. He now calls the attention of his six Jewish companions (Acts xi, 12), to the fact that the house of Cornelius was baptized by the Lord Jesus himself, with the same Spirit which had been poured upon the Jews on Pentecost; and with an emphatic pause, challenges objection. There being none, the apostle, then, in the name and by the authority of Christ, proclaims the doors of salvation thrown open to the world. He "in the name of the Lord Jesus, commanded them to be baptized;" and afterward vindicated the action by the demand, "What was I, that I should withstand God."—Acts xi, 17.

Epi, in this connection, has the general meaning of, because of,—on account of,—with reference to,—*for*; and the phrase as thus constructed means, "for the sake of." Thus, "Whoso shall receive one such little child (*epi 'onomati mou*), *for my name's sake.*"—Matt. xviii, 5; Mark ix, 37. "They called him Zacharias (*epi*), *for the sake of* his father's name."—Luke i, 59. "That repentance and remission of sins should be preached (*epi*) *for his name's sake.*"—Luke xxiv, 47. "That they speak henceforth to no man (*epi*) *for the sake of* the name."—Acts iv, 17. From these illustrations, it will be seen that in connection with baptism, the rendering, of *epi*,—"*in the name*,"—altogether misses the idea of the sacred writer. It occurs but once. On the day of Pentecost, Peter, in reply to the cry,—"What shall we do?" answered,—"Repent and be baptized every one of you (*epi*), *for the sake of* the name of Jesus Christ (*eis*), *unto* the remission of sins."—Acts ii, 38. Jesus had said, "He that believeth and is baptized, shall be saved." Peter, therefore, tells the multitude, "Repent and be baptized. Do this, in honor of the Lord Jesus; and unto the remission of sins; since repentance, and obedience shown by receiving baptism, are pledges of remission."

In the text of Matthew, which stands at the head of this section, the word is, *eis*,—"Baptizing them (*eis*), *into* the name of the Father and of the Son and of the Holy Ghost." This is the preposition ordinarily used with relation to baptism, both real and ritual. In connection with the baptism of the Spirit, its signification is so fully explained and illustrated as to admit of no doubt or question. They that are "baptized (*eis*) *into* Christ" (Gal. iii, 27; Rom. vi, 3), are united to him,—"by one Spirit baptized (*eis*) *into* one body," "the body of Christ."—1 Cor. xii, 13, 27. Those who are "baptized (*eis*) *into* his death," are thereby "dead with him."—Rom. vi, 3, 8. So, it is said of the children of Israel that they were "baptized (*eis*) *into* Moses, in the cloud and in the sea," as the passage of the Red Sea, the destruction of the Egyptians and the deliverance of Israel by the hand of Moses released them finally and forever from the Egyptian yoke, and united them to Moses in subordination to his mediatorial authority. "They believed the Lord and his servant Moses."—Ex. xiv, 31. This is viewed by the apostle as a figure of the work of grace by which the people of Christ are released from Satan's bondage and brought under his saving scepter; and he, therefore, uses the same form of expression, "Baptized *into* Christ," "Baptized *into* Moses."

The style in which the real baptism is thus spoken of is a key to the meaning of the Lord Jesus, in his language concerning the ritual ordinance. The visible church is the representative and type of that invisible body of Christ, the members of which are incorporated therein by the baptism of the Spirit. Baptism with water is a symbol, merely, of that spiritual grace. The recipient may be truly united to the Lord Jesus. But such union is not produced by the ritual ordinance. The effect can ascend no higher than the cause. A symbolic baptism can accomplish no more than a symbolic union, a union in outward semblance and name. Its ground is *profession* of the name of Christ, and the characteristic designation of those who have received it is, — that they "have *named the name* of Christ" — (2 Tim. ii, 19), that is, they have professed to take hold of his covenant, and have thereupon had his name named upon them. They are Christ's. If, therefore, baptism *"into Christ,"* by the Spirit, means spiritual union with Christ, and with his invisible body, then, manifestly, baptism with water *"into the name of Christ,"* can mean nothing else but ritual identification with his name, and with that visible body which is known by his name, and embraced by profession in the bonds of his covenant. To effect such union is all that Christ's ministers can do. It is what they are commissioned to do. The rest remains with the Great Baptizer himself. Intimately related to this subject is that remarkable word of God which instructed Aaron and his sons to bless Israel with that threefold benediction which is believed to refer to the doctrine of the glorious Trinity. "The Lord bless thee and keep thee. The Lord make his face shine upon thee, and be gracious unto thee. The Lord lift up his countenance upon thee, and give thee peace," — and then adds, — "And *they* shall *put my name* upon the children of Israel, and *I* will bless them." — Num. vi, 23-27.

The form of expression used by the Lord Jesus, — "baptizing them into the name," is a perpetual rebuke of every doctrine or pretense which would attribute to the rite, in itself, any higher or other efficacy than that of changing the outward and professed relation of the baptized to Christ and the Godhead. The view here presented is further involved in the relation between baptism and discipleship, intimated in the words of Jesus, — "Disciple all nations, baptizing them into the name." Christ came as the revealer of the Godhead, the Prophet of Israel, as well as her royal Priest. The preaching of the gospel is the fulfillment of his prophetic function, and those whether Jews or Gentiles, who accept it are to be enrolled as disciples of Christ, by being baptized into the name or profession of the faith of the triune Godhead, as revealed by him, in the gospel. It will thus be seen that the translation invariably given to the phrase in question, in our common English version, entirely fails of exhibiting a true idea of the meaning of the original. See Matt, xxviii, 19; Acts viii, 16; xix, 5; 1 Cor. i, 13, 15. Baptizing *"in* the name," can only mean, dispensing the rite by the authority of the Persons named. The command is, to "baptize *into* the name."

2. "The name of the Father, and of the Son, and of the Holy Ghost." In other places, baptism is said to be "into the name of the Lord Jesus." — Acts ii, 38; viii, 16; xix, 5. Nor are the other Persons of the Godhead ever mentioned in such con-

nection with the real baptism. That is always described as being into Jesus Christ. Rom. vi, 3; 1 Cor. xii, 13, 27; Gal. iii, 27. How is this diversity of expression to be explained? It is abundantly plain, as respects the real baptism. In it, each Person is signally present, in appropriate relation. In it, Christ, the Royal Administrator, by whom the Spirit is poured out, is also the Head into which by that one Spirit all are baptized as members. The Spirit appears as the Spirit of life in Christ Jesus, the Renewer and Sanctifier. And as to the Father, "Ye are all the children of God, by faith in Christ Jesus; for as many of you as have been baptized into Christ have put on Christ."—Gal. iii, 26, 27. "As many as received him to them gave he power to become the sons of God, even to them that believed on his name."—Joh. i, 12. In a word, thus is fulfilled the petition of Jesus. "As thou Father art in me and I in thee, that they also may be one in us.... I in them and thou in me, that they may be made perfect in one."—John xvii, 21, 23. By the real baptism, therefore, the believer is united to each Person of the Godhead,—a fact, nevertheless, expressed by baptism into one, Jesus Christ.

The same principle governs the forms of expression used with reference to ritual baptism. Jesus Christ is the Word of God, and can not be truly apprehended except in that relation. "No man hath seen God at any time. The only begotten Son which is in the bosom of the Father, he hath declared Him."—John i, 18. He came to make known the Father. He returned to impart the Spirit. And, as he was thus apprehended by the apostles, a baptism into his name was a baptism into the name of the Father, and of the Son, and of the Spirit. It only ceases to be so, when Jesus ceases to be appreciated as him in whom "dwelleth all the fullness of the Godhead bodily."—Col. ii, 9.

It is an illustration of the essential deficiency of the theory of immersion that it has no explanation for the diversity of expression here considered.

Section XCI.—"*He that believeth and is baptized.*"—It refers to ritual baptism; and is a caution against trust in it. Faith is the essential thing

In the great commission, as recorded by Mark, Jesus said to his disciples, "Go ye into all the world, and preach the gospel to every creature. He that believeth and is baptized shall be saved, but he that believeth not shall be damned."—Mark xvi, 15, 16. Dr. Dale denies that ritual baptism is here referred to.—"We accept the real baptism by the Holy Spirit as the sole baptism directly contemplated by the passage; in general, because it meets in the most absolute and unlimited manner, *as a condition of salvation*, the obvious requirement on the face of the passage, having the same breadth with belief, and universally present in every case of salvation."[122] To this view the objections are obvious and conclusive. (1.) The clause which the author has emphasized with Italics, is inaccurate. The baptism with the Holy Ghost is not "*a condition of salvation;*" but is the very salvation itself. It is the casket in which are bestowed repentance, faith, remission of sins, justification, adoption, sanctification, the resurrection and eternal life. (2.) The interpretation would not only make this baptism a condition of salvation, but puts it in the position of a co-ordinate but secondary condition with faith.—"He that *believeth* and is

[122] Christic Baptism, p. 393.

baptized." Whereas faith, as just remarked, is one of the immediate phenomena of this baptism. (3.) The text as thus explained represents the Lord Jesus as commissioning his ministers to offer salvation to sinners *upon conditions* one of which is to be performed by them; but the other belongs to his own peculiar prerogative, to which, in no circumstances, can they assume an efficient relation. It interprets the message to be preached thus: "Whoever believeth shall be saved; *provided* I, Jesus, shall see fit to baptize him!"

The text is a statement to the apostles, and through them to the ministry in all ages, of their duties and the results of their labors. With baptism as a ritual ordinance of the gospel they had been familiar from the beginning of John's ministry, and of Christ's in coincidence with it. They had been fully instructed, as to the baptism of the Spirit, which Christ was about to dispense, and which they were to await; and as to the typical relation to it which the ritual ordinance sustained. They are now commanded to go forth and preach that gospel; not, as heretofore, to Israel, only, but to every creature, in all the world; and whereas, until now, none could be baptized,—none could receive the token of the covenant, except those who were, by circumcision, identified with Israel after the flesh,—he indicates the removal of that restriction,—"Go teach all nations, baptizing them." Baptizing them with water, which, only, they could administer; and in token of that *profession* of faith, of which only they could take cognizance. It is in view of these things, that the declaration is made, "He that *believeth* and is baptized shall be saved; but he that believeth not shall be damned." The repetition shows that the emphasis of the passage rests on believing. "You are to preach, and baptize those who *profess* to believe. But let all, both preachers and hearers, beware of trusting in the baptismal shadow. He that *believeth* and is baptized, shall be saved. But he that believeth not,—his baptism will not avail,—He shall be damned." Assuredly, had the Lord Jesus been stating conditions of salvation, as concerning baptism, he knew how to set it on both sides of the alternative.

> Section XCII.—*The Formula of Baptism.*—Ritualistic view. No formula
> prescribed by Christ, nor used by the apostles

It is proper and necessary that such words be used in the administration of Baptism, as shall give an intelligent announcement of the nature and intent of the ordinance. For this purpose nothing can be more appropriate than the formula in universal use, in all the churches. But the question arises whether the words thus employed were given to be uttered as a formula necessary to the rite.

1. There is nothing whatever in the language of the Lord Jesus, on the subject, to give countenance to the suggestion in question. "Go ye, and *disciple* all nations, *baptizing* them into the name of the Father, and of the Son, and of the Holy Ghost; *teaching* them to observe all things whatsoever I have commanded you." We have already seen that "baptizing into the name" means, not the utterance in the baptism of any words or formula; but instruction and consecration to the faith and service of the Triune God, identified with the baptismal rite and signified by it. But if such be the meaning of our Savior's words, it excludes the idea in question. "Baptizing them into the name," then, means something very different from "ut-

tering the name." In fact, the more carefully the language in question is examined, in itself, in its immediate connection, and in its relation to the general scope of the gospel and its history, the more evident will it appear that it was not *words* that were present to the mind of Jesus, or by him put into the mouths of his ministry, but the great doctrine of baptism, in which the whole gospel is summed,—that doctrine which was heralded by the baptist, and expounded by the Lord Jesus in his discourse and prayer at the supper. One who should teach that the Holy Spirit is not a coequal Person of the Godhead, or that the Lord Jesus is not the eternal and coequal Son, might administer the rite, in the use of the formula. Yet would it not be baptism in the intent of Jesus as here set forth.

2. The silence of all of the evangelists except Matthew as to the words in question, is wholly inconsistent with the supposition that they were given as a formula. The importance of the rite is of common agreement. And resting as it does as an obligation on every soul that hears the gospel, it is the first and foremost of all the practical duties of those who receive it. If, therefore, the formula was now given as an element in the administration of the ordinance, it is of the first and universal moment. How then is it possible for three of the evangelists to have ignored it, in their several versions of the gospel. Evidently they attached to it no such significance as obtains with those who hold it as of the essence of baptism.

3. The fact that it is not once used or alluded to, in the whole subsequent history and epistles, is conclusive. Those records are a testimony;—as much by silence, often, as by utterance. But, on this subject, they are not silent. On the day of Pentecost, Peter calls upon the inquirers to be baptized "(*epi*) for the name's sake of Jesus Christ."—Acts ii, 38. The Samaritans and the twelve disciples of John at Ephesus were baptized "into the name of the Lord Jesus."—Acts viii, 16; xix, 5. And Paul distinctly implies that the Corinthians were baptized into the same name. "Is Christ divided? was Paul crucified for you? or, were ye baptized into the name of Paul?"—1 Cor. i, 13. How these facts are consistent with obedience to Christ's command we have already seen. The only interpretation which will harmonize the record is deduced from that doctrine of baptism which has been unfolded in these pages. He that is spiritually baptized into Jesus Christ, thereby receives the Spirit and is united in Christ to the Father. He is baptized into the Three.

Here, the doctrine of immersion is radically defective. The form may be administered with the utterance of the names of the Trinity. But its doctrine contains no testimony to the Triune, nor recognition of any Person of the Godhead. It relates altogether to the humanity of Christ, whose burial it represents.

Section XCIII.—*The Administration on Pentecost.*—There was a baptism
    with water. Dr. Dale's objections

On the day of Pentecost, in reply to the cry of the repentant multitude,—"What shall we do?" Peter said, "Repent and be baptized every one of you (*epi to 'onomati*), *for the name's sake* of Jesus Christ (*eis*) *unto* the remission of sins; and ye shall receive the gift of the Holy Ghost. For the promise is to you, and to your children, and to all that are afar off, even as many as the Lord our God shall call.... Then, they that gladly received his word were baptized; and the same day there were added unto them about three thousand souls." — Acts ii, 37-41. Dr. Dale denies this baptism to have been ritual, and demands, — "Was there a visible Christian church in existence at Pentecost? Was there any one competent to organize a Christian church before Pentecost? Did not the divine Head of the church himself furnish the materials for a church organization, officers, and members, 'that day?' Was there a Christian organization effected, as well as a tri-millenary baptism administered 'that day?' Were they organized and then baptized, or baptized and then organized?"[123] These questions, coming with the authority of the learned writer, are entitled to respectful consideration. And although they have, in effect, been answered, already, a few words will here be added, in direct response. The Jewish church, as organized, according to the law of Moses, under the ministry of the elders, was the Christian church, on the day of Pentecost. But as that church had become largely corrupt and apostate, and its rulers had betrayed and crucified the Lord Jesus, her King, a separation had become necessary, and the preaching and baptism of the apostles was the means appointed by Him for eliminating the apostate elements. The one hundred and twenty who remained together in Jerusalem after the ascension were but a small part of believing Israel, even then; for the Lord Jesus was seen of above five hundred brethren at once, after his resurrection. (1 Cor. xv, 6.) But they, or the apostles alone, or one of them, would have been abundantly sufficient as a center for gathering the believing from among the apostate. They stood precisely as did Moses in the midst of the congregation of Israel, at the time of the apostasy of the golden calf, saying, — "Who is on the Lord's side? Let him come unto me." — Ex. xxxii, 26. Hence the style in which the historian of the Acts writes of the converts of Pentecost. "Then they that gladly received his word, were baptized; and the same day there were added about three thousand souls." — Acts ii, 41. They are not said to have been "added to the church;" for they were the church, obeying the call of her Head, — "Come out from among them, and be ye separate, saith the Lord, and touch not the unclean thing." — 2 Cor. vi, 17. They are, therefore, said to have been "added (to them)," — that is, to the apostles; or more literally "associated together," — joined in one body. By that act, they stood forth, the church of Jerusalem, divested of the unbelieving elements. Accordingly, we read, immediately after, that "the Lord added to the *church* daily such as should be saved." — Vs. 47. For all the purposes of the occasion, on the day of Pentecost, there was no farther organization necessary than that which existed in the sanhedrim of the apostles, men inspired of the Holy Ghost, and endowed by the Lord Jesus with authority for presiding over his church in this transition period of her history.

The baptism of the Spirit on the day of Pentecost has been already illustrated fully. That there was also a ritual baptism, with water, I venture to regard as equally certain. (1.) We have just seen that the apostolic commission contained a command to baptize the disciples. Peter, therefore, in inviting his hearers to repent and be baptized, was simply following the literal terms of his instructions. And had he omitted baptism, — that ritual baptism which alone the apostles could administer — he would have been acting in direct violation of his commission. (2.) In his exhortation, the baptism is secondary to repentance. This is the proper order of ritual baptism, which is predicated on profession of repentance. But it is the

---

[123] Dale's Christic Baptism, p. 162.

reverse as to the real baptism, which precedes repentance and is its cause. (3.) The language used in describing the result of the exhortation is conclusive.—"Then they that gladly received his word were baptized." The glad reception of the word is stated as the antecedent ground of receiving the baptism; the reverse, again, of the order in real baptism. (4.) In the case of Cornelius and his house, Peter based their baptizing with water upon the fact that the spiritual phenomena were identical with those of the day of Pentecost. "The Holy Ghost fell on them as on us at the beginning."—"Can any man forbid the water, that these should not be baptized, which have received the Holy Ghost, as well as we?"—Acts x, 47; xi, 15. This argument would have been wholly inappropriate had there been no water baptism on Pentecost.

But Dr. Dale urges another objection.—"While the reception of these thousands that day into the church by dipping into water, is improbable to absurdity, for reasons both moral and physical, their reception by any ritual form whatever, is, for moral considerations mainly, not without embarrassment. These thousands were all personally strangers to the apostles, mostly from foreign lands, Parthians, Medes, Elamites, Mesopotamians, Cretes, Arabians, etc. An hour before, they were mockers of the work of the Holy Ghost, and declared the apostles to be drunk. Now, is there moral fitness in the reception of such men into the church, by a rite without any personal intercourse, to learn their moral condition? But the passage states that the baptism was grounded in the 'glad reception of the word' preached. If the baptism was the work of the apostles, then this knowledge must also be the knowledge of the apostles; and if so, then it must have been obtained, either by divine illumination, or by personal intercourse touching repentance and faith, the knowledge of Christ and the duty of baptism; then, how could the addition of three thousand be made 'that day?'"[124] The theory that, the baptism here in question was spiritual and not ritual, is, here, self-condemned, by the statement which truly represents it to have been "grounded in the glad reception of the word preached." That word was, "Repent and be baptized." Its glad reception, therefore is equivalent to the exercise of repentance, which is the immediate fruit of the spiritual baptism, and therefore of necessity follows, but can not precede it. The baptism, therefore, which was "grounded in the glad reception of the word," can have been no other than ritual baptism. The fundamental fallacy of the argument lies in the assumption, which we have before noticed, that the Pentecostal transactions were incident to the organizing of a new church; instead of being, as we have shown, the separating of the existing church from the corrupt and ungodly elements which had taken possession of it.

It is asserted respecting the three thousand that, "an hour before, they were mockers of the work of the Holy Spirit." A kindred statement is frequently heard, in illustration of the fickleness of the multitude,—that those who yesterday filled the air with shouts of "Hosanna!" to-day cry, "Away with him." Both representations are erroneous, and tend to obscure the true state of the case. In the Pentecostal scene, there were "some" mockers, and possibly, nay, probably some of these were made trophies of grace that day. But to represent the assembly as characteristically

---

[124] "Christic Baptism," p. 158.

of that class, involves an utter misconception of the case as expressly stated by the sacred historian. He represents them as "Jews, *devout men*, out of every nation under heaven."—Acts ii, 5. It was they, who came thronging to the assembly of the apostles. It was characteristically they who gladly received the word and were baptized. Nor is the language of Peter to them incongruous to this view. "Him ye have taken, and by wicked hands, have crucified and slain."—v. 23. Their rulers had done it, and the whole people were responsible and polluted with the crime of his blood, until they purged themselves, by separation and baptism. So, the multitude who cried, "Hosanna!" were "the multitude of the disciples," from Galilee. (Luke xix, 37; compare Ib. xxii, 59.) For fear of the people, the conspirators seized Jesus by betrayal, by night; and the cry against him was uttered, at the instigation of the rulers and priests, by their retainers and dependents. (Mark xv, 11.) "It was early," when they brought Jesus before Pilate. (John xviii, 28.) And it is probable that the sentence was already passed and Jesus in the hands of the executioners, before the Galileans who were accustomed, at the feasts, to encamp on Olivet, had any knowledge of the fearful tragedy of that day. These facts are all of importance, in order to a just conception of the real nature of the separation which began in Jerusalem on the day of Pentecost, and ultimately extended throughout Judea, Galilee, and Samaria, and to all parts of the world, where a synagogue of the Jews was to be found. We do no service to the truth, by underestimating the number of those who in that day, were waiting for the consolation of Israel, and "gladly received the word" of the rising of the Sun of righteousness, in the person of the Lord Jesus.

From the foregoing considerations, we conclude it to be certain that the three thousand converts of the day of Pentecost were baptized with water. The order of occurrences, as it appears from the record was this: The preaching of Peter was accompanied with the promised power, the baptism of the Spirit being bestowed upon his hearers, by the Lord Jesus. By that baptism was given to them repentance and remission of sins. (Acts v, 31.) Upon their correspondent profession, they were baptized with water; and thereupon, they received the gifts of tongues and of prophecy, in fulfillment of the promise of Christ (Mark xvi, 17), and in accordance with the assurance given them by Peter;—"Repent and be baptized, and ye shall receive the gift of the Holy Ghost. For the promise is to you and to your children,"—the promise, to wit, which he had before quoted from Joel, in explanation of the Pentecostal signs.

Section XCIV.—*Symbolic Meaning of this Baptism.*—It could but symbolize the baptism of the Spirit. The two formulas thus reconciled

The rite of immersion is inseparably identified with the theory that ritual baptism is designed to symbolize the burial of the Lord Jesus. By the advocates of this theory, the baptism administered to the converts of Pentecost is held to have been the original of the institution. By all, that baptism must be recognized as a most conspicuous and normal exemplification of the rite. We are perfectly willing to stake the whole issue upon the question of the symbolic meaning of the ordinance, as determined by the Scriptural statements concerning that baptism.

It has been shown that the Old Testament baptisms symbolized the gift from on high of the Spirit of life from God. We have seen that John administered his baptism as an announcement and symbol of that which the coming One should dispense,—the baptism of the Holy Ghost. We have heard the Lord Jesus appropriate to himself the testimonies of John, and promise their fulfillment, in terms by which the baptism to be administered by him was distinctly identified as the antitype of that of John. "John truly baptized with water, but ye shall be baptized with the Holy Ghost."—Acts i, 5. We have seen the promise fulfilled, and heard the testimony of Peter, that therein was accomplished the prophecy of Joel,—a prophecy in which and the kindred language of the other prophets, the baptisms of the Old Testament were so clearly interpreted. We have seen that his baptizing office was the great end of Christ's exaltation, and the consummate function of his scepter,—that by which he begins, carries on, and accomplishes the salvation and the glory of his people; and that this, his exaltation and saving power, were, on the day of Pentecost, preached as the express ground of the call to repent and be baptized, for his name's sake. In view of these facts, how is it possible, by argument or by sophistry, to avoid the conclusion that the ritual baptism to which Peter's hearers were thus called, was designed to signify that real baptism with which it was thus so closely identified? But the evidence is more specific.

1. The sum and substance of the preaching of John and of Jesus was the same, and reported by the evangelists in the same words:—"Repent, for the kingdom of heaven is at hand."

2. In both cases, this preaching was accompanied with a ritual baptism, which was as identical as was the preaching. Else, have we a house divided against itself,—the one doctrine, attested by two rival rites, which, under one and the same name, competed for acceptance with the Jews!

3. Of this baptism, Paul says, that "John verily baptized with the baptism of repentance, saying unto the people, that they should believe on Him which should come after, that is on Christ Jesus."—Acts xix, 4. Of it, Mark and Luke state that "John did baptize in the wilderness and preach the baptism of repentance for the remission of sins."—Mark i, 4; Luke iii, 3. And John himself declares,—"I indeed baptize you with water, unto repentance: but He ... shall baptize you with the Holy Ghost, and with fire."—Matt, iii, 11. It thus appears that this baptism was identified with a doctrine the cardinal elements of which are (1) repentance, and (2) faith in the Lord Jesus; as the conditions precedent; and (3) the remission of sins, as the result. These were what the ordinance meant. From them it took its name,—"The baptism of repentance for the remission of sins."

4. On the day of Pentecost, this, precisely, was the preaching and baptism of Peter. "Repent, and be baptized every one of you, for the name's sake of Jesus Christ, unto the remission of sins."—Acts ii, 38.

5. Peter had already proclaimed that the Lord Jesus, "being by the right hand of God exalted, and having received of the Father the promise of the Holy Ghost, hath shed forth this, which ye now see and hear."—Ib. 33. A few days afterward, he explained more precisely to the rulers, the significance of this great fact.—"Him hath God exalted with his right hand to be a Prince and a Saviour, for *to give* to

Israel *repentance* and (*aphesin hamartiōn*) *remission of sins."* —Ib. v, 31.

From these things it irrefragably follows, (1) that whereas, Christ's baptizing office is fulfilled by shedding down his Spirit upon his people, the baptisms of John and the disciples prior to the day of Pentecost, as well as that administered by Peter and the twelve on that day, were all proclaimed symbols of this the great reality; (2) that, while the intent and end of Christ's baptism is, through the bestowal of the Spirit, to give repentance, faith, and the remission of sins—the other baptisms and conspicuously, that of the apostles on Pentecost, were designed to signify and bear witness to that very thing. Not only are these conclusions manifest and incontrovertible; but by them and the facts on which they rest the idea of the burial of Christ, as included in the symbolism of baptism, is not merely ignored, but utterly excluded, as incongruous and unmeaning, in that connection.

This impregnable conclusion is further fortified by the fact already shown, that in this meaning of the rite and in it only can be reconciled the two forms of expression, "Baptizing into the name of the Father, and of the Son, and of the Holy Ghost;" and,—"into the name of the Lord Jesus." Baptism shows forth the Triune Godhead united in the salvation of man, and uniting the saved with that blessed Godhead.

Section XCV.—*The Mode of the ritual Baptism on Pentecost.*—Immersion incongruous and impossible. They were baptized in groups with a hyssop bush

As to the mode of the baptism of that day the evidence is not doubtful. The assembled throng were "Jews, devout men out of every nation,"—men whose cherished faith and hopes all centered on Moses and the covenant made and sealed with their fathers at Sinai. The baptismal seal of that covenant, perpetuated in the sprinkled water of separation, was familiar to them everywhere. They were conversant with the prophecies which assured them that in the latter days God would "sprinkle clean water upon them,"—that the Messiah would "sprinkle many nations," and "pour out of his Spirit upon all flesh." They are now told by the apostles that these prophecies are announcements of the baptizing office of the Lord Jesus,—that he, being by the right hand of God exalted, and having received of the Father the promise of the Holy Ghost, had, in the exercise of his baptizing office, shed forth this, which they saw and heard. And, in response to their penitent cry, they are required to be "baptized for the name's sake of the Lord Jesus." Is it possible to avoid the conclusion that the baptism thus propounded was the sprinkled baptism which was familiar to them all? Or, are we to accept the opposite assumption? Then must Peter have explained to the multitude.—"Our fathers, at Sinai, were sealed to the covenant with the sprinkled blood and water. In all generations of our race, the same seal has been familiar, in the same office; as it is, this day, to you. The prophets have explained the affusion of water as being a symbol of the official work of the Messiah. In that office and work, the reality of the Sinai rite is to-day fulfilled. And now, ye are to be baptized into the name of the Lord Jesus; but with another baptism,—a baptism dislocated from all relation to the past,—a baptism severed from all analogy, even, or association of ideas with that of the

Spirit, which is this day dispensed by the Lord Jesus. He baptizes by outpouring; but ye must be dipped. He baptizes by a pouring out of the Spirit, of which, in the prophecies, and in the baptisms of our fathers, living water was the constant symbol; but to you, dipped in that living water, it is to become the symbol of the sepulchre of Joseph, in which the body of Jesus was laid. His baptism gives repentance and remission of sins; and the baptism to be received by you might seem to mean this very thing; for it is conditioned upon repentance and is 'unto remission.' But it means not that; but the burial of the dead body of Jesus."

And now, where shall the water be found, for the immersion of these thousands? And by what miracle shall the rite be performed, "decently and in order," within the hours of that day? For, not only is the record specific, which limits the time,—but the supposition of a delay implies the encumbrance of after time, of which each day had its own duties and labors, its own converts and baptisms. It is demonstrably possible for the twelve apostles to have baptized the entire multitude by sprinkling in the ordinary manner in which we administer the rite within four or five hours. But such was not, as I conceive, the manner of the administration. No mere rite could without disparagement endure such repetition for hour after hour. The reiteration must obscure and obliterate the spiritual significance of the rite. The attention of the witnesses would become exhausted and diverted, and the monotony of the form would inevitably become a weariness and an offense. By such a manner of observance, the very intent of the ordinance would be lost, and this as much in one form, as in another.

But we are not reduced to the necessity of encountering these obvious embarrassments. We have seen the millions of Israel baptized by Moses, in the hours of one morning, they receiving the rite either collectively in one body, or by tribe-families or tribes. It is very probable that this was the manner in which the rite was ordinarily administered by John to the throngs that attended on his ministry, and by the disciples of Christ, when he "made and baptized more disciples than John." The Jews were familiar with the use of the hyssop bush as appointed in the law, for administering the rite. There was nothing in the nature of the ordinance, nor in the circumstances of the occasion, to render inappropriate or improbable a resort to that mode. On the contrary, every consideration, of convenience, of dignity, propriety and edification, united to commend it as the most suitable way, the water being sprinkled with a hyssop bush, and the recipients of the rite presenting themselves in companies of suitable size, by scores or by hundreds. Thus was set forth by a joint baptism the doctrine of Paul. "By one Spirit are we all baptized into one body."—1 Cor. xii, 13.

Such is the conclusion to which the analogy of the Scriptures points. Such, I doubt not, was the form of administration that day. For the present purpose, however, this much is clear and sufficient,—that the record of Pentecost contains nothing incongruous to the previous history and doctrine of baptism,—that on the contrary, the Spirit-baptism of that day and all the circumstances, concur to the same conclusion which the foregoing history indicates. *"Not immersion; but affusion"* —is the unambiguous voice of Pentecost.

Section XCVI.—*Other Cases Illustrating the Mode.*—The eunuch. The apostle Paul. The house of Cornelius. The jailer. None of these look to immersion

The next case that illustrates the mode, is the baptism of the eunuch. "As they went on their way, they came unto a certain water. And the eunuch said, See, here is water, what doth hinder me to be baptized?... And he commanded the chariot to stand still; and they went down both into the water, both Philip and the eunuch, and he baptized him. And when they were come up out of the water."—Acts viii, 36-39. To what has been said already concerning this passage, one or two points only need be added. Dr. Dale has pointed out the fact that the verb (*katebēsan*), "they went down," has primary reference to the chariot, out of which they descended. He refers to the Septuagint of Judges iv, 15, "And Sisera (*katebē*) *stepped down* from his chariot;" and to Matt. xiv, 29,—"Peter (*katabas*) *stepping down* from the boat walked on the water, to go to Jesus." The essential point, however, is that the descent was not the baptism,—that, with the style of clothing, then as now, worn in the east, nothing would have been more natural and convenient than that they should have stepped into the water, as the most convenient way of access, even though the baptism was to be performed by sprinkling or pouring. "The place" (*periochē*, the section), which the eunuch was reading, begins with Isa. lii, 13, and includes the whole of liii. It is a continuous prophecy of the Messiah, under the designation of God's servant. In the fifty-third chapter, down to the eleventh verse the pronoun "*he*" is used to designate the subject of the account. It refers back to lii, 13, to which we must look for the theme of the prophecy. "Behold *my servant* shall deal prudently.*" When, therefore, the eunuch read liii, 7, 8,—"He was led as a sheep to the slaughter," and asked, "Of whom speaketh the prophet this?" Philip must of necessity have turned back to the beginning of the section, for the answer. In so doing, he finds this among the first things said of the person described:—"As many were astonied at thee, his visage was so marred more than any man, and his form more than the sons of men, ... so shall he *sprinkle* many nations."—lii, 14, 15. This prophecy, thus coinciding with that of Joel, which was the text of Peter's Pentecostal discourse, could not be overlooked by Philip, in his instructions to the eunuch. The latter, although himself a Jew, was identified with a Gentile nation. He was chamberlain, or treasurer, to Candace, the queen of Meroe, in upper Egypt.[125] The prophecy, therefore, "So shall he *sprinkle many nations*," could not fail to arrest his attention and elicit the story of Pentecost, as the beginning of redemption to the Gentiles. That, with Christ's baptizing office brought thus into view, his ordinance concerning ritual baptism should be announced, was not only a necessary result of the circumstances, but was an essential part of that office which Philip was to perform. "Disciple all nations, baptizing them." In favor of the hypothesis that the eunuch was immersed, there is nothing but the fact that they went down to, or into the water. On behalf of his being sprinkled, is the explicit testimony of the prophet as to the manner of the real baptism, of which the ritual ordinance is the symbol.

2. The baptism of the apostle Paul next presents itself. Of it we have two brief

[125] Pliny (Hist. Nat. vi, 35) states this kingdom of which Meroe, on an island in the Nile, was the chief city, to have been "now for a long time," governed by queens, who transmitted to each other the name of Candace.

accounts which are mutually supplementary. (Acts ix, 10-20; xxii, 12-16.) After his vision of Jesus, on the way, he had lain for three days in the house of Judas, in Damascus, blind, fasting and prostrate. To him Ananias was sent and said to him—"And now, why tarriest thou?" Why liest thou thus prostrate and desponding? "Arise, and be baptized, and wash away thy sins, calling on the name of the Lord."—Acts xxii, 16. Literally "(*Anastas, baptisai, kai apolusai*), *Rising, be baptized, and let* thy sins *be washed away*, calling upon the name of the Lord." Says Alexander, "Be baptized, is not a passive, as in ii, 38, but the middle voice of the same verb, strictly meaning, 'baptize thyself,' or, rather, 'cause thyself to be baptized,' or suffer (some one) to baptize thee. The form of the next verb [*apolusai*] is the same, but can not be so easily expressed in English; as it has a noun dependent on it. This peculiarity of form is only so far of importance as it shows that Paul was to wash away his sins in the same sense that he was to baptize himself; *i. e.* by consenting to receive both from another. As his body was to be baptized by man; so, his sins were to be washed away by God. The identity, or even the inseparable union, of the two effects, is so far from being here affirmed, that they are rather held apart, as things connected by the natural relation of type and antitype, yet perfectly distinguishable in themselves, and easily separable in experience."[126] The exhortation, "Let thy sins be washed away," is intimately dependent upon the next clause,—"calling upon the name of the Lord."—Calling not as a mere reverential invocation; nor as a mere profession or act of faith. But "calling on him to purge away thy sins with the washing of regeneration, and renewing of the Holy Ghost; and accepting the baptism of water as the symbol and pledge of the other."

In the parallel account, it is stated that "he received sight forthwith (*kai anastas, ebaptisthe*) *and rising up, was baptized*."—Acts ix, 18. Thus, in both of these accounts, the same form of expression is used as to the manner of the baptism,—a form which indicates that the administration was immediate, upon his rising from his couch. "Rising up, be baptized." "And he, rising up, was baptized." In the original, the force of the expressions is even stronger, to the same effect. The circumstances coincide with this interpretation. The prostration, resulting from the vision by the way, from the blindness, and the three days in which he was "without sight, and neither did eat nor drink" (Acts ix, 9), must have been very great; and it was not until after his baptism that "he received meat and was strengthened."—Ib. 19. There is no intimation of leaving the place. There is no word of such preparation as an immersion would require. But the whole case stands in the expression twice employed, from which but one meaning can be deduced,—that he was baptized immediately, in his chamber, as he rose from his couch, and stood before Ananias. Whatever the mode, it can not have been immersion.

It has been asserted that Paul's baptism was not ritual but spiritual. The supposition is encumbered with the same difficulties which attend the like idea respecting the baptism of Pentecost. The occasion of Ananias being sent to him was the fact attested by the Lord Jesus,—"Behold he prayeth."—Prayer so attested lacked neither repentance nor faith. He had, therefore, already received the baptism of the Spirit,—that is his renewing grace; although not his miraculous gifts.

---

[126] Alexander, *in loco*.

Moreover, the baptism which he received in his chamber was something to which the ministry of Ananias was requisite, and for which his rising from his couch was preparatory. None of these things harmonize with the idea that it was the baptism of the Holy Ghost. Nor was it implied in the language of Ananias,—"That thou mightest receive thy sight and be filled with the Holy Ghost."—Acts ix, 17. With this is to be compared the previous statement concerning him, made in vision by Jesus to Ananias, "He hath seen in a vision a man named Ananias coming and *putting his hand upon him*, that he might receive his sight."—Ib. 12. It was through the laying on of the hands of Ananias that Paul's sight was restored and the miraculous gifts of the Holy Ghost conferred upon him. Such was the ordinary manner, as we have already seen, of the imparting of those gifts; which was undoubtedly the nature of the present endowment of Saul of Tarsus.

3. The baptism of the house of Cornelius is equally unfavorable to the idea of immersion. (Acts x, 44-48.) The words of Peter admit of but one construction. "Can any man forbid (*to udōr*) *the water*; that these should not be baptized."—Acts x, 47. We have already pointed out that this language means that the water, as an instrument, was to be brought to the place, in order to the baptism. Moreover, the baptism of this company, thus, with water, was by Peter expressly predicated upon the fact that they had been already baptized with the Holy Ghost, by his outpouring upon them. "The Holy Ghost fell upon all them which heard." "On the Gentiles also was poured out the gift of the Holy Ghost." "Can any man forbid the water, that these should not be baptized, which have received the Holy Ghost as well as we?"—Acts x, 44, 45, 47. And lest there should be any possible doubt about the meaning of all this, Peter explains himself to the church in Jerusalem,—"Then remembered I the word of the Lord, how that he said, John indeed baptized with water, but ye shall be baptized with the Holy Ghost."—Ib. xi, 16. Here again the facts are decisive in favor of affusion.

4. The Philippian jailer and his family are the only remaining instance in which illustrative circumstances are recorded. (Acts xvi, 25-34.) As bearing upon the mode, these are, that at midnight, in the jail, upon his professed repentance and faith, the jailer was baptized, "he and all his straightway."—Acts xvi, 33. This too was before he had taken Paul and Silas out of the jail proper, into his own apartments. The impossibility of the rite, administered in such circumstances, having been immersion, would seem evident. Nor is it admissible, as proposed by Baptist writers, to suppose that the jailer and his family with the prisoners went out to the river and were there immersed. The suggestion is not only contradicted by the record, which describes the baptism as having been (*parachrēma*) "straightway," with neither time nor action intervening. But it would have been an act of official dereliction, involving peril to the jailer's life, and rendering the message of Paul to the magistrates, the next day, an impudent pretence. They sent the sergeants to the jailer, saying, "Let these men go." "But Paul said unto them, They have beaten us openly, uncondemned, being Romans, and have cast us into prison. And now do they thrust us out privily? Nay, verily, but let them come themselves and fetch us out."—Ib. 37. Is this the language of men who had already stolen out of the prison, by night?

We have thus passed in review every instance of Christian baptism mentioned in the New Testament, in which any particulars are given. The only other cases named are the Samaritans (Acts viii, 12, 13, 15), Lydia (Ib. xvi, 15), the Corinthians (Ib. xviii, 8; 1 Cor. i, 14-17), and the twelve disciples of John at Ephesus (Acts xix, 1-5). Of them we are only informed that they were baptized. As to the cases which we have examined it is certainly remarkable and significant that with the exception of the eunuch, they each present physical difficulties in the way of immersion, serious if not insurmountable; and that in the excepted case, the utmost that can be said is, that nothing appears to render immersion physically impossible; while the connection of the occasion points distinctly to a sprinkled baptism.

The cumulative argument arising out of these baptisms is overwhelming. They can not have been by immersion.

> Section XCVII.—*"Baptized into Moses."*—Moses and Israel were types.
> Dr. Kendrick contradicts the record. By this baptism Israel were
> brought into a new state of faith and obedience

The baptism of Israel into Moses, is pertinent here, as illustrating the apostolic style of conception and language on the subject. "All our fathers were under the cloud, and all passed through the sea; and were all baptized (*eis*) *into* Moses, (*en*) *by* the cloud and (*en*) *by* the sea."—1 Cor. x, 1, 2.

We have already seen the typical relation which Moses and Israel, and the covenant with them sustained to the Lord Jesus and the true Israel, and the better covenant, as expounded by Paul to the Hebrews. The language here cited from the same apostle derives its form from the same conception. Israel in the bondage of Egypt,—Moses sent to them as a deliverer,—the passage out of the land of bondage, through the Red Sea,—the destruction of Pharaoh in the sea and the cutting off thus of Israel from all dependence or subjection to him,—their consequent faith in Moses and submission to his authority,—the covenant made with them through him as Mediator,—their nourishment in the wilderness on the bread of heaven, and the water from the Rock,—and their final passage through the Jordan and entrance into the promised land,—are the elements of a typical system the antitypes of which are to be sought, not in the visible church and its ritual ordinances, but in Christ and his body, the invisible church, and the spiritual and heavenly realities which it enjoys. According to this conception, the "baptism into Moses" finds its antitype in the baptism into Christ, by which his people are emancipated from the bondage of Satan and brought under the yoke of Christ. And as that baptism is instrumentally accomplished by the Spirit, whereby they all are baptized into one body of which Christ is the Head, so the baptism of Israel was instrumentally effected "*by* the cloud and *by* the sea;" they being by the cloud protected from the Egyptians and directed through the receding sea; while "the Lord looked unto the host of the Egyptians, through the pillar of fire and of the cloud, and troubled the Egyptians, and took off their chariot wheels," and the returning sea swallowed them up.—Ex. xiv, 23-28. Here was an immersion. But it was of the Egyptians. Here was a baptism,—of the children of Israel,—into Moses,—not into water,— not into cloud, or sea or both together. There were not two baptisms, but one, and in order to make it an immersion "in the cloud and in the sea," the baptism "into Moses" must be obliterated. The Baptist figment which we have seen stated by Dr. Kendrick, of the "double wall of water rolled up on each side, and the column of fiery cloud stretching its enshrouding folds above them," is not merely an idle imagination. But it is an imagination in direct and palpable contradiction to the record of Moses. The Israelites were indeed under the cloud. But it was *before* they entered the sea, and not during their march through it. "The Angel of God which went before the camp of Israel, removed and went behind them; and the pillar of the cloud went from before their face, and stood behind them. And it came between the camp of the Egyptians and the camp of Israel; and it was a cloud and darkness to them; but it gave light by night to these; so that the one came not near the other all the night. And Moses stretched out his hand over the sea ... and the waters were divided. And the children of Israel went into the midst of the sea."—Ex. xiv, 19-22. Thus, before the sea was divided, Israel were "under the cloud," as it passed back from their front, to become an intercepting barrier between them and the pursuing host. But, during the march through the sea, the cloud was *between* the two hosts, and not "enshrouding" Israel above. Thus, as by the touch of Ithuriel's spear, the figment of immersion vanishes in the presence of the word of truth, and in its stead appear the ransomed tribes marching upon the sands between walls of water, miles apart, the open heavens above them and the cloud moving as a protecting curtain, in their rear. The attempt to find immersion here, is futile.

That the preposition, *en*, is rightly here translated, *by*, as indicating the instrumental cause, in the baptism, is illustrated by an example a little farther on in the same epistle. "*By* one Spirit, are we all baptized *into* one body."—1 Cor. xii, 13. Here, Christ is the Baptizer, the Spirit is the instrument, and union with Christ and his body the result. So, of Israel, Jehovah was the Baptizer, the cloud and the sea were the instruments, and union with Moses the result. Just before, they had been in a state of open mutiny. (Ex. xiv, 11, 12.) But now, says the record, "the Lord saved Israel that day out of the hand of the Egyptians; and Israel saw the Egyptians dead upon the sea-shore. And Israel saw that great work which the Lord did upon the Egyptians, and the people feared the Lord, and believed the Lord and his servant Moses."—Ib. 30, 31. Their changed state of mind was attested by the song of their triumph which rang out over the unconscious and now peaceful waters. "Sing ye to the Lord, for he hath triumphed gloriously; the horse and his rider hath he thrown into the sea."—Ib. xv, 1-21. Thus have we a signal example of such a change of state or experience as even Dr. Conant admits to have been designated by the word, *baptizo*. From under the power and fear of Pharaoh, they came into the trust and obedience of Moses. They were "baptized into Moses." The only intimation of instrumental mode in this baptism, to be found in the Scriptures, occurs in the Psalmist's vivid description of the scene. "The clouds poured out water, the skies sent out a sound, thine arrows also went abroad."—Ps. lxxvii, 17.

PART XVI.

THE FAMILY AND THE CHILDREN.

Section XCVIII.—*Christ and the Children.*—A retrospect. Christ's attitude toward the lambs. Peter's commission. The Jews predominant in the church. The Sinai covenant recognized the children and made place for the Gentiles

At this stage of our inquiry, we note the following points which have important bearings upon the relation of the children to the church. (1.) We have seen that, in the establishing of the covenant with Abraham,—the promises of which were blessings to the natural offspring of the patriarch, and through them, salvation to the world,—its seal was set upon all the males of his household,—through whom the descent was to be counted,—at the age of eight days. (2.) We have seen that in the Sinai covenant, by which in fulfillment of the promises to Abraham, the church was constituted in the family of Israel, the same fundamental principles of family unity and parental headship were recognized and incorporated in the constitution of the church; and that in accordance therewith, the children and bondservants, both male and female, were included in its terms, with the family head; endowed with all its rights and privileges; bound under its responsibilities; and sealed with its baptismal seal. (3.) We have seen that it was into this church, as thus constituted and existing, and without change in its constitutional principles, or form of organization, that through the ministry of the apostles, the Gentiles were graffed; thus fulfilling the promise to Abraham, that in his seed should all families of the earth be blessed; a promise fulfilled not only in salvation accomplished through the promised Seed of Abraham, but in the reception thus of the Gentiles into the bosom of the church of Israel.

It now remains to be ascertained whether there is any thing in the principles of the gospel, as set forth in the New Testament, in the practical rules therein recorded, or in the facts of its history, to require or justify the extruding of the children from the place and privileges hitherto enjoyed;—whether there is any thing to lead us to the conclusion that the coming of Christ has straitened the grace of God, and withdrawn from the babes of us Gentiles that privilege of acceptance which was enjoyed by the little ones of Israel, from the day of the covenant at Sinai.

1. As the place of the children was originally conferred and secured by express statute and repeated enactments of confirmation, we have a right to expect the abrogation of the privileges thus established to be accomplished in terms as specific and imperative as were the laws by which they were conferred. But no one has

ever pretended to produce such a statute of abrogation. Confessedly the New Testament is absolutely silent as to such an act,—a silence fatal to the theories which deny a place to the babes in the family of God.

2. The facts and principles set forth in the New Testament supply no argument for the exclusion of the children. First, is that touching incident which is recorded with more or less fullness in each of the synoptical gospels. In reply to the question who of the apostles should be greatest in the kingdom of heaven, Jesus, being in a house in Capernaum,—probably in the house of one of them, several of whom lived there,—he "called a little child unto him and set him in the midst of them,"— "and (*enagkalisamenos*) *having folded it in his arms*, he said unto them," "Verily I say unto you, Except ye be converted, and become as little children, ye shall not enter into the kingdom of heaven. Whosoever, therefore, shall humble himself as this little child, the same is greatest in the kingdom of heaven. And whoso shall receive one such little child in my name receiveth me."—Matt. xviii, 1-5; Mark ix, 36; Luke ix, 46-48. With this is to be connected that kindred fact which occurred a few days afterward, and is also recorded in each of the three synoptical gospels. "Then were there brought unto him little children, that he should put his hands on them and pray; and the disciples rebuked them. But Jesus said, Suffer little children and forbid them not to come unto me; for of such is the kingdom of heaven. And he laid his hands on them, and departed thence."—Matt. xix, 13-15. Mark and Luke add that he said, "Verily I say unto you, whosoever shall not receive the kingdom of God as a little child, he shall not enter therein. And (*enagkalisamenos*) *folding them in his arms*, he put his hands upon them, and blessed them."—Mark x, 13-16; Luke xviii, 15-17. Of these little children, Luke tells us that they were (*brephē*) *babes*. That these incidents in the life of our Savior were of special significance is indicated by the fact that they are both given by each of the evangelists, Matthew, Mark, and Luke. As to their meaning,—(1.) These children all were, at the time, actual members of that visible kingdom of God the church of Israel, in the bosom of which Jesus himself lived and died. (2.) That church was the type and representative of the invisible church and kingdom. (3.) Of all members of the visible church, Jesus selects the little child of the first incident and the babes of the second, as the fittest types or representatives of the temper and spirit which will have admittance and honor in the heavenly kingdom. (4.) He was much displeased, that his disciples should attempt to prevent their being brought, in their unconsciousness and helplessness, into his personal presence, for recognition and a blessing from him. (5.) Both the child in the house, and the babes brought to him, he folded in his arms, and upon the latter he laid his hands and blessed them. He was the great Shepherd, as himself testifies,—"I am the good Shepherd."—John x, 11. Of him the prophet wrote,—"He shall gather the lambs with his arm, and carry them in his bosom."—Isa. xl, 11. And we ask,—Can any one venture to deny that, by these acts, so distinctly referring to the prophecy, Jesus designed to recognize and claim the babes as lambs of his fold? As before remarked, these babes were undeniably members of the church, at the time of these occurrences. If the Lord Jesus designed to leave them in undisturbed possession of the rights and privileges heretofore enjoyed, with his benediction added thereto, all this is clear and intelligible. But, if they were to be deprived and excluded, how are these things to be reconciled?

Another incident, in circumstances even more significant, presents itself. After his resurrection, Jesus met with his disciples at the Sea of Galilee. "When they had dined, Jesus saith to Simon Peter, Simon, son of Jonas, lovest thou me more than these? He saith unto him, Yea, Lord; thou knowest that I love thee. He saith unto him, Feed my lambs."—John xxi, 15. Peter was present in the house in Capernaum, when Jesus took the child in his arms. Nay, it is not improbable that it was Peter's house, and Peter's child. He was present when the babes were brought for blessing, and saw and heard all that then occurred. He was a Hebrew of the Hebrews,—the chief apostle of the circumcision. When he received this charge from the Master, in which were commended to his love and care, first, the lambs, and afterward the sheep; and when he pondered this charge and legacy, in the light of the fifteen centuries during which the place of the children had been unquestioned and unquestionable, and in remembrance of those demonstrative facts which he had seen and heard,—would he understand it as implying a command to purge and renovate the fold, by the exclusion of the lambs? And when, a few days after, or, possibly on this very same occasion, he as the apostle through whom the doors of the gospel were to be opened to the Gentiles, with the rest, received that great command,—"Go disciple all nations, baptizing them,"—are we to conceive it possible that he understood it to mean that he must be very tender of the Jewish lambs, bringing them into the fold and school of Christ, but must drive out the children of the Gentiles as unclean?

3. Under the ministry of the apostles, the Gentiles were called and graffed into the church of Israel. In the church, thus constituted as already shown, some congregations were composed of Jews alone, some, of Gentiles, and some, of the two classes associated together; but in them all Jewish influences were pervasive and paramount. Now, is it to be imagined that without a word of command from Christ or the apostles, the Jewish believers would unanimously, gratuitously, and in silence, surrender the place of their children in the church, just at the moment when the privileges thereto incident had become so much more manifest, by the coming of Christ, and the brightness, by his rising, shed upon the gospel day? And even if such a thing could be imagined possible, what else would it have been but a wicked apostasy and rejection of the grace given them? But, that no such apostasy did take place, is assuredly testified by the silence of the record, and by all the circumstances. That, in the churches of the circumcision, and among Jewish believers everywhere, the children occupied their old status is beyond controversy or question. Of this, their circumcision is of itself conclusive proof. And as, from the days of Abraham, that rite certified them seed of the patriarch and heirs of the promises,—and at Sinai they were introduced, by baptism, into the pale of the church and the privileges of that covenant,—so their continued enjoyment alike of the privileges and the seals must stand forever certain, till some prophet shall arise to tell us when, and how, and for what cause, they were divested of rights once bestowed by Him whose "gifts and callings are without repentance."

And if, by a special clause in the very covenant of Sinai itself, grace to the Gentiles was reserved, in harmony with abundant grace to Israel, the baptism of Israel's babes into the fold of that covenant, that day, was a foretokening and pledge of the same grace to the children of the Gentiles, when the times of the Gentiles shall have come. They are not the seed of Abraham, and therefore receive not the seal of his covenant in their flesh. But baptism is theirs,—the seal of the Sinai covenant, in which, now, the rights of the Gentiles are equal. "For there is no difference between the Jew and the Greek: for the same Lord over all is rich unto all that call upon him."—Rom. x, 12.

Section XCIX.—*"Now are they Holy."*—Unclean, and holy. Israel a holy nation. "The saints." The Baptist exegesis of the language

We have the express testimony of inspiration, to the children's right within the pale of the church. Says Paul to the Corinthians,—"The unbelieving husband is sanctified by the wife, and the unbelieving wife is sanctified by the husband. Else were your children *unclean*; but now are they *holy*."—1 Cor. vii, 14. The significance of this declaration, as concerning the children, depends upon the meaning of the words, *unclean* (*akathartoi*), and *holy* (*hagioi*.) Both of them come into the New Testament, from the Septuagint version of the Old. In the Greek of that version, the word (*akathartos*) does not appear in the books of Moses until we come to the laws of ritual uncleanness and purifying, which have been so largely discussed in these pages. Then, beginning with the fifth chapter of Leviticus, it occurs in that book in about eighty-seven places, in all of which it designates the ritually unclean; being applied alike to things and persons. In Numbers and Deuteronomy, it appears about thirty times, in the same sense. In the entire Old Testament, the word is used about one hundred and forty times; and with the exception of half a dozen passages in which it indicates the moral offensiveness of sin, it is invariably employed in one and the same sense,—to designate persons and things that by virtue of ritual defilements were excluded from the pale of the covenant and the sanctuary. If we add to this the related noun (*akatharsia*) the force of these considerations is greatly increased. It, in like manner, first occurs in Leviticus, as the designation of the *uncleannesses* which were described by the adjective (*akathartos*), *unclean*. It occurs about fifty times, and with a few exceptions in which it describes the vileness of sin, is constantly used in the ritual sense.

The other word (*hagios*) *holy*, has a history and meaning, equally clear and well defined. It has primary reference to the sum of the divine perfections, in view of which God is designated, the *holy* One. Thence, it is transferred to designate those moral attributes in men which are after the likeness of God's holiness; as, in the admonition which is often repeated in the books of Moses, "Be ye holy, for I am holy." Again, it is used to denote the relation sustained to God by things devoted to his use or service. Thus, the tabernacle and all its parts and furniture were holy. In this sense, the word was used in the covenant with Israel. "Ye shall be unto me a *holy* nation (*ethnos hagion*.")—Ex. xix, 6. The acceptance of this covenant, and the seal of baptism by which it was confirmed established Israel as "holy" unto the Lord. Prior to that covenant the word had never been applied to men. But from that transaction forward Israel was recognized in that character. Thus, alluding to the covenant, Moses says to them,—"Thou art a holy people unto the Lord thy God; the Lord thy God hath chosen thee to be a special people unto himself above all people that are upon the face of the earth."—Deut. vii, 6. Upon this title and the covenant ground of it, Moses insists with great emphasis, recurring to the theme again and again. (See Deut. xiv, 2, 21; xxvi, 19; xxviii, 9.) It is in view of this covenant provision that the distinctive appellation of Israel in the prophets is, "the holy people;" and to the same source is to be referred the familiar designation of "saints," that is, holy ones, which is constantly employed, especially in the Psalms. Thus, the Lord says in Ps. 1, 5,—"Gather my saints together unto me; those that have made a covenant with me by sacrifice." Here, not only is the title used, but the ground of it is stated. It is that public profession and covenant of which sacrifice was essential as a seal, and incorporated as such in the baptismal rite.

Such is the testimony of the Old Testament, respecting these words. The church of Corinth was composed largely of Jews, who as we have seen still maintained the ordinances of the synagogue after as well as before their conversion to Christ. In those assemblies, James declares that "Moses of old time hath in every city, them that preach him, being read in the synagogues every Sabbath day."—Acts xv, 21. The Corinthian disciples, therefore, never attended those services without hearing the words in question used; and used in this continual sense of ritual uncleanness and ritual purity.

In the New Testament, the words in question are employed in strict accordance with the Old Testament usage. But as the ritual law here sinks into comparative obscurity, *akathartos*, more frequently means the loathsomeness of sin. Of the twenty-eight places in which it is found, it in twenty, describes *"unclean* spirits," or demons. But when the question arises of the right of the Gentiles to a part with Israel, in the covenant and the church, the ritual meaning of the word, again comes forward. Peter in his vision pleads that he had "never eaten any thing common, or *unclean."*—Acts x, 14. The lesson which that vision taught him was, that he "should not call any man common or *unclean."*—Ib. 28. And he afterward said of the house of Cornelius that God "put no difference between us and them, (*katharisas*) *cleansing* their hearts by faith."—Ib. xv, 9. Except the place in question, in which the relation of the children to the church is in view, and that of Peter, concerning the like relation of believing Gentiles, the word is invariably used in the New Testament to designate that moral character of which ritual uncleanness was the figure.

So, too, as to (*hagioi*) *"holy,"* or "saints"—it is the peculiar and distinctive appellation in the New Testament, as in the Old, for those whom we would call "members of the church." In the Acts of the Apostles, some half a dozen times, the title of "disciples," is used; once, Peter employs the name of "Christian" (1 Pet. iv, 16); and Paul once speaks of "the believers." (1 Tim. iv, 12.) But, with these exceptions, the appellation universally used is (*hagioi*) "saints." It thus occurs about fifty-six times, of which forty are in the epistles of Paul, the author of the passage in question. In fact, this is the designation which he uniformly employs in this very epistle and his second to the same church to designate the members of the church. "Dare any of you, having a matter against another, go to law before the unjust and not before the *saints*?"—1 Cor. vi, 1. "As in all the churches of the *saints*." (Ib. xiv, 33.) "Paul ... unto the church of God which is in Corinth, with all the *saints* which are in all Achaia."—2 Cor. i, 1. The source of this title, moreover, as derived from the Sinai covenant, is indicated by Peter, who quotes the terms of that covenant and applies them to the New Testament church. "Ye are a chosen generation, a royal priesthood, a *holy nation* (*ethnos hagion*), a peculiar people."—1 Peter ii, 9. As in the Old Testament, so in the New, the word, *hagios*, invariably means, either, that holiness which is essential in God, and which, in his creatures is a bond of consecration to him; or, the characteristic of persons and things separated by a peculiar dedication and appropriation to his use and service.

The alternative to which the facts reduce us, is this:—that Paul, master as he was of the Mosaic system and of the language in which it is recorded,—in his reference to the children, used the words, *akathartoi*, and, *hagioi*, in their familiar ritual signification; or that he meant to deceive his readers. For, that the heirs of the covenant were in fact a holy people to God, was an express and fundamental specification in the covenant. And that the children were comprehended in this provision was no more questionable than was the existence of the covenant itself. Whatever therefore the meaning of Paul, his readers could not possibly understand his language in any but one way:—"*Else were your children excluded from the pale of the covenant; but now are they embraced in it.*"

The attempt is made to evade the overwhelming force of the facts, on this point, by a most extraordinary interpretation. It is asserted that Paul means,—"Else were your children illegitimate, but now are they legitimate." The doctrine thus attributed to the apostle, is in the first place, false and abominable in morals. It is an assertion that no child is legitimate, unless one or other of its parents be a Christian. In the second place, it is an interpretation false to the whole testimony of the Scriptures as to the meaning of the words. In all the multitude of places in which they are to be found, there is not one to give the slightest color of sanction to it. It is nothing less than a desperate and unscrupulous attempt to silence the voice of God's testimony because it is in terms of grace to our children.

Paul's language is, in fact, an application to the children, of the same general principle of divine grace, which governed him in the circumcision of Timothy. The Hebrew blood of Timothy's mother was held to entitle him to part in the Abrahamic covenant, although his father was a Greek. So, Paul pronounces the children of believers, Gentiles and Jews, to be *clean*, as comprehended in the Sinai covenant, and the gospel church, even though one parent should be an unbeliever.

It is only to be farther considered, that as those only who are baptized of the Spirit are spiritually clean, so the Scriptures know nothing of ritual cleanness, except by baptism with water; and that the command, "Go, disciple all nations, baptizing them," makes the baptizing co-extensive with the discipleship,—that is, with admission to the school of Christ, and pale of the covenant.

Section C.—*Household Baptisms.*—Not "infant," but "family baptism." Lydia's house. The jailer and all his. The house of Stephanas. These, in the light of fifteen centuries preceding, and of the everlasting covenant

We have seen the grace of God expressed toward the children of his people, under the Mosaic economy, by their being embraced with their parents in the terms of the covenant. We have seen their admission thereto announced and confirmed by the seal of baptism. We have seen no token of the withdrawal of that grace by the Lord Jesus when in person on earth. We have heard, on the contrary, his confirmation of it in terms as strong as language can furnish. We have seen that same covenant, its terms unchanged, and its seal the same, thrown open, through the ministry of the apostles, to the Gentiles, and heard the testimony of the apostle, that our children are not unclean,—offensive to God, but holy,—acceptable before him. We now proceed to consider the facts and principles involved in the household baptisms, which are described in the New Testament. First, however, it is proper to make an important correction in the aspect in which the subject is commonly viewed and discussed. The principle which the Scriptures set forth and establish is not that of the baptism and membership of *infants*, as such. The fundamental element of the visible church, as conceived and set forth, in Scripture, is not the individual, but the family. As God planted the earth in families, so in the covenant with Abraham he laid down the family society as the foundation stone, on which, at Sinai, the church was builded; and hence the organization of the church of Israel upon the family principle, and its government by the eldership, the representatives of its families. Under this constitution, the infants, were of course included. But the designation and discussion of the subject, under their name, as if it were a question of *infant* baptism and *infant* membership, distinctively, does injustice to the subject, as it leaves out of sight and practically excludes the fundamental principle involved. That principle is, parental headship, and the consequent grace of God bestowed on the *families* of his people,—their children and bond servants,—as identified in and represented by them.

1. The first case of household baptism mentioned is that of Lydia,—"whose heart the Lord opened, that she attended unto the things which were spoken of Paul. And when she was baptized, and her household, she besought us saying, If ye have judged me to be faithful to the Lord, come into my house and abide there."—Acts xvi, 14, 15. Here, the essential facts are, (1.) that the house of Lydia were by the inspired historian, recognized in no other capacity than as being (*oikos autēs*) *her house.* Their number, their names, their ages, their distinctive relation to her, whether as children or servants, their several or joint sentiments toward the gospel,—on all these points he is silent. The one single fact to which he directs our attention is Lydia's property in them. (2.) Of Lydia alone it is said that the Lord opened her heart; and upon this fact exclusively is predicated her baptism and that of her house. Should any surmise that her house also believed, we do not object, provided the surmise is not to be made an essential part of the record. If it be insisted that they believed and therefore were baptized, we reply that had such been the conception of the sacred writer, it would have been as easy, and far more important for him to have stated their faith, as he has recorded their baptism. The supposition that they did in fact believe, only renders his silence on that point the more significant. (3.) These facts occurred in the ministry of that same Paul whom we have just seen to testify that the children of believers are holy. In a word Luke states the fact of the baptism, and the ground of it. Lydia believed, and she was

baptized and her house. Because of her faith, to her and to her house the old, the everlasting, covenant was fulfilled, — "to be a God to thee and to thy seed after thee."

2. The baptism, which soon followed, of the jailer and his house is equally explicit on this point. He said to Paul and Silas, "Sirs, what must I do to be saved? And they said, Believe on the Lord Jesus Christ, and thou shalt be saved, and thy house. And they spake unto him the word of the Lord, and to all that were in his house. And he took them the same hour of the night, and washed their stripes, and was baptized, he and all his straightway. And when he had brought them into his house, he set meat before them, and (*ēgalliasato panoiki, pepisteukōs tō Theō,*) rejoiced with his house, he believing in God." — Acts xvi, 30-34. Here, again, we have a construction which remarkably ignores the question whether his house, as well as he, believed. It may he assumed that they were all of an age to hear and understand the gospel. It may be assumed that they, so understanding, believed also. But it may not be assumed that such knowledge and faith were the ground of their baptism, because the sacred writer puts it upon a different ground. It was as identified with him — as belonging to him, that they were included in the rite. "He was baptized, — he and all *his*." Thus their relation to him is the defining term. "He and *all* that were his." — He and *none but* his; and they *because* they were his. Such is the force of the expression as it stands. In the same direction looks the closing expression. "He rejoiced with all his house, — he believing." That his house did not believe we neither assert nor deny. The point of importance is, that their faith is no element of the case, as stated on the record, upon which was grounded their baptism. The alternative is clear and inevitable. Either he, only, of all his house did in fact believe; or, if his household shared in his faith, the remarkable manner in which, in the narrative, they are associated with him in his baptism and joy, but omitted from the statement which describes him alone, as believing, was an express and designed intimation that his personal faith was the controlling element in the case, according to the terms of the everlasting covenant, — "to be a God to thee, and to *thy seed* after thee," and the assurance given him by Paul, — "Believe, ... and thou shalt be saved and thy house." He was recognized and dealt with as the head of his house, precisely as was Abraham.

3. Paul declares that he "baptized (*ton Stephana oikon*) the house of Stephanas." — 1 Cor. i, 16. Here, again, there is no discrimination of individuals. The characteristic upon which he predicates the baptism is the relation which he indicates. It was the house of Stephanas, as such, whom he baptized.

Respecting these cases, it may be admitted that if taken separately, they would constitute no conclusive evidence to the present purpose. But such is not their position. They stand as one element in a series of facts and principles which together present a cumulative argument conclusive and unanswerable. These begin with the Abrahamic covenant and the family principle there established. They include the Sinai constitution, in which the same principle was ineffaceably engraved. They comprehend the opening of the doors of the church thereon founded, to the Gentile world, with this principle unimpaired. They reveal the love of Christ to the babes, in the history and instructions of his personal ministry, and in his parting commission to Peter. They hold up the testimony of Paul, that the babes of believers are "saints." It is in the presence of these great facts, inscribed in letters of light upon the records of fifteen hundred years; and in the absence of any thing whatever to contravene their testimonies, or to set aside the conclusions thence following, that the household baptisms in question are to be considered. The children and household were once unquestionably embraced in God's covenant with his church. "*Everlasting*," was by His finger written on the face of that covenant. (Gen. xvii, 7.) In its terms, as announced at Sinai, place for the Gentiles was expressly reserved; and upon their ultimate admission, no trace of change, in these respects, appears in the record. On the contrary, in the cases just examined, we have the most conclusive evidence, in view of the foregoing facts, that the position of the family has not been changed by the coming of Christ, and the giving of the gospel to the Gentiles. It still continues a unit under the parental head; and the same grace which blessed the seed of Abraham because of his faith, — the same which, at Sinai, embraced the children with their parents, in the covenant and the fold, still extends those privileges to the children of Gentiles who believe. They are holy.

CONCLUSION.

Christ's real baptism with the Spirit is the criterion of all baptismal
doctrines and rites. Baptismal regeneration tried and rejected. The
evidence against immersion cumulative and overwhelming

And now, at the goal, we turn to survey the broad field of our explorations,
and to note the accumulated results. From this vantage point, many things appear
in a light of peculiar instructiveness and beauty. But one feature stands out in proportions of loftiness, and glory, which cast all else into the shade of insignificance.
As with rapt spirits, we gaze, the high throne is revealed where sits the Son of
man,—his human form robed in the Father's glory,—his countenance blending the
infinite majesty of God, with the fullness of grace and truth,—his brow adorned
with a diadem of many crowns, and all power in heaven and earth, in his hand.
The heavens are astonished at the presence of his glory, and the adoring angels,
prostrate, await his bidding. The fullness of the Spirit is his; and his office thus exalted it is, to baptize us sinners with that Spirit,—to give us thus, repentance and
remission of sins and sanctifying grace, and to raise us up from the dead and make
us sit with him in the heavenly places where he reigns. This is the central sun of the
system which we have explored. From this baptism of the Spirit all the ordinances
here examined, derive their instructive light and beauty. It is the original,—the
heavenly pattern whence their form and office were divinely transcribed. It is,
therefore, the rule and standard to which all baptismal rites and doctrines must
be brought.

Tried by this rule, the figment of baptismal regeneration stands exposed in
naked falsehood and dishonor; arrogating to men a share of the sovereign prerogatives of our glorious Baptizer; subordinating the functions of his grace to their
will and wisdom, their fidelity and zeal.

The rite of immersion too,—already discountenanced by the united voice of
the Scriptures,—when brought to this supreme and final test, is utterly wanting.

It is discountenanced by the transaction at Sinai, in which the church was separated out of the world and consecrated to God by a baptism of sprinkled water
and blood.

It is discountenanced by the rites which certified and sealed the restoration of
the healed leper to the communion of Israel.

It is discountenanced by the water of purifying with which the Levites were
sprinkled, in their consecration to the service of God's sanctuary.

It is discountenanced by the ordinance which appointed the water of separation, to be sprinkled as the ordinary and perpetuated form of the Sinai baptism, for sealing admission to the benefits of the Sinai covenant.

It is excluded by the declaration of the son of Sirach that the sprinkling of the unclean with the water of separation was a baptizing.

It is discountenanced by the sprinkled baptism of the thirty-two thousand infants and youths of Midian, whereby they were received into the fold of the covenant and the church.

It is condemned by every voice in the Psalms and the prophets which breathes a sense of the sinner's need, or anticipates the blessings of Messiah's grace, in the language of these ordinances.

It is excluded by the explicit testimony of the apostle Paul, that these ordinances were baptisms.

It is condemned by the implacable war which it of necessity wages against the identity of the church from the day of the assembly at Sinai, — by its repudiation of the Old Testament church — the church of Moses and the prophets, which was for fifteen centuries a lone beacon light among the nations, God's only witness amid the gloom of thick darkness which enshrouded the world.

It is discountenanced by the voice of John's baptism which heralded and symbolized the outpouring of the Spirit on Pentecost; and is excluded by all the circumstances of his ministry, which show that he could not have immersed his disciples, and that he would not have done it, though he could.

It is discountenanced by the whole style of the evangelists and apostles, who speak of baptism and its relations in the language of the Old Testament, and recognize it as a symbol of the outpouring of Pentecost.

It is excluded by the records of Christian baptisms as given by Luke, which, beginning with the three thousand of Pentecost and ending with the jailer of Philippi and his house, present an array of difficulties in the way of immersion, which are severally inexplicable, and together overwhelming.

It is condemned by its association with the kindred denial of the place which God has assigned to the family and the children in his fold and his covenant; and by all the facts which demonstrate their God-given and inalienable rights therein.

It is utterly condemned by the fact that it maims the symmetry and completeness of the sacramental system of the Christian church. Whilst the Old Testament sacraments exhibit in just proportions every part and feature of the plan of grace, and whilst the genuine ordinances of the New Testament, in like proportions, abbreviate the whole, exhibiting in the holy supper the sacrament of Christ's humiliation and sacrifice, and in baptism that of his exaltation and glory, his power and grace, — the system in question, recognizes indeed, with us, in the Lord's supper, the memorial of Christ's suffering and death, but in baptism can see nothing but the symbol of his burial, and so leaves him and all our hopes shut up and sealed in the sepulchre of Joseph.

It is signally discountenanced by the remarkable fact that in every rite and every figure in which the Scriptures represent the active exercise by the Messiah of his official functions, the form of action is affusion, whether it be with the blood of atonement at the sanctuary of Israel,—the water, mingled with ashes or blood, which sprinkled the unclean,—the anointing oil poured upon the head; or the fires of justice rained down from heaven.

But why dwell upon minor particulars! The rite in question is condemned and excluded by the whole tenor of the Scriptures, which demonstrate that *baptizo* as there used *does not* mean, to immerse, and which reveal no vestige of other testimony in behalf of the rite, but everywhere show evidence abundant and conclusive against it.

But the capital and paramount consideration still remains, in the fact that this rite will not assimilate with, nor recognize the baptism which Christ dispenses from his throne. It ignores the exaltation whence that baptism descends, and refuses to testify of its outpouring of grace. And hence, although administered with the use of the words, it is not in the sense intended by the Lord Jesus, baptism "into the name of the Father and of the Son and of the Holy Ghost;" for its doctrine has no relation to those blessed Persons, nor to our union with them. It is wholly occupied with another theme. Whilst the true baptism exultingly points upward to the throne of Christ's glory, this rite looks downward ever to the grave.

To our readers we leave the question,—What one trait or characteristic of Scriptural baptism is traceable in this rite of immersion, in doctrine, or in form?

In entire consistency with a spirit of true Christian love and fellowship toward our brethren of the Baptist churches, we can not but realize an indignant revolt against this rite, so imperious in its claims, so devoid of evidence, so hostile to the true baptism of the Christian church, so efficient in creating division therein,—this rite in the zeal of which, those who reject it have been denied any part in the church of God, or place at his table, or portion in his covenant. Not such the ordinance which her glorious Head has bestowed upon his church, nor such the principles which he has taught her to cherish;—an ordinance in which is shown forth and celebrated the glory of his exaltation and his grace,—an ordinance which baptizes us into his name and that of the blessed Godhead, by setting forth the doctrine of that Godhead and of our union with it in Christ by the Spirit,—an ordinance which seals upon the brows of our babes that same blessing which they received in His own arms and from His own hands, in the days of his flesh;—and principles which teach us to recognize and embrace in the bonds of love and the fellowship of the covenant and of the church all those who in every place call upon the name of Jesus Christ our Lord, both their Lord and ours, even though they may grievously err respecting outward rites and forms.

Now to Him, the King eternal, immortal, invisible, the only wise God, be honor and glory, for ever. Amen.

SCRIPTURES ILLUSTRATED
IN THE FOREGOING PAGES.

Genesis.—i, 26;—ii, 10;—iii, 15;—xii, 1-3;—xv, 1+;—xvii, 1-21;—xvii, 7;—xxii, 16-18;—xxxvii, 31

Exodus.—vi, 2-8;—xix, 3-5;—xix, 3-21;—xix, 5;—xix, 6;—xx, 24;—xxiv, 5, 8;—xxv, 21;—xxv, 40;—xl, 12

Leviticus.—i, 9;—xiii, 45, 46;—xiv, 7-9;—xiv, 8, 9;—xxiii, 36

Numbers.—vi, 9;—vi, 18;—viii, 7;—xix, 1-22;—xix, 2-19;—xix, 12, 13, 19;—xxix, 12-38;—xxxi, 19-24;—xxxi, 23

Deuteronomy.—iv, 10;—xvi, 13-15;—xxi, 3-9;—xxi, 12

2 Kings.—iii, 11;—v, 10, 14

Job.—ix, 30, 31

Psalm.—viii, 4-8;—li, 2-10

Isaiah.—i, 16,17;—vi, 5-7;—xix, 19;—xxi, 4;—lii, 15

Ezekiel.—xvi, 8, 9;—xxii, 24;—xxxvii, 1-14;—xxxvii, 12-15;—xlvii, 1-12

Haggai.—ii, 11, 14

Zechariah.—xiv, 8

Malachi.—iii, 2, 3;—iv, 1-4;—iv, 4

Matthew.—iii, 5, 6;—iii, 11;—iii, 13-15;—xvii, 3;—xviii, 1-5;—xix, 13-15;—xx, 20-23;—xxvi, 28;—xxvii, 24;—xxviii, 19, 20

Mark.—i, 4;—vii, 1-4;—vii, 3, 4;—ix, 4;—ix, 36;—x, 13-16;—xvi, 15, 16

Luke.—i, 17;—ii, 22;—iii, 16;—iii, 21, 22;—vii, 37, 38, 44;—ix, 31;—ix, 46-48;—xi, 29;—xi, 38;—xii, 49-53;—xviii, 15-17;—xxiv, 44-46

John.—i, 33;—ii, 18-22;—iii, 5;—iii, 23;—iv, 14;—vii, 37, 38;—ix, 4;—xi, 25, 26;—xiv, 16,17, 25, 26;—xv, 26;—xvi, 7-15;—xvii, 22;—xx, 17

Acts.—ii, 2;—ii, 3;—ii, 4;—ii, 38;—viii, 36-39;—ix, 18;—x, 47;—xv, 10;—xvi, 14, 15;—xvi, 30-34;—xvi, 33;—xviii, 18;—xix, 1-7;—xix, 2;—xix, 4;—xxii, 16

Romans.—vi, 1-11;—vi, 4;—xi, 17-24

1 Corinthians.—i, 16;—vii, 14;—x, 1, 2;—xii, 13;—xv, 4;—xv, 25-27;—xv, 29

2 Corinthians.—iii, 2, 3, 6

Ephesians.—iv, 3-16;—iv, 5;—v, 25-27

Colossians.—ii, 9-13

Titus.—iii, 4-7

Hebrews.—ii, 5-8;—iv, 4-9;—vi, 7-9;—vi, 17-20;—ix, 8, 9;—xiii, 11-13

1 Peter.—ii, 9;—iii, 17-22

1 John.—v, 18, 19

Revelation.—i, 12, 13;—xxii, 1, 2

INDEX.

A

B

J

K

L

Lector House believes that a society develops through a two-fold approach of continuous learning and adaptation, which is derived from the study of classic literary works spread across the historic timeline of literature records. Therefore, we aim at reviving, repairing and redeveloping all those inaccessible or damaged but historically as well as culturally important literature across subjects so that the future generations may have an opportunity to study and learn from past works to embark upon a journey of creating a better future.

This book is a result of an effort made by Lector House towards making a contribution to the preservation and repair of original ancient works which might hold historical significance to the approach of continuous learning across subjects.

HAPPY READING & LEARNING!

LECTOR HOUSE LLP
E-MAIL: lectorpublishing@gmail.com